From Sinai to Ethiopia
The Halakhic and Conceptual World of the Ethiopian Jews
including
Shulhan ha-Orit: A Halakhic Guide for the Beta Israel Community

Dr. Sharon Shalom

From Sinai to Ethiopia

The Halachic and Conceptual World of Ethiopian Jewry

Translated by Jessica Setbon

Copyright © Sharon Shalom
Jerusalem 2016/5776

All rights reserved. No part of this publication may be translated, reproduced, stored in a retrieval system or transmitted, in any form or by any means, electronic, mechanical, photocopying, recording or otherwise, without express written permission from the publishers.

Scripture quotations are modified from *The Holy Scriptures According to the Masoretic Text*, published by the Jewish Publication Society in 1917.

Cover Design: Pini Hamou
Typesetting: Raphaël Freeman, Renana Typesetting

ISBN: 978-965-229-637-5

1 3 5 7 9 8 6 4 2

Gefen Publishing House Ltd.
6 Hatzvi Street
Jerusalem 94386, Israel
972-2-538-0247
orders@gefenpublishing.com

Gefen Books
11 Edison Place
Springfield, NJ 07081
516-593-1234
orders@gefenpublishing.com

www.gefenpublishing.com

Printed in Israel

* * *

Library of Congress Cataloging-in-Publication Data

Names: Shalom, Sharon, author. | Setbon, Jessica, translator.
Title: From Sinai to Ethiopia : the halakhic and conceptual world of the Ethiopian Jews : including Shulhan ha-Orit: a halakhic guide for the Beta Israel community / Rabbi Dr. Sharon Shalom ; translated from the Hebrew by Jessica Setbon.
Other titles: Mi-Sinai le-Etyopyah. English
Description: Springfield, NJ : Gefen Books, 2016.
Identifiers: LCCN 2015039462 | ISBN 9789652296375
Subjects: LCSH: Jews, Ethiopian--Religious life. | Jews, Ethiopian--Israel. | Jews, Ethiopian--Customs and practices. | Jews, Ethiopian--Rites and ceremonies. | Jewish law--Philosophy.
Classification: LCC DS113.8.F34 S542513 2016 | DDC 296.40963--dc23 LC record available at http://lccn.loc.gov/2015039462

This work is dedicated to the memories of my grandfather, Abba Gideon (Dejen) Mengesha, of blessed memory, and my grandmother, Toru (Yafa) Tefery, of blessed memory. They were a shining example of simple, innocent Jews who believed in the truth of their path. In their humble way, they sanctified the Name of Heaven, and sacrificed their lives in glorification of His Name.

This work is also dedicated to the memories of the thousands of Jews who were martyred on their way from Ethiopia to the promised land they called Jerusalem – the Land of Israel.

– Sharon Shalom

* * *

This book is also dedicated to the eternal memory of my father Menachem Manale ha-Levi ben Yehuda and Clara. Menachem was born in Austria in 1926 and came to America in 1939. From the moment he arrived in America he worked – and gave – until his last day. He helped build the wonderful Yeshivat Ramaz, in New York City, where all his children and most of his grandchildren went to school. He also helped support his first cousin Zeev Lev (Willie Low), who started and built Machon Lev in Jerusalem.

– Joey Low

* * *

May their memories be blessed.

Contents

Foreword by Rabbi Dr. Daniel Sperber	xi
Foreword by Rabbi Dr. Yehuda Brandes	xv
Author's Preface to the English Edition	xxv
Acknowledgments	xxxi
Introduction: The Spiritual World of Ethiopian Jewry, Then and Now	1
Shulhan ha-Orit	
The Halakhah of Ethiopian Jewry, Then and Now	73
1. Daily Practices	75
2. Blessings	105
3. Shabbat	117
4. Holidays and Festivals	143
5. Bride, Groom, and Family	189
6. Foundations of the Jewish Home	223
7. Dietary Laws	249
8. Societal Relationships	257
9. Laws of Mourning	267
In Memoriam	283
Reaction to the Book	287
Approbations	291

FLESH OF OUR FLESH
By Rabbi Sharon Shalom

A tribe exiled beyond the Sambatyon
Traveled thousands of miles from Jerusalem to Zion
They shunned non-Jews and the idols of pagans
Waited for the exiles to be gathered in
Never ceasing to tell of Jerusalem.
Shepherds of goats, donkeys, and cows
They kept the mitzvot, lenient and severe, no matter how
When the sign was given, they left behind home and beast
Crossing mountains, hills, and borders without cease
And witnessed God's unbounded miracles.
On foot through forest, river, and thorn
Despite the obstacles, they refused to mourn
Lifted heads in prayer to God in Heaven
Voicing their plea – morning, noon, and even'
For Him to bring them to Jerusalem.
Death overcame men, women, children, and the old
Yet they did not lose hope, but kept their hold
Prayed for Him to save them in their need
And take them to the city beloved, with speed
Jerusalem of dreams, where all paths lead.
Hear, God, their shout and cry
Send Your messengers of good works to fly
Lift these people in Your palms
By land, air, and sea,
And bring them to Jerusalem the free.
Exiled for 2,500 years
Filled with prayer, dream, and tears
Now they live among us in the Holy Land
No longer strangers, we take their hands,
In Zion, city of our delight, they stand.

Foreword by Rabbi Dr. Daniel Sperber

The Sages and scholars of the past insisted on the supreme importance of the continuity of tradition. Among other support, they based their opinion on the verse in Proverbs 1:8, "Hear, my son, the instruction of your father, and do not forsake the Torah of your mother." During the Middle Ages, they formulated a saying that became well known and widespread in halakhic literature: "Jewish tradition is Torah."[1] Scholars have determined that we must not change the melodies of the prayers or the Torah reading,[2] or even the accent and pronunciation of Hebrew in the prayers and Torah reading that we have received from our ancestors.[3] This principle also applies to varying methods of interpreting and deriving halakhah. Each individual should uphold the law of his community – whether it be Ashkenazic, Sephardic, Edot ha-Mizrach, or other.[4]

At the same time, if a person moves from a place where the residents followed a certain custom to a place where the residents follow a different custom, and he intends to settle in the new place permanently, then "He is subject to the rigor of the custom, either of the place he came from or of that to which he went. Thus it is always proper not to act differently from the established customs of a place, on account of the disputes to which such conduct may lead" (Mishnah, *Pesahim* 4:1). In other words, there are circumstances in which a person strays

---

1. Rishba (Rabbi Shlomo Aderet, 1235–1310), commenting on Ramban (Nahmanides), par. 260, Rabbi Yitzhak son of Rabbi Yehuda, *Shibbolei ha-leket ha-shalom*, par. 271:129b. See explanation in my book *Minhagei Yisrael* [Jewish customs], vol. 1 (Jerusalem, 5749/1989), 235–37.
2. See, for example, in *Sefer hassidim*, ed. J. Wistinietski, par. 8:17, and *Minhagei Yisrael*, vol. 2 (Jerusalem, 5755/1995), chapter 9, 264–65.
3. *Shu"t har Zvi, Orah Haim*, par. 4; *Mishpatei Uziel, Orah Haim*, par. 1; *Shulhan Arukh ha-Rav, Orah Haim* 128:45; *Birkhei Yosef, Orah Haim* 53:5; *Nohag ke-tzon Yosef* 68; *Shu"t yabia omer*, vol. 6, *Orah Haim*, 11:33–39.
4. See, for example, Rabbi Yehuda Zarhia Halevy Segal, "Birurim be-gidrei minhagei ha-edot ha-shonot" [Explorations of the boundaries of customs of various communities], *Ha-Torah ve-ha-medinah* 11–13 (5720–22/1960–62): 268–407.

from the tradition of his forebears to a certain extent, and takes upon himself another custom.

But what about an entire community that moved from one place to another, and which has its own ancient tradition based on biblical verses, which developed and was apparently fixed before the period of the Sages and their halakhic interpretations? Must they completely neglect the tradition of dozens of generations and thousands of years? Or may we adopt the Sages' saying: "In the town of Rabbi Yose ha-Gelili, they ate chicken with milk" (Babylonian Talmud, *Hullin* 116a)? Is the rule applying to an entire community that was cut off from its origin similar to the rule for an individual who moves from one place to another?

Such weighty questions have been widely discussed in the halakhic literature, particularly during the periods of expulsion and migration of populations, such as the exile from Spain and in recent generations after the Holocaust, and, at the other end of the spectrum, after the public miracle of the ingathering of the exiles to our Holy Land.

These questions become even more complex when we refer to the sudden uprooting of an entire community with a unique culture, character, and skin color that is completely different from what was accepted previously in Israel. Despite the great variety in our state, and the obvious difficulties of adaptation to a way of life so vastly different from what the community knew in the past, how can we expect it to change its cultural and religious skin overnight, or even in a year or two, and become similar to its brethren? And to which brethren should it become similar – Ashkenazic Jews, Sephardic Jews, or Jews from Edot ha-Mizrach (Eastern communities)? How can the elders of the community, both fathers and mothers, accept with equanimity when their sons and daughters abandon the ways of their ancestors? What will be the fate of these torn and shattered families, and what will be the social, emotional, and spiritual results of such a scenario?

The multifaceted halakhic aspects of these questions are related to halakhic policy and the method of practical halakhic decision making. Is unity equivalent to uniformity, or does it mean mutual responsibility that tolerates the concept of *nehara nehara u-fashtei* ("Every river has its own course" – Babylonian Talmud, *Hullin* 18b; 57a)? What is more, are we able to and is it appropriate for us to act with such "liberal tolerance" regarding issues that are biblically prohibited,[5] when some of these are agreed upon by all other Jewish communities?

---

5. Compare, for example, the various opinions on *helev ha-kesalim* (fat on the upper pelvis of an animal) given in Tur and Beit Yosef on *Yoreh De'ah*, par. 64.

Clearly, then, we must differentiate between biblical law, rabbinic law, and community tradition. Perhaps we should also distinguish between halakhic rulings for individuals and rulings for the public. Similarly, we might also consider the consequences of the attempt to impose far-reaching changes on the communal and familial fabric. Some of the necessary halakhic discussions are fundamental, while others address details, but these categories combine into one under the general rubric of halakhic policy.

For this reason, Rabbi Sharon Shalom – a member of the Ethiopian community who has rabbinic ordination and also serves as a rabbi in practice – has made a positive contribution in taking on the weighty task of offering his community a guide to halakhah, a kind of *Kitzur Shulhan Arukh* for the Ethiopian community. He has done this out of a deep understanding of the needs of the community, its distresses and cries for relief, and in light of sensitivities that we, members of other communities, are not necessarily aware of and do not feel. Toward this purpose, he has labored at this holy project, researching and interpreting halakhah, customs, and traditions according to the elders of his Beta Israel community and his own ancestors, and comparing them to the *halakhot* and customs practiced among the majority of Jewry. He proposes methods of contending with these issues and appropriate halakhic decisions for each detail.

Rabbi Shalom is deeply aware of the process experienced by the youth of the community as they are educated in Israeli institutions. They naturally accept the practices of these institutions and of their comrades, and are gradually being integrated into general Israeli society, particularly during service in the Israel Defense Forces. Awareness of this process has led Rabbi Shalom to distinguish between generations, between parents and children – in other words, between the present period and the more distant future, and he has differentiated between them in his suggestions for halakhic decisions.

In writing this book, Rabbi Shalom has performed a labor of sanctity. He presents it to his community clearly and discerningly, out of involvement and a sense of responsibility, along with understanding of the need for unification with the rest of the Jewish people. Undoubtedly, there will be those who will question his halakhic decisions, details as well as principles. The book may invite illuminating and significant comments that will pave the way for additional discussion. Perhaps this is but the beginning of the path, and not its end. New editions of the book will address additional issues, and even mandate changes in halakhic understanding and decision making. I believe that those who are truly committed to the preservation of tradition but are also aware of the necessity of social and religious integration of the various Jewish communities, those who are disturbed at communal differences in all their manifestations, will benefit by studying this book in depth and by recognizing its wisdom and utility.

On a personal level, I take pride in this work of Rabbi Shalom, my former student, and pride in the small part I played in this significant project. I pray that his efforts will lead to no error, and that his work will lead to a strengthening of love for Torah and observance of the mitzvot, and to love for fellow human beings, as *kol Yisrael arevim zeh la-zeh* ("all Jews are responsible for each other").[6] If even a small portion of this is fulfilled, we will have earned our reward.

---

6. Babylonian Talmud, *Shevuot* 39a.

Foreword by
Rabbi Dr. Yehuda Brandes

We accept the halakhic decision of the Ridvaz[1] that the Beta Israel community of Ethiopia are Jews in the full sense of the word.[2] The Israeli heart is uplifted by the encounter with their dedication and faithfulness to tradition that has spanned many generations. In the last few years, I have participated in the Sigd holiday celebration, held on the hill across from Mount Moriah to the south. This site is first referred to in the Bible in the verse "Abraham lifted up his eyes, and saw the place far off" (Genesis 22:4). The choice of this site at which to celebrate the holiday of the Ethiopian community is exacting and faithful to the community's ancient tradition, for throughout their history, they lifted their eyes in longing from afar, to Jerusalem.

The members of the community, and with them, the entire Jewish people, have merited fulfillment of the verse "I will say to the north: 'Give up,' and to the south: 'Do not hold back; bring My sons from afar, and My daughters from the end of the earth…'" (Isaiah 43:6). This prophecy of comfort in Isaiah seems a particularly appropriate description of the path of those who came to Israel from far in the south, and of the miraculous route they followed through the desert, over the sea, and even through the air, in order to return and gather the dispersed of Israel to their land. The arm of God is the one that "hewed Rahab in pieces, that pierced the dragon…that dried up the sea, the waters of the great deep, that

---

1. Rabbi Yaakov Dovid Wilovsky (1845–1913), responsa, part 7, par. 5.
2. Without addressing the question of the community's history, as per the halakhic decisions of Rabbi Ovadia Yosef (former Sephardi chief rabbi of Israel) and Rabbi Shlomo Goren (former Ashkenazi chief rabbi of Israel). According to Rabbi Avraham Shapira, *ztz"l*: "The decision of the Chief Rabbinate of Israel does not rely on articles or research studies, even religious or rabbinic ones, but rather on halakhic decision making." "Be-inyan tzorekh be-hatafat dam brit be-gerut olei Etiopiah," *Barkai* 3 (5746/1986): 144.

made the depths of the sea a way for the redeemed to pass over" (Isaiah 51:9–10), so that they might fulfill the prophecy "And the ransomed of the Lord shall return, and come with singing to Zion" (Isaiah 51:11). Many individuals took part in this mitzvah – diplomats and Foreign Ministry officials, soldiers of the Israel Defense Forces and members of the security forces, governments of Israel and ordinary Jews. Countless individuals worked indefatigably, sometimes even endangering their lives, both in public and hidden from view. All participated along with the Holy One, blessed be He, in this miraculous deed of salvation and redemption. As in the Exodus from Egypt and the days of Joshua and the Judges, as in the days of the return to Zion, so is this modern redemption. The miracles of redemption represent the conclusion of a protracted chapter of Diaspora and enslavement. But they do not lead to complete serenity and inheritance of the Jewish heritage. A long road begins from here, paved with the challenges of building the Jewish people in the Land of Israel, according to the Torah of Israel, or as we might say – building God's people in God's land, based on God's Torah.

The Beta Israel Jews have a special challenge, unlike any other in the history of the Jewish people. On one hand, this community preserved their Jewish identity and observed the mitzvot devotedly for many generations, despite many obstacles, physical and spiritual, and despite ceaseless attempts to convert them. On the other hand, their tradition of observance is significantly different from the accepted tradition of other Jewish communities, which was influenced by rabbinic writings from the Mishnah and the Talmud and up to the *Shulhan Arukh* and modern authorities. Most agree that Ethiopian tradition reflects ancient halakhah (Jewish law), exhibiting a very loose relationship with the Oral Torah as known to us from the time of the Sages (Hazal).

Some explain this as due to the fact that the Beta Israel community was founded during the time of the dispersion of the Ten Tribes, who had no knowledge of later rabbinic tradition or even of the Oral Torah (codified beginning in the days of the return to Zion, Ezra and Nehemiah, and the members of the Great Assembly, and continuing with the Tannaim and Amoraim), nor of the entire chain of halakhah that relies on them. Some give other reasons. But all agree that there is a significant disparity between Ethiopian tradition and the accepted halakhic tradition of the majority of Jews, much greater than the differences among any of the communities that developed within the Jewish people in the Diaspora, following the destruction of the Second Temple.

The Ridvaz notes that the way the Habash (Abyssinian) Jews, as they were called in his day, observed the Torah bears more similarity to Karaite practice than to rabbinical tradition. However, he recognizes a considerable difference from the Karaites, since the Karaites diverged from rabbinical Judaism and the Oral Torah out of heresy and denial of the Sages' authority. By contrast, the Habash Jews had no direct contact with rabbinic teachings. Thus although they differ from accepted halakhah on many points, this should in no way be considered as *apikorsut* or heresy.

The encounter with Ethiopian tradition poses several fascinating challenges to the world of halakhah, both in the field of academic study as well as for practical halakhic decisions. From an academic point of view, surprising questions and insights arise regarding the existence of an extra-rabbinical halakhic tradition. For example, Beta Israel is the only community that continued to offer the Passover sacrifice many generations after the destruction of the Second Temple, and to this day. Although accepted halakhah does not permit this sacrifice, we may glean foundations for such a tradition from authoritative halakhic sources. *Me-ikkar ha-din* (according to the essence of the law), one may offer the Passover sacrifice without the Temple, in modern times as well, and some recent halakhic authorities have attempted to renew this offering. This issue was raised emphatically by Rabbi Zvi Hirsch Kalischer in the nineteenth century. His proposal inspired a dynamic rabbinic polemic, which remains on the agenda today.

Regarding offering the sacrifice outside Jerusalem, we may rely on the opinion that the prohibition against using local altars for worship is annulled when there is no Temple. The phenomenon most similar to the Beta Israel tradition is Beit Honya (the Temple of Onias at Leontopolis), which operated in Egypt during the Second Temple period. The attitude of the Sages toward this temple was not categorically negative, to the extent that some thought that the Judaism of Beta Israel was directly influenced by the earlier settlement of Jews at Elephantine in Egypt.

For this reason, the Beta Israel tradition of the Passover sacrifice offers a fascinating opportunity to peek behind the screen of two thousand years of sacrificial tradition. Even if it was not preserved in exactly the same way as when the Temple existed, the practical aspects were maintained to a certain extent, as well as something of the spiritual climate that surrounded the sacrifices.[3]

---

3. We must admit that something of the Passover sacrifice has also been preserved in the Passover sacrificial ceremony of the Samaritans. Although the heretical sects were expelled from the Jewish people at the end of the Mishnaic period, the Sages determined that the sects were more exacting in their performance of each mitzvah than the followers of rabbinical Judaism. If so, even if one says that they are sacrificing to honor "a dove" or "to Mount Gerizim" and

Another example is the Ethiopian halakhah regarding the obligation of eating on Yom Kippur that falls on Shabbat. According to the Sages, this has no validity. But the conceptual and practical foundation of this halakhah is related to rabbinical halakhah. The tension between the value of the fast and the mitzvah of *oneg Shabbat* (enjoying the Shabbat) is well known from discussions in the Talmud and the Rishonim, regarding Shabbat in general, and regarding Shabbatot during the Elul period of repentance and the Ten Days of Repentance between Rosh Hashanah and Yom Kippur. In the final account, the Sages forbade fasting on Shabbat, except for unusual exceptions, such as fasts of exceptional Hassidim and fasting following a dream.

The idea that the fast of Yom Kippur does not overrule the sanctity of the Shabbat and the mitzvah of enjoying the Shabbat has some basis, if we study the sources and refuse to rely merely on knowledge of the final ruling practiced today. The existence of a community that implements this concept, although it opposes rabbinic halakhah, recalls the significant differences in halakhic practice developed by disparate Jewish communities, which have led to the creation of diverse customs for other holidays and festivals. One example of this is the differences in Passover foods, between Orthodox Jews who avoid *matzah shruyah* (matzah that has come into contact with water) and those who do not observe this stringency, and between Ashkenazic Jews who refrain from eating *kitniyot* (legumes) and Sephardic Jews who do eat them. Another example is the differences in the laws of *kashrut* for meat, between those who stringently observe the custom of checking the lung for defects (*glatt* kosher – applies to Sephardic and some Ashkenazic Jews), following the opinion of Rabbi Yosef Caro (the Beit Yosef), and those who observe the lenient position on this ruling, following the Rema (Rabbi Moses Isserles, 1520–1572). Some stringent Sephardic *poskim* compare the consumption of non-*glatt* meat to transgression of the biblical prohibition against eating *nevelot* (carcasses of kosher animals not killed in accordance with halakhah) and *terefot* (food ritually unfit for consumption), which is equal in severity to the prohibition against eating on Yom Kippur.

Interestingly, the laws of Shabbat observance that were preserved by the Ethiopian community are closer to the Shabbat laws in the book of Jubilees than to those recorded by the Sages. Researchers accept that "ancient halakhah," practiced by some of the sects during the Second Temple period and during the period

---

not to the God of Israel, in the act of their mitzvah we may identify components of the way it was performed during Temple times.

of the Sages, ruled more strictly on Shabbat laws than did the Sages. These laws, which until now were known only from the literature, were partially implemented in the halakhah of Beta Israel. Under Beta Israel halakhah, many prohibitions of *shvut* (cessation of work) that rabbinical Judaism considers *de-rabbanan* (rabbinically mandated) are considered biblical prohibitions.[4]

In summary, the theoretical and scholarly challenges that Beta Israel halakhah raises for traditional Talmudic halakhah are as follows: (1) understanding the sources and assumptions that formed the underpinnings of Beta Israel halakhah; (2) comparison with general Jewish halakhah and identification of the sources within accepted Talmudic law that are close to the Beta Israel approach; (3) explanation of the Sages' position and its reasoning, as opposed to Beta Israel halakhah and its reasoning, following the approach of "These and those are the words of the living God."[5]

I think that every scholar and researcher will welcome these findings as a great treasure, as they have the potential to enrich and deepen the study of halakhah and of works of Torah scholarship. This in no way intends to undermine, not even by a hair's breadth, the stability and strength of the Oral Law or the obligation to the tradition of halakhic practice, just as studying the opinion of the House of Shammai does not undermine the obligating validity of halakhah that was decided according to the House of Hillel.

The practical halakhic challenge posed by the Beta Israel community is more complex. The question that arises from every paragraph in the chapters of this book is how we must contend with this Beta Israel halakhic tradition. At first glance, three main possibilities arise. First, we may obligate the Beta Israel community to accept mainstream halakhah. Second, we may obligate the members of this community to maintain full loyalty to the tradition they have received. The third possibility is a compromise, which suggests some integration between the first two options.

Under the first option, we recognize that the vast majority of the Jewish people accepted the tradition of the Sages and of halakhah as it was consolidated from the Mishnah to the *Shulhan Arukh* and its commentators. Therefore, Ethiopian immigrants who wish to observe the mitzvot properly are obligated to join existing halakhic practice, and thus abandon their own halakhic tradition.

This position has several important motives: (1) uniformity of the halakhah;

---

4. Gilat Yitzhak, *Perakim be-hishtalshelut ha-halakhah* (Ramat Gan, 5752/1992).
5. Babylonian Talmud, *Eruvin* 13b.

(2) acceptance of the majority opinion as halakhically binding and as an expression of divine will; and (3) prevention of a societal and national rift.

The second option requires strict preservation of Ethiopian halakhah to the extent possible, both in terms of the self-understanding of the community and as binding halakhic-rabbinic teaching. For according to the law of "Do not forsake the Torah of your mother" (Proverbs 1:8), every Jew is required to follow the halakhic tradition of his ancestors. Such is the tradition of the members of the Beta Israel community. Following another interpretation, we may base this position on the halakhah of *minhag ha-makom*, "Whoever goes from a place where the people followed a certain tradition...to a place where they followed another tradition."[6] Such a person is required to accept the stringent rulings of the place that he left (in other words, the stringencies of Ethiopian halakhah) as well as the stringencies of the place to which he went (in other words, the stringencies of mainstream halakhah).

The third possibility, as mentioned, is a compromise position, and this is the position proposed by the author of this book. This position attempts to combine preservation of Ethiopian custom with integration of the community into Israeli society. In the following paragraphs, I will attempt to explain the value of this solution over the others.

The demand that the Beta Israel community accept Talmudic halakhah is not the same as the demand that an individual who has entered another community follow its customs. The foundation of the vitality and endurance of this community is in its stubborn preservation of the customs of its ancestors, and sometimes in the extreme stringencies to which they dedicated themselves on a daily basis. In this sense, "Do not foresake the Torah of your mother" is not a saying from the book of Proverbs or an adage that was adopted by halakhah for the rules governing traditions, but rather the foundation of the community's existence. The demand to abandon the ancient traditions and the authority of the *kesim*, their spiritual leaders, and to "convert" to Orthodox, rabbinic Judaism, is, from their point of view, intolerable. At the very least, it represents a personal injury on the level of deceit and humiliation, disrespect toward the *kesim*, and discredit of the Rishonim. Furthermore, we also have good reason to assume that the societal and spiritual significance of such a process will be the complete abandonment of religion by the youth of the community, who will lose the remaining fragment of their faith, which relies on the ancestral traditions. This is indeed happening

---

6. Babylonian Talmud, *Hullin* 18b.

before our very eyes, as it did in the previous generation of aliyah from Islamic countries, until the inception of the movement *le-hahzir atarah le-yoshnah*, "to return the crown of Torah to its ancient glory," which restored the traditional foundation of faith and mitzvot to these communities.

From a purely halakhic aspect, we must discuss this question: If a Jewish community was disconnected from the Jewish people and was not party to the halakhah decided by the majority, should it be required to accept the majority halakhah? Possibly, we must differentiate between the period in which the Great Sanhedrin was active in ancient Israel, when its authority and the validity of its laws applied to the entire Jewish nation without exception, and the period that followed. Possibly, because the Ethiopian Jews did not live under the authority of the Sanhedrin during the Second Temple period, they hold no obligation to its rulings.

On the other hand, we may use the prohibition of *lo titgodedu* (self-mutilation in mourning for the dead) to guide an approach of forbidding the community from following some of its customs, particularly when these conflict with a law accepted as a basic principle of the Torah. Certainly in the past, when the Sanhedrin was active, the aspiration developed that the great court which met in the Lishkat ha-Gazit (Chamber of Hewn Stone) would formulate one overall body of halakhah for the entire Jewish people. But after the Temple was destroyed and the Sanhedrin sent into exile, the Jews were unable to reach agreement on a uniform halakhah for the nation, or to enforce it. Other mechanisms replaced the Sanhedrin, and despite the enormous variety of communal traditions, one central halakhah was created that applies to the entire Jewish people. Even in the postmodern world, there is no justification to practice a variety of traditions. The halakhah does not take a favorable view of individuals and groups practicing their own traditions. "There shall be one law…for you" (Numbers 15:16) is a fundamental value derived from the Torah that supports one mode of behavior for the entire Jewish people, not for each individual. This is especially so after the Jews have come together in the Land of Israel, and we aspire to the restoration of our judges as in ancient times and to the establishment of one Torah law in the State of Israel for all Jews.

For this reason, we must pave an intermediate path that will balance between both concepts. This path should enable practice and respect for the customs and traditions of the community, but also enable integration of the community and its practices into mainstream halakhah. Wherever the differences touch on fundamental questions in halakhah, particularly issues in which the Ethiopian custom is considered forbidden under mainstream halakhah, or when general Jewish custom is considered forbidden under Ethiopian halakhah, we must make an effort to adapt practice so that preservation of the Ethiopian tradition will not create a fundamental conflict with accepted halakhah.

Rabbi Sharon Shalom has done well to present in this book a model for a system enabling peaceful coexistence of these two *atzei hayim*, "trees of life," of Torah, whose roots and trunk are shared, but whose branches have grown apart. In the first part of his book, Rabbi Shalom discusses the theoretical questions underpinning his work. But the principal significance of the book is in the second section. For each clause of the entire scope of halakhah, he suggests a practical solution for compromise between mainstream and Beta Israel halakhah, integrating the historical decision of the Jewish majority with the obligation to respect and preserve the traditions of the minority.

Rabbi Sharon Shalom is well suited to this task, both through his education and through his personal talents. As a member and leader of the Beta Israel community on the one hand, and on the other, as a long-standing student of Torah in Israeli yeshivas who was ordained by the Chief Rabbinate of Israel, he is well acquainted with these two worlds, and lives within them. In his personal life, he is able to integrate his origin in the particular community of Beta Israel with full absorption into Israeli religious society, at once both traditional and modern. Aside from his education, he is gifted with sensitivity, and has the social and communal ties that enable him to attend to the human and social implications of halakhic and leadership decisions.

I do not believe that this book was written as a binding book of halakhic decisions, as *ka-zeh re'eh ve-kadesh*.[7] The writer has provided us with a kind of *Shulhan Arukh*, a table laden with bountiful delights, but he does not dictate "accept my decision" on every detail and issue he discusses. In many details, the solutions he offers are refined and astute, and have the capacity to settle the disputes between the two traditions. In some cases, the difficulties are too severe to expect easy solutions, and his opinion may not be accepted – sometimes by the *kesim* and the community, at other times by the *poskim* and rabbis. At any rate, a leader who accepts this book as general instruction may use it to direct his community, formulate community guidelines, and instruct individuals who consult with him, and will find it to be a great blessing.

On the other hand, some representatives of both sides may view the general

---

7. Babylonian Talmud, *Rosh Hashanah* 20a.

direction of this book as a concession that is not at all legitimate. The author gives many examples of rigidity and insensitivity on the part of public leaders and halakhic experts, and we may add a range of other individuals to this list. We can only hope that this book will also serve to heighten awareness of the Jewish and human aspect that lies beyond the halakhic rigidity imposed on every leader of the Jewish public, even for those who do not agree with his central assumptions. This applies both to those who disagree with the decree of the Ridbaz and who do not accept the Judaism of the Beta Israel community, and to those who consider it forbidden to concede even the smallest point of their ancestors' traditions – either way, one tradition is undermined, either rabbinic or Beta Israel.

A fundamental principle of the Torah is *derakheiha darkhei noam ve-kol netivoteiha shalom* – "Her ways are ways of pleasantness, and all her paths are peace" (Proverbs 3:17). This book was written out of deep faith in the value of peace. For this reason, beyond the halakhic details and the deep philosophical discussion, every page of this book emits a powerful call for peace and pleasant ways. As Rabbi Akiva said, "This is a major principle of the Torah: 'Love your neighbor as yourself.'"

Author's Preface to the English Edition

❧ Between Preservation and Renewal

When *From Sinai to Ethiopia* was published in Hebrew by Yediot Publishing, no one estimated the extent of its influence on interreligious dialogue within and without the Ethiopian community. It was clear to Yediot, a well-respected publishing house in Israel, that this book was targeted to the Ethiopian sector. But we were greatly surprised that the concepts the book presents attracted the interest of many Israelis, religious and secular, from many sectors. On first analysis, we might ask, why should such a book meet with success, engaging a wide spectrum of groups and ages in such a modern, free society? Apparently, Israeli society is deeply interested in questions about the identity of the Beta Israel community. The questions of identity that engage Beta Israel represent an additional facet of the questions of self that concern many members of Israeli society. In other words, this book addresses the dilemmas of immigrants in carving out a new path in their new home, and in a new age – in other words, it delves into the tension between preservation and renewal.

❧ Between Modernity and Tradition

In the past two decades, the world has taken a dramatic turn, unlike any previous change. Electronic communications technology has transformed people around the world who were previously disconnected from each other into participants in the information age and consumers in the global market. Still, when we say "village," we mean a small settlement, and when we say "global," we refer to something that encompasses the entire world. A conflict is created between the small village and the global one. People do not remain in the place where they began their life's journey, but migrate to wherever they think they will be well-off and comfortable. Today, 20–40 percent of the populations of most Western countries were not born in their country of residence.

The revolution of modernity has led to rejection of an entire world of tradition – a world that upheld the ideal of following ancestral tradition. Human beings now view their environment as subject to their own design, and assert that they are permitted to change it. Individuals do what they think is best for them. The free, modern individual no longer fears threats and bans as practiced in the Jewish world in the past, or persecution and censure as once practiced by the authorities of the Catholic Church. Against this background, we face the challenge of defining the boundaries between local and universal culture. Tensions arise between the aspiration to preserve the culture of origin and the desire to integrate into the new one, between assimilation and integration, between nationality and religion. Questions such as these occupy millions of people in Israel and around the world.

Still, despite the freedom of citizens of the modern world to make autonomous decisions about their lives, the decisive majority prefer to view themselves as part of something continuous, as belonging at the root of their souls to something larger. Many times, it seems that grasping onto tradition is the solution for this existential need. *From Sinai to Ethiopia* has succeeded in touching on these questions, in a significant manner. From the reactions to the book in Israel, it is clear that these questions interest substantial numbers of people, from all sectors.

Difference, Equality, and Responsibility

The Bible describes the creation of the world, the heavens and the earth, light and darkness, land and water, and animals. Then it tells how God created all of humanity in His image: "And God created man in His own image; in the image of God He created him; male and female He created them" (Genesis 1:28). In the Jewish world, the concept of the creation of humanity in the image of God is one of the foundations of faith. As Rabbi Akiva would say, "Human beings are beloved because they were created in the image of God, as in the verse, 'In the image of God He made man' (Genesis 9:6)" (Mishnah, *Avot* 3:14). *From Sinai to Ethiopia* expresses this concept in a straightforward manner: in all the ways of worshipping God there is no one truth, but rather a variety of equal truths. Each person must discover his own way of connecting to the God in Whose image he is individually made.

This book adopts a pluralistic understanding, supporting integration but not the annulment of different cultures. In my opinion, difference between human beings is a priori ontological, just as it is in the natural world. It is in this sense that we may comprehend the blessing *Hakham ha-razim* ("The Knower of all secrets") – "One who witnesses 600,000 Jews gathered together should recite the blessing *Hakham ha-razim*, for just as each of their faces is different from the others, their personalities are also different from each other, and each one has his own individual personality."[1] This book calls for integration and mutual, egalitarian respect, and a renewed kind of melting pot that is not destructive. Pluralism accepts difference as part of human nature, with each individual facet expressing itself in an equal manner.

In Jewish sources, the individual is considered, first and foremost, as bearing responsibilities, and not enjoying rights. The Torah educates us for personal responsibility in every situation. On one hand, minorities bear responsibility toward the majority. What is considered to be prejudice against minority groups is actually damaging to the personal responsibility of that group. On the other hand, the majority bears responsibility toward minority groups, and what is considered assistance to the weak may in fact be damaging to them.

✣ A Call for Pluralism

The Mishnah asks, why was Adam created alone – why did humanity begin with one person? To teach us, the Mishnah explains, that a person should never say, "My father is greater than yours," as we are all descended from the same person (*Sanhedrin* 4:6). We thus have a firm basis to argue that a person who considers himself greater than another is committing a serious error, which borders on immorality. It follows that a person who does not value himself, who considers himself significantly inequal in value to other human beings who were created in the image of God, is also in error, and approaching immorality. The common denominator is that both are harming the image of God. The fact that a person is white, black, short, disabled, Jewish, Christian, or Muslim says nothing about whether he or she is a person who reflects the image of God. Everything is determined by the manner in which a person understands himself as a person created in the image of God.

This is not a call for monolithic religion or society, but rather for multiculturalism anchored in individual responsibility and mutual respect. The call for pluralism does not mean anarchy, as in the verse "There was no king in Israel, and

---

1. *Midrash Tanhuma* (Buber), Parashat Pinhas, par. 1b.

every man did what was right in his eyes" (Judges 17:1), or blurring of the lines that divide groups, but rather preservation of uniqueness along with mutual personal responsibility. The Torah's dictum "Love your neighbor as yourself" is an expression of this personal responsibility. "As yourself" means that you should be capable of looking at the world through the eyes of the other, just as you have become accustomed to looking through your own eyes. We find an example of this in the relations between non-Jews and Jews in Ethiopia. The Jews of Ethiopia strictly upheld the custom of avoiding contact with non-Jews. Yet at celebrations and public events, they invited their Christian neighbors, just as the Christians invited the Jews to their events, without any bias. The groups sat separately and each group slaughtered according to its custom, but Jews and Christians respected each other. This custom teaches us that the Ethiopian Jews' customs were based on a moral foundation, according to which all individuals are equal before God. Perhaps this is another reason that many readers have identified with the theological spirit of this book, in which uniqueness is not the opposite of unity, but rather its synonym.

❧ Toward the Next Book

There is a story about a certain rabbi who used to receive a constant stream of followers throughout the day. One day, the *shamash* asked him, "Why do you sweat so much when you receive people?" The rabbi answered, "Each time I meet someone, I try to strip my emotional clothing and don his, so that I can truly understand him. I do this for each and every person. That is why I sweat." In today's reality in Israel, we aspire to achieve a reality in which "Each person takes upon himself the yoke of the kingdom of Heaven, one from another" (*malkhut shamayim zeh mi-zeh*). According to Rabbi Samson Raphael Hirsch, this means that Jews will accept the yoke of the kingdom of Heaven through their relationships with each other – in other words, their openness to each other brings them closer to God. In this manner, everyone wins. People develop a sense of belonging; they feel that they are contributing and that others trust them. Thus they are educated for strong, healthy interpersonal relations, free of jealousy and competition, firmly anchored within an atmosphere of responsibility and tolerance. *From Sinai to Ethiopia* was written out of a deep sense of faith in the concept that both sides are the words of the living God, and that there are many channels for worshipping God. How do we create such a theological-social reality? How do we create a society founded on trust and mutual respect? How do we form a society based on pluralism and egalitarianism? How do we form a consciousness based on the deep understanding that human uniformity is contrary to nature and outside of morality? And through this, aspire to human unity? In my next book, we will attempt to contend with these questions.

Acknowledgments

I wish to thank all the wonderful people who supported me over the many years since I made aliyah without my immediate family, and who continue to do so to this day – in elementary school at the Emunah Sarah Herzog Children's Center in Afula, the Shafir Youth Aliya dormitory in Shapira Center, Har Etzion Yeshiva in Alon Shvut, Herzog College, Michlalah – Jerusalem College, the Department of Talmud and the Ludwig and Erica Jesselson Institute for Advanced Torah Studies at Bar-Ilan University, and Beit Morasha in Jerusalem. To all I offer thanks from the depths of my heart. The tolerance and trust I received from these institutions gave me the feeling that I can, and that I am able. I am certain that a large portion of my achievements is the result of great investment on the part of the teaching staff, counselors, and rabbis. May God be with them in all their efforts. I also wish to extend my special thanks to Rabbi Aryeh and Ahuvah Shalom, who were like a second family to me. They served as the model of a Western family, and as a source of inspiration, support, and advice, and continue to encourage me to this day.

This is the place to thank those who assisted me in the work of writing, particularly in the section *Shulhan ha-Orit*.[1] First of all, I would like to express my heartfelt thanks to Rabbi Dr. Daniel Sperber, for his exemplary advising. His comments, recommendations, and emendations assisted me to reach this point. My teachers Rabbi Shabtai Rappaport, *shlita*, and Rabbi Yehuda Brandes, *shlita*, in addition to encouragement and support, provided a wealth of illuminating comments that contributed to improving this work, especially the halakhic section. Rabbi Nachum Rabinowitz, *shlita*, received me warmly and recognized the significance of this work. He took from his valuable time to read over the entire manuscript, and made important comments, many of which are incorporated

---

1. This is a play on the name of the well-known codification of Jewish law the *Shulhan Arukh*, written in the sixteenth century by Rabbi Yosef Caro. *Orit* is the Ge'ez word for Torah.

into the book. I also thank the members of the Basic Jewish Studies Program, and members of the Department of Philosophy at Bar-Ilan University, as well as the members of the Department of History at Orot Israel College-Elkana, Dr. Amnon Hever for his brilliant ideas, and my teacher Professor Binyamin Ish Shalom.

Without the support of my doctoral advisors Rabbi Dr. Noam Zohar and Dr. Nissim Leon, I would not have been able to write this book or to reach the advanced stage in writing my dissertation. David Nigel provided support in the course "Ethiopian Jewry" in the Basic Jewish Studies Program. I am grateful to my friends from the Tzohar Rabbinical Association, and in particular to Rabbi Ronen Neuwirth. I also thank the Tzohar Rabbinical Association for initiating, along with Baruch Keisler and the congregation committee, my service as rabbi of the Kedoshei Yisrael congregation. The association continues to support me in this holy work. This community is a wonderful example of tolerance in accepting the "other." The members of the Kedoshei Yisrael congregation, and the mayor of Kiryat Gat, who is attentive to the needs of the residents in general and of the congregation in particular, are all deserving of thanks.

I also thank the researchers of SOSTEJE, the Society for the Study of Ethiopian Jewry, in Israel and around the world. I thank my friends and comrades from Har Etzion Yeshiva, as well as Rabbi Reuven-Tal Iasso, *shlita*, whose enthusiasm over the manuscript and support of the concept assisted me greatly and served as a source of strength throughout the lengthy journey. Dr. Dov Herman's three books (*Ma'agal hayei ha-yom yom ba-bayit ha-yehudi* [Daily life in the Jewish home; Prolog, 2006], *Ma'agal ha-hagim ve-ha-mo'adim ba-bayit ha-yehudi* [The cycle of the holidays and festivals in the Jewish home; Prolog, 2005], and *Ma'agal ha-hayim ba-bayit ha-yehudi* [The life cycle in the Jewish home; Prolog, 2005]) assisted me in writing this book, and I have quoted from them numerous times. My deepest thanks go to Amihai Berholz, chief editor of Yediot Aharonot Publishing: from the moment the manuscript reached him, Amihai paved the way for publication of the book in a professional, reliable, and responsible manner. Throughout the process, Rabbi Avraham Wengruber served as my study partner, and his comments helped me to elucidate issues that I previously had thought were clear.

I thank the researchers of Ethiopian Jewry and members of the Ethiopian community whom I interviewed for the purpose of writing this book. Some are my family members, and unfortunately some of them are no longer living. My grandfather and grandmother, Abba Gideon (Dejen) Mengesha and Toru (Yafa) Tefery, of blessed memory, from whom I had the merit to learn Torah. To the spiritual leaders of the community – the wise men, the *kahanotsh* (*kesim*).

In particular, I thank Kohen Werede Nega, of blessed memory; Kohen Trune Salomon, Kohen Kes Tefesahaku Malchi Zedek Fkadu, Kohen Kes Brahan Iheis, Kohen Kes Mentosnot (Eli) Wende, and Kohen Kes Rafael Hadana, may they live long lives. I thank Avraham Yardai, who read the book carefully immediately after publication and offered informative comments on his own initiative, which I have incorporated into the English version. Hezi Ovadia, of blessed memory, granted me much of his time – I learned much from him about his battles with the Israeli-religious establishment regarding the aliyah of Ethiopian Jewry.

To all the individuals who gave me their time and answered my questions, and to the spiritual leaders of the community who serve their flock day and night, in celebrations and mourning, memorial days and holidays, I wish long lives.

Thanks to my friend Joey Low. His significant contribution toward this book allowed us to begin to translate the book.

I'd like to thank Dina Hahn, chairperson of World Emunah, which ordered a sizeable number of copies of the English edition of the book, and thus made a significant contribution to its publication. This is also the place to offer my heartfelt thanks to my friend Shlomo Kassel, director of Emunah Sarah Herzog Children's Center in Afula; to Leora Minka, chair of Emunah Israel; and to my teacher, Rabbi Dr. Daniel Sperber, for the financial assistance they granted me and for their rapid sponsorship of this project.

I would also like to thank my friends in Montreal – Steve and Saryl Gross, Ilan Gewurz and Julie Shugarman, and Samuel and Brenda Gewurz – who helped make this publication possible.

This is my second year of participation in the Beit Midrash program for the Israeli rabbinate, sponsored by the Shalom Hartman Institute and Oranim College. It has been my great privilege to be included in this special group, which demonstrates a heightened sensitivity to the "other." This group succeeds in implementing a spiritual vision that integrates the values of individuality and solidarity, that emphasizes unity but disdains uniformity. I would like to take this opportunity to express my sincere thanks to my friends and colleagues in the program.

Many thanks to Ilan Greenfield, publisher of Gefen Publishing House, who saw great importance in promoting the publication of this book. He recognized the significance and value of the book and the unique voice it represents, and he personally handled and shepherded its publication with patience and professionalism. In this vein I'd like to thank my translator, Jessica Setbon, and editor, Kezia Raffel Pride. Beyond just translation and editing, working with them was like a *havruta*, a scholarly exchange.

May God grant them health and success in all their endeavors, and may their worthy deeds be rewarded.

Last but not least, I thank my family. I offer my thanks and appreciation to my mother and father, who have enveloped me with love and concern, from the journey from Ethiopia to Sudan to the reunion here in Israel. I also thank my parents' relatives, Bituali and Asresu Tespay, who agreed to take on the heavy responsibility of taking me with them on our aliyah, without my parents, from Sudan to Israel. I thank my wife's family, and particularly Grandmother Batsheva Adolph – to me her life is an example. Despite everything she underwent as a Holocaust survivor, Grandmother Batsheva continues to demonstrate powerful faith in the Master of the universe, and continues to take personal responsibility in all aspects of her life. May God grant her a long life in full health.

I thank my in-laws, Dr. Aharon and Tzameret Gavlinger, for their unending support throughout the entire process, for their deep concern and warm embrace filled with compassion and respect. They have been and continue to be an anchor and source of security for myself and my family. May God grant them success in all their efforts.

Finally, I thank my wife Avital, who has supported me in her wisdom from the conception of this project until its birth. Throughout, she has constantly offered me her assistance, encouragement, and support, until I was privileged to see it through to completion. Words cannot express my thanks for her help. I pray to the Master of the universe that we and our children – Roi Gideon, Nadav Mordechai, Ziv Yehuda, Gil Haya, and Tohar – will enjoy long lives in full health, and may God be with us in all our paths. May we enjoy mutual respect and Torah learning along with love and tolerance. May it be His will that we merit worshipping God with full intent and pureness of heart. We thank God for the grace He constantly bestows upon us. May it be Your will our God, that no harm will be done by our actions. May we not fail in mitzvot between ourselves and our fellow human beings, whether in halakhah or *aggadah*. May our fellows be pleased with us, and we be pleased with them.

I thank the Holy One, blessed be He, Who remained by my side throughout the travails of the journey from Ethiopia to Israel, Who saved me from dangers and pitfalls, and Who sheltered me under His wing. Illnesses, plagues, and thousands of enemies surrounded me, but they did not approach me, and only looked into my eyes. To paraphrase the Psalm (91:11), For He commanded His angels on my behalf to guard me in all my ways. Moses did not have the privilege of entering the Land of Israel, and countless generations of Jews dreamed of Jerusalem but did not merit witnessing the return of God to Zion. I thank God for granting me the merit to enter the Land of Israel. Why did I merit this? I cannot know. But I do know that I have a duty – "I shall not die, but live, and declare the works of the Lord" (Psalms 118:17), and the astounding story of religious Zionism, whose stubborn path led to the rebirth of the State of Israel and the Jewish people. "With long life will I satisfy him, and make him to behold My salvation" (Psalms 91:16).

I pray that this book will open for Ethiopian Jewry a channel through which they may discover the philosophical world of the Beta Israel community, and that it will carve a path for dialogue between communities and a meeting between worlds. I pray that Beta Israel will become an inseparable part of the mosaic of the Jewish people and Israeli society. May the love of Heaven and love of humanity increase, for beloved is humanity who was created in His image.

Introduction: The Spiritual World of Ethiopian Jewry, Then and Now

This book was born out of a personal need to find a particular path for worshipping God. In my opinion, many members of the Ethiopian community, of the first generation and especially of the second generation, share this need. The move to another country burned the Ethiopian community deeply. Apparently, many Ethiopian Jews do not view their tradition as a link connecting their past to their present and future in the State of Israel. The community's ancient traditions, bound by a strong cord to the time of the Mishnah, made it unique and separated it from mainstream Judaism. Against this background, the community wavers between the commitment to preserving its tradition (and thus being defined as different) and the longing to join the majority, without particular characteristics. The lack of a spiritual path that connects past, present, and future has led many Ethiopian Jews to a theological crisis, disorientation, and a sense of helplessness.

My esteemed teachers (Rabbi Shabtai Rappaport, *shlita*; Rabbi Yehuda Brandes, *shlita*; Rabbi Nachum Rabinowitz, *shlita*; Rabbi Dr. Daniel Sperber, *shlita*; and Rabbi Reuven-Tal Iasso, *shlita*) proposed that I separate the fields of halakhah and philosophy. Thus the present book addresses the halakhic field, while a philosophical book that will examine questions of identity is expected for publication in the near future.

I view this book as a window through which readers may peek into the world of Ethiopian tradition and halakhic interpretation, and understand contemporary halakhic decisions, as presented below in *Shulhan ha-Orit*. In writing this book, I have essentially created "something from something," as I have collected already existing written material that was scattered throughout many articles and books, and organized it into a structured composition. Thus I am not stating anything new here. The interviews with community and spiritual leaders, which demanded intense attention and much patience and tolerance, proved a significant addition to this work.

As the author of *Mesillat Yesharim* (Path of the Just), Rabbi Moshe Haim Luzzatto, wrote:

> I have written this work not to teach men what they do not know, but to remind them of what they already know and is very evident to them, for you will find in most of my words only things which most people know, and concerning which they entertain no doubts. But to the extent that they are well known and their truths revealed to all, so is forgetfulness in relation to them extremely prevalent.[1]

What brings intelligent people, wise and knowledgeable individuals, linguistic artists, to ignore the simple and well-known principles upon which the world is based, such as mitzvot *bein adam le-haveiro*, the laws that govern interpersonal relationships?

The author of *Mesillat Yesharim* provides us with an answer to this question:

> A consideration of the general state of affairs will reveal that the majority of men of quick intelligence and keen mentality devote most of their thought and speculation to the subtleties of wisdom and the profundities of analysis, each according to the inclination of his intelligence and his natural bent. There are some who expend a great deal of effort in studying creation and nature. Others devote all of their thought to astronomy and mathematics, and others to the arts. There are those who go more deeply into sacred studies, into the study of the holy Torah, some occupying themselves with halakhic discussions, others with Midrash and others with legal decisions. There are few, however, who devote thought and study to perfection of Divine service – to love, awe, communion with God, and the other aspects of *hassidut* [saintliness].

Failure to attend to such simple issues also causes distance from the Divine path:

> This state of affairs results in evil consequences both for those who possess wisdom and for those who do not, causing both classes to lack true saintliness,

---

1. Rabbi Moshe Haim Luzzatto, introduction to *Mesillat Yesharim*, trans. Aryeh Kaplan (5734/1974).

and rendering it extremely rare. The wise lack it because of their limited consideration of it and the unwise because of their limited grasp. The result is that saintliness is construed by most to consist in the recitation of many Psalms, very long confessions, difficult fasts, and ablutions in ice and snow – all of which are incompatible with intellect and which reason cannot accept.

Rabbi Moshe Haim Luzzatto addresses the phenomenon of ignoring issues that are well known and evident. The more evident they are, the more they are ignored, and people forget them. What is the cause of this? According to the author of *Mesillat Yesharim*, the cause is that most intelligent people invest their energy in studying "the subtleties of wisdom and the profundities of analysis," such that they forget and even distance themselves from *hassidut* and ethical interpersonal relations.

Yet Rabbi Luzzatto did not answer the question of what causes people to invest their energy in refined halakhic arguments. Further, in the final analysis, everyone is aware that "true saintliness" is the basis for a just society. So why do such people not repent and admit that they have erred?

I believe the solution to this question lies in the words of Rabbi Elazar Hakapor about the qualities that lead a person to the grave: "Jealousy, and lust, and ambition, drive a person out of the world."[2] Here Rabbi Elazar teaches us that in the presence of one of these characteristics, no human being is left. The person is erased. Human intelligence does not function at all. As Rabbi Moshe Almozalino says, "driving a person out of the world" means the loss of common sense, because it is as if he has abandoned the human side of himself, and thus he is erased from the world.[3]

In other words, excessive preoccupation with "the subtleties of wisdom" is only a symptom of a greater problem: having been "driven from the world" by jealousy, lust, and ambition (in other words, ego). Still, the solution is not to flee from such traits. A dichotomous understanding of the world is invalid, as it is based on despair and fear. Inner exploration of egotistical characteristics reveals that they have two sides. On one hand, they detach the person from grasping onto the grounding of reality – they "drive a person out of the world." On the other hand, these qualities serve as an anchor for creative activity, and give a person power and majesty. The root of creativity is also the root of destruction. It is

---

2. Mishnah, *Avot* 4:21.
3. *Midrash Shmuel*, Avot 4.

incorrect to adopt a passive lifestyle and to make it into an ideology. The significance of such an approach is to amplify one side of life, the dark side, garbed in a cloak of misfortune and lack of vision or creativity. This spirit is inappropriate for intelligent human beings, certainly not for the Jew, who is commanded to fashion himself in the image of God. How can this be accomplished?

> Rabbi Yehuda Bar Simon began, "After the Lord your God shall you follow" (Deuteronomy 13:5). But can human beings follow the Holy One, blessed be He, He about whom it is written, "Your way was in the sea, and Your path in the great waters" (Psalms 77:20)?... Can human beings ascend to the heavens and cling to the Divine Presence, about whom it is written, "For the Lord your God is a devouring fire" (Deuteronomy 4:24)?... Rather, from the beginning of creation the Holy One has been occupied first with planting – "And the Lord God planted a garden eastward, in Eden" (Genesis 2:8). Similarly, when you enter the Land, you should occupy yourself first with planting – "When you shall come into the Land and shall have planted" (Leviticus 19:23).[4]

Thus the solution is not found in the depths of the ocean nor in the heavens above, but rather deep within ourselves, in our self-awareness – in the ability to distinguish between envy, lust, and the search for honor that lead a person to creativity and humanity, and envy, lust, and the search for honor that reduce a person to glorification of the ego, such that "There is no other but myself." An extremely thin line separates these two states. Nothing but the tip of a letter *yud* separates between "*Ein od milvado*" (There is no other but Him) and "*Ein od milvadi*" (There is no other but myself). Thus Rabbi Yosef Dov Soloveitchik describes the dichotomous character of a person who grasps these two modes of being:

> It is in this light that we can understand the deep contradiction pervading the spiritual self-evaluation of *homo religiosus*. On the one hand, he senses his own lowliness and insignificance, his own frailty and weakness; he knows that even "a gnat precedes him, a snail preceded him." He sees himself as...the one biological creature who has misused his own talents for destructive ends, who has failed in the task assigned to him. On the other hand, he is aware of his own greatness and loftiness, how his spirit breaks through all barriers and ascends to the very heights, bores through all obstacles and descends to the very depths. Is he not the crown of creation to whom God granted

---

4. *Leviticus Rabbah* 25.

> dominion over all the work of His hands?...In the depths of his consciousness he is entangled in the thicket of two contradictory verses. One verse declares, "When I behold Your heavens, the work of Your fingers, the moon and the stars which You have established; what is man, that You think of him?" (Psalms 8:4–5), while the other verse declares, "Yet You have made him but a little lower than the angels, and have crowned him with glory and honor. You have made him to have dominion over the works of Your hands; You have put all things under his feet" (Psalms 8:6–7).[5]

We thus find that the individual faces a challenging task, if not an insurmountable one. He must find the path between "There is no other but myself" and "There is no other but Him." With an understanding of the fine difference between these two perspectives, we may now understand Rabbi Luzzatto's proposal for correcting the problem, which he presents in his introduction:

> Though the beginnings and foundations of saintliness are implanted in every person's heart, if he does not occupy himself with them, he will witness details of saintliness without recognizing them and he will trespass upon them without feeling or perceiving that he is doing so.[6]

Several reasons brought me, as an Ethiopian Jew, to write this book. The first reason, as I have mentioned, is out of personal need, as in the verse "I will speak, that I may find relief" (Job 32:20). The second reason is the complete ignorance of Israeli society regarding the entire traditional world of the Ethiopian Jewish community. It is thus necessary and valuable to teach our customs and explain our beautiful tradition. The third reason is related to the community's spiritual leaders, the *kesim*, who sense a delegitimization of the spiritual customs of the community as a way of worshipping God. In addition, I believe that the customs and traditions of the Ethiopian community are an important source of knowledge that stands on its own, that can shed much light on Jewish tradition as a whole.

From a certain viewpoint, aliyah for the Beta Israel community was equivalent to the destruction of the Temple. For this reason, recording the customs of Ethiopian Jewry in a manner that is organized according to modern halakhah is important now – it is "A time to act for God; they have made void Your law" (Psalms 119:126). The final reason is on behalf of the young generation growing up

---

5. Rabbi Joseph B. Soloveitchik, *Halakhic Man*, translated from the Hebrew by Lawrence Kaplan (Philadelphia: Jewish Publication Society, 1983), 67–68.
6. *Mesillat Yesharim*, introduction.

in Israel, who are mostly forgetting our customs. For all these reasons, I decided to write this book, *From Sinai to Ethiopia: The Halakhic and Conceptual World of the Ethiopian Jews*, including the *Shulhan ha-Orit*, to teach all of humanity what it has never known, and for the Ethiopian Jews, to remind them of what they already know, but "forgetfulness in relation to them is extremely prevalent."[7]

In the natural course of things, so I believe, the halakhic solutions proposed in this book will lead many fellow Jews, even Ethiopians, to raise an eyebrow. In certain places, there will be those who will even denounce some of the statements and ideas here. Whatever the resistance or criticism, know that I am working from pure motivations, while remaining faithful to the people and the Torah of Israel. At the same time, I ask that the call for unity be just that, and not a call for uniformity. The reader should try to stand in the other's shoes, and from there, he will find tolerance toward the "other" as other. This demand is not new – it is a demand for a basic norm of behavior. The demand for uniformity, by contrast, conflicts with nature and with Jewish tradition, which throughout history has supported unity while granting room for autonomy of the individual, at least for expressing opinions. This is the image that arises from every page of the Talmud.

Further, every attempt of Jewish tradition to create a monolithic society, as far as I am aware, has created an apologetic society, shallow and defensive, and has led to baseless hatred that ends in destruction. In short, we are never obligated to agree with everything, especially in relationships between the individual and God. Every person is unique and special before the Holy One, blessed be He, and for this reason, each of us attempts to relate to God in his own special way. We conclude that there is no one way to worship God. We must demonstrate tolerance – instead of apathy or yielding of the path – toward those who think differently.

The support, understanding, and instruction that I received from my teachers in writing this book are an excellent example of healthy tolerance. Their attitude toward this book made a deep impression on me. My teachers and rabbis studied the content from a point of view of Jewish tolerance, with no apologetics or veneer of doubt. In my opinion, a lack of tolerance expressed in physical and verbal militancy or in dogmatic apologetics of the sort we might call the "self-appointed religion police" originates in instability of faith, insecurity in one's way of life, or in lack of coherent understanding of life in general and the history of

---

7. Ibid.

Jewish tradition in particular. Apparently, the source of my teachers' tolerance for this work is located deep within their world of faith, and in their desire to emulate the qualities of God. According to the Kabbalah, God is full of tolerance toward the world in which we live. God, Who is omnipotent, infinite, and manifold, limited Himself and enabled the material world to come into being. This is the "secret of limitation" (*tzimtzum*) explained at length in the works of the kabbalists of Safed. The meaning of this secret, to put it concisely, is that everything that exists is part of the Divine. But in order for all created things (angels, animals, plants, dust) to exist, instead of pure Divinity in its unique essence, the Divine must limit itself, in a manner of speaking, and refrain from appearing in its full power. The Divine Power influences every single creature only according to the measure that it can tolerate.[8]

From this we learn that tolerance is derived from the concept of limitation. Further, this unique perspective of my teachers, of power on one hand and limitation on the other, enabled me to feel that this book was a legitimate path to worshipping God. "Just as He is merciful, so should you be merciful" (Rambam, *Hilkhot De'ot* [Laws of personal development] 1:5–6).

Since I made aliyah, I have had the privilege of meeting many Jews in Israel and around the world. I have been amazed at the great distance that seems to separate various groups, and simultaneously, the solidarity that bonds these groups. In each place, I searched for similarities, but found differences – differences that lead to a world that is deep and full of growth and personal development. During my travels, even more than I learned about others, I learned a great deal about myself. I thank the communities and families I met abroad in the past ten years through World Mizrachi, Emunah of America, British Emunah, Israel at Heart, Zohar Organization, Tzohar Rabbinical Association, Bar-Ilan University, and other private organizations. Undoubtedly, their humane, tolerant, and loving behavior toward the "other" inspired my admiration and served as a personal example for empathy, caring, and solidarity. Every meeting with Jews left a powerful impression on me of determination, Jewish power, and particularly Jewish solidarity.

Over the years, I discovered that admiration for the ways of the Jewish people has been expressed by many. As Winston Churchill, former British prime minister, declared, "Some people like the Jews, and some do not. But no thoughtful

---

8. Avraham Regelson, *Or ha-Kabbalah be-shirat Milton* [The light of Kabbalah in the poetry of Milton], http://www.benyehuda.org/regelson/milton.html.

man can deny the fact that they are, beyond any question, the most formidable and most remarkable race which has appeared in the world."[9] Similarly, Mark Twain (1835–1910) marveled at the relationship between the number of Jews in the world and their influence:

> If the statistics are right, the Jews constitute but *one per cent.* of the human race. It suggests a nebulous dim puff of star-dust lost in the blaze of the Milky Way. Properly the Jew ought hardly to be heard of; but he is heard of, has always been heard of. He is as prominent on the planet as any other people, and his commercial importance is extravagantly out of proportion to the smallness of his bulk. His contributions to the world's list of great names in literature, science, art, music, finance, medicine, and abstruse learning are also away out of proportion to the weakness of his numbers. He has made a marvelous fight in this world, in all the ages; and has done it with his hands tied behind him. He could be vain of himself, and be excused for it. The Egyptian, the Babylonian, and the Persian rose, filled the planet with sound and splendor, then faded to dream-stuff and passed away; the Greek and the Roman followed, and made a vast noise, and they are gone; other peoples have sprung up and held their torch high for a time, but it burned out, and they sit in twilight now, or have vanished. The Jew saw them all, beat them all, and is now what he always was, exhibiting no decadence, no infirmities of age, no weakening of his parts, no slowing of his energies, no dulling of his alert and aggressive mind. All things are mortal but the Jew; all other forces pass, but he remains. What is the secret of his immortality?"[10]

In my view, the answer to Twain's question lies in one sentence: "Love your neighbor as yourself." If so, then the power of solidarity, creativity, and personal and national responsibility form a significant portion of the secret of the Jewish people. In every place I have visited, both in Israel and around the world, beginning with the meeting with the Mossad and the IDF elite naval commando unit, Shayetet 13, in 1982 on the beach of Sudan, I have been privileged to witness special moments in which individuals revealed enormous personal sacrifice, dedication, and boundless responsibility. I view them all as models for emulation.

---

9. Cited in Rabbi Mordechai Greenberg, "*Hen am le-vaded yishkon*" [A nation dwells apart], http://www.inn.co.il/Articles/Article.aspx/968.
10. "Concerning the Jews," *Harper's Magazine* 99, no. 592 (September 1899).

INTRODUCTION: THE SPIRITUAL WORLD OF ETHIOPIAN JEWRY, THEN AND NOW • 9

✡ From Dream to Reality

As a child in Ethiopia, I thought that Jerusalem was made of gold. I dreamed of a land of milk and honey, in which everyone was Jewish and the gentiles did not hate them. My friend Mesphin Iasu, of blessed memory, and I decided to do what every Ethiopian Jew dreamed of doing: to make aliyah, to go up to Jerusalem, which was our term for Eretz Yisrael. At dawn, without saying a word to our parents, we two children awoke and left our village of Irer in the Godolo region, on our way to the Promised Land. This decision was the climax of many stories we had heard from our fathers and mothers. Mesphin and I began to run. We didn't know in which direction to go. We only knew that we had to run, and we believed that if only we ran far enough, in the end we would reach Jerusalem. In the afternoon, after we left the Godolo region, we were detained by locals from the adjoining region who suspected that we were spies. Mesphin managed to escape from prison, but I remained behind.

An elderly local came to prison. He asked me, "Boy, tell me – who are you?"

"I'm the grandson of Abba Dejen Mengesha," I answered.

The old man replied, "You're his son?! You're the son of an *agoway – wedy Israel*?! *Giratam kaila*!" These are all derogatory words that the non-Jewish Ethiopians use for the Jews. "You're a Jew who drinks the blood of Christians and eats them!" I was confused by this accusation. "Release him so he'll leave this place!"

The old man did not order my release out of the goodness of his heart, but in the hopes that I would fall prey to wild beasts. I was released in the middle of the night. I didn't know where to go. I thought about my friend Mesphin. I had no idea what had happened to him. (I later found out that he had escaped on his own and returned to the Jewish village.) It was pitch-black outside, and the sounds of the animals intensified my fear. I pounded on a door in the town and pretended I was a non-Jewish shepherd who had lost his way. The next day, I woke up and asked how to get to the village of Irer. My hosts gave me directions, and I began to run again. In the evening I reached my village. My family had no idea where I had been. They were afraid that I had been devoured by animals or harmed by evil spirits. I arrived exhausted and panting heavily, but unharmed. For me, this was a first attempt. Although it ended in failure, I held onto the vision of reaching Jerusalem, postponing it to another, more successful opportunity.

In the village, we continued dreaming of Jerusalem. Less than two years after my first failed attempt to go to Jerusalem, a second opportunity arose. Rumors began to fly around our village and others that Jews from Jerusalem had come to Sudan in order to help the Ethiopian Jews, the Beta Israel community, to go to Israel. The gates were open, and whoever wanted to leave could go ahead. None of the villagers thought of waiting. We all did everything possible to get organized and start moving in order to go up to Jerusalem. Every item that could be sold, we sold. Whatever we couldn't sell, we left behind in our clay huts. After two thousand years, we began to internalize the idea that the road to Jerusalem was open. One night, when the sign to begin the journey was given, the residents of several villages gathered at a meeting point and began the great trek to Jerusalem.

Our hasty departure led to complications. In my family, we kept our donkeys, so sometimes we rode, but most of the group journeyed on foot. We walked for over two months from Ethiopia to Sudan, exposed to the dangers of the road. People were certain they would reach Jerusalem within a short time, but in reality, some of them were forced to wait in the Twawa refugee camp in Sudan for as long as six years. Conditions in the camp were harsh – it was overcrowded, and sanitary conditions were deplorable. The path from this situation to outbreaks of infectious diseases was short. Thousands died of disease. In consideration of this situation, the Mossad and Jewish Agency aliyah representatives did their best to help the interned Ethiopian Jews. They worked to improve conditions and speed up the stream of aliyah, all the while operating under stressful conditions and a heavy pall of secrecy and fear. On the one hand, they tried to push up the pace of aliyah, while on the other, they had to be careful not to arouse the attention of the soldiers of Jaafar Nimeiri, president of Sudan.

My family was in the camp, and we were told we would have to wait two or three years for our turn. The mortality rate among children in the camp was particularly high, so some of the parents decided to send their children ahead of them to Israel, to try to save their lives. I was the eldest child in my family. At eight years old, I was told to go with my aunt and uncle to Jerusalem. I was torn between my love for my family and my love for Jerusalem. I followed my parents' wishes. Along with hundreds of other children, adults, and elderly, I was packed into a crowded truck. The bed of the truck was covered with a heavy tarp, and we were off.

Conditions inside the truck were foul. It was terribly crowded and hot. People vomited, and the smell was unbearable. No one dared to make a sound. Even the children and babies were silent, as if they also realized they had to keep silent, or else put all of our lives at risk. We didn't know where they were taking us or how much longer we would have to travel in this horrific state. Finally, the truck stopped, and we heard a powerful racket outside. The tarp was lifted from the truck bed, and we climbed out. The roar intensified. I had no idea what it was. Then I saw an amazing sight, something I had never seen before. I saw water, more and more water that erupted and writhed fearfully. This was the shore of the Red Sea – my first glimpse of the ocean. It looked like a wild beast that hadn't been fed for weeks, and it moved toward us, jaws open, but from inside a cage that confined it. I can hardly describe my fear at the sight of the powerful waves pounding toward me – I didn't know they would stop the moment they reached the shore. Then suddenly a miracle happened. From out of this nowhere, from deep within the darkness and the fog, the tumult and the confusion, commandos from unit 13 of the Israeli navy rose up out of the sea. They shed tears, and we cried along with them. It was a meeting of two brothers who had been separated for two thousand years.

The soldiers loaded us onto rubber boats. It was a dark night, and the boats floated silently into the sea. After a while, the boat reached what I thought was a large, well-lit building – an Israeli naval ship. The boat passengers climbed up through the belly of the boat onto the high deck. Some of them kissed the deck, convinced they had arrived in Jerusalem. Only the next day, when the sun rose, did we realize that we were on the deck of a boat in the middle of the ocean. We sailed to Sharm el-Sheikh in the southern Sinai Peninsula. Then we were taken off the boat and driven in buses to the local airport. From there, we flew to Ben-Gurion airport, our gate to the promised Jerusalem – the first step in a reality that for many years had been only a dream.

In January 1982, I stood in front of an Immigration Ministry clerk at Ben-Gurion Airport. Through a translator, I was asked my name and age. But I was at a loss for words. Two years previously, I had acted without a word, and here again I lost the power of speech. I barely managed to pronounce my name in a whisper.

In his 1966 Nobel Prize acceptance speech, Shai Agnon wrote:

> As a result of the historic catastrophe in which Titus of Rome destroyed Jerusalem and Israel was exiled from its land, I was born in one of the cities of the Exile. But always I regarded myself as one who was born in Jerusalem. In a dream, in a vision of the night, I saw myself standing with my brother-Levites in the Holy Temple, singing with them the songs of David, King of Israel, melodies such as no ear has heard since the day our city was destroyed and its people went into exile.

For over two thousand years, our people recited the prayer "May our eyes behold Your return to Zion in mercy." After an absence of 2,500 years, the Ethiopian Jewish community has merited the return to our homeland. We have returned to our home. This is why, when I stood before the Immigration Ministry clerk at the airport and was asked my name and age, my throat was choked and I could barely utter my name.

I went to live in a children's home in Afula. At one point, I received the bitter news that my parents were no longer alive. For two years, I lived with the knowledge that I would continue in this world without my family. The Emunah Children's Center provided for all my needs, and my aunt and uncle, Btouli and Tedu Sisay, whom I did not know in Ethiopia, became my family. Then one day, the children's center director, Baruch Vasen, called me to his office urgently. I went in and sat down cautiously, petrified I had done something wrong. Then he told me that the news I had received two years earlier about my parents' death had been a mistake. My entire family was alive, and the night before they had made aliyah in a major IDF operation (Operation Moses).

I took a shower and put on new clothes in preparation for the meeting. My counselor, Gabi Ohayon, drove me to the immigration office in Or Akiva. That trip, which took just half an hour, seemed like an eternity to me. We got out of the car and walked toward the immigration center. Tense with anticipation, we quickly found the right house. We knocked on the door, and my mother opened it. We embraced and wept, and I felt that I was experiencing the miracle of the Resurrection.

When I arrived in Israel, there were very few Ethiopian Jews in the country, and I felt foreign and strange. I had the constant feeling that people were looking at me, thinking I was a character who had come out of a popular Israeli children's book, *The Little Black Boy Goes to Kindergarten*. I felt different, foreign. I remembered that feeling of otherness from when I was still in Ethiopia, from the other side of the coin. When a representative of the Jewish Agency came to our village, we considered him a *feregi* – a foreigner. Still, we desperately wanted to meet him, because he was a Jew who came from Jerusalem. In Israel, it was difficult for me to reconcile the difference between the dream of Jerusalem and the reality. But I know it was harder for the adults than it was for me, a child.

My identity became a central question. Who was I? In Ethiopia I was identified as a Jew of Beta Israel. They called me "Israel." But ironically, here in Israel I was called "Ethiopian." To me, it was a jarring experience to discover I was an Ethiopian. Later, I discovered that my Ethiopian name, Zaude, had been changed to the Israeli name of Sharon. I was pleased to have this name, because people explained to me that this was a new name from Jerusalem. Wonderful, I thought, but that led me to ask: Who am I, an Israeli or an Ethiopian? What does it mean to change your name to an Israeli one? Or on the contrary, to keep your Ethiopian name? Was society a factor that pulled me down and kept me back, or was it a motivating factor that pushed me forward? I also asked, why am I different? Is difference a blessing or a handicap? Is this society racist or not? I had to reformulate my identity – how should I go about it? I was confused.

Furthermore, I constantly heard conflicting voices. Some said that Israeli society was racist, while others said it wasn't. Some said we had to throw our Ethiopian identity out the window, but some said we should preserve our traditions. I heard these two voices even within my own family.

I remember walking with my grandfather, Abba Dejen Mengesha, of blessed memory, in the central bus station in Be'er Sheva. As we walked around, we saw an uncomfortable sight: a young man and woman sat on a bench, one on the other's lap, kissing. My grandfather was surprised, and asked, is this what people do in the Holy Land? But he wasn't angry. He asked me, do you know why the dog does not get along with the cat? No, I said. "I'll tell you," he continued. "The animosity between them began back in the time of the Flood, when Noah forbade all the animals from having sexual relations. The male and female dogs couldn't control themselves, and they went into a corner together. The cat caught them in the act and told Noah. Noah cursed the dogs, saying, 'You will be punished an eye for an eye. You mated in hiding, so from now on you will mate in public for all to see.'" My grandfather added, "Ever since, the dog doesn't like the cat." That was my grandfather's response to this encounter with Israeli social reality.

Eight years after hearing this story, I asked him, "Grandfather, how old are you?" He replied, "I'm eight years old." I was astonished. "Eight years old? How can that be?" He answered that the moment he set foot on the ground of Jerusalem, he began to count the years of his life anew. I was thrilled. With all the complex reality of life after aliyah, my grandfather still saw the light of Jerusalem.

One day, my uncle (my grandfather's son) came to me and asked, "Do you think we have democracy in Israel?" "Of course we have democracy," I replied. He countered, "No! We have no democracy in Israel. The only place where there is democracy is in the cemetery." I asked him why he thought that. "While my father was alive, he lived in a small apartment in the immigrant absorption center, while the mayor of our city lived in a fancy neighborhood, in a large house. After my father's funeral, I saw who was buried next to him – the mayor! Finally they became neighbors." He continued, "You see, democracy exists only in the cemetery." I listened to both my grandfather and my uncle, and I asked, which one of them is right?

My grandfather's death had a profound effect on me. He was a man I esteemed greatly, who had a powerful fear of God. He was righteous and honest. He knew the book of Psalms by heart, and he was a Jew with all his heart and might. He had a pure soul. I asked myself, where does he sit now – in the Garden of Eden? I thought that beyond any doubt, my grandfather must be sitting in the same room with Abraham, Isaac, and Jacob, Aaron, David, and Solomon. He was sitting with all the *tzaddikim*, the Prophets, the Tannaim, and the Amoraim. Then I reached an earth-shattering conclusion: a man like my grandfather, whose worship of Heaven was based on the Ethiopian tradition, had reached the status of sitting up there with all the righteous people. For the first time, I understood that there were many channels to worshipping God, and all of them are equally legitimate.

Over time, I learned that everyone in the world has difficulties and challenges along the way. I tried to avoid asking questions like "Why did they do that to me?" "Why did God do that to me?" "Why is it my fault?" None of the immigrants to Israel have had it easy, no matter what country they came from. Countless Jews suffered indescribable horrors in the death camps in Germany in the Second World War. Some were saved and came to Israel. But they weren't expecting government aid for new immigrants. They picked up weapons and went out to fight in the War of Independence, in order to establish a state. Many of them met their deaths. This had a big impression on me. People might call me naïve, but this quality is what has pushed me to examine the reality of Israeli society and discover that society is a given condition. Society does not make personal claims against certain individuals or groups. Each individual determines how to interpret society, whether in a positive or negative light. I, like my grandfather, have chosen to emphasize the good side of Israeli society, and I have found much to appreciate.

Today I have a PhD in Jewish philosophy from Bar-Ilan University, where I teach courses titled "Culture, Halakhah, and Tradition in the Ethiopian Community" and "Tolerance and Pluralism in Jewish Sources." I am also a lecturer at Tel Aviv University in the African Studies Department, where I teach "Ethiopian Jewry: From Ghetto to Segregation." I also serve as rabbi of Kedoshei Yisrael, a community in Kiryat Gat that was established by Holocaust survivors. I am married to Avital, a highly educated woman (she has a degree in social work from Hebrew University of Jerusalem and a master's degree in art therapy from

Lesley University) who made aliyah from Switzerland as a young girl. We are parents to Roi, Nadav, Ziv, Gil, and Tohar. After over two thousand years of exile and wanderings, we are proud to live in Kiryat Gat in the Holy Land. It is truly a miracle, a miracle of the revival of the Jewish people, and a sign that the redemption will soon be coming.

Finding My Way to Worshipping God

On one of my first days at Har Etzion Yeshiva, a *hesder* yeshiva combining Talmud studies and army service, I approached the two yeshiva directors with a serious question. Why were the Ethiopian Jews required to immerse themselves in a *mikveh*?[11] My teacher, Rabbi Yehuda Amital, did not try to win me over with intricate and convoluted halakhic justifications. Rabbi Amital was not surprised by my question, but I was startled by his answer. "If someone comes to me tomorrow and expresses an interest in you for a *shidduch*, I don't want to have to hesitate when recommending you for a match. People here ask questions, and we want you to be an inseparable part of the student body in the *beit midrash*." I thought this was an honest answer.

The obligation of immersion *le-humrah*, on the strict side of halakhah, for the Ethiopian community led to a deep rift in relations between the community and the state. In fact, to this day a holistic solution to this problem has yet to be found, and the community considers it the elephant in the room. My teachers, the two rabbinic directors of Har Etzion Yeshiva, required every immigrant of Ethiopian Jewish origin to immerse himself as a prerequisite for admission to the yeshiva. Personally, I did not have to perform this act when I entered the yeshiva, as I had immersed myself on arrival in Israel. Eventually, I did have the merit to feel an inseparable part of the student body in the *beit midrash*, as Rabbi Amital described.

Rabbi Lichtenstein gave a more technical and nuanced explanation based on halakhic foundations for why we should immerse, and his explanation was given with great respect and humility. To my estimation, many communication problems between people arise not because of what is said, but because of how it is said. Both yeshiva directors, each in his own way, were attentive to the "how," giving me the feeling that they recognized that standing before them was a Jew who needed sympathy and tolerance. Indeed, their words fell on attentive ears.

---

11. Immersion in a ritual bath or *mikveh* is one element in the process of conversion to Judaism. Requiring Ethiopian Jews to immerse implies that something is amiss in their status as Jews.

As is said when entering a *beit midrash* to study, "I thank God for placing me among the students in the *beit midrash*, and for not placing me among the idlers."[12] I thank God for granting me the privilege to study and to practice the mitzvot, and to become a full-fledged student in the *beit midrash*. I was able to grow and acquire an education in the epicenter of religious Zionism. I studied halakhic decision making for many years in a yeshiva that was built on the basis of the Lithuanian yeshiva ideal, and I was ordained as a rabbi by the Chief Rabbinate of Israel. I thus assumed that I should follow in one of the normative paths, either Ashkenazic or Sephardic. However, I thought that opting for the Ashkenazic tradition would be "obeying the letter but not the spirit of the law," because I was told upon making aliyah that I was considered to be Sephardic. But opting for the Sephardic approach was also problematic. Although in practice I did take upon myself Sephardic customs, this choice did not stem from self-awareness, but rather from a technical reason. In all the institutions in which I had studied at the outset of my educational path, and in my neighborhood, almost everyone came from a Sephardic background. Yet I felt that this was not my path to serving God, and that it did not fit my spiritual world or my soul.

At some point when I was in the *hesder* yeshiva, I began to feel a pull toward the Ashkenazic hassidic world. The Yiddishkeit appealed to me: sitting around the Shabbat table with friends at a *tisch* eating kugel and singing the melodies. But in truth, I felt that I could not fully adopt for myself even this spiritual world. For years I defined myself as having two sides – one side was Sephardic halakhah, the other was Ashkenazic soul. Then two things happened that transformed this worldview significantly.

The change took place during my studies at Beit Morasha of Jerusalem and in the Department of Talmud at Bar-Ilan University. A number of factors led me to reexamine how I served God. At one opportunity, I asked my teacher, Rabbi Dr. Yehuda Brandes, director of the *beit midrash* in Beit Morasha, whether I should follow Sephardic tradition, despite the fact that many of its *halakhot* did not fit the halakhic phenomenology of traditional Ethiopian Jewry. Rabbi Brandes's reply surprised me. I expected him to give me a standard answer – "You should follow either Sephardic tradition or Ashkenazic tradition, but you must never grasp the rope from both ends," as in the statement "Be either like the House of Shammai in their leniencies and stringencies, or like the House of Hillel in their

---

12. Babylonian Talmud, *Berakhot* 28b.

leniencies and stringencies."[13] I was astonished when he answered, "Who said you have to follow Sephardic or Ashkenazic tradition? You can be a Jew who follows the *Shulhan Arukh* standard code of law." I said that I feared I would be following the letter but not the spirit of the law, and he replied, "I have faith that you truly want to serve God. You cannot be following only the letter but not the spirit of the law. Either your priority is the way of Torah, or you are immoral."

Rabbi Brandes's reply expanded my horizon and opened up new space for my service of God: serving God not through awe alone, and not through fear, as if I were walking a tightrope. All at once, I felt an easing. I felt that serving God was not a burden or an encumbrance. There was a way to pave a unique path to serving God that reflected my complex inner world.

A second encounter cemented my new spiritual framework. While writing my master's degree thesis, under the professional and compassionate advisorship of Rabbi Dr. Daniel Sperber of the Department of Talmud at Bar-Ilan, I was exposed to a new interpretation. Up to that point, I had thought that the "red line" for an Orthodox Jew was the *Shulhan Arukh*. In other words, following the decisions of the *Shulhan Arukh* was a clear sign of what I call a "Talmudic Jew," one who observes the mitzvot, while one who questioned its authority removed himself from the ranks of Talmudic Jewry. Professor Sperber answered me, "Why do you think that? The Yemenite community has always followed the Rambam in its halakhic decisions, and not the *Shulhan Arukh*. Yet the Yemenite Jews have been accepted without a shadow of a doubt into the realm of Talmudic Judaism. Although at the outset, major rabbis did not agree with their method, over the years their customs and traditions have earned approval and have even become assets. Today, no one would question that this group belongs to Talmudic Judaism."

"If so," I asked Rabbi Dr. Sperber, "what should I learn from this?"

"Who says that the red line is the *Shulhan Arukh*?" he responded.

"So what do you think is Judaism's 'red line'?"

"The Talmud," he answered, "because the Talmud is accepted by the entire Jewish people. We have reason to think that the Talmud should become the red line."

This surprised me even more. Then I understood the breadth of the space that had opened before me. Paradoxically, the replies of Rabbi Brandes and Rabbi Sperber were not foreign to me at all. On the contrary, I felt that they offered

---

13. *Yalkut Shimoni*, Ecclesiastes 2.

me an answer to an inner vacuum, and quenched my thirst. "My soul thirsts for God, for the living God; when shall I come and appear before God?"[14] Now! Suddenly I felt that I had the tools, the way, and the personal pace with which to meet my God.

When I first thought about writing this book, naturally I consulted with Rabbi Dr. Sperber. He gave me his support and encouragement to pursue the process of recording and preserving the traditions of the Ethiopian community. He even directed me on how to proceed. After writing the first draft, I showed it to him. Professor Sperber emphasized the particular customs of the community, and based on this, he supported the radical halakhic decisions in my project. On the other hand, he did not hesitate to warn me of points that he felt might be damaging to the community.

When I began to write this book, I contacted Rabbi Shabtai Rappaport, head of the Beit Midrash of the Jesselson Institute for Advanced Torah Studies at Bar-Ilan University. I received his blessings, and throughout the writing process, he guided me in a pleasant and professional manner, offering cheerful encouragement and broad knowledge on a variety of topics. My conversations with him contributed greatly to this composition.

When I finished writing, I sent the draft to Rabbi Yehuda Brandes. I asked him to read the work, and I anxiously awaited his comments. His comments were edifying and very practical. Rabbi Yehuda represents those *talmidei chachamim* who are expert in halakhah but maintain a deep connection to the present reality. Finally, Rabbi Yehuda advised, "This is a very important work. Its importance cannot be underestimated. It must be published and publicized."

Personal need along with the support of my rabbis for this step provided the impetus for this work, *From Sinai to Ethiopia: The Halakhic and Conceptual World of the Ethiopian Jews*. I have no doubt that many members of the Ethiopian community will find it meaningful. I am certain that every Jew will find it valuable; some may even find it a path toward serving God.

May we be privileged to learn and to teach, to observe, perform, and fulfill the will of the Holy One, blessed be He, as we say, "Cleanse our hearts, that we may serve you in truth."[15]

---

14. Psalms 42:3.
15. From the Amidah prayer for Shabbat and festivals.

✣ Toward an Ethiopian Jewish Halakhah

Preserving the Mystery

The purpose of religion today seems to be similar to that of philosophy: to determine definitions, to search for truth, to address formalism, to decide what is true and what is false. The symbols, the framework, and the institution are transformed from a means of worshipping God into an end. In such a situation, religion becomes irrelevant. As Abraham Joshua Heschel wrote, "It would be more honest to blame religion for its own defeats."[16] In his view, "Religion declined not because it was refuted, but because it became irrelevant, dull, oppressive, insipid." Why? "When faith is completely replaced by creed, worship by discipline, love by habit; when the crisis of today is ignored because of the splendor of the past; when faith becomes an heirloom rather than a living fountain; when religion speaks only in the name of authority rather than with the voice of compassion – its message becomes meaningless."[17] Still, as the philosopher Ludwig Wittgenstein asserts,

> Tradition is not something a man can learn; not a thread he can pick up when he feels like it, any more than a man can choose his own ancestors. Someone lacking a tradition who would like to have one is like a man unhappily in love.[18]

Still, we must remember that a very thin line separates preserving tradition in its dogmatic-symbolic form and preserving it in a more meaningful way. Wittgenstein continues:

> Something of the irrational reverence for the past is preserved in the pomp and ceremony of the British monarchy, even though no subject of the United Kingdom regards this form of government as anything more than a medieval relic.[19]

We may certainly preserve the continuity of tradition "as a living and dynamic organism that can only grow by positive acceptance and affirmation of its

---

16. *God in Search of Man: A Philosophy of Judaism* (New York: Farrar, Straus and Giroux, 1955), 3.
17. Ibid.
18. Ludwig Wittgenstein, *Culture and Value*, trans. Peter Winch (Oxford: Basil Blackwell, 1980), 76, cited in Tamar Ross, *Expanding the Palace of Torah: Orthodoxy and Feminism* (Waltham, MA: Brandeis University Press, 2004), xxi.
19. Ibid.

historical and intellectual legacy."[20] We must ensure that our world stands on a halakhic approach based as far as possible on objective truth. Still, our relation to the "other" should come through intimacy, from the personal-humane dimension – *mentschlichkeit*. Any contact with the "other" in the name of the establishment or of "institution," in the name of halakhah as objective truth, from a perspective of *frumkeit* ("religiosity" in Yiddish), may arouse antagonism. Those who observe tradition clearly tend to follow this approach, due to its analytic and formal nature, but this approach does not relate to tradition as a living entity that must be passed down to the next generation.

As Leo Strauss writes, "Genuine fidelity to a tradition is not the same as literalist traditionalism and is in fact incompatible with it. It consists in preserving not simply the tradition but the continuity of the tradition."[21] In fact, this is the significance of *Shulhan ha-Orit* – to preserve the tradition of the community and to conduct an in-depth analysis of the drastic changes it underwent in the wake of aliyah to the Land of Israel. This is not out of an apologetic approach, not in order to act as an advocate for one tradition or another, but rather to represent the understanding that one cannot criticize the other – not because this is unpleasant, but because it is not right. Further, each side must demonstrate openness and understanding for the other side. If we act in this way, we can redeem tradition from a past that has become stale, and disconnect it from the context of institution and slogans, so that it will no longer be considered burdensome. I hope that this book will contribute to the preservation and continuity of tradition, not in a closed manner that remains unaware of reality and surrounding events, but rather with openness to the world around it.

Unity or Uniformity?

A believing Jew is a person who lives with doubts, uncertainties, and questions. In an ideal reality, religion would never be satisfied with one decision, but would always strive for more. An angel that lives in a perfect, ideal world has no doubts, but humans who live in the pre-messianic world do have doubts. Indeed, doubt is a component of belief. For this reason, any attempt to construct a perfect world through a single decision remains only an illusion. Judaism speaks of a mysterious world full of doubt, and its goal is to enable a life of faith in such a world. The impulse to try to make clear, absolute decisions originates in the scientific

---

20. Ibid., xix.
21. Leo Strauss, *Spinoza's Critique of Religion* (New York: Schocken, 1965), 24.

world, as science strives to give unconditional, universal answers about life. But it cannot give the individual what Judaism does – the awareness that he lives in a world full of mystery and wonder. As Heschel writes:

> Religion…goes beyond philosophy, and the task of philosophy of religion is to lead the mind to the summit of thinking; to create in us the understanding of why the problems of religion cannot be apprehended in terms of science; to let us realize that religion has its own scope, perspective and goal; to expose us to the majesty and mystery, in the presence of which the mind is not deaf to that which transcends the mind.[22]

The debate among the spiritual leaders of the Ethiopian community, the *kesim*, and the rabbinic world focuses on exactly this point. Within the Beta Israel community, religion is understood as a mysterious, spiritual entity, personal and transcendent, not something that can be understood with the mind. Thus their religious world is not expressed in precise definitions or exact *halakhot*. This is a world of spontaneity, of individuality.

Here is an example that illustrates the conflict between the formal, analytic view of Talmudic Judaism and the more spontaneous, individually oriented biblical tradition. In the nineteenth century, an Ethiopian Jew named Daniel ben Hananiah visited the Land of Israel. When the rabbis in the Land of Israel heard that the Ethiopian community was in a dire state, both spiritually and physically, they decided to send an empathetic letter of solidarity through Daniel ben Hananiah:

> Your situation has touched our hearts, and we have decided to take the following steps: when Daniel ben Hananiah returns, call a meeting, listen to him, and learn what he saw us doing and how we observe God's mitzvot according to the traditions of the Sages. If you conclude that until now, you have not behaved properly, then appoint three or four talented individuals and send them to us, to the Holy City, and we will teach them the practicalities of observing the mitzvot.[23]

---

22. Heschel, *God in Search of Man*, 18.
23. "Leaders of the Jerusalem Community 1855," in Menachem Waldman, *Me-Etiopiah le-Yerushalayim: Yehudei Etiopiah ba-et ha-hadashah* [From Ethiopia to Jerusalem: Ethiopian Jewry in the new age] (Jerusalem, 5752/1991).

The community leaders and priests received the letter. They were enthusiastic, but they also felt a threat to the foundations of their leadership and traditions. Confident of their path, they sent a reply that rejected the attempt at external interference:

> We have heard that there are many Jews in Egypt and Jerusalem whose religion and customs are different from ours. It would behoove them to send us knowledgeable representatives who will learn the principles of Judaism accepted among us, and we will show you the path that you should follow.[24]

Division or Unification?

The biggest challenge of the rabbinic leaders of our generation is to enrich religion with spirituality, to grant it a personal and mysterious status. Instead of the lavish attention paid to framework and symbol, we should encourage the confrontation with content, spirituality, and the Jewish world, with the understanding that the mitzvot enable the individual's encounter with God and with other human beings. In my opinion, this opportunity has been sorely missed. To me and many others, Judaism has been responsible for unifying the Jewish people over thousands of years of Diaspora and distance. The problem is that today more than ever, the religious world divides the Jewish world. Religious and non-religious Jews cannot eat together, they cannot manage a business together, live in the same neighborhoods, or marry each other. Even within religious groups, a hierarchy prevails, with well-defined divisions. Today we might find four observant Jews sitting together but who cannot eat each other's food, due to *kashrut* laws. In such a miserable reality, the definition of the Jew becomes external, not one of meaning or value. To which stream does one belong? Haredi, knitted *kippah* (religious Zionist), secular, "Talmudic," Reform, Conservative, Ethiopian, Yemenite, Russian, formerly religious, and the list goes on.

Shortly after I completed my studies at Har Etzion Yeshiva, I contacted one of the religious councils regarding a position as a rabbi. The council chairman's reply came as a shock: "I can't give you the job, because you are not 'black' enough." I answered naively, "You know that I am Ethiopian. Do you mean that my brown skin is not dark enough?" He continued with a smile, "I'm not referring to your skin color. I mean *this*," he said, pointing to the black *kippah* on his own head. When he realized that I was completely in the dark, he continued, "I'm sorry, but I am faithful to the public that elected me."

---

24. "Priests of the Habash Community 1858," in Waldman, *Me-Etiopiah*.

A Judaism that is motivated by self-interest can go astray, and we may now see how the strength of the Jewish people in Israel and around the world has been harmed. A striking example of this damage is the "quiet Holocaust," meaning the overwhelming phenomenon of assimilation in the United States. If a Jew does not accept Judaism through significant choice, his Judaism has no meaning,[25] even though formally he is a Jew. In other words, the root of the disease lies in the fact that when religion focuses on ideas, the personal and ethical dimensions disappear, and formal faith comes at the expense of interpersonal faith. The world of observing mitzvot becomes a stock exchange, and the connection with God becomes a business. I do not in any way mean to negate the study of ideas or formal definitions, but we must ascertain that personal awareness, so vital to the formation of Jewish identity, is not pushed aside in favor of formality.

Keeping Halakhah Relevant

In encounters I organize with the members of the Ethiopian community, with the first generation and the second as well, I find that the tension between their subjective, personal feeling as true Jews and the halakhic definitions they encountered in Israel has caused them intense frustration. "Everything here is politics," they say. We must build a spiritual vision, out of power and humility, which will offer an appropriate answer for this sad reality. The Sages in their genius annulled a law in the Torah when its fulfillment became irrelevant and hypocritical. Yet today, the spiritual aspect has moved aside for the benefit of definitions and symbols.[26]

We read in the Torah, "If a slain person be found in the land...lying in the field, [and] it is not known who slew him" (Deuteronomy 21:1) – in such a case, the guilt lies with the public. A frightening and impressive ceremony is held in order to provoke shock. The elders of the town nearest to the corpse meet and hold a ceremony called *eglah arufah*, in which the neck of an unworked heifer is broken. Some fifteen hundred years after this mitzvah was given, the Mishnah (*Sotah* 9:9) records: "When murderers multiplied, the ceremony of breaking a heifer's neck was discontinued [since it was assumed that the murderer was known]." We find another example in the laws of adultery. According to the Torah, when a woman is suspected of adultery, she should be given bitter water to drink

---

25. Eliyahu Zarur, *Yeshayahu Leibowitz: Ish ha-ruah ve-ha-hagut* [Yeshayahu Leibowitz: Man of spirit and philosophy] (Israel, 2001).
26. See *Minhagei Yisrael*, vol. 2, "The place of the symbol in the world of tradition," 113.

in order to verify her innocence. But the Rambam states that this mitzvah was annulled.[27] In this context, Professor Yeshayahu Leibowitz writes:

> This religious ceremony is significant in a society in which murder is a revolting and exceptional occurrence. In a corrupt society in which murder is frequent, there is no reason to pretend that we are repulsed by a murder that we are not able to decipher. In such a society, this ceremony would be hypocritical.... If the society is filled with licentiousness and sunken in lust, there is no reason to be shocked by a certain incident in which there is a suspicion of adultery.... In a civilized society in which murder is an exceptional occurrence, we should respond with the *eglah arufah* ceremony in case of an unsolved murder. In a society in which ethical behavior is the norm, we should respond with the bitter waters for an exceptional incident of a suspected adultery. But if the society is corrupt, there is no reason for these ceremonies.[28]

God's Laughter – Humanity's Victory

The primary message of this work is reflected in the well-known legend of "Akhnai's oven."[29] The background of this legend is a halakhic argument between Rabbi Eliezer and other sages about the method of purification of a clay oven:

> On that day Rabbi Eliezer brought forward every imaginable argument, but the Sages did not accept any of them.... Again Rabbi Eliezer then said to the Sages, "If the halakhah agrees with me, let it be proved from Heaven." Sure enough, a divine voice cried out, "Why do you dispute with Rabbi Eliezer, with whom the halakhah always agrees?" Rabbi Joshua stood up and protested: "[The Torah] is not in Heaven!" (Deuteronomy 30:12). What does "it is not in Heaven" mean? Rabbi Yirmiya said: "That the Torah was already given on Mount Sinai, and we do not pay attention to a heavenly voice, because long ago at Mount Sinai You wrote in Your Torah at Mount Sinai, 'After the majority must one incline' (Exodus 23:2)." Rabbi Nathan met [the prophet] Elijah and asked him, "What did the Holy One do at that moment?" Elijah: "He laughed [with joy], saying, 'My children have defeated Me, My children have defeated Me.'" (Babylonian Talmud, *Baba Metzia* 59b)

---

27. Rambam, *Mishneh Torah*, Hilkhot Sotah 3:17–19.
28. Yeshayahu Leibowitz, *Sheva shanim shel sichot al parashat ha-shavuah* [Seven years of conversations on the weekly Torah portion] (Jerusalem, 5760/2000).
29. M. Waltzer, M. Lorberboim, N. Zohar, and Y. Lorberboim, eds., *Ha-masoret ha-politit ha-Yehudit* [The Jewish political tradition] (Jerusalem, 5767/2007).

Rabbi Eliezer calls upon supernatural phenomena in order to convince his colleagues of the validity of his position. In contrast, the Sages, led by Rabbi Joshua, insist that "It is not in Heaven," while the Holy One laughs over how His children "defeated" Him.

Why does God laugh? I would like to propose a new direction for the interpretation of the reason for God's laughter, following the question of the Tosafot on this story. The Tosafot note the difference between the argument Rabbi Eliezer conducts with the Sages, and the argument between Beit Hillel and Beit Shammai. Both stories record the intervention of a *bat kol* (heavenly voice). In the debate between Hillel and Shammai, the Sages rely on the intervention of the *bat kol* in deciding the halakhah, while in the story of Akhnai's oven, the Sages reject the opinion of the *bat kol*, stating that "We pay no attention to a heavenly voice." The Tosafot give their answer. In my opinion, what leads to opposite results in these two stories is mainly the rhetoric, the way the *bat kol* addresses the Sages.

In the argument between Hillel and Shammai, the *bat kol* makes its first statement out of respect and esteem for the dissenting opinion. "These and those are both the words of the Living God,"[30] says the *bat kol*, and then declares that the halakhah is according to Beit Hillel. With this statement, the *bat kol* appeases the representatives of Beit Shammai. By contrast, in the story of Akhnai's oven, the *bat kol*'s statement seems to contain a measure of reproach toward the Sages – "Why do you dispute with Rabbi Eliezer, with whom the halakhah always agrees?" In other words, who are you, anyway? Perhaps it is for this reason that the Sages reply, "It is not in Heaven." God's laughter expresses agreement or even embarrassment, because He placed His creatures to a test that led them to disgrace.

> Rabbi Abba said in the name of Samuel: For three years the House of Shammai and the House of Hillel disagreed. These said that the halakhah was according to us, and those said the halakhah is in accordance with us. A heavenly voice emerged saying: "Both these and those are the words of the living God, and the halakhah is in accordance with the school of Hillel."
>
> Since both these and those are the words of the living God, why was the halakhah established in accordance with the House of Hillel? Because they were polite and forbearing (*aluvin*), and would teach both their own views and the views of the House of Shammai. Moreover, they would place the views of the House of Shammai before their own. (Babylonian Talmud, *Eruvin* 13b)

---

30. Babylonian Talmud, *Eruvin* 13b.

Rashi comments (there) that *aluvin* means "forbearing." The justification that the Talmud gives for deciding the halakhah according to Beit Hillel demands explanation:

> The explanations that the Talmud offers for the victory of Beit Hillel recall ad hominem arguments.... What is the relationship between the ethical honesty of a sage and the legal validity of his opinions?... The concept that "nice sages finish first" comprises an important ethical lesson: not only does God appreciate humility and lead the humble toward truth, but a natural connection exists between ethical qualities and legal credibility.... The more respect he gives his enemy and the more humble he is, the higher the possibility is that he will succeed in assimilating his opponent's assertions.... We may propose another explanation of how the positive qualities of Beit Hillel led to decision of the halakhah according to their opinion. Beit Hillel's practice of considering the other demonstrates greater esteem than Beit Shammai revealed for the importance of the dispute and the principle of "both these and those." The sages of Beit Hillel were more committed to the process of discussion, and this commitment causes their positions to represent a well-functioning conscious method. This process even serves as a good example for such a method, to a greater extent than that of Beit Shammai.[31]

This book attempts to adopt the method of Beit Hillel, and to consider the other – the Ethiopian Jewish community. This is not an organized *Shulhan Arukh* that pretends to gather the entire Jewish world under one umbrella; history has taught us that there is no such thing. But I am certain that every Jew will be able to find within tools for serving God.

The Evolution of Ethiopian Jewish Custom

Custom as Cultural Category

"Our idea of dirt is compounded of two things, care for hygiene and respect for conventions. The rules of hygiene change, of course, with changes in our state of knowledge."[32] Dirt is a derivation of a social judgment, and its definition depends on the environment. We may compare this to Aristotle's ancient question, what gives "good" the quality of being good, or "evil" the quality of being

---

31. Waltzer et al., *Ha-masoret ha-politit ha-Yehudit*.
32. Mary Douglas, *Purity and Danger: An Analysis of the Concepts of Pollution and Taboo* (London and New York: Routledge, 2002), 7.

evil? Is it a result of human agreement and choice, or is there a priori good and a priori evil? In my opinion, it is very difficult to determine, and I do not know if we will ever find an answer. I do not necessarily connect good and evil to dirt and impurity, but the methodology for both is the same. In other words, just as dirt and cleanliness are not universal concepts, so good and evil are not universal concepts. Still, for both, the ability of the individual or the group to choose one or the other can reveal something about the nature of the society or the individual within that group.[33]

Who is the individual? What is culture? What creates cognitive cultural differences between human beings? We know that there are genes that determine physiological characteristics, such as bone structure and the color of one's skin and hair. In the past, people made attempts to find significant differences between various groups; for example, between the mentality of "primitives" and the mentality of modern Western people, or between logical and mythical thinking.[34] If we accept the difficulty in deciphering the riddle called "humanity," the following questions arise: Where can we search for the universal? How does the universal – once we have found it – become unique? In other words, what is the turning point that transforms a value shared among human beings to a value that separates them?

The basic assumption of these questions is that human beings reach some kind of arbitrary agreement that is not dictated by nature, regarding the meaning of things and the reason for the order that they themselves create.[35] In the beginning, a human being is a blank page, and he himself fills in the content in accordance with his understanding of the social environment. Herein lies the turning point that creates differences between individuals; the fact that we find different ways to understand reality shows that this agreement differs from one society to another.

We give an interpretation to reality using cultural categories of our own creation. Below we will give examples of Jewish customs that support this assertion. Many customs are based on logical principles, and any stricter or looser

---

33. *Minhagei Yisrael*, vol. 3, "The economic factor in the formulation of custom," 65; vol. 1, "Local external influences on the customs of Moroccan Jewry," 235.
34. H. Hazan, *Ha-siach ha-antropologi* [The anthropological dialogue], ed. Malka Tal (Tel Aviv, 5753/1993), 42.
35. A. Rapp, *Humanism: ha-ra'ayon ve-toldotav* [Humanism: history of an idea], ed. Tirza Yovel (Tel Aviv, 5751/1991), 41–48.

interpretation of such a custom is based on a logical principle that explains Jewish culture and society.

Rabbi Avraham Yitzhak Hacohen Kook writes:

> The minutiae of laws and customs, and the strict interpretations that the Jews have taken upon themselves, represent the intricacies of the inner love of the Jewish people for their God, their Torah, their peoplehood and land, bound together inseparably as one. Inner love and sacred longing attempt to expand in all that they encounter.... We fulfill with love the Jewish customs that we know we were not commanded to perform by any prophecy, due to love for our nation.... The everlasting foundation is the acceptance of Torah throughout history as our way of life. We find, for example, that the ban of Rabbenu Gershom, where this tradition spread, remains as firm in the heart of the nation as the other prohibitions of the Torah, although he was neither Tanna nor Amora, but because he had the support of the Jewish people.[36]

According to Rabbi Kook, the definition of a custom is based on two components:

- The nation creates a custom out of an emotional need, the longing and desire to express the love of God and His mitzvot.
- The custom becomes obligatory only if it is accepted by the entire nation.

From the positive, we may deduce the negative. If a new custom leads to separation and disagreement within the nation, it cannot be valid.[37] The creation of a custom is a good example of agreement within a certain culture regarding the meaning of an object or situation.

One example of such a custom is *yayin nesekh* – wine produced by non-Jews that is designated for use in a ritual of idol worship. Use of such wine is forbidden by the Torah. Extrapolating from this, the Sages forbade the wine of non-Jews for drinking or any type of enjoyment, even if it is not meant for use in idol worship – this is the principle of *stam yeynam*. However, in certain locations, rabbis relaxed part of the prohibition due to special conditions in those places. In the early Middle Ages, the rabbis forbade commerce in *stam yeynam*, and completely prohibited the use of any wine belonging to a Jew that had come into contact with a non-Jew, or the wine of a non-Jew that was taken as repayment of a debt.

---

36. Cited in *Ha-mahshava ha-Yisraelit*, ed. Elchanan Clemenson (Jerusalem, 5727/1967), 4.
37. See also *Minhagei Yisrael*, vol. 4 (Tel Aviv, 5755/1995), 24–25.

Yet in the sixteenth century, they permitted the use of such wine, mainly in Polish towns near the Hungarian border and in Moravian communities.[38] The reason for this was that non-Jewish wine had become an important source of income.

Clearly, every religious group is strongly influenced by the environment in which it lives. We may note many examples of this, but we will limit ourselves to one example in which the geographic element has a direct influence on the development of certain customs. During biblical times,[39] mourners would wrap their heads in a shawl, like the head covering that the Muslims call *kaffiyeh*. Later in history, this ancient custom was annulled, as the Tosafot records: "Today we do not practice wrapping of the head…as it would lead to mockery, like the wrapping of the Ishmaelites" (Tosafot, *Moed Katan* 21a).

Certainly, wrapping the head "like the wrapping of the Ishmaelites" would not lead to mockery by the Ishmaelites. But in Christian provinces, the non-Jews would laugh at the Jews for wrapping, and so the Jews did not follow this practice. Thus the annulment of this custom could only develop on Christian territory.[40] For this reason, Yemenite Jews who came from a Muslim environment followed this practice until recently.[41]

Before entering their synagogue (*masjid*), the Jews of Ethiopia would remove their shoes, and only after that were they permitted to enter the synagogue (according to the testimony of my grandfather, Abba Gideon Mengesha, *ztz"l*). I remember this event from my childhood – hundreds of pairs of shoes arranged neatly at the entrance to the synagogue. The congregants stood barefoot. I also recall that the floor of the synagogue was covered with carpets or tree branches. The synagogues in Ethiopia had no chairs or benches – the congregants stood throughout the entire service. I asked my grandfather about the source for this tradition, and he replied that according to the sources, it is forbidden to enter a holy place wearing shoes. Indeed, the Mishnah records that wearing shoes was forbidden in the Temple: "One may not enter the holy mount with his staff, or with his sandal, or with his belt-pouch, or with dust on his feet" (Mishnah, *Berakhot* 9:5).

The synagogue is considered a *mikdash me'at*, a miniature Temple. The rabbis

---

38. Y. Katz, *Masoret u-mashber* [Tradition and crisis] (Jerusalem, 5718/1958), 30–31. See also *Minhagei Yisrael*, vol. 2, 49–59.
39. Ezekiel 24:17.
40. *Minhagei Yisrael*, vol. 3, "The economic factor in the formulation of custom," 65.
41. Y. Razhabi, *Be-ma'agalot Teiman* [Among Yemenite circles] (Tel Aviv, 5748/1988), 44. See also *Minhagei Yisrael*, vol. 4, 62–63.

instituted prayer in the synagogue as a replacement for the ritual practiced in the destroyed Temple, and yet wearing shoes was not forbidden inside the synagogue. The Rambam writes: "A person is permitted to enter a synagogue [holding] his staff, [wearing] his shoes, wearing [only] lower garments, or with dust on his feet."[42]

The question again arises, why did the custom change among rabbinic Jewry? And why did Ethiopian Jewry continue to follow the original custom? In order to answer this question, we must explore two conceptions of the connection between the individual and God in prayer.

In today's *siddur*, we find that the individual's relationship with his Creator is ambivalent.[43] On the one hand, it is respectful, and on the other, submissive.

> The two forms of consciousness recognize the existential gap between God and the individual, but each views it in a different light. This difference is expressed in the concept of God, the concept of human beings, and of the relationship between them. For the inferior side, a consciousness of respect creates the need to raise himself so that he will be worthy of an encounter with that which is greater than he. The inferior side, in this case, the human being, must adapt himself in a temporary, artificial manner to the status of respect, in order to bridge the gap between himself and God and to be worthy of meeting with Him. By contrast, a consciousness of submission creates for the inferior the need to diminish his appearance and to emphasize the chasm that exists between himself and the person greater than he. Through his inferiority and self-debasement, the inferior expresses his dependence on the other. Only by emphasizing this dependence is the inferior eligible to stand before one who is greater than he.[44]

From my knowledge of the Ethiopian Jewish religious world, I may say that it is characterized by a relationship of submission, as opposed to what is accepted in Western culture. For this reason, the Ethiopian Jew's worship of God focuses on the difference between him and the construct that is greater than him (God). Removing one's shoes is an expression of the inferiority of human beings. Therefore, when Ethiopian Jews enters a place that symbolizes the distance and

---

42. *Mishneh Torah*, Hilkhot Tefillah ve-Nesiat Kapayim 11:10.
43. Y. Heineman, *Ha-tefillah bi-tekufat ha-Tannaim ve-ha-Amoraim* [Prayer in the period of the Tannaim and Amoraim] (Jerusalem, 5724/1964).
44. Waltzer et al., *Ha-masoret ha-politit ha-Yehudit*, vol. 1.

difference between human beings and God, they must remove their shoes, and in places where the worship of God migrates to a mode of respect, the custom of removing shoes is annulled. Annulment of this custom expresses the change a society experiences in its understanding of the relationship between humanity and God.

In summary, we have seen how the accepted values of one society may be rejected by another society. The changing relationship has no objective explanation; rather, it is a cultural and environmental change.[45] This distinction forms the background of this book.

The Ethiopian Church

Ethiopia is one of the most ancient Christian countries in the world. King Ezana of Ethiopia was one of the earliest rulers to convert to Christianity, in 333 CE, preceded only by the conversion of the ruler of Armenia in 301 CE and the conversion of the Roman emperor Constantine in 312 CE.[46] The many years that have passed since then have granted Christianity an important place in Ethiopian culture. Christianity penetrated Ethiopia when the basic components of Ethiopian life were first being defined, and ever since, it has formed an inseparable part of the state's foundations and cultural-political fabric. In traditional Ethiopia, only two institutions have tried to define and lead the daily life of the population on a national basis, and only they had the ability to do so. These were the emperor and the Ethiopian church, which he headed.[47]

The Ethiopian Christians were the only Ethiopians who regularly attempted to document and preserve their history in writing. Other population groups in Ethiopia preserved detailed traditions, but they did not record these in writing in a methodical fashion. The monopoly over written culture, in combination with political authority, granted the Christians almost total hegemony over consolidation and preservation of the historical narrative. Until recently, non-Christian groups occupied a marginal, even negligible, position in the history of the country.[48]

---

45. Douglas, *Purity and Danger*.
46. Hagai Erlich, *Etiopiah ve-ha-Mizrah ha-Tihon: Tarbut matzor ve-alpayim shnot* [Ethiopia and the Middle East: A besieged culture and two thousand years], ed. Hagai Boaz (Tel Aviv: Broadcast University, 5768/2008).
47. However, the relationship between the church and political life was much more complex than the fact that all members of the ruling classes were Christians (ibid.).
48. Ibid.

What do we know about Beta Israel, which has been considered a Jewish community ever since ancient times?[49] In the heart of the state of Habash,[50] which is Ethiopia, lived a unique tribe, different in its religion from the rest of the population. The Habesha people called them *falashim*, meaning "exiled," while the members of the tribe preferred to call themselves Beta Israel.[51] For hundreds of years, the Beta Israel community maintained a complex network of ties with neighbors and Ethiopian rulers, Christians and members of other religions, and in modern times the community encountered the European Protestant missions. In addition to internal ties, the community developed connections with Jews in other countries, which led to complex relationships. These ties had far-reaching consequences for the formation of their identity and the character of their life as Jews in Ethiopia.[52]

In the ancient chronicles of the Habash kings, we read with bated breath of the cruel wars against the Falasha, who denied the basic principles of Christianity. These wars continued for almost five hundred years. Their enemies had to admit that the Beta Israel defended themselves heroically against their persecutors. Unintentionally, the authors of the chronicles express amazement and admiration at the courage of the men, women, and children who chose martyrdom over conversion.[53]

During the period called *Kifu Qen* (the Terrible Days, 1888–1892), about half of Beta Israel perished in a severe famine.[54] Members of today's community are a thin remnant of a numerous people that played an important role in the history of Habash.[55] The national tradition of the Habash and their leaders documents the influence of Judaism on the formation of the spiritual and social image of

---

49. H. Erlich, H. Salmon, and S. Kaplan, *Etiopiah, Natzrut, Islam, ve-Yehadut* [Ethiopia, Christianity, Islam, and Judaism] (Tel Aviv, 5763/2003).

50. See Rabbi Haim David Shlush, *Nidhei Yisrael yikanes: Al Yehudei Habash* [Gathering the far-flung remnants of Israel: On the Habash Jews] (Tel Aviv, 5748/1988). The beginning of this book discusses the origin and meaning of the name Habash.

51. For more on the meaning of the name Beta Israel, see Aharon Ze'ev Eshkoli, *Sefer ha-Falashim* [The book of the Falasha] (Jerusalem, 5703/1943), chapter 1, 1–12; Haim Rosen, *Falashim, ka'ila o Beit Yisrael* [Falasha, ka'ila, or Beta Israel].

52. Erlich et al., *Etiopiah, Natzrut, Islam, ve-Yehadut*.

53. M. Wurmbrand, *Sefer mitzvot ha-Shabbat shel Beta Israel* [The book of Shabbat mitzvot of Beta Israel], *Mahut* 8–9 (1991–1992).

54. Erlich et al., *Etiopiah, Natzrut, Islam, ve-Yehadut*, 292.

55. Today the community numbers over 121,000 individuals. Most of them are immigrants to Israel and their offspring, who came to Israel during two major aliyah operations: Operation Moses (1984) and Operation Solomon (1991). As of 2009, some 81,000 Ethiopian residents

Habash culture. According to several Ethiopian traditions, before the arrival of Christianity, about half of the population of Aksum[56] was Jewish. We may assume that this is a gross exaggeration, but still, the penetration of knowledge of the Bible and basic biblical Hebrew texts had a deep influence on ancient Ethiopian culture. For many years, the Christians in Ethiopia circumcised their sons on the eighth day after birth. They observed Shabbat and followed biblical laws of *kashrut*, and considered themselves the descendants of the ancient Israelites.[57]

Ge'ez: The Sacred Language

We do not know what language the ancient ancestors of Beta Israel spoke. Did they have prayers and sacred writings in Hebrew? Did they understand it? Clearly, in Habash they spoke the local language of Agaw in its various dialects. Today, the Beta Israel speak Amharic or Tigrinya, according to their place of habitation. The sacred texts in their possession and other books are written in the ancient Ethiopian language of Ge'ez, which remains the language of the Habesh church today. Bishop Samuel Gobat relates that he heard from Falashas about books in Hebrew that were buried in the city of Gondar to protect them from falling into enemy hands.[58] But to this day, no Hebrew texts have been found among the Falashas. Filosseno Luzzatto relates that the last king of Beta Israel burned their history books before he died, during the war of destruction waged against them by Emperor Susenyos (c. 1617).[59] If such books did indeed exist, we cannot know in what language they were written. We may only estimate that the persecutions, which did not succeed in destroying the Falashas, did succeed in completely destroying their literature.[60] At any rate, in the fourteenth century

---

of Israel were born in Ethiopia, while 38,500 (32 percent of the community) were native-born Israelis.

56. The Kingdom of Aksum was the cradle of the Ethiopian nation, where the first cultural patterns were established in 100–940 CE. Researchers accept that it grew out of the proto-Aksumite Ethiopian period, circa fifth century BCE to first century CE. Aksum was the first capital of the Habash state (Erlich et al., *Etiopiah, Natzrut, Islam, ve-Yehadut*).

57. The Jewish influence during the pre-Christian period also produced many words and basic terms in Ge'ez (Erlich et al., *Natzrut, Islam, ve-Yehadut*). On this, see also Yitzhak Greenfeld, "Masoret ha-tefillot shel Yehudei Etiopiah" [The prayer traditions of Ethiopian Jewry], *Mahut* 22 (5761/2001).

58. Greenfeld, "Masoret ha-tefillot shel Yehudei Etiopiah"; Samuel Gobat, *Journal of Three Years' Residence in Abyssinia* (New York, 1850).

59. Filosseno Luzzatto, *Mémoire sur les Juifs d'Abyssinie ou Falashas* (Paris, c. 1852).

60. Wurmbrand, *Sefer mitzvot ha-Shabbat shel Beta Israel*, 8–9. See also Michael Corinaldi, *Yehadut Etiopiah: Zehut u-masoret* [Ethiopian Jewry: Identity and tradition] (Jerusalem,

Amharic replaced Ge'ez as the spoken language, but Ge'ez remained the liturgical language, for the Ethiopian church as well as for Beta Israel. To this day, any religious ceremony, whether prayer services, songs, reading the Torah, blessings, or memorial service, is held in Ge'ez. We should note that the vast majority of Beta Israel do not know Ge'ez, and so every religious ceremony is entirely dependent on the *kes*, who is proficient in the language.

First Contact with Other Jews

The appearance of the Protestant mission in Ethiopia in the mid-nineteenth century represented one of the most significant turning points in the history of the Beta Israel community. Until then, Ethiopian Jewry had no contact with other Jewish groups, and they were not even aware of the existence of a Jewish Diaspora worldwide. Ironically, it was the encounter with the Western missionaries that began the period of contact with the general Jewish world and the initial definition of their Jewish identity. The encounter of the Christian mission also led to the initial awareness and interest of world Jewry in the Ethiopian Jewish community. Contacts between world Jewish organizations and the community were established, leading to changes in the definition of its identity from an internal Ethiopian group to a Diaspora community of "Ethiopian Jewry."[61] As mentioned, until the eighteenth century, knowledge of the lost Jewish tribe in Ethiopia was vague and limited, based on rumor and legend. The Ethiopian Jews never viewed themselves as belonging to the locals spiritually – rather, they considered themselves foreigners who had been exiled from their city of origin, Jerusalem, and who awaited the moment when they could return there.[62]

In the mid-nineteenth century, relations with the Jewish community outside Ethiopia developed and a process of material assistance for Habash Jewry began. Still, we may say that the main stimulus for awareness of Beta Israel and granting them assistance was missionary activity. As M. Eliav writes, "The main factor in arousing public awareness was missionary activity in Habash. In the early nineteenth century, European Jewry noted with deep concern the expanding activities

---

5749/1989); S. Kaplan, "Historiyah ketzarah shel Yehudei Etiopiah" [A short history of Ethiopian Jewry] in Natalya Berger, ed., *Beta Israel: Sippuram shel Yehudei Etiopiah* [Beta Israel: The story of Ethiopian Jewry] (5748/1988).
61. Erlich et al., *Etiopiah, Natzrut, Islam, ve-Yehadut*.
62. The prayers of Ethiopian Jewry are interlaced with expressions of longing for Jerusalem. This explains why the prayers of Sigd, the community's special holiday, focus on supplications and longing for the return to Zion.

of the missions in hunting for souls among Jews in various countries.[63] In 1862, at the yearly assembly of the missionary society in London, Henry Aaron Stern (a German Jew from Hessen, Germany, who had converted to Christianity) reported on his journey to Habash. He noted the success of missionary activity among the Falashas, and emphasized that he himself had underestimated the potential for the mission's success.

At the end of his speech, he announced his plans for a second trip, and stressed that there was no reason to fear the reaction of European Jewry. Even if the Jews wanted to send a mission, the representatives would encounter great difficulty should they try to convince the Falashas to accept traditional or Reform Judaism, "more than our difficulty in convincing them to accept Christianity."[64] Another reason that contributed to the interest of world Jewry was the surprising appearance of two Habash Jews in Jerusalem, Daniel ben Hananiah and his son Moshe, who arrived in 5615/1855. Their story spread throughout Jerusalem and led to an exchange of letters between the sages of that city and the Ethiopian priests.[65]

Zionism Comes to Ethiopia

Abba Mahari was born into the Beta Israel community in the early nineteenth century in the Kawara district. After he was ordained as a *kes*, Mahari became a monk and lived a life of isolation in which he wandered from one village to another, teaching Torah to Jews. Henry Stern first met Abba Mahari in 1860, about two years before Mahari led the Beta Israel community in an attempt to make aliyah. Stern gives the following description of their meeting:

> Abba Mahari, the leader, appeared in a turban white as snow and garments of the same color, holding a long bamboo staff, like a bishop's staff, and moving with hushed weightiness. There was something imposing and majestic in the appearance of the man, which one could scarcely behold without admiration and reverence. In my opinion, he was about sixty years old, his appearance noble and authoritative, his forehead high and expressive, his eyes sad and restless, and his expression, which before had undoubtedly been moderate

---

63. M. Eliav, "Hitorerut shel Yehudei Eiropa le-ezrat ha-Falashim" [The awakening of European Jewry to aid the Falashas], *Tarbiz* 35 (5727/1967).
64. Ibid.
65. M. Waldman, *Me-ever la-Nahar Cush* [Beyond the River Cush] (Tel Aviv, 5749/1989).

and attractive, had become quite strange and other-worldly as a result of self-training and abstinence.[66]

Mahari's messages were based on principles of messianism and Zionism, and he informed the Beta Israel of the inception of Zionism. Most of his pronouncements were directed toward one goal – aliyah to Israel and ending the Diaspora. Factors that influenced Abba Mahari included the civil war taking place at that time among district princes and noble families, and the missionary activity that affected the Jews. But above all, Abba Mahari was influenced by the ascendancy of Emperor Tewodros II, who valued the Jews and aspired to conquer Jerusalem from the Muslims. He is known for declaring, "Jerusalem is the wife and Ethiopia is the husband." Abba Mahari viewed these events as signs of the approaching end of the Diaspora. According to tradition, the God of Israel revealed Himself to Abba Mahari in a dream and said, "The time of redemption has arrived. You must lead the Jews to the Land of Israel."

Abba Mahari gathered thousands of Beta Israel and told them about the vision. They followed him on a tortuous journey. When they reached the Red Sea, they stood gazing at the water, but it refused to part. Many began to doubt the reliability of the dream, and begged Abba Mahari to return to Ethiopia. Abba Mahari tried to calm the public, and spoke to them about Zionism: "We must believe that God is testing us, as he did our forefathers during the Exodus from Egypt. He parted the sea then, and He will do so now as well." He believed that God was with him, watching over the community. Abba Mahari raised his staff over the water, but it did not divide. He entered the sea first, followed by thousands who believed that God would part the waters. Instead, many drowned. The survivors returned to Ethiopia, settled in villages, and established a Jewish community in the Tigray area. The first attempted journey of Ethiopian Jewry to the Land of Israel was thus a stinging failure that claimed many victims. It also represented an attempt at transition from imagination to rationality, and left behind stories of heroism of simple people who believed that the time would come when their children would cross the ocean and return home to the Land of Israel, to build and be strengthened there.

This attempted aliyah was transformed into myth for many of the Beta Israel. Some 120 years later, it inspired them to leave their villages and march toward

---

66. Shoshanah Ben-Dor, "Ha-masa le-ever Eretz Yisrael: Ha-sippur al Abba Mahari," *Pa'amim* 33 (5748/1987). The original is found in Stern's "Communities," published in the missionary journal *Jewish Intelligence*, July 1, 1861.

INTRODUCTION: THE SPIRITUAL WORLD OF ETHIOPIAN JEWRY, THEN AND NOW · 37

Israel. This journey, which began with Abba Mahari, continues with Ethiopian immigrants who undertook the journey to Israel.

The State of Israel

After the State of Israel was established, mass aliyah began. Hopes were rekindled of bringing the Ethiopian Jews to Israel – "the far-flung and remote members of our people,"[67] as documented in this letter, sent by the Ethiopian Jewish community to the president of the nascent State of Israel:

> For thousands of years, we have waited for the coming of the Messiah to take us away from here and bring us back to Jerusalem, the goal for which our fathers and forefathers fought. Now that the redemption has arrived, and we are left as a remnant of a numerous people, the waiting is very difficult for us.[68]

This letter inspired an enthusiastic response. Leaders of the Jewish state and heads of the Jewish Agency held discussions late into the night, and finally a historic decision was made: "We must help them!" The directors of the Department of Religious Education and Culture in the Diaspora were charged with implementing the decision.[69] Still, due to uncertainties surrounding the Ethiopian Jews' origin, no practical steps were made to carry out the decision. The Jewish world adopted an ambivalent stance toward the community, with the reaction wavering from extremes of encouragement and support to turning its back and ignoring the community's existence, from displays of unrelenting curiosity to disappointment and indifference.[70] Only in 1973 did a turning point take place in the attitude toward the community. The spearhead for this change was a declaration made by the former Chief Sephardic Rabbi of Israel, the late Rabbi Ovadia Yosef:

> I have thus come to the conclusion that the Falashas are the descendants of Israelite tribes who moved south to Cush. It is beyond doubt that the above-mentioned sages who determined that they are from the tribe of Dan have researched and studied the issue, and reached this conclusion based on

---

67. This was thanks to the efforts of Dr. Jacques Faitlovitch, then director of the International Pro-Falasha Committee.
68. Y. Azrieli and S. Meizlisch, *Ha-mesimah Etiopiah* [Mission Ethiopia] (Jerusalem, 5749/1989), 18–59.
69. Ibid.
70. S. Kaplan, "Al ha-temurot be-heker Yehadut Etiopiah" [Contributions to Research on Ethiopian Jewry], *Pa'amim* 58, 5754/1994.

very reliable evidence. As a young member of the Israelite tribes, I have also researched and studied this issue intensively, after Falasha leaders asked me to join them to their fellow Jews in the spirit of Torah, both Oral and Written, and of halakhah, without restriction, and to enable them to keep all the mitzvot of the Holy Torah according to the instruction of our rabbis, by whose words we live. I have thus decided that in my humble opinion, the Falashas are Jews, whom we must save from assimilation. We must encourage their rapid aliyah to Israel, educate them in the spirit of our Holy Torah, and involve them in the building of our Holy Land, "and your children shall return to their own border" (Jeremiah 31:16).[71]

Practically speaking, Rabbi Yosef instructed that the Ethiopian Jews undergo conversion according to strict interpretation of the halakhah, due to uncertainty over intermarriage with non-Jews,[72] even though in his opinion there was no reason to fear the status of *mamzerut* (illegitimate birth, as defined in halakhah – see "Strict Conversion and the Status of Mamzer" in chapter 5), as their marriage ceremonies were not halakhically valid. After Rabbi Yosef's decision, a historic decision was made in the Israeli Knesset, recognizing the Falashas as Jews in every way, and determining that they should be brought to Israel as immigrants under the Law of Return. The Ethiopian Jews were enthusiastic – more than ever, they felt that their heart's desire was about to be fulfilled. The path to the Land of Israel was finally approaching. One of the community leaders expressed the joy over this decision as follows:

> As in the words of the prophet, "How beautiful upon the mountains are the feet of the messenger of good tidings, that announces peace, the harbinger of good tidings, that announces salvation" (Isaiah 52:7). In the past weeks, we, the Jews of Ethiopia, the Falashas, have received the good tidings that the government of the State of Israel has decided to include the Ethiopian Jews

---

71. *Shu"t yabia omer*, part 8, *Even ha-Ezer*, par. 11. This response was written in reply to a letter addressed to Rabbi Ovadia Yosef by First Sergeant Hezi Ovadia, an Ethiopian-born Jew of Yemenite origin. In the letter, Hezi asks the rabbi to make a final decision regarding the Jewish status of the Beta Israel community. I would like to take this opportunity to thank Hezi for his efforts on behalf of the Ethiopian community.

72. After further investigation into the issue of Jewish-non-Jewish relations in Ethiopia, and after learning that the Ethiopian Jews were very careful about maintaining insulation from the Christian environment, this strict ruling was annulled. Instead, a special bureau was established under the direction of Rabbi Yosef Hadana, chief rabbi of the community, to conduct an additional investigation into each case individually.

among the Jewish people as enjoying rights under the Law of Return, like any other immigrant from Diaspora nations.[73]

The aliyah of the Ethiopian Jews intensified Israel's character as a museum representing different periods and cultures. Wondrously, members of a people that had dispersed more widely than any other nation, thousands of years ago, and that was living in all corners of the world, came together and united into one body. The ability of the Jewish people in Israel and the world to cooperate to solve the seemingly impossible problem of saving Ethiopian Jewry is triumphant evidence of Jewish solidarity. Solidarity and love for others as they are is the secret of existence for the entire Jewish people throughout its history, as well as of the modern State of Israel.[74]

Religious Literature

The halakhic tradition of Beta Israel was passed down from father to son, from *kes* to *kes* and community to community. There are no books other than this one that collect the halakhic tradition in an organized fashion. There is one exception, in the form of twenty-two verses of the tenth chapter of the book *Te'ezaz Senbet*. These verses, which are apparently a copy or reconstruction from the book of Jubilees, are the only halakhic source in the Beta Israel literature. Despite the almost complete absence of halakhic works, the community does possess some sixty-eight sacred works, most of which are apocalyptic. The Tanakh is one of these. The others are apocryphal works in the order accepted by the Church according to the Lucan version of the Septuagint, and other works of biblical and aggadic nature.

Most of the sacred works that the community possesses were borrowed from the Ethiopian church. The manuscripts were purchased or copied from church literature in the Ge'ez language. The community sages would then "convert" them, meaning they chose texts of a biblical character that were acceptable to both religions and did not emphasize Christian themes. For example, they chose stories of the deaths of the forefathers, keeping Shabbat, reward and punishment, and the fate of the soul after death. Then the community's scribes made changes in the body of the text. They distorted figures of crosses on the book covers, replaced

---

73. Azrieli and Meizlisch, *Ha-mesimah Etiopiah*, 38.
74. Y. Ephraim, "Ha-solidariyut ha-Yehudit ve-Yehudei Etiopiah" [Jewish solidarity and Ethiopian Jewry], in *Solidariyut Yehudit leumit ba-et ha-hadashah* [National Jewish solidarity in modern times], Binyamin Pinkus and Ilan Trowan, eds. (5748–49/1988–89).

mention of the Christian Trinity with the blessing "Blessed is He, the God of Israel, God of all spirit and body," and exchanged the name of Jesus with the name Egziabher ("Master of All," a name for the Creator of the universe). Later scribes improved on the work of their predecessors and deleted allusions to Christianity that survived after the first redaction.[75]

A Unique Halakhic Tradition

Many researchers have expressed interest in the history and culture of Ethiopian Jewry. Expression of this is found in the extensive travel literature describing the lives of the Falashas.[76] Steven Kaplan provides a comprehensive survey of the history of Beta Israel from its inception to the twentieth century.[77] Against the background of the waves of aliyah from Ethiopia in the last few decades, we find heightened interest of social science researchers in the issue of the move to Israel and its influence on customs and traditions, in changes in social structures such as the family, and in the question of the young generation's identity in its encounter with the Israeli educational institutions and the army.[78] We also find studies of the story of the journey of Ethiopian Jewry to Israel, and the place of this narrative

---

75. Yossi Ziv, "Hilkhot Shabbat shel 'Beta Yisrael' lefi *Tataza Sanvet*," doctoral dissertation, Department of Talmud, Bar-Ilan University (5769/2009); Kaplan, *Motzam shel Beta Yisrael: Hamesh he-arot metodologiyot* [Five methodological notes], Pa'amim 33 (5748/1987): 33–49.
76. James Bruce, *Travels to Discover the Sources of the Nile*, 2d ed. (Edinburgh, 1805). This is a description of James Bruce's journey to Ethiopia in the late eighteenth century, and includes many references to the Falashas. See also Y. Halevy, "Masa be-Habash le-gilui ha-Falashim" [Journey to Habash to discover the Falashas], Pa'amim 58 (5754/1994): 5–66. This article gives Halevy's full report of his travels among the Ethiopian Jews, with notes by Professor Steven Kaplan. See also Azrieli and Meizlisch, *Ha-mesimah Etiopiah*; Y. Kahane, *Ahim shehorim hayim be-kerev ha-Falashim* [Black brothers live among the Falashas] (Tel Aviv, 5738/1978).
77. Steven Kaplan, *The Beta-Israel (Falasha) in Ethiopia: From Earliest Times to the Twentieth Century* (New York: NYU Press, 1995).
78. S. Weil, *Emunot u-minhagim shel Yehudei Etiopiah be-Yisrael* [Beliefs and customs of Ethiopian Jews in Israel] (Jerusalem, 5749/1989); S. Weil, *Yehudei Etiopiah ba-ma'avar bein tarbuti: Ha-mishpahah ba-ma'agal ha-hayim* [Ethiopian Jewry in transition between cultures: The family in the life cycle] (Jerusalem, 5754/1994); Waldman, *Me-ever la-Nahar Cush*; Corinaldi, *Yehadut Etiopiah: Zehut u-masoret*; Shlush, *Nidhei Yisrael yikanes: Al Yehudei Habash*; D. Bodovsky and Y. David, *Sugiyot be-nosei mishpaha shel Yehudei Etiopiah* [Issues on the subject of families among Ethiopian Jewry] (Jerusalem, 5752/1992); M. Shabbtai, *Hakhi ahi: Masa ha-zehut shel hayalim olim me-Etiopiah* [My best bro': The journey of identity of new immigrant soldiers from Ethiopia] (Tel Aviv, 5765/2005); M. Shabbtai, *Bein reggae le-rap* [From reggae to rap] (Tel Aviv, 5761/2001).

in the collective and cultural memory of the group.[79] Some of the studies that address the traditions and beliefs of Beta Israel are part of early research in this field.[80] Among recent studies, we find an attempt to compare the customs of the Ethiopian community practiced today to ancient customs practiced among the Jewish people.[81] Among these studies, we find the overwhelming assertion that the Beta Israel community was cut off from halakhic development based on the Sages' rulings. In other words, Beta Israel was completely uninfluenced by the fundamental historical events that accompanied the development of the Jewish people after the destruction of the Second Temple. The Beta Israel community continued Jewish tradition anchored in the biblical spirit, as opposed to the Talmudic way of thinking.

In the State of Israel: Rebuilding after the Destruction

From Biblical to Talmudic Template

Researchers accept that the religious identity of the Beta Israel community does not recognize the Mishnah or the Talmud. Rather, it is based on the spirit of the Tanakh. While tradition throughout the Jewish world today draws from Talmudic, rabbinic halakhah, the customs of the Ethiopian community are mainly based on the Torah – the Orit, the Prophets, the Writings, and the Apocrypha. The transition from biblical to Talmudic tradition in mainstream Judaism took place following the destruction of the Second Temple. The destruction sent shockwaves throughout the Jewish world, but had no influence whatsoever on the Ethiopian community, which remained unaware of it and continued to follow biblical tradition. We find interesting evidence of biblical Ethiopian tradition in a nineteenth-century letter sent from the Karaite community to the Beta Israel community:

---

79. G. Ben-Ezer, *Kemo or ba-kad: Aliyatam u-klitatam shel Yehudei Etiopiah* [Like light in a pot: The immigration and absorption of Ethiopian Jewry] (Tel Aviv, 5752/1992).
80. Eshkoli, *Sefer ha-Falashim* [The book of the Falashas] (Jerusalem, 5733/1973). See also Aharon Ze'ev Eshkoli, "Ha-halakhah ve-ha-minhag bein Yehudei Habash le-or ha-halakhah ha-rabbanit ve-ha-Karait" [Halakhah and custom among the Jews of Habash in light of rabbinic and Karaite halakhah], *Tarbiz* 7 (5796/1936): 31–134; Wolf Laslau, *Falasha Anthology: Translated from Ethiopic Sources* (New Haven, CT: Yale University Press, 1979), an introduction on Beta Israel customs and beliefs, with discussion of the sacred texts.
81. S. Shalom, "Minhagei brit ha-milah etzel Beta Israel" [Circumcision customs among the Beta Israel], MA thesis, Bar-Ilan University; Y. Ziv, "Tumah ve-taharah etzel ha-kehillah ha-Etiopit" [Impurity and purity in the Ethiopian community], MA thesis, Bar-Ilan University.

> Our brothers, children of Israel, fellow members of the Karaite religion.…
> Greetings to you, our dear brothers, sons of Abraham, Isaac, and Jacob.…
> We have heard and also read that some of our fellow children of Israel are living in the land of Cush, which is Abyssinia, and that the foundation of their religion and faith is the holy Torah of Moses, given on Mount Sinai by God's servant, Moses. When we heard that you are called "Falash" and also "Kara," we thought that the name *kara* [lit., "read"] was given to you because you believe only in the Written Torah of Moses, the only text that is read, and that you do not believe in the Torah that was given orally to Moses on Sinai, as most of the Jews believe. For this reason, our sages call them "masters of the received [word]" or rabbis, because they believe in the Mishnah and the Talmud, which were recently written and added to the Torah. We therefore inform you that we are also Jews who believe only in the Torah of Moses, and we are therefore called *kara*, Karaites, or people of the written word.

From the Ethiopian community's point of view, the destruction of the Temple took place when they made aliyah to Israel. In order to support this statement, we must trace the status of the Jewish people immediately following the destruction of the Second Temple.

The Role of the Temple in Jewish Life: A Brief History

AFTER THE DESTRUCTION

After the destruction of the Second Temple, the Jewish people sank into deep despair and shame.[82] Many did not believe that the Jewish people would continue to exist. The literature of that time describes a miserable reality of a people barely able to recover. The Sages of the generation of the destruction felt that the reality of that time could not continue. The Midrash describes a discussion among the Sages about abstinence following the destruction:

> When the Temple was destroyed for the second time, large numbers in Israel became ascetics, refraining from eating meat and drinking wine. Rabbi Joshua felt compelled to address them: "My children, why do you refrain from eating meat and drinking wine?" They said: "How can we eat meat, when the *tamid* offering can no longer be offered daily on the altar? Drink wine, when libations cannot be offered?" He said: "Maybe we should not eat figs or grapes,

---

82. Dr. Yeshayahu Gafni, *From Jerusalem to Jabneh: The Period of the Mishnah and Its Literature* (Tel Aviv: Everyman's University Publishing House, 5740/1980).

since the first fruits cannot be offered. Maybe we should not eat bread, as we brought bread as an offering on Shavuot and the bread offering every Shabbat. We should not drink water, since water libations can no longer be offered on the altar on Sukkot." They were silent [since he proved to them that their behavior was problematic]. Rabbi Joshua said to them, "Not to mourn at all is not possible, for the Temple has been destroyed, but to mourn too much is also not possible, since we do not impose on the community a hardship which the majority cannot bear." ... So the Sages suggested that when one paints his house, he should leave a portion unpainted. When a person makes a banquet, he should leave out a few dishes. What should this be? Rabbi Pappa said, "the hors d'oeuvre of salted fish." A woman can put on all her jewelry, but she should leave off some. What should this be? Rav said, "[She should not remove] the hair at the temple, as it is said, 'If I forget you, Jerusalem, may my right hand lose its cunning.'"[83]

Rabbi Joshua stands in opposition to those who supported abstaining from worldly pleasures. Rabbi Joshua is not alone in the struggle, as we discover; his statement is only one example of the process of rehabilitation of the Jewish people and establishing its daily practices on new foundations.[84]

Why did the destruction of the Second Temple have such a profound influence on the Jewish people?

The destruction landed a powerful blow on the religious system in which the Jewish people lived and acted. In the Jewish consciousness, the Temple was understood as the place where God "atoned for Israel's sins." When the sacrificial rites in the Temple disappeared, the direct connection between the people and their God was severed, and there was no way to atone for sins. One of the Sages of the Mishnah expressed this situation as follows: "On the day that the Temple was destroyed, an iron wall was erected between Israel and their heavenly Father."[85] In the early Second Temple period, Shimon ha-Tzaddik, listed three elements on which the existence of the world depended: Torah, sacrificial ritual, and charitable deeds.

According to this understanding, the destruction of the Temple called into question one of the basic foundations of the world. But this does not fully

---

83. *Ecclesiastes Rabbah* 2, *Lamentations Rabbati* 1:32. See also Babylonian Talmud, *Baba Batra* 60a.
84. Gafni, From Jerusalem to Jabneh, 5.
85. Babylonian Talmud, *Berakhot* 32a.

describe the elements of the crisis. We must recall that many mitzvot and traditions, even those that were not dependent on the Temple in their essence, were connected in the public consciousness with the sacrificial ritual. The Temple served as a foundation for the national unity of the Jewish people. Jews from all over the Diaspora sent yearly donations for its continual upkeep. Even a Jew who lived in the Diaspora his entire life made sure to send a half shekel every year to Jerusalem, and by doing so, he gave material expression to his national involvement. Pilgrims from the Land of Israel and abroad met at the Temple; the pilgrimage was both a personal and public experience, and it aroused powerful nationalist emotions.[86] Further, "the political activity of the Jewish people was mostly centered on the Temple … [;] various institutions and even those who by nature were unconnected to the sacrificial ritual in the Temple drew substantial ethical authority from their connection and proximity to the Temple."[87]

NEW PATTERNS OF WORSHIP

Having established the position of the Temple in the life of the Jewish people, we may now

> …hold in proper esteem the serious task that a number of leaders in the generation of the destruction took upon themselves. The revival of the nation, both spiritually and organizationally, can be attributed to the rapid and daring action of the generation of the Sages of Yavne, and first and foremost, to the activity of Rabban Yochanan ben Zakkai.[88]

The main task was to fill the empty space created by the destruction, in the worship of God as well as in the national leadership. In parallel to the cultivation of the conceptual unity of the entire nation, compensation began to be felt in the Yavne generation through the world of the Sages. For the first time, the need arose to determine a normative halakhah that would unite the entire people. The sages of the Yavne generation, aware of this trend, emphasized the necessity of deciding halakhah. Out of concern for the completeness of the tradition that they and their teachers had cultivated for hundreds of years, the sages of Yavne saw a need to revise and organize it. This process led to heated battles among

---

86. Gafni, From Jerusalem to Jabneh.
87. Ibid.
88. Ibid.

the Sages, and even to conflicts between the Nasi and the Sages. At the end of the process, we may conclude that

> ...the act of Yavne influenced the character of the Jewish Diaspora. The foundations for the adaptive ability of the Jew, which is the first condition for his ability to survive in foreign lands, are located in this period, and draw significantly from the acts of the Sages at Yavne. The transition from Jerusalem to Yavne is based first and foremost on the recognition that Jewish life can flourish in every place and at every time. In this sense, Yavne is no more than a station in a long chain of exiles from Jerusalem.[89]

EXTRA-BIBLICAL HOLIDAYS

The Sages of Yavne determined several days of joy, praise, and thanksgiving, and days of mourning and fasting. For the days of celebration, the Sages set aside appropriate mitzvot, and for the days of mourning and fasting, they determined patterns of grieving. The days of celebration they established are Purim and Chanukah, which commemorate events in Jewish history during the Second Temple period. Purim marks salvation from the decrees of destruction that threatened the Jews in the Perisan Empire during the fifth century BCE. Chanukah commemorates the victory over the Hellenizing Jews and the Greeks, and the repurification of the Temple during the Hellenistic period, in the second century BCE. The days of mourning and fasting are the Fast of Gedaliya, the Tenth of Tevet, the Fast of Esther, the Seventeenth of Tammuz, and Tisha be-Av. These fasts, except for the Fast of Esther, were established in commemoration of events in the Land of Israel – the destruction of the Temple and the Exile. According to the book of Zechariah, in the future these fasts will be annulled and transformed into days of joy and celebration.[90]

ALIYAH AND THE NEED FOR NEW PATTERNS

The crisis felt among the Ethiopian community after aliyah led to a destruction of its religious world, and in this way, the Ethiopian aliyah can be compared to the destruction of the Temple. The move to Israel was accompanied by the total collapse of the religious, authoritative, and family system within which the Ethiopian community lived. When they came to Israel, the traditional balance between men and women was undermined. The sensitive relationship between

---

89. Ibid., 29.
90. Zechariah 8:9.

the community and its spiritual leadership was disrupted, and the observance of mitzvot was damaged. For this reason, we may state that some of the negative social phenomena we observe today, such as abandoning the practice of Judaism out of depression and discouragement, interest in the Afro-American world, and leaving Israel and immigrating to other countries, are the results of the crisis of aliyah. Yet the majority of the Israeli public remains unaware of the deep religious crisis that continues to affect the Ethiopian community.

> In Ethiopia, most of the Beta Israel Jews lived in small communities, with only a minority in the cities. Each village or community numbered between eight and ten families. The family structure was patriarchal, and it was part of the intergenerational communal family, whose members took responsibility for each other for seven generations. The division of roles within the family was clear: the man held the authority, and he represented the family toward community members and leaders. As the most respected member of the family, he was responsible for its economic status, the division of roles, education, tradition, religion, and spirituality. The woman, who was married at a very young age, went to live with her husband's family and was considered his property. She performed hard physical labor and was responsible for cooking and raising the children. Community life followed a traditional pattern and was led by spiritual leaders who drew their power from Judaism. The need and demand to adapt to the Western lifestyle in Israel led to many changes in the traditional lifestyle. Their dream of spiritual fulfillment was dashed. The *kesim*, the community's spiritual leaders, were not recognized by the Israeli establishment, and their status was weakened. They found themselves out of place in terms of their culture, mode of dress, and dark skin. The status of the traditional community institutions was eroded, and they lost their efficiency in leadership and problem solving. For example, the *shmaglotz* [community sages], who in Ethiopia had been responsible for solving family disputes, lost their status, particularly among the women and youth, who preferred the Israeli establishment over the traditional one.[91]

To paraphrase the Mishnah cited above, I will permit myself to say that the world of Ethiopian Jewry stands on three principles: on the religious support of the *kesim*, family support, and the longing for a better future. With the aliyah to Israel,

---

91. Leah Kassan and Shabbtai Malkah, "Zion she-hikhzivah: Yehudei Etiopiah be-Yisrael; gevarim mi-Etiopiah, nashim mi-Yisrael," *Eretz Aheret* 30 (2005).

these foundations were damaged and are no longer stable. Seemingly, therefore, the situation of the Ethiopian community today recalls that of many Jews after the destruction of the Second Temple. For this reason, they can learn methods of recovery and coping from the Jewish people of that time.

To illustrate the deep crisis of Ethiopian Jewry that accompanied the transition to Israel, I will relate a story that expresses this rift in a concrete manner. Following Operation Moses, the *kesim*, the spiritual leaders of the community, were taken on a tour of Jerusalem, the city of their dreams. The last stop of the day was at the Western Wall Plaza. One of the *kesim* lifted his hand and asked, "Where is Jerusalem?" Ya'akov from the Jewish Agency answered, "We've been in Jerusalem all day long, and now we're at the Western Wall." The *kes* continued, "Where is the Temple?" Ya'akov pointed at the Temple Mount and said, "That is where the Temple used to be." The *kesim* fell on their faces to the pavement of the plaza, and began to weep like children.[92]

A Living *Genizah*

A *genizah* (repository for sacred texts) preserves everything exactly as it was placed inside. In a sense, we may call the Beta Israel community a living *genizah*, as it brought with it an ancient tradition. Because its members are a living people, the Jewish people have inherited a precious legacy. By studying the ancient traditions of the community, we may come to understand and value the reasons for some of their halakhic decisions. The problem is that since their aliyah, the Beta Israel spiritual leaders have sensed coercion on the part of the religious establishment. They sense that they cannot publicly express their opinion on halakhah or tradition. They feel a controlling attitude from above, instead of a joint debate on the most serious issues. This approach on the part of leaders in the rabbinic institution has indicated to the spiritual leadership that they do not intend to include the Ethiopian customs. As a result, the community has created a defensive, closed world in order to preserve its unique tradition and past.

In every process of integration among various groups, we may identify two stages: the first stage requires understanding and listening, while the second stage involves implementation. Although this method may seem like ignoring the problem instead of coping with the painful issues, in the end we find that this is the only way to create a deep, internal connection between the two sides, and that difference expresses abundance and mutual productivity.

---

92. Personal story of an employee of the Jewish Agency.

A *Shulhan Arukh* for Ethiopian Jewry

Since the *Shulhan Arukh* was written by Rabbi Yosef Caro, no Jewish group has ever disputed it. This work was accepted unanimously by all Jews, except for annotations and corrections made in accordance with time and place. Acceptance of this work is a clear sign of recognition of a Talmudic Jew. Anyone who questions its authority has apparently not found his place among the ranks of Talmudic Judaism. Yet in the past century, a group of Jews – the Yemenites – asserted that they did not rule according to the *Shulhan Arukh*, but rather according to the Rambam alone. Still, the Yemenite Jews were accepted without any doubt into the rubric of Orthodox Judaism. At first, major contemporary rabbis did not agree with their halakhic practice, but today no one questions their belonging. Today the Yemenite Jews represent an integral part of the mosaic of the Jewish people throughout history. They represent a valuable legacy for the Jewish people for the very reason that they preserved the uniqueness of their tradition.

In recent times, we have been privileged to encounter a group with a very special tradition – the Beta Israel Ethiopian community. This group does not resemble any of the groups that comprise the mosaic of Talmudic Jewry, not even the Yemenite Jews. While the Yemenites recognized the world of the Mishnah, Talmud, the Geonim, the Rishonim, and the *Shulhan Arukh*, the Beta Israel community did not recognize any of these. Its tradition is based entirely on the biblical text and additional halakhah that was preserved orally. This group also demanded recognition as an integral part of the Jewish people. The Ethiopian community must be connected to the Jewish people and to the *beit midrash*, and needs a clear and practical halakhah for the second generation of Ethiopian immigrants living in Israel.

The precious treasure that is Ethiopian tradition is dwarfed by the intensity of the crisis, and overwhelmed by the negative images that have become attached to the community. Members of the community have a powerful desire to grasp onto something from their tradition, but they do not know much about it. What is more, they feel embarrassment because the community they would like to identify with is known for its negative, weak side. This unhappy reality has encouraged me to write a book of halakhah that presents the community's custom, the history of this custom in the rabbinic world, and finally the appropriate halakhic decision. I do so in the hopes that the community will become an integral part of the Jewish people and participate in building it, not through an act of charity or kindness, but as their inherent right.

❧ Ethiopian Jewry and Talmudic Law

The Model of the Jerusalem Talmud

Since the early days of the Ethiopian aliyah, the topic of religious tension between Orthodoxy and Ethiopian Jewry has been painful and loaded. Since then, the community's spiritual leaders have felt unable to express their opinion on halakhah and tradition. The tension still exists today as well, and it seems that as time goes on, the anger and conflict increase. On the other hand, we also find understanding and rapprochement between the two worlds.

One year when Yom Kippur fell on Shabbat, the *kesim* ruled that members of the community should make Kiddush and even take a small bite to eat, in honor of the sanctity of the Shabbat. In doing so, they attempted to compromise between two conflicting *halakhot*. On one hand, the Beta Israel work the *Tataza Sanvet* (Laws of Shabbat), which is based on the book of Jubilees, specifies that any individual who fasts on Shabbat is liable for the death penalty; on the other, one who eats on Yom Kippur is liable for *karet* (untimely death or eternal excommunication). Yet the local religious council was quick to accuse the *kesim*: "Your acts are leading the public to sin," "This ruling is an act of heresy."

I will give another example of tensions surrounding halakhah. In Ethiopian culture, it is acceptable for men and women to exchange greetings by shaking hands or kissing the cheek. Many parents have difficulty adjusting to the fact that their male children who have become religious no longer greet women in these ways, even within the family. The parents scorn this practice and consider those who follow it to be uncultured. Many parents do not understand it, not only because it is opposed to their cultural world, but also because it does not follow the spirit of the Torah, whose "ways are ways of pleasantness, and all her paths are peace" (Proverbs 3:17).

But in my opinion, the most shocking issue is the debate about giving money for charity during the prayer services on Shabbat. According to Ethiopian tradition, during the morning services on Shabbat, the congregants place bills and coins on the synagogue platform. This is the custom practiced today in a synagogue in Kiryat Gat. According to the *kes* of the synagogue, Kes Barhan, this practice is based on the principle of not coming to the synagogue empty-handed – "every man shall give as he is able" (Deuteronomy 16:17). Yet this practice has led to complaints, anger, and degradation of the *kesim*. I have heard people say, "They're *goyim*," "It's like eating pork," "I'm embarrassed to pray there," "They are defiling the sanctity of Shabbat," and other harsh criticisms.

What will lead to a change in the attitude of the rabbinic establishment toward the Ethiopian community and its leaders? What will lead to an attitude of respect toward their customs and leaders?

I believe that the root of this intense conflict between the rabbis and the *kesim* lies in their differing worldviews, which may be compared to the worldview expressed in the Babylonian Talmud as opposed to that presented in the Jerusalem Talmud. Many sources in the Talmuds point to differing attitudes toward the nature of the individual. While the Babylonian Talmud adopts a suspicious, skeptical approach toward the individual, as in the first half of the verse in Psalms 34:15, "shun evil," the Jerusalem Talmud promotes a positive attitude and believing in others – as in the second half of the same verse, "do good." Below we will give several examples in support of this distinction.[93]

The first example addresses the issue of sleeping in the sukkah. Both Talmuds debate the law regarding taking a nap (*sheinat arai*) outside the sukkah. The Babylonian Talmud completely forbids napping outside the sukkah, even if one appoints a guard whose job is to prevent one from falling into a deep sleep, if one should happen to fall asleep at all.[94]

The Jerusalem Talmud reaches the same halakhic conclusion, but not out of doubt. Rather, its position is that "taking a nap" cannot be defined, since a person might be refreshed after sleeping for only a short time.[95]

Another example is the issue of blowing the shofar on Rosh Hashanah when it falls on Shabbat. In Temple times, they blew the shofar even when Rosh Hashanah fell on Shabbat. But after the Temple was destroyed, the Sages ruled that we should not blow shofar on Shabbat. Why? The Babylonian Talmud cites the likelihood that a person who is not proficient in blowing the shofar might carry it to one who is proficient in blowing, in order to learn. He thus might be tempted to carry it four cubits in the public domain, which would be a violation of the Shabbat.[96] But the Jerusalem Talmud forbids blowing the shofar on Shabbat for another reason:

> They taught that on the holiday of Rosh Hashanah that falls on Shabbat, they would blow in the Temple but not elsewhere... Rabbi Shimon ben Yochai

---

93. My friend Rabbi Avraham Blas assisted me greatly in locating the sources in the Jerusalem Talmud.
94. Babylonian Talmud, *Sukkah* 26a.
95. Jerusalem Talmud, *Sukkah* 2:53, column 1, halakhah 5.
96. Babylonian Talmud, *Rosh Hashanah* 29b.

taught, "You shall sacrifice"(Leviticus 24:25) – [this means] the place where the sacrifices are made.[97]

Rabbi Shimon ben Yochai is addressing the question of whether it is permitted to make a sacrifice outside the Temple. Based on the biblical citation, he rules against this – one may sacrifice only in the Temple. The Jerusalem Talmud applies the same principle to blowing the shofar on Shabbat – it is permitted only in the Temple. According to the Jerusalem Talmud, blowing on Shabbat depends on the existence of the Temple and sacrificial worship, and not on the suspicion of a possible violation, as in the Babylonian Talmud.

Another example of the differing attitudes is found in the discussion of the *sotah* (a woman accused of betraying her husband). According to the Torah, the *sotah* must be taken to the Temple, where her husband's accusation is verified in a special ceremony. The Mishnah describes the process:

> They bring her [the *sotah*]…to the entrance of Nicanor's gate, where they gave the *sotah* the water to drink, where they purified the women who had given birth and purified the lepers. A priest seizes her garments – if they tear, they tear, and if they shred, they shred – until he uncovers her bosom and undoes her hair. Rabbi Judah says: If her bosom was beautiful, he did not uncover it, and if her hair was beautiful, he did not undo it.[98]

The Babylonian Talmud explains that the basis for Rabbi Judah's statement is the suspicion of arousing impure thoughts. In the Jerusalem Talmud, however, in the discussion of waving the meal offering of the *sotah*, we encounter a different approach:

> The priest places his hand under hers and waves it [the meal offering], but this is unseemly. He brings a cloth, but it does not properly conceal. Then he brings an elderly priest. You may even say that they bring a youth who is not drawn by desire at that time.[99]

According to the biblical text, the priest must wave the meal offering together with the accused woman. The Jerusalem Talmud states that this may even be done by a young priest, for *"ein yetzer hara matzui le-sha'ah"* ([he] is not drawn by desire at that time). That is, because he is involved in performing a mitzvah,

---

97. Jerusalem Talmud, *Rosh Hashanah* 4:59, column 2, halakhah 1.
98. Mishnah, *Sotah* 7a.
99. Jerusalem Talmud, *Sotah* 3:1.

there is no fear that he will stray from the goal. There is no need to worry that a person who acts for the sake of heaven will wander into forbidden territory. Likewise, it is not an assumption that a man has no desire for women that makes a woman feel secure that her husband will not be unfaithful; rather, it is the love and trust between them that fosters this faithfulness. In the same way, the Jerusalem Talmud trusts that the priest will not stray because his love for and fealty toward God and the mitzvot overrides any other desire.

According to Rabbi Avraham Blas, this is additional evidence for the significant difference between the two Talmuds: while the Babylonian Talmud reveals a suspicious attitude toward the worshipper of God, the Jerusalem Talmud expresses full trust in the world of the faithful.

A good example that sharpens our understanding of the difference between the two Talmuds is the issue of the beautiful female prisoner of war:

> [When you go out to war]…and see among the captives a woman of goodly form, and you desire her, and would take her as a wife, then you shall bring her home to your house; and she shall shave her head, and pare her nails; and she shall put the raiment of her captivity from off her, and shall remain in your house, and bewail her father and her mother a full month; and after that you may go in unto her, and be her husband, and she shall be your wife. (Deuteronomy 21:11–13)

Is it possible that the Torah permits a soldier to take a foreign woman, even though she may be already married? Yes, the Torah permits this, as "The Torah only provided for man's evil inclination."[100] The question is, at what point was the beautiful woman permitted? Rashi writes (based on the Babylonian Talmud): "beautiful – because his evil inclination desires her for her beauty, the Torah permits it to him, but grudgingly, since it is preferable for Israel to eat flesh of animals about to die, yet ritually slaughtered, than flesh of animals which may not have been ritually slaughtered."[101] According to the Babylonian Talmud, the beautiful woman is permitted on the battlefield, because "The Torah only provided for man's evil inclination." The Jerusalem Talmud, on the other hand, does not permit this:

---

100. Babylonian Talmud, *Kiddushin* 21b.
101. Ibid.

Rabbi Yochanan sent to the rabbis over there [in Babylonia]: Two things you say in the name of Rav and they are not so. You say in Rav's name: "A beautiful captive woman – permitted in her case is only the first act of sexual relations." But I say that it is neither the first nor any later act of sexual relations that is permitted, except after all the required preparations have been carried out – as specified, "After that, you may be intimate with her and possess her" – that is, after the specified deeds.[102]

As opposed to the Babylonian Talmud, which permits intercourse with the beautiful woman during battle, the Jerusalem Talmud forbids the practice entirely. According to the Jerusalem Talmud, it is completely forbidden to have relations with a beautiful war captive. Only after one month, after the prisoner has made all efforts to become repulsive to the man who captured her, if he decides that he still wants her, then he is permitted to take her. A fundamental controversy lies at the root of this issue. One approach is that man is weak in character, and if the beautiful woman is not permitted to him, he will go to her when she is forbidden, and therefore we will permit it – this is the educational approach of the Babylonian Talmud, which considers how to protect man. In contrast, the approach of the Jerusalem Talmud is revolutionary, and expresses powerful faith in man's powers. This approach asserts that even though the prisoner is in the man's hands, he can overcome his sexual desire during battle and even afterward, for an extended period. Human beings have strong spiritual powers, and we believe in them.[103]

Through the distinction we have identified between the two Talmuds, we can now argue that the Ethiopian halakhah is based on a principle similar to that of the Jerusalem Talmud, as opposed to the rabbinic establishment, which supports the Babylonian model. This is no controversy between institution and gender, between hegemony and the fringes of society, between strong and weak. Rather, it is a controversy between two Talmuds, found on the same shelf in the *beit midrash*. According to the Jerusalem approach, we can understand why a man greeting a woman with a kiss on the cheek is not shocking. This is also the way to understand a person who makes Kiddush on Yom Kippur that falls on Shabbat without suspecting him of eating plentifully (I am not arguing that the Jerusalem Talmud permits eating on Yom Kippur that falls on Shabbat). This is

---

102. Jerusalem Talmud, *Makkot* 2:6, trans. Jacob Neusner.
103. Avraham Hacohen Blas, *Otzarot ha-Yerushalmi* [Treasures of the Jerusalem Talmud] (Jerusalem, 5768/2008), 133–34.

54 · FROM SINAI TO ETHIOPIA

also the key to understanding a person who gives charity on Shabbat because he believes that this is a mitzvah, without suspecting him of engaging in commerce, because the money is used only for sacred purposes. The Ethiopian community, like the Jerusalem Talmud, believes in humanity's goodwill, and that his intention in both cases is to serve God. I am not arguing that we should adopt the Jerusalem Talmud instead of the Babylonian Talmud in a wholesale manner, but we can and should use the Jerusalem Talmud's approach as an example of how we may relate to differing opinions.

Many rabbis assert that the approach of the Jerusalem Talmud is appropriate for our generation, the generation of the redemption.[104] In this book, I will present a method for building a civilized world founded on the experience of the Jerusalem Talmud.

Can the Ethiopian Jews Continue Their Customs?

Usually, when halakhic questions arise, we refer to halakhic works such as the Rambam's *Mishneh Torah* or Rabbi Yosef Caro's *Shulhan Arukh*. But a *posek halakhah*, a rabbi who makes halakhic decisions, cannot rely on texts alone.[105] Reality is complex, and in order to find the appropriate answer he must use good judgment, as we find in the responsa literature. Sometimes, this is not enough, and he must proceed to a third stage in order to answer the question. At this point, rabbis rely on certain fundamental halakhic principles, such as *et la-asot*

---

104. Avraham Hacohen Blas, *Orot ha-Yerushalmi* [Lights of the Jerusalem Talmud] (5770/2010), 26–27.
105. D. Sperber, *Minhagei Yisrael*, vol. 1, "Le-makor tokef ha-minhag" [The origin of the validity of custom], 20; ibid., "Mahut ha-minhag u-tokpo" [The significance of custom and its validity], 1. See also Rabbi Yehuda Amichai, "Eikh poskim ka'asher ein masoret mesuderet shel pesika?" [How do we rule when there is no organized tradition of ruling?] in *Kumi ori* [Rise, awake] (Shevat 5767/2007); ibid., "Ha-pesharah ba-minhag" [Compromise in customs], 23; ibid., "Hisardutam ve-he'almutam shel minhagim" [Survival and disappearance of customs], 227; ibid., part 3, "Al ma'amado shel minhag etzel miktzat gedolei ha-Aharonim" [The status of custom according to some great Aharonim], 3.

le-Hashem heferu Toratekha,[106] *kavod ha-briyot*,[107] *mutav she-yehu shogegin*,[108] and *ein gozrim*.[109] This means that a *posek* must take into account the entire range of sources in order to find the necessary balance between universal morality and the halakhah, which is based on defined principles. This is particularly true for issues concerning communities that have immigrated to Israel, such as the Beta Israel community. The final result, the practical halakhic decision, may seem like an exception. But on a deeper level, we find that it derives from one root. A person who reads the halakhah with this awareness will understand that the halakhic decisions of Ethiopian Jewry, whether strict or lenient rulings, come from a recognized source and are all firmly founded on the Torah, the Talmud, and the decisions of the Rishonim.

The path I propose is influenced by the Ethiopian values and traditions I absorbed from my grandfather, Abba Gideon (Dejen) Mengesha, of blessed memory. This is the way of all halakhah. For example, the halakhic decisions of the religious Zionist rabbis are influenced by their study of faith and their openness to Western culture, and thus are different from the decisions of the haredi rabbis. Sometimes, cultural difference influences the choice of sources and arguments, and sometimes the interpretation of sources may differ. How is the personal aspect expressed in the halakhic decision? In my view, the answer is, *kabbalat ol malkhut shamayim*, "accepting the yoke of Heaven." Where there is *yirat shamayim*, fear or awe of God, there is room for the personal aspect, because the individual wants to do God's will. When we see the faithful of Beta Israel, we find that they

---

106. "Time to act in the name of the Lord, because they violate Your Torah" (Psalms 119:126). Under this principle, rabbis may make innovations in halakhah under unique circumstances when Torah law as a whole is endangered. For example, after the destruction of the Second Temple, the rabbinic leadership used this principle to overturn the law forbidding transcription of the Oral Law.

107. Mishnah, *Avot* 4:1, and elsewhere. This concept permits exceptions to rabbinic decisions under circumstances that would lead to an undignified situation. For example, rabbinic prohibition forbids carrying any object across a private property line on Shabbat, but the Talmud records that the rabbis created an exception for carrying as many as three small stones if needed for wiping oneself in a latrine, on the basis of *kavod ha-briyot* (*Shabbat* 81b, 94b).

108. Babylonian Talmud, *Beitzah* 30a, specifies that it is preferable not to protest against someone who is sinning unintentionally, if the listener will not heed rebuke, as by doing so one transforms the listener into an intentional transgressor.

109. "*Ein gozrim gezerah al ha-tzibbur ela im ken rov ha-tzibbur yeholim la-amod bah*" (We do not enact a decree upon the community unless a majority of the community is able to comply with it), *Baba Batra* 60b and elsewhere.

are rich in awe of God. The existence of varying traditions among the Jews is not a sign of weakness, but rather of greatness – the greatness of a living people.

In the *Shulhan Arukh*, Rabbi Yosef Caro (the Beit Yosef) attempted to outline a single body of halakhah that drew from a variety of traditions. In his book, he set out the rules that he used to determine halakhah:

> The Jewish people rely on three major teachers as the pillars of their instruction – Rabbi Yitzhak Alfasi (the Rif), Rabbi Moshe ben Maimon (the Rambam), and Rabbi Asher ben Yehiel (the Rosh), of blessed memory. I have decided that when two of them agree on one point, the law should follow their opinion, except in the few areas where all or most of the Jewish sages disagreed with that opinion, and so the opposite tradition became popular.... When we do not have an opinion from these three pillars, we will follow the well-known sages who did write opinions on that particular law. This is the correct path of compromise that avoids the likelihood of failure. If in some countries the Jews prohibited some acts, even though we decide the opposite, they should continue to follow their customs, because they have already accepted the sages' decision to forbid, and so they may not permit it.[110]

Rabbi Moses Isserles (the Rema)[111] objected to Rabbi Yosef Caro's methodology in deciding halakhah according to the majority opinion of two out of three. According to the Rema, one should decide halakhah according to the traditions that developed after the time of the Rif and the Rambam, based on the principle of *halakhah ke-batrai* (following the later decisor), since the Aharonim (rabbinic authorities after the *Shulhan Arukh*) were aware of the practices of the Rishonim (eleventh to sixteenth centuries, following the Geonim and preceding the *Shulhan Arukh*), but ruled against them. According to Rabbi Yehoshua Volk Katz, z"l, the source of the controversy lies in the geographic and cultural differences between the Rema and Rabbi Yosef Caro.

> Rabbi Yosef Caro lived in Arab countries, where the Jews followed the rulings of the Rif and the Rambam, who agreed on one opinion except for minor details of the law. For this reason, he wrote that we must follow two out of three, so that the residents of those countries would continue to follow their traditions. In contrast, the Jews of Ashkenaz [central Europe], Poland, and

---

110. Introduction to Tur, *Orah Haim*.
111. Introduction to *Darkhei Moshe*.

Russia, who followed the sages of Ashkenaz and France, did not accept the decisions of the Rif or the Rambam, and so *Darkhei Moshe* specifies the customs of the Ashkenazic Jews.[112]

The two central branches of contemporary Judaism grew out of this controversy. The Sephardic Jews follow the opinion of the Beit Yosef, while Ashkenazic Jews accept the halakhic decisions of the Rema.[113] Each community followed its own customs and did not deviate from the customs that developed over history.

At this point we ask whether acceptance of the decisions of a certain *posek* by a community obligates their descendants to follow these practices as well. The Torah commands us to go "to the judge that shall be in those days" (Deuteronomy 17:9); each generation should follow the rabbinic authorities of its time. We must distinguish between two types of customs: those related to location and those related to community.[114] Regarding geographically dependent customs, the Talmud relates[115] that the citizens of Beyshan were accustomed not to travel from Tyre to Sidon on Shabbat eve, even though Friday was market day in Sidon, so as not to interrupt Shabbat preparations. Their children wanted to annul this custom, as they were not as wealthy as their parents. They went to Rabbi Johanan, but he forbade them from annulling it, based on the verse, "Hear, my son, the instruction of thy father, and forsake not the teaching of thy mother" (Proverbs 1:8). The custom of the citizens of Beyshan applied to the local residents, and therefore their descendants were also obligated to follow it.[116] Another type of decree that obligates descendants is the acceptance of Talmudic authority. As the Rambam writes:

> Everything in the Babylonian Talmud is binding for all the people of Israel; and every city and town is required to observe the customs observed by the Talmud's sages, their restrictive legislations and their positive legislations. For all those matters in the Babylonian Talmud received the assent of all of Israel. All of Israel's sages, or a majority of them, are the ones who enacted the positive and negative legislations, enacted binding customs, made the rulings, and found that a certain understanding of the Law was correct. It was they who received the traditions of the Oral Law concerning the fundamentals

---

112. Introduction to his books *Perisha* and *Derisha*.
113. See *Shem ha-gedolim*, s.v. "Beit Yosef," *Sde Hemed Klalei ha-Poskim*, part 6, 13:31, 14:18.
114. Amichai, "Eikh poskim ka'asher ein masoret mesuderet shel pesika?"
115. Babylonian Talmud, *Pesahim* 50b.
116. *Shu"t havat Yair* [Responsa of Rabbi Shimon Yair Bacharach], par. 126.

of the whole Law, in unbroken succession back to Moses Our Teacher, may he rest in peace.[117]

After the Jews were exiled, they could no longer unite in one place, and thus they split into numerous communities. Just as all Jews were obligated to accept Talmudic authority, each community was obligated to follow the decrees of its own sages: "The laws that a community accepts are binding for them and their descendants."[118] As Rabbi Yitzhak bar Sheshet decreed, "Every law accepted by the community obligates them and their descendants."[119] In other words, when a community accepts a law, this is comparable to a communal vow that cannot be annulled. In this manner, Ashkenazic Jews have accepted the leadership of the Rema, while Sephardic Jews have accepted the teachings of the Beit Yosef. The acceptance of the law of these authorities applies to them and their descendants, and cannot be exchanged. But when a Jew from one community goes to another community, how should he behave? This question arose when Ashkenazic Jews came to Eretz Yisrael, where they encountered Sephardic communities that had lived there for many years. Rabbi Avraham ben Yehiel Michael Danzig wrote, "Regarding those who come to Eretz Yisrael, I think that if they settle in a city that has a *minyan*, even though the newcomers are numerous, they should follow one law. They must follow the stringencies of their new location. The stringencies that they followed in their home location are no longer valid."[120]

There are many points of friction between the customs of the Ethiopian community and the Talmudic-rabbinic world. This book attempts to carve a path through the thicket of halakhic sources, sometimes relying on an individual opinion, which will lead to acceptance of the Beta Israel as a legitimate, normative stream within the Jewish people. Acceptance of the community is a sign that there are *poskim* who accept the strength of the Jewish people, and are thus willing to open the door to this community, not as an act of sympathy but through recognition of their right.

The first way to do this relies on theological-philosophical arguments that justify changes and developments in the world of religious philosophy and halakhah. Another way is to attempt to act through the mechanisms of halakhic decision making. There are additional principles according to which we can

---

117. Introduction to *Mishneh Torah, Yad ha-hazakah* [trans. based on Mechon Mamre website].
118. See Nachum Leam, *Halakhot ve-halikhot* [Laws and customs] (Jerusalem, 5750/1990), 144.
119. Shu"t Ribash [Responsa of Rabbi Yitzhak bar Sheshet], par. 399.
120. *Hokhmat adam, Sha'ar mishpatei ha-aretz* 11:23.

accept changes in halakhah on a certain point, and in parallel, we can attempt to find halakhic precedents. Even if these precedents were written in a completely theoretical manner at the time, they enable us to formulate new models of religious behavior that can reduce the gap between these two groups. Halakhic decision making is not just a deductive process of reaching practical decisions based on textual study. Alongside the intellectual pursuit that relies on books stand fundamental values that guide the *posek* on his path. Based on these values, the *posek* can find an opening and address every problem that arises in the context of its time and place.

I come from within the world of Ethiopian tradition, which I absorbed from the *khanokh* (spiritual leaders of the Ethiopian community), as well as from my grandfather and family. I am aware of the spiritual needs of this community in the most profound sense. In light of the problems arising among the second generation, I intend to offer a response to the spiritual distress of today, out of respect and deep appreciation. Any person who did not grow up within the world of Ethiopian halakhah, but through study and patience is able to see the positive sides of this world, is graced with greatness of soul.

I hope that in this manner, I will succeed in raising the tradition of Ethiopian Jewry to the level of the "royal table," and to grant it the status it deserves.

Respect for Particularity

Recently, I had the opportunity to listen to a Torah lesson given by a great rabbi who argued that today's halakhic reality of multiple customs and traditions is an ex post facto reality. His ideal was conformity of halakhah, in which everyone would accept the halakhah of the great sage of Eretz Yisrael, the Beit Yosef, as recorded in the *Shulhan Arukh*. In his opinion, Jews from other Middle Eastern countries should change their ancestral customs and adapt them to the laws of the *Shulhan Arukh*. Ashkenazic Jews should also accept the rulings of the *Shulhan Arukh*. As for the work of changing customs, the rabbi left this for the Messiah. This approach, which aspires toward a monolithic world of halakhah, left me astonished and angry, for it is likely to plunge us deep into the halakhic politics that led to the destruction of the Second Temple.

During another class given by a young yeshiva scholar, one of the listeners, a woman who had emigrated from Morocco, asked a question about her mother's custom of lighting Shabbat candles first and then reciting the blessing. The yeshiva scholar replied decisively and with excessive brutality: "Your mother's practice is based on a mistaken custom, and so you must cease this practice immediately.

You should follow the *Shulhan Arukh* and the decision of Rabbi Ovadia Yosef – first recite the blessing and then light the candles." I could not remain silent over such an answer. I told the woman that she could continue to follow her mother's custom, because several traditions exist on this issue. The yeshiva scholar attacked me and dismissed everything I said with a wave of his hand, asserting that I did not understand anything. I deeply lament such incidents. In this context, I would like to cite an interview with Rabbi Uri Sherki, who addresses the attempt to enforce a monolithic halakhic world:

> I am from Algiers, which is not in the Middle East at all. In general, I think that one of the central factors in the cultural decline of Sephardic Jewry is the halakhic uniformity imposed on it in the spirit of the expression "Eastern Jews," or if you will, the spirit of the *Shulhan Arukh* alone....
>
> This is a crime against how I grew up, against the tradition of my ancestors and rabbis over generations. My *beit midrash* includes Rabbi Judah Halevi, the Rambam's *Guide for the Perplexed*, and the traditions of my ancestors, who were scholars of Kabbalah, philosophy, halakhah, and poetry – and not just liturgical poetry! Rabbi Judah Halevi or Rabbi Avraham Ibn Ezra wrote poems, and I'm not sure whether they would allow someone in a yeshiva today to write such things. They would probably banish such a person from the yeshiva. This is a very rich world, and the attempt to create uniformity instead of unity has destroyed it.
>
> The Sephardic Jews did not have the polarity of religious versus secular that we find today in the Ashkenazic world. I grew up in a European country, in France, and I knew the terms *religious* and *secular* from French. I did not know they existed in Judaism. I knew all kinds of Jews, and I knew there were some who kept many mitzvot, and others who kept only a few. Only when I came to Israel did I discover that Jewish society lived according to such codes.
>
> In the Ashkenazic world, you have to define yourself by a certain ideology. For example, an Ashkenazic Jew who does not wish to follow the mitzvot punctiliously has to define himself as Conservative. For the Sephardic Jews, this need was never felt, because every Jew was accepted for what he was, and therefore a Jew who traveled on Shabbat or on Yom Kippur to the synagogue felt he belonged in the synagogue....
>
> Once Rabbi [Shlomo Zalman] Auerbach was asked whether it would be permitted to conduct an aliyah seminar outside of Israel, even though some of the participants would arrive on Shabbat, and they would push children in

strollers without an *eruv* [a boundary that encloses a large area and makes it into a single domain, to avoid transgressing the prohibition against carrying objects from one domain to another on Shabbat]. He answered, "A woman is drowning in a river, and you're asking questions?!"

Rabbi Auerbach also thought that halakhah should be decided according to tradition. When he was asked if it was permitted to prepare egg salad on Shabbat – as this involved many actions that might be forbidden – he answered, "It is permitted, because my grandmother used to make egg salad on Shabbat." He added, "Even if I don't find a satisfactory halakhic explanation, it will still be permitted, because my grandmother did so." Such a position is unique in today's halakhic landscape, as today halakhic decisions are made by the book, not according to tradition, and what your grandmother did is no longer relevant and [is considered] halakhically incorrect.[121]

Rabbi Sherki notes that Sephardic Jews used to follow this custom when the Torah scroll was removed from the ark: "The women would kiss it. Even further, in many Sephardic communities outside Israel, on Yom Kippur, during the priestly blessing of the concluding Ne'ilah service, the women would go into the men's section and stand under their husbands' *tallitot*. Feeling deep emotion at the conclusion of the holy day, the family wanted to be together, and the rabbis chose to overlook this. Today no rabbi would permit such a thing."

Shulhan ha-Orit was written out of faith in Jewish law and tradition. I live and breathe the entire Jewish people, with all 248 limbs and 365 sinews of my body. I view each stream within the Jewish people as part of one heterogeneous family, and each in its own way is created in God's image.

No matter what kind of society we have, if alongside the laws and halakhah that it legislates, natural morality is overrun – such a society cannot endure.

❧ A Short History of Ethiopian Jewry

Overview

A number of theories have been proposed regarding the origin of the Ethiopian Jews:

1. A legend known among Ethiopian Jewry relates that the marriage of King Solomon and the Queen of Sheba produced a son named Menelik. When

---

121. Hagit Bartov and Shraga Bar-On, "Normaliut Sefardit" [Sephardic normalcy], *Kippah*, November 16, 2010, http://www.kipa.co.il/jew/41133.html.

the Queen of Sheba returned to her country with the boy, the king decided to send the firstborn sons of Israel to accompany her. When they arrived in Sheba, her escorts decided to remain there. According to this legend, the Ethiopian Jews are indeed Jews.[122]

2. The Ethiopian Jews are the descendants of the tribe of Dan from the Ten Lost Tribes. They wandered to Ethiopia from the tenth century BCE until the destruction of the Second Temple.[123]

3. The Ethiopian Jews are the descendants of Jews who emigrated from Egypt from the seventh century BCE to the second century CE.[124]

4. The Ethiopian Jews are descended from Jews who emigrated from southern Arabia (Yemen) between the second century CE and the war between Ethiopian Christian king Kaleb and Yemenite king Joseph Dhu-Nuwas, a convert to Judaism, in the sixth century CE.[125]

5. The Ethiopian Jews are descendants of the Agaw tribe, which converted or adopted a unique form of Judaism in the fifteenth century CE.[126]

6. The Falashas appeared as a separate group between the fourteenth and sixteenth centuries.[127]

7. "The Jews had several periods of immigration to Habash, and did not arrive there all at once, The Jews there came mainly from Egypt, and they were later joined by their brothers who came from the west. Over time, these Jews intermingled with the Agaws. The Falashas were citizens of a free Jewish state until the seventeenth century."[128]

Timeline

- **5th–6th centuries** – Translation of the Tanakh from the Septuagint into Ge'ez. The Orit has words in Hebrew and in Judeo-Aramaic.

---

122. *Kebra nagst* [Glory of kings], early fourteenth century. See also Rabbi Kashani, *Ha-Falashim: Korot, mesorot, minhagim* [The Falashas: History, traditions, customs] (Jerusalem, 5736/1976).
123. Waldman, *Me-ever la-Nahar Cush*.
124. Eshkoli, *Ha-halakhah ve-ha-minhag*, note 8.
125. Ibid.
126. Here we note that in their external appearance, particularly their facial features, the Ethiopian Jews mostly resemble the local residents. However, sometimes we may identify differences in skin color and in the facial features, which may be similar to those of the Yemenite and Cuchin Jews (Eshkoli, note 4).
127. S. Kaplan, "Al temurot be-heker Yehadut Etiopiah" [Changes in the study of Ethiopian Jewry], *Pa'amim* 58.
128. Eshkoli, *Ha-halakhah ve-ha-minhag*.

- **9th century** – Eldad ha-Dani ("the Danite") appears in Kairouan, Tunisia (about 180 kilometers south of Tunis, the capital city). He claims he is from Ethiopia, and relates that Jewish communities exist there. His stories about the dispersed tribes and the Sambatyon River rely partially on ancient sources, descriptions in the Bible and midrashic material, but he also gives descriptions that have no parallels in rabbinic literature. Rabbi Zemach Gaon accepts ha-Dani's statements in principle, and considers him a member of the tribes of Israel who preserve the ancient tradition of the Oral Torah. But most people do not believe ha-Dani's stories, and consider him a fraud.[129] Regardless of the truth of his statements, they ignite the hopes of many Jews, who believe that the tribes of Israel have been found. His story has more significant influence in the fifteenth and sixteenth centuries, when other rumors and evidence of Jews in Ethiopia appear. At that time, Eldad ha-Dani's assertions serve as an inspiration for the search for the tribes of Israel and their kingdom.

- **10th–16th centuries** – Between the responsa of Rabbi Zemach Gaon in the tenth century and that of the Ridbaz in the sixteenth century, the rabbis are silent on the status of Ethiopian Jewry.

- **1270–1632** – Period of anti-Semitic persecution in the Seamen and Wegera districts of Ethiopia. Heavy pressure is placed on "those behaving like Jews" for them to convert or be killed. In response, the Jews adopt the ascetic practices of their neighbors. In addition, the rights of Jewish landowners are annulled. The Jews who are expelled from their lands are forced to change their trades, and they become builders, ironworkers, carpenters, and weavers. Following the expulsion, they are given the derogatory name Falasha, meaning "intruders" or "foreigners."[130]

- **Letter of Rabbi Eliyahu of Ferrara** – In the fifteenth century, Rabbi Eliyahu, a respected Torah scholar from Italy, makes aliyah to Eretz Yisrael, passing through Egypt along the way. After a tortuous journey, he finally reaches Jerusalem on 26 Iyyar 5196 (May 1, 1437). He makes a pilgrimage to Jerusalem, and in parallel tries to verify rumors that had reached Italy about the Ten Tribes overcoming their enemies. Below is his description of the Jews of Habash and the Ten Tribes:

---

129. Waldman, *Me-ever la-Nahar Cush*.
130. Kaplan, "Historiyah ketzarah shel Yehudei Etiopiah," 11–16.

> I think I have already told you what a young Jewish man told me about the residents of his area, who are their own masters and not subservient to others. They are surrounded by a great nation called Hubash [sic]... These Hebrews have their own language, which is not Hebrew or Arabic. They have the Torah and an oral commentary, but they do not have the Talmud or our *poskim*. I studied several of their mitzvot, and found that some follow our opinion while others follow the opinion of the Karaites. They have the Scroll of Esther but not Hanukkah. They are a distance of three months away from us, and the River Gozen runs through their land.[131]

- **1488** – Rabbi Ovadia of Bartenura, commentator on the Mishnah, travels from Italy to Eretz Yisrael. On the way he meets two Ethiopian Jews, whom he describes as follows:

  > I saw two of them, almost black but not like the Cushites, and I could not tell what they were, or whether they observed the Karaite law.... They said they were related to the tribe of Dan. They said that most of the pepper and the spices that the Cushites sell come from their land. I saw this with my own eyes and heard it with my own ears. However, the two men did not know the holy language [well], only a tiny bit, and their Arabic was barely comprehensible to the residents of Eretz Yisrael.[132]

- **15th–16th centuries** – The Ridbaz (Rabbi David ben Zimra, 1479–1573), chief rabbi of the Egyptian community and considered one of the great *poskim*, writes a halakhic response about the community's status:
  - > Those Habishish [sic] who live in the land of Cush follow the religion of the Karaites, who are Sadducees and Boethusians, and we are not commanded to redeem them or to save them. In any case, it seems to me that those who live among the rabbis and observe what the sages do but insult and ridicule them, of these and their likes it is said, "We lower them [into a pit in order to cause their death] but do not raise them up" (Babylonian Talmud, *Avodah Zarah* 26b). They are the accursed group that the Rambam mentions. But those who come from the Land of Cush are undoubtedly from the tribe of Dan, and because there were no sages among them who had received the Oral Law, they followed the simple meaning of the texts. If they had studied [the Oral Law], then they would not have denied the

---

131. Waldman, *Me-ever la-Nahar Cush*.
132. Ibid.

decrees of our rabbis. They are like "captured infants" who lived among the idol worshippers. Know that the Sadducees and the Boethusians lived in Second Temple times, while the tribe of Dan was exiled previously. One might question whether redeeming them is a mitzvah. But regarding their genealogy, I doubt the validity of their marriages, and their divorce contracts do not follow the laws of the sages, as they know nothing about the nature of divorce and marriage contracts.[133]

- **Shlomo Molcho (1500–1532)**[134] – He believes that the Jews of Cush are the people who will realize redemption for the Jewish people:

  Regarding the verse, "Woe to the land [shaded by wings, which is on the other side of the rivers of Cush]" (Isaiah 18:1), this means, Woe will come to the land of the foreign nations, as in the verse, "For the day of the Lord over all the nations is near" (Obediah 1:15). When will this take place? When the boats arrive with a great uproar from Ethiopia, beyond the River Cush, they will take revenge against the Christian nation and save the remaining tribes from Christian slavery, and those Jews will bring about redemption. Thank God, this day of our redemption is near, in fulfillment of what is written about the war of God, who will throw arrows at the foreign nations that fought with His children, and bring distress upon them. They will battle among themselves, as the verse says, "One against his brother, and everyone against his neighbor, city against city, and kingdom against kingdom. And the spirit of Egypt shall be made empty within it; and I will make void the counsel thereof…" (Isaiah 19:2–3).[135]

- **War and adaptation (1270–1632)** – Emperor Amda Seyon ("Pillar of Zion," 1314–1344) sends soldiers to fight local enemies in the district where Jews lived. The motivation for the war is political and cultural, but not religious. These wars and battles between the Ethiopian kings and the Jews provoke a social change among the Beta Israel. The Christian king Isaac (1413–1430) leads his soldiers in a war against the Beta Israel. After he defeats them, he forces them to convert to Christianity. Whoever does not do so can lose his land. The Jews adapt to Christian culture, found an ascetic institution (fifteenth century), and practice new purification customs such as *attenkun* ("Do not touch me" – see

---

133. Ibid.
134. Born in Portugal, he was an outstanding personality and kabbalist who wrote about the redemption of Israel.
135. Waldman, *Me-ever la-Nahar Cush*.

below). In addition, they are forced to work in low-status professions such as pottery-making, iron-working, weaving, and construction.[136]

- **Gondar Period, 1632–1769** – Zemene Mesafnt (Period of the Judges). During this period, the political center of the kingdom begins to migrate to the Gondar region. The Jews who were expelled from their lands are forced to participate in the construction of fortifications and churches in the new capital of Gondar. In recognition of the women of Beta Israel, who are known for their talents in preparing dyes and decorative items, the Jews are again granted land, and their general status improves.[137]

- **Period of the Princes (1755–1855)** – After the murder of Emperor Iyo'as in 1769, an extended period of unstable rule begins, and the power of local military leaders grows. Beta Israel loses all the economic, social, and religious advantages they had achieved during the Gondar period. This period is a difficult one in the religious life of Beta Israel, and according to tradition, they are unable to practice religious rituals for forty years.[138]

- **1855** – Daniel ben Hananiah, an Ethiopian Jew, visits Eretz Yisrael for the first time, and meets with leading rabbis in Jerusalem. The leaders of the community give him a letter addressed to the Beta Israel (cited above in "Toward an Ethiopian Jewish Halakhah: Unity or Uniformity?").

- **1862** – The first Ethiopian Zionist, Abba Mahari (discussed above in "The Evolution of Ethiopian Jewish Custom: Zionism Comes to Ethiopia"), an ascetic and leader of the Ethiopian Jewish community, attempts to make aliyah to Jerusalem with many members of the community. The journey fails, and many perish along the way.[139]

- **1864** – Protestant Christian missionaries are active among the Ethiopian Jews. Leading rabbis of Europe make a public call to use all possible ways to save the Ethiopian Jews. The Jews who converted to Christianity are known today as "Falashmura." I have heard two explanations for this. First, Falashi + *mumar* ("converted") = Falashmura. Second, the converts settled in a place called Falashmura, and are named after this location.[140] Yet Avraham Yardai

---

136. Kaplan, "Historiyah ketzarah shel Yehudei Etiopiah."
137. Ibid.
138. Ibid.
139. Ben-Dor, "Ha-masa le-ever Eretz Yisrael: Ha-sippur al Abba Mahari."
140. M. Eliav, "Hitorerut shel Yehudei Eiropah le-ezrat ha-Falashim" [The awakening of

has noted that in fact conversion to Christianity was completely unknown in that area.

- 1864 – **Rabbi Azriel Hildesheimer** is one of the first to take practical action, during his tenure as rabbi of the Austro-Hungarian community of Eisenstadt. In his letter to Rabbi Shai Rappaport, rabbi of Prague, dated Shushan Purim 5624/1864, he states that "the desire to do good for my people burns within me. My heart says that I must take this holy burden upon my shoulders, formulate my intentions, implement this plan, reflect, and make a beginning, and that I must lead this great event." He sends letters to Jewish leaders to encourage them to participate in the rescue efforts, concluding his letters with the words of the Sages: "Whoever saves one Jewish soul, it is as if he saved an entire world." Six months later, on 11 Tishrei 5625/1865, he makes a "public appeal to all our fellow Jews," which is published in the major Jewish publications.[141]

- 1865 – **Rabbi Zvi Hirsch Kalischer** addresses a letter to Rabbi Hildesheimer, Rabbi Kalischer expresses his support:

  "As often as I speak of him, I do earnestly remember" (Jeremiah 31:19) that he has done very well… on the issue of the Falashas, to arouse the spirit of our fellow Jews, to teach the wayward knowledge of how they should worship the Lord, our God, according to the holy Written Torah and the Oral Torah, and to preserve them from straying into the ways of the inciters, the missionaries, God forbid. This is certainly a great mitzvah.… We must act on behalf of these souls, to grant knowledge to the ignorant among the people in distant lands, to bring them under the shadow of the Divine, and to prevent the hunters from snaring their human prey.

  Further in his letter, Rabbi Kalischer makes practical proposals for action. In Germany in 1864, Rabbi Marcus (Meyer) Lehmann's Yiddish publication *Der Israelit*[142] nominated prominent rabbis as candidates for the central committee for rescue operations – the nominees include Rabbi Nathan Adler, chief rabbi of England; Rabbi Solomon Ullman, chief rabbi of France; Rabbi Jacob Ettlinger, chief rabbi of Altona; Rabbi Yitzhak

---

European Jewry to aid the Falashas], *Tarbiz* 35 (5727/1967).
141. Waldman, *Me-ever la-Nahar Cush*, 138–47.
142. Major publication of Orthodox Jewry in Germany in the 1860s.

Dov (Seligman Baer) Halevi Bamberger of Wurzburg; and Rabbi Samson Raphael Hirsch of Frankfurt.[143]

- **1867** – Professor Yosef Halevi is sent to verify the rumor of Jews living in Habash. He is deeply moved by the encounter with the Jews of Ethiopia, but they refuse to believe he is a Jew. Below is Halevi's description of his attempt to convince them:

  > You should know, dear brothers, that I am also a Falashi, I am one of you! I believe in no other God but the one God Himself, and my religion is none other but the heritage of the Jewish people from Mount Sinai.... Finally the masses called out together, "You are a Falashi! A Falashi with white skin! You are mocking us! Who has ever heard or seen such a thing? Are there white Falashas under the sun?" I tried to tell them and to pledge on my faith that all the Falashas in Jerusalem and in the other countries of the world were white, and that their skin was no different from that of the other peoples among whom they lived. My mention of the word "Jerusalem," which I uttered coincidentally, immediately annulled any doubt the Falashas may have had regarding my words. Like lightning in the dark of night, the word "Jerusalem" lit up the eyes and hearts of my lost brothers. With eyes full of tears, they cried, "Ah, have you also visited Jerusalem the holy, blessed city? Have you seen the beautiful Mount Zion with your own eyes, and our magnificently built Temple, the admired and exalted palace in which the God of Israel loves to dwell in honor within? Ah, have you perhaps seen with your own eyes the grave of our foremother Rachel? Have you been in Bethlehem and in the city of Hebron, where our holy forefathers are buried?[144]

- **1879** – Rabbi Meir Leibush ben Yehiel Mikhel Weiser (the Malbim), rabbi and theologian born in the Ukraine. While in Paris, the Malbim writes a letter to the heads of the Alliance Israélite Universelle, recommending that Professor Yosef Halevi, a European Jewish Orientalist, lead the rescue mission, calling it "a mitzvah mission." In his words to one of the organization's directors, he says that in his opinion, the Falashas are undoubtedly of Jewish origin, and that the Diaspora Jews should work to rescue them.

---

143. Ibid.
144. Ibid.

- **1888–1892** – Kfu Ken (The Terrible Days). Drought, cattle plagues, and invasion of the Darvish people of Sudan. Up to two thirds of the Beta Israel community dies in the plagues. As the great *kes* Abba Yitzhak reported to a researcher, "In the beginning, people refused to eat the meat of the cattle that had died in the plague. Not long afterward, they were fighting to eat its skin."[145]

- **1896** – The Karaite community in St. Petersburg, Russia, buzzes with excitement on hearing rumors of Jews who do not follow the Talmud, and sends an expressive letter to the spiritual leaders of Beta Israel (cited above in "In the State of Israel: Rebuilding after the Destruction; From Biblical to Talmudic Template").[146]

- **1904** – Dr. Jacques Noah Faitlovitch, a historian and student of Professor Yosef Halevi, visits the Jews in Ethiopia and develops a strong attachment to the community. He confirms the view that Beta Israel is an entirely Jewish community, and through various means, informs world Jewry of their existence.[147]

- **1913** – Dr. Faitlovitch establishes a Jewish school in Gondar province.[148]

- **1923** – A second Jewish school is founded in the capital of Addis Ababa. Emmanuel Tamrat, a member of the community, is appointed principal of the school.[149]

- **Early 20th century** – **Rabbi Avraham Yitzhak Hacohen Kook** – As part of his work to aid the Falashas, Rabbi Samuel Hirsch Margulies (1858–1932), rabbi of the Jews of Firenze, Italy, contacted rabbis and leaders in the Jewish world. Beginning in 5672/1912, we find correspondence between him and Rabbi Kook, who was in Jaffa. In his replies, Rabbi Kook writes profusely and warmly about the magnitude of the mitzvah involved: "With all my being, I wish to encourage those performing this mitzvah of supporting them in all their needs and working for the eternal good of our distant brothers. The Rock of Israel in His mercy has awakened the hearts of these remnants, pure souls of this generation. We must work to remedy them and save them from the

---

145. Erlich et al., *Etiopiah, Natzrut, Islam, ve-Yehadut*.
146. Waldman, *Me-ever la-Nahar Cush*, 168–71.
147. Waldman, *Me-ever la-Nahar Cush*.
148. Ibid.
149. Ibid.

grave of extinction."[150] In 5682/1922, before Faitlovitch sets out on another publicity campaign in Europe and America, he asks Rabbi Kook for a letter of recommendation. Rabbi Kook, then chief rabbi of Eretz Yisrael, gives him a letter entitled "Public call to our fellow Jews everywhere!" After describing the miserable condition of this distant tribe and Faitlovitch's activity, Rabbi Kook concludes:

> Fellow Jews, save our brothers the Falashas from extinction and assimilation! Help bring back these exiled brothers! No tribe of Israel shall be wiped out from under God's heavens. Return our exiles to their fortifications; save fifty thousand holy souls of Israel from annihilation. Grant strength and courage to the building of our people and reinforce our strength. The Rock of Israel will arise with the help of Israel. Gather our exiles from the four corners of the earth, and let them come and rejoice on Zion's heights, and "worship the Lord on the holy mountain in Jerusalem" (Isaiah 27:13).

Rabbi Kook signs this letter alongside his colleague, the Sephardic chief rabbi of Palestine and Rishon Le-Zion, Rabbi Ya'akov Meir.[151]

- 1936–1941 – The Italian army occupies Ethiopia. War and destruction leads to the cessation of Jewish activity for several years.
- 1941 – The Italian army retreats and Emperor Haile Selassie returns to Ethiopia. The situation of the Jews improves and Jewish activity is renewed.
- 1954 – President Yitzhak Ben Zvi of Israel asks Emperor Haile Selassie to permit several young Jews to visit Israel.
- 1956 – The first Jewish boarding school is established by Jacques Faitlovitch. The director is community member Yona Bogale.
- 1956 – Two groups of young men and women from the community visit Israel in secret in order to learn Hebrew and serve as Hebrew teachers in villages in Ethiopia.
- 1973 – Based on the halakhic decision of Rabbi David ben Zimra, Chief Sephardic Rabbi Ovadia Israel determines that Ethiopian Jews are Jews according to halakhah.
- 1975 – The Israeli Knesset decides that the Law of Return applies to Ethiopian

---
150. *Iggerot Ha-Re'ayah*, part 2:432.
151. Waldman, *Me-ever la-Nahar Cush*.

INTRODUCTION: THE SPIRITUAL WORLD OF ETHIOPIAN JEWRY, THEN AND NOW · 71

Jewry. The significance of this decision is that Ethiopian Jews can make aliyah to Israel as Jews, with no need for immigration permits or visas.

- **1977** – Israeli prime minister Menachem Begin instructs the heads of the Israel Security Agency and the Mossad: "Bring me the Ethiopian Jews." The Mossad strikes a deal with Ethiopian dictator Mengistu Haile Mariam – arms for Jews. The first 120 Jews reach Israel, including *kes* Brhan Baruch.

- **1978** – Following media reports that Israel was supplying weapons to Ethiopia in exchange for Jews, Mengistu decides to cancel the deal due to pressure from Arab states.

- **1979** – The Mossad decides to bring the Jews to Israel through Sudan, and many Jews begin to walk in the direction of Sudan. The Mossad makes secret contact with community leader Fereda Aklum, and soon after, aliyah operations begin.

- By **1984**, some 8000 Jews have been brought to Israel – by sea, in Operation Bat Galim of the navy's commando unit, and by air, with Hercules transport planes landing in improvised airfields.

- **November 1984–January 1985** – Operation Moses. In a secret agreement signed between the Sudanese president and the Israeli government, six thousand Jews are brought to Israel.

- **March 1984** – Operation Queen of Sheba. Five hundred Jews are brought to Israel in Hercules transport planes of the US military.

- **1985** – The immigration and absorption of the Jews brought to Israel in Operation Moses leads to a renewed examination of the halakhic status of the Beta Israel. The Chief Rabbinic Council of Israel decides that "the Ethiopian Jews are Jews from the tribe of Dan." However, due to doubts in the wake of their disconnection from the rest of the Jewish people for hundreds of years, the Chief Rabbinate rules that the Ethiopians must undergo *giyyur le-humrah*, precautionary conversions, requiring circumcision, immersion in a *mikveh*, and acceptance of the *mitzvot*, in order to remove all doubts about the status of the Ethiopian Jews. In any case, the rabbinate declares, "It is a mitzvah to save them from annihilation and danger, as for any Jew … and we must help and support them in all their daily needs, both material and spiritual."

- By **1990**, the Mossad has carried out additional secret operations, bringing the total number of Ethiopian Jews brought to Israel to seventeen thousand.

- **May 1991** – Operation Solomon. Under an agreement signed with Ethiopian dictator Mengistu, a mass exodus is authorized in exchange for 35 million dollars. In forty-eight hours, fifteen thousand Jews are brought to Israel from Addis Ababa in an unprecedented operation.

- With Operation Solomon, the story of the aliyah of Ethiopian Jewry ends. But with this arises the problem of the Falashmura, which is still ongoing. Initially denied aliyah due to their status as Christian breakaways from the original Beta Israel community, the Falashmura gathered in Addis during Operation Solomon in the hopes of being allowed to go to Israel with their Beta Israel brethren. Since Operation Solomon, groups of Falashmura have periodically been allowed to make aliyah on the basis of family reunification. For years large numbers of Falashmura have been gathered primarily in a transit camp in Gondar, in very difficult conditions, waiting for a decision on their aliyah status. Concluding in 2013, Operation Dove's Wings brought to Israel nearly eight thousand additional Falashmura, and the government of Israel declared the matter closed, but there are still thousands more who feel connected to the Jewish people, have family in Israel, and long to make aliyah. There is an urgent need for the Israeli government to address the plight of the Falashmura, via private organizations in the first stage, while in the second stage, the government must establish a government committee made up of representatives of various groups (*kesim*, rabbis, Knesset members, activists, researchers, and representatives of the government of Ethiopia) to finally find a definitive and complete solution.[152]

---

152. For more information on the situation of the Falashmura, see Mitchell Bard, "Ethiopian Jewry:The Falash Mura," *Jewish Virtual Library*, https://www.jewishvirtuallibrary.org/jsource/Judaism/falashmura.html, and Michal Shmulovich, "The Last of the Falash Mura?" *The Times of Israel*, August 26, 2013, http://www.timesofisrael.com/the-last-of-the-falash-mura. For more information on all the historical events described in this timeline, see the following: Waldman, *Me-ever la-Nahar Cush*; Erlich et al., *Etiopiah, Natzrut, Islam, ve-Yehadut*; Wurmbrand, *Sefer mitzvot ha-Shabbat shel Beta Israel*. See also Michael Corinaldi, *Yehadut Etiopiah – zehut u-masoret*; S. Kaplan, "Historiyah ketzarah shel Yehudei Etiopiah"; Azrieli and Meizlisch, *Ha-mesimah Etiopiah*.

Shulhan ha-Orit
The Halakhah of Ethiopian Jewry, Then and Now

- *Shulhan ha-Orit* was written out of a personal need, in a search for a way to serve God. Thus the reader should not consider this work as intended for the public. Still, some may find it useful for paving personal paths within their respective spiritual worlds.
- The goal of this work is to collect the customs of the Beta Israel community and to preserve customs that were transmitted orally.
- This book presents a halakhic method that "returns the crown of Torah to its ancient glory" for Ethiopian Jews. It does not intend to negate other methods.
- To show the connection between different customs, I give the Talmudic halakhah alongside the Ethiopian Jewish custom.
- Ethiopian Jewish customs are very ancient, apparently preceding the Talmudic era. Thus Torah scholars can use them to study Talmudic issues.
- Preservation of these customs is a value, while keeping them is an emotional need. Therefore we should not feel obligated to keep the customs in any situation.
- This work intends to remove barriers and promote friendship, not to create obstacles. Therefore in case of conflict, unity precedes other considerations.
- In this work, educational and social concerns are factors in the halakhic decision of whether to keep a custom or annul it.
- A custom that creates a conflict between a married couple should be annulled.

- If a custom creates a conflict among members of the Ethiopian community and there is no solution other than to annul it, then the unity of the community takes precedence, and the custom should be annulled.
- The first generation of Ethiopian Jews in Israel will continue to practice their customs, without consideration for other issues. We must demonstrate maximum understanding toward these customs.
- The second generation should be permitted to continue their ancestral customs, but with other considerations applying (mentioned above).
- Some customs that were practiced in Ethiopia should be ceased completely, even among first-generation Ethiopian immigrants to Israel. Among these are certain Ethiopian customs that give precedence to keeping mitzvot over saving a life.
- The Talmud, not the *Shulhan Arukh*, takes precedence as the halakhic guide for Ethiopian Jewry.

1. Daily Practices

❧ Washing the Feet

Ethiopian Halakhah

The Beta Israel followed the practice of washing their feet when they left the house early in the morning to go to work, and when they returned home, for reasons of personal cleanliness and human dignity.

Past and Present in Talmudic Halakhah

Jews in Eretz Yisrael did not follow the practice of washing the feet. This practice is mentioned in versions of the Talmud from the periods of the Geonim and the Rishonim. But it was not accepted as halakhah, because today people do not usually walk barefoot.[1]

The Recommended Custom in Israel

There is no obligation to wash the feet because today people do not usually walk barefoot. Still, if a person wants to wash his feet, he is certainly permitted to do so. He should wash his feet himself, and not have his wife do it for him, as was the practice in most locations in Ethiopia.

❧ Covering the Head – *Kippah*

Ethiopian Halakhah

In Ethiopia, only the *kesim* (priests) covered their heads. The head covering was white. The *kesim* began to cover their heads during their student years. In addition, persons of high social status also covered their heads, but this was not obligatory. Usually the *shmaglotz*, respected community leaders, did so. But most

---

1. Babylonian Talmud, *Shabbat* 50b.

of the community did not wear a head covering or a hat. The custom of covering the head signified respect, and the reason for doing so was cultural more than religious.

Past and Present in Talmudic Halakhah

The *Shulhan Arukh* delineates: "A man should not walk four cubits with his head uncovered."[2] Today it is accepted for a Jewish man to cover his head with a *kippah*, and according to the major *poskim*, this also applies during prayer and reciting blessings. The rabbis are divided over whether a *kippah* that covers only part of the head should be considered a head covering, but the major *poskim* have agreed to permit invoking God's name in prayers and blessings while wearing a *kippah* only. There is no specified size for a *kippah*, although it is advisable to wear one that is visible from all around the head. Note that according to some *poskim*, covering the head is not obligatory but *middat hassidut*, a practice of the pious or exemplary conduct. Others find that the practice is obligatory, but only outside the home. On the other hand, some are careful to wear a *kippah* even while sleeping, and they teach their young boys to do so as well. Today the *kippah* has become a symbol, and a man who does not cover his head is likely to be considered rebellious.

The Torah, however, does not mention head covering for men, except for the *kohanim* – both the *kohen hedyot* (lay priest; Exodus 29:9) and the *kohen gadol* (high priest; Leviticus 8:9) wear special hats. During the periods of the Talmud and the Mishnah, mourners and excommunicated Jews wrapped their heads. During the Hellenistic and Roman periods, uncovering the head was a sign of respect. In Babylon in the third century, the Sages developed the custom of covering the head and not walking four cubits with the head uncovered, as a sign of respect and awe before God. This custom spread throughout Babylon, and thus the Jews covered their heads during prayer or whenever mentioning God's name. From Babylon, the custom gradually spread to Eretz Yisrael. During the Middle Ages, the custom was not universal, but it slowly developed to include covering the head throughout the day as well as when mentioning God's name. After that period, an uncovered head became a sign of recognition for non-Jews, while covering the head became a sign of recognition for Jews.[3]

---

2. *Orah Haim*, ch. 2, par. 6.
3. Herman, *Ma'agal hayei ha-yom*.

The Recommended Custom in Israel

As we have seen, the Beta Israel preserve the ancient custom – only the *kohanim* who serve the community wear a head covering as a sign of God-fearing character, while the *shmaglotz* do so as a sign of honor. But the ordinary community members do not follow this practice. Thus for purposes of halakhah, it seems that we should not obligate any Ethiopian Jew to cover his head, even for prayers and blessing. However, an Ethiopian Jew who wishes to follow the local practice, for whatever reason, should wear a head covering, at least for prayer and blessings. But according to halakhah, this is not obligatory. Thus we must not suspect that the Ethiopian Jew who does not wear a head covering is rebelling against Jewish precepts, because this is the custom, even though today head covering is a clear sign of a Torah-observant Jew.

Laws of *Tzitzit*

Ethiopian Halakhah

The Beta Israel custom on this issue is very interesting. There was no obligation for a man to wear a *tallit* until his wedding. An unmarried man walked around without a *tallit* to cover him. After the wedding, he wore the *tallit* everywhere except for during work. This covering symbolizes respect, dignity, maturity, and responsibility. The *tallit* is made of wool or linen. The Beta Israel did not attach *tzitzit* (fringes) on the four corners – instead they wove small threads around the *tallit*. The Ethiopian *tallit* is called a *natleh*, and is usually white, with or without stripes. After their wedding, women also wrapped themselves in the *natleh*, in addition to covering their heads. But the woman's *natleh* is different from the man's.

Past and Present in Talmudic Halakhah

The Torah specifies the mitzvah of *tzitzit* in two places: "Speak to the children of Israel and bid them that they make ... fringes on the corners of their garments" (Numbers 15:38), and "You shall make yourself twisted cords upon the four corners of your garment with which you cover yourself" (Deuteronomy 22:12). Several interpretations have been given for the word *tzitzit*. According to one, the word *tzitzit* is derived from the word *yetziah* (going out), and refers to threads that extend like branches from the sides of the garment.[4] Others consider the *tzitzit* to be a symbol of status. A relief from the ninth century BCE shows nobles from the ancient Near East wearing a top garment with fringes on the

---

4. Rashi, Numbers 22:12.

corners. The Torah does not explain the importance of the garment, how the fringes should be tied, what should be tied, or the significance of the ties. It only remarks that the obligation of *tzitzit* is "on the four corners of the garment with which you cover yourself." The Sages of the Mishnah and the Talmud supplied the necessary details.

The *tallit katan* (literally, "small *tallit*," a four-cornered piece of cloth with fringes attached) first appears in the period of the Rishonim. During the time of the Mishnah, men wore a four-cornered garment to which they attached the *tzitzit*. For this reason, the blessing over *tzitzit* mentions wrapping: "*le-hitatef ba-tzitzit*" (Who has commanded us to wrap ourselves in the *tzitzit*). Over time, clothing habits changed and people stopped wearing four-cornered garments. Thus during the period of the Rishonim, the Sages ruled that a man should wear the *tallit katan* in order to fulfill the mitzvah of *tzitzit*. Some believe that one should not recite the blessing of *le-hitatef ba-tzitzit* over the *tallit katan*, because it is not the same as the four-cornered garment mentioned in the Torah. During the period of the Geonim, the custom spread of wrapping oneself in the *tallit* during the prayer service, in addition to wearing the *tzitzit*.[5]

The Recommended Custom in Israel

In Ethiopia, *tzitzit* are a sign of respect, dignity, and responsibility. After a person is married, responsibility increases, and thus the custom in Ethiopia was to wrap oneself in the *tallit* only after marriage. Thus in Israel, in my view, Ethiopian Jews are not obligated to wrap themselves in the *tallit* until after they are married. Regarding the *tallit katan*, this should be worn after a boy becomes bar mitzvah. The *tallit* should be worn following marriage, during all three prayer services – Shaharit (morning), Minhah (afternoon), and Arvit (evening). This was the custom in Ethiopia, and this should be the practice in Israel as well.

Laws of Tefillin (Phylacteries)

Ethiopian Halakhah

The Ethiopian Jewish community was unaware of the mitzvah of tefillin. However, some assert that in ancient times, they did wear tefillin. According to legend, the Jews were not permitted to fulfill the mitzvot for forty years. Due to this decree, many mitzvot were forgotten, and even the community sages were unable to reconstruct them. The mitzvah of tefillin was among these forgotten

---

5. Herman, *Ma'agal hayei ha-yom*.

mitzvot. My late grandfather, Abba Gideon (Dejen) Mengesha, upheld this belief. He used to tie small phylacteries to his forearm. They were not black, and they looked like a charm with a piece of parchment inside. He wore these phylacteries all day long. This custom serves as supporting evidence for the assertion that in the past, Ethiopian Jews did practice the mitzvah of tefillin in a certain manner. On the other hand, some community members state that they had no knowledge of this mitzvah. Community elders also recognize this opinion. The fact that wearing tefillin was not known to the Beta Israel community, which left Eretz Yisrael during the First Temple period, arouses many questions about the history of this mitzvah.[6]

Past and Present in Talmudic Halakhah

The Torah commands us: "And it shall be for a sign upon your hand and for frontlets between your eyes" (Exodus 13:16). In Deuteronomy, the verse reads, "And you shall bind them for a sign upon your hand, and they shall be for frontlets between your eyes" (6:8). The Oral Torah completed the details of this mitzvah. Many laws of tefillin were determined after the destruction of the Second Temple and during the Second Temple period – for example, that the tefillin should be written on parchment in black ink, that they should be square, and that the straps should be black. According to the historical findings, we may assume that the shape of the tefillin as we know it today became unified over time. An Aramaic document from the Jewish community of Elephantine from the early third century BCE mentions a silver box tefillin. Tefillin found in the Qumran caves were dated at the first century, during the Great Rebellion (66–73/74 CE). These tefillin contain a number of Torah portions, including the Song of Moses (*Ha'azinu*, Deuteronomy 32) and the Ten Commandments. In the Qumran tefillin, the texts are different from the traditional ones – only some follow the Masoretic text. Remains of tefillin from Bar Kochba's time (132–136 CE), which were found in Nahal Ze'elim in the Judean Desert, contain selections from only two Torah portions, and their text is almost identical to the Masoretic text.

The accepted view among researchers is that during the period of the Tannaim, the wearing of tefillin was not a widespread custom. Apparently, the Pharisees,

---

6. My teacher, Rabbi Dr. Noam Zohar, believes that the practice of laying tefillin began in a later period. Until then, the mitzvah was understood as conceptual only – "And you shall bind them for a sign upon your hand, and they shall be for frontlets between your eyes" – meaning that the mitzvot should be engraved upon or bound to the heart and intellect. In a later period, this mitzvah was expanded beyond the allegorical dimension and transformed into a practical act.

who referred to themselves as *haverim* ("friends" or "members"), did follow this practice. The Talmud severely reprimands those who do not do so: "Who is an *am ha-aretz* [Jew who is ignorant of Torah law]?...One who does not lay tefillin," "Jews who sin with the body, who are they? Rav says: 'Skulls that have not worn tefillin.'"[7] From these references, we understand that not everyone wore tefillin, and the severity of the statements provides a clue as to the extent of the phenomenon. By contrast, the Talmud describes Rabbi Yochanan ben Zakkai, Elisha Ba'al Knafaim, and Rabbi Akiva walking around all day wearing tefillin. The Talmud further relates that the warriors of Bar Kochba at Beitar went out to war decorated with tefillin. Neither the Mishnah nor the Talmud gives an exact description of tefillin or the method of preparing them or wearing them. The method of laying tefillin known today is first described in a halakhic work from the period of the Geonim entitled *Shimusha Rabba*.

The Recommended Custom in Israel

Today, the mitzvah of tefillin is one of the symbols marking the uniqueness of the Jewish people throughout its communities. Most Jewish men have worn tefillin at least once in their lives. Thus we must explain to the Ethiopian community the importance of this mitzvah, with courtesy and respect. Experience demonstrates that when we address the other with politeness, the response is more positive. At the same time, we must use caution and avoid pressuring those who remain unconvinced. Further, it is completely forbidden to behave disrespectfully or with superiority toward those who do not wear tefillin. When an individual migrates from one culture to another, we cannot demand that he make a drastic change in his culture. In the same way, we cannot ask a believer who was accustomed to a certain practice, such as the Ethiopian tradition, to leave everything he knows behind and begin to follow new practices, as per the Talmudic *halakhah*. A person is not an object or a robot. We cannot force the Ethiopian community to abandon their ancient traditions and immediately accept mainstream *halakhah*. Who are we, and in which direction would we proceed without those sages who inspired in us the belief in the Rock of Israel and His Redeemer? Those who are not convinced to wear tefillin undoubtedly share this same belief. "Man looks at the outward appearance, but the Lord sees into the heart" (1 Samuel 16:7). Still, as noted, we should encourage the Ethiopian Jews to wear tefillin as is practiced among all other Jewish communities, or at least to follow my grandfather's

---

7. Babylonian Talmud, *Rosh Hashanah* 17a.

practice. The straps of the tefillin should be black, following rabbinic halakhah,[8] while the boxes may be a different color.[9]

The Synagogue

Ethiopian Halakhah

In Ethiopia, the synagogue was called *masgid* or *beit mikdas* or *yetzulot bayit*. People related to the synagogue with awe, as a real Temple. Villagers lived in huts, but the synagogue in every village was a stone structure, quite large, stable and respectable. The building stood out in its form, and could be seen and identified from afar. In large villages, the synagogue was built in the center of the village. It could be identified from afar by the red clay pot attached to a pole in the middle of the roof. My grandfather used to say that whoever came from afar to participate in the prayer services had great merit – long distances were not a disadvantage, but rather an advantage. The synagogue structure was divided into three parts – the courtyard, the hall, and the *kadesta kedusan* (*kodesh ha-kodashim* or "Holy of Holies"). Only the *kohanim* entered the Holy of Holies, and the Orit (Torah scroll) was placed there.

The public gathered in the hall. There were no chairs in the synagogue. Prayers were conducted while standing, and lasted many hours. Thus many people carried walking sticks, on which they leaned when they grew tired of standing, as in the verse, "Your rod and Your staff, they comfort me" (Psalms 23:4). The synagogue courtyard also served as a gathering place for sermons, study, offering sacrifices, reading the Torah, and any event of sacred character. The inside of the synagogue was used for prayer services only. When praying, the congregants faced Jerusalem. Before entering the synagogue, congregants removed their shoes in respect for the sanctity of the site. They spread leaves on the synagogue floor, so as not to have direct contact with the floor. Inside the Holy of Holies stood the *tevot* (ark), and the Orit stood on top. Next to the Orit were additional garments for the *kohanim* and two jars – one with ashes from the *parah adumah* (red heifer), the other with holy water for sprinkling on the sacrifices.

Up until the aliyah to Eretz Yisrael, the Beta Israel had a continuous tradition

---

8. Because this is a halakhah given to Moses at Sinai. See *Shulhan Arukh* 33:3.
9. In most Jewish communities, using black boxes is considered a *hiddur mitzvah* (particularly meticulous performance of this mitzvah). But in the cultural understanding of Ethiopian Jewry, black has negative connotations. For this reason, the Ethiopian Jews wore white, and so for them, using black boxes is not considered to have additional merit.

for the observance of all the biblical laws of purity and impurity. This included the laws of impurity relating to *tumat hamet*, contact with a dead body, and the means of purifying oneself from it with the ashes of the red heifer. In Ethiopia, some animals met the biblical qualifications of a *parah adumah*. Against this backdrop, we must ask why the rabbinic and Talmudic tradition testifies that the *parah adumah* no longer exists. Was it the intention of the Sages to cease the observance of all laws of purity and impurity in the wake of the destruction of the Holy Temple? Perhaps they felt that since the destruction of the Second Temple ended the use of the *parah adumah* in Jerusalem, therefore the practice should be halted everywhere. In Ethiopia, however, the Beta Israel were careful to observe all laws of purity and impurity as specified in the Torah.

Past and Present in Talmudic Halakhah

The term *beit knesset* (synagogue; literally, "house of assembly") or simply *knesset* appears in rabbinic literature. The term is based on the Hebrew root *kuf, nun, samekh* (k-n-s), meaning "gathering." The Aramaic term is *kenista*. The rabbis also called the synagogue a "miniature Temple," due to its sanctity and comparison to the actual Temple. The term *synagogue* appears in the Septuagint as a translation of the biblical terms *kahal* (assembly), and *eda* (congregation), and is used in Christian literary sources. In the Middle Ages, in Roman and Slavic countries as well as in Hungary, the synagogue was called temple, from the Latin word *templum*. In Germany and in Yiddish-speaking communities, the term *shul* was used.[10]

Some researchers assert that the first synagogues were established during the time of the First Temple, for the benefit of those who lived far from the Temple in Jerusalem. They think that the early origins of the ancient synagogues lay in the gathering of the people in the time of Ezra, for the purpose of reading the Torah and reciting the prayers. Others believe that synagogues were begun by the Pharisaic rabbis during the Hasmonean period in the second century BCE, in order to gather the people together and deepen their knowledge of Torah and religious belief in response to the spread of Hellenism in ancient Israel. At any rate, the first epigraphical evidence of the existence of a synagogue in the Diaspora is found in inscriptions discovered in the Schedia section of Alexandria, and these are dated to the period of Ptolemy III Euergetes (247–221 BCE).

---

10. Herman, *Ma'agal hayei ha-yom*, 152.

The oldest synagogues in the Land of Israel are from the Hasmonean period and were discovered in 1998.

Literary sources note that synagogues played a number of roles: assembly for the purpose of reading and studying the Torah, teaching, administering justice, collecting charity, and festive meals.[11] The halakhah states that in a place where there is no synagogue, the residents must oblige each other to build one.[12] Although every synagogue is technically open to every Jew, they are usually divided according to two main principles: the prayer ritual of the majority of the community (Ashkenaz, Sefard, Chassidic styles; Sephardic, Yemenite, Jerba, Halab, Moroccan, Iraqi, Ethiopian) and the stream of observance (Orthodox, Conservative, Reform, etc.). Despite the differences in the texts and tunes of the prayers, all Jews are equal.[13]

The Recommended Custom in Israel

Today, just as we cannot speak of Ashkenazic and Sephardic Jews, or Conservative and Reform Jews as a unified whole, so, too, we cannot describe the Beta Israel community as a cohesive unit. We must therefore distinguish between the collective thinking and the inspirational communal approach of the Beta Israel, and the individualistic mode of thinking, in which each person tries to succeed through his own merits and character. Life in Israel and the world of current events should arouse us to complex, courageous, and truthful thinking. We must all realize that no individual or group has a monopoly on the truth. Thus today, each person should follow the customs of his ancestors, and should be permitted to open his own synagogue and pray according to his own will. Each person should be allowed to pray in any synagogue he wishes. Today, ethnic origin does not determine prayer style – for example, an Ethiopian Jew may pray in Moroccan style.

A good example of this took place in a synagogue for Ethiopian Jews, in which respected *kesim* prayed. This synagogue was closed by the State of Israel, due to the assertion that the *kesim* were anti-Semitic, as they did not permit some Ethiopian Jews who had abandoned Ethiopian traditions to perform circumcisions in their synagogue. But a *kes* cannot permit Ethiopian Jews to perform circumcisions in the synagogue, since according to Ethiopian tradition, it is forbidden

---

11. Herman, 152–54.
12. *Shulhan Arukh, Orah Haim* 150a.
13. Herman, *Ma'agal hayei ha-yom*, 153–54.

to perform circumcisions there. To ask a *kes* to perform circumcision in a synagogue is like asking a traditional Jew to eat pork. The only way this would be possible is if the *kesim* decided to begin a new tradition.

The State of Israel and halakhic decision makers must enable every Jew, under law and halakhah, to live according to his own choice of halakhic style, under one umbrella – the Chief Rabbinate of Israel. We must aspire to unity, but not uniformity. The fact that two brothers pray in two different synagogues is not a deficiency – rather, it is an advantage. Still, if they do not respect each other, then it becomes a disadvantage. In short, it is the attempt to create uniformity that led us to the destruction of the Temple and to exile. If there is a synagogue for Beta Israel Jews, we must respect the site and pray according to the style accepted there, and not try to impose another style. This applies to every synagogue.

Sacrifices

Ethiopian Halakhah

The altar was located behind the synagogue, in the courtyard. It was square and built of stones, with a stone cornice surrounded by a fence. The altar was a sacred site, and no non-Jew was permitted to touch it. On it, the *kohanim* offered sacrifices. The main ceremony related to the altar was Pesiha (Pesah). A woman who gave birth offered a sacrifice of a goat, chicken, or bread at the conclusion of her days of impurity (forty days after giving birth to a boy or eighty days after giving birth to a girl, as specified biblically). Other sacrifices the Ethiopian Jews practiced included the biblical thanksgiving offering and the sin offering.

In the nineteenth century, Protestant missionaries went to Ethiopia. These missionaries were converted Jews, and they brought with them religious books written in Amharic. They established schools and taught the population to read these books. The missionaries' skill in religious debate succeeded in undermining the authority of the Beta Israel sages, as well as the community's confidence in the biblical origin of their beliefs. Some of the community stopped performing the sacrificial offerings after they were taught that the Bible specifies that sacrifices should not be offered in any location, but only in the place that God has chosen, in Jerusalem. The *kesim* (spiritual leaders) were unable to offer a satisfactory response to this argument. Thus the practice of offering sacrifices diminished.

Past and Present in Talmudic Halakhah

Sacrifices appear in the Bible from the beginning of human history. Cain and Abel were the first to offer sacrifices, leading to a struggle between them, and Cain's murder of Abel. Noah offered a sacrifice of thanks to God for saving him from the Flood – "And Noah built an altar to the Lord; and took of every clean beast, and of every clean fowl, and offered burnt offerings on the altar" (Genesis 8:20). Sacrifices were offered on altars both in the Temple and outside it as well. But when the Israelites entered the Land of Israel, they were commanded to offer sacrifices in the Temple alone. The *korban* (whose grammatical root is *kuf, resh, bet* [k-r-b]) is thus called because through it, humans become closer (*mitkarev*, from the same root) to God. Offering sacrifices was a central part of religious ritual. The altars and shrines served as spiritual centers for the Jewish people for a long period. Most of the sacrificial laws are found in the book of Leviticus, and in the Mishnah, in Tractate Kodashim.

After the destruction of the Temple, the sacrifices were annulled, and the Sages determined that the prayer services would replace them, following the verse "so will we render for bullocks the offering of our lips" (Hosea 14:3). They organized the prayer services based on this principle, for example, "so that the number of prayer services would equal the number of sacrifices."[14] During Second Temple times, there was no framework for regular prayers, because worship focused on the sacrificial offerings in the Temple. The text and number of the prayers were determined only after the Temple's destruction, by Rabbi Gamliel and his religious court at Yavne. Some assert that Rabbi Gamliel and the Men of the Great Assembly only determined the obligation of prayer and the framework and general content of the blessings, but that the exact text was codified in a later period.[15]

The Recommended Custom in Israel

While in the rest of the Jewish world, the practice of offering sacrifices ended with the destruction of the Second Temple, and they were replaced by prayer, for Ethiopian Jewry, sacrificial practices remained unaffected by the Temple's destruction. Still, in my view, the ceremony of offering sacrifices cannot remain as it was practiced in Ethiopia. Instead of actually offering sacrifices, I suggest reading the verses on sacrifices that appear in the *siddur* (prayer book), and this will serve as a commemoration of the sacrificial offerings.

---

14. Rambam, *Mishneh Torah*, Hilkhot Tefillah 1:1–5.
15. Herman, *Ma'agal hayei ha-yom*.

✻ The Prayer Book and Liturgy

Ethiopian Halakhah

The Beta Israel did not pray from a prayer book, as we do today. Instead, the *kesim* used a book called *Yetzukot Mishaf*, which contained selections from the Bible, mainly from Psalms, and additional compositions of request and praise. Most of the prayers were thanks and praise of God. The prayers of praise specifically mention Jerusalem and the longing to see it and return to it. The prayers also contain requests with well-known motifs: redemption, the return to Zion, the rebuilding of Jerusalem, the expectation to see the *kohanim* and the Levites performing the priestly service, God's kingship over all the nations, and vengeance for the spilled blood of the Jews. We note that the individual prayers of the Beta Israel, as opposed to the versions of the other Jewish communities, contain almost no mention of material issues such as long life, livelihood, and health. Rather, the Beta Israel prayer focuses mainly on remembering destroyed Jerusalem, remembering enslavement among the nations, and similar topics. Thus the national foundations that differentiate Jewish prayer from Christian prayer all became part of the prayers of Ethiopian Jewry. In addition, the principle of praise of the forefathers also entered the Ethiopian service, although this is shared with Christians in general and the Ethiopian church in particular. This principle is particularly strong in the structure of Ethiopian Jewish prayer.

The prayers are written in the liturgical language Ge'ez, an ancient language usually known only to the *kesim*. Some of the congregation prayed from memory; most did not understand the prayers. All participated by listening, responding "Amen," and reciting the few selections they did know, mostly songs. The text of the blessings is the same version that is repeated in all the sacred writings: *Itbarech Egziavher Amlake Israel* (Blessed is the Lord God of Israel). This is the short version. Sometimes, the ending of this blessing is *Amlake zekul sga zekul menfest* (God of all living flesh and spirit). Some add *Amlake zekul zemidr vezebesemay* (God of everything on the earth and in the heavens), *Melekh marusemi* (God of the earth and the heavens). Sometimes the blessing begins: *Itbarech Egziavher Amlachan Amlekh* (Blessed is my Lord, our God, my God). This is the usual version. Prayers of praise follow another version: *Itsabach veitachot*, meaning "May He be praised and glorified." Sometimes other descriptions are used, such as "May He be exalted and elevated."

This text is fundamentally Jewish and is based on the sacred texts. A few researchers believe that in the first half of the fifteenth century, a significant religious-cultural change took place, in which the Beta Israel borrowed melodies from their Christian neighbors. After a process of adaptation, these melodies were integrated into the Jewish prayers. To this day, the Ethiopian Jews accompany the prayer services on Rosh Hodesh and holidays with musical instruments, drums and cymbals. This is not done on Shabbat or Yom Kippur. Kes Rachamim Nega, of blessed memory, informed me that the text of the prayers, prayer customs, and the use of musical instruments is an ancient tradition from the First Temple period, and that the tunes are the same as those of the Levites.

Past and Present in Talmudic Halakhah

The obligation of prayer is first mentioned in the Tannaitic literature. Sifre comments on the verse "And [you shall] serve Him with all your heart" (Deuteronomy 11:13): "'Serve Him' – this means the Amidah prayer."[16] The Torah does not give a regular format for the Amidah, while the Sages' writings offer a number of statements regarding who determined the text and when. One statement indicates that the Amidah was determined by Ezra and his religious court, who were members of the Great Assembly. A *baraita* states, "One hundred and twenty elders, including several prophets, determined eighteen blessings in a certain order."[17] We understand from the statement of the Amora Rabbi Yochanan that "the Men of the Great Assembly determined for the Jewish people blessings and prayers, sanctifications and *havadalot*."[18]

An indication of the ancient character of the Amidah prayer can perhaps be found in the texts of certain blessings in the book of Ben Sira,[19] which are similar to the blessings of the Amidah known to us. Evidence for an Amidah text at the end of the Second Temple period is found in the controversy between Beit Shammai and Beit Hillel regarding the number of blessings in the Amidah for Rosh Hashanah that falls on Shabbat, and that of the Amidah for a holiday that begins on Shabbat, as recorded in the Tosefta: "When the Rosh Hashanah holiday falls on Shabbat, Beit Shammai say one should recite ten [blessings], while Beit Hillel say one should recite nine [blessings]. When a holiday falls on Shabbat, Beit Shammai say one should recite eight [blessings], while Beit Hillel say one should recite seven."[20]

---

16. Sifre, Deuteronomy 11:13.
17. Babylonian Talmud, *Megillah* 17b.
18. Babylonian Talmud, *Berakhot* 33a.
19. Ben Sira 51:21–35.
20. *Rosh Hashanah* 2:17.

We find another tradition in which the Amidah was formulated only after the destruction of the Second Temple, and this is upheld by the following *baraita*: "The rabbis taught, Shimon ha-Pakuli formulated eighteen blessings in their proper order before Rabban Gamliel at Yavne."[21] As we know, after the destruction of the Second Temple, the Sages congregated at Yavne. The Babylonian Talmud resolves the conflict between the *baraitot* above by stating, "They were forgotten, and then he reformulated them"[22] – in other words, the Amidah prayer was formulated by "one hundred and twenty elders, including several prophets," but with time it was forgotten, until Shimon ha-Pakuli reconstructed them. The Rambam writes that reciting the Amidah every day is a biblical injunction, but that the text of the Amidah and the number of blessings that should be recited each day were determined in a later period by Ezra and his court, who were members of the Great Assembly.[23]

Tannaitic and Amoraitic literature give several versions of the Amidah blessings, and of additional prayers that were recited before and after the Amidah. The number of blessings in the Amidah prayer in Eretz Yisrael was eighteen, while Babylonian Jews recited nineteen blessings. We also find differences in the Babylonian and Eretz Yisrael versions of the endings of some of the Amidah blessings. The texts of the prayers known to us today are a result of the dispersal of Jewish communities and their distance from the great centers of Torah learning in Eretz Yisrael and Babylonia. Some assert that the differences between the texts of the Amidah and other prayers reflect the differences between the Eretz Yisrael version and the Babylonian version. Others believe that the Babylonian version is an early version of the Eretz Yisrael text. The appearance of the written *siddur* made a significant contribution to the formulation of the final version of most of the prayers. Booklets of prayers began to be recorded in writing only after the sixth century. The first booklet did not follow the framework of the *siddur* known today, and it was written based on the practical implantation of the general halakhah determined by the Tanna Rabbi Meir that "a person must recite one hundred blessings each day."[24]

In the last third of the ninth century, Rabbi Amram bar Sheshna Gaon recorded a booklet of prayers entitled *Seder Rav Amram Gaon*, at the bequest of

---

21. Babylonian Talmud, *Berakhot* 28b; Babylonian Talmud, *Megillah* 17b.
22. Babylonian Talmud, *Megillah* 18a.
23. Rambam, *Hakdamah le-perush ha-Mishnah*, Mossad Ha-Rav Kook.
24. Babylonian Talmud, *Menahot* 43b.

the Barcelona community. This composition included a version of the prayers and prayer customs. A century later, Rabbi Sa'adia Gaon also followed this practice, composing *Siddur Rav Sa'adia Gaon*. The Rambam also published a collection of prayers at the end of his *Sefer Ahavah*, entitled *Seder Tefillot Kol ha-Shanah* (Order of prayers for the entire year). The Eretz Yisrael version influenced the custom in Ashkenaz, and the sages of Ashkenaz in the Middle Ages formulated the final character of the rite known today as Nusah Ashkenaz, as appearing in the Vitry Machzor. The Ashkenazic Jews of Europe followed this rite. Later, following the influence of Kabbalah as taught by the Ari (Rabbi Isaac Luria), the Sefard rite developed. It was based on the Ashkenaz text, with changes and additions according to the Ari. Here we should note that the Kabbalah had a great influence on the *siddur*, contributing many sections of prayer.

Included under the Ashkenaz rite is the version of the Gaon of Vilna, who made changes and corrections to the service for which he found halakhic support. His version was accepted by the Ashkenazic Jews. The Sefard rite also includes the Ari text, as formulated by Rabbi Shneuer Zalman of Liadi. The Chabad hassidim follow this text today.

Another version is that of Sephardic Jewry, which is mainly based on the *siddur* of Rabbi Amram Gaon. The Sephardic text was accepted by the communities of the East and the Balkans. Yet another version is that of Italian Jewry, which is an ancient rite, and has language and expressions not found in other versions. An additional version is that of Yemenite Jewry. Rabbi Shlomo Goren, in his term as Chief Rabbi of the Israel Defense Forces, instituted a uniform version for the IDF, which follows the Sefard rite.[25]

The Recommended Custom in Israel

The *kesim* should continue to pray according to the Ethiopian custom. Anyone who understands the prayers in Ge'ez may participate in the service together with the *kesim*. This prayer brings us closer to God, and there is no need to add any additional prayers. But the second generation of Ethiopian Jews in Israel who have no knowledge of Ge'ez should pray using a *siddur* written in a language they understand. At any rate, they are not obligated to uphold either of these customs, but are permitted to pray according to whichever version they choose. Those who wish to continue the Ethiopian tradition and pray in Ge'ez are permitted to do so, on condition that they learn the language and the prayers. As the *Shulhan Arukh*

---

25. Herman, *Ma'agal hayei ha-yom*.

rules, "he may pray in any language he wishes" (*Orah Haim* 101:4). The *Mishnah Berurah* adds that an individual may pray in any language, on condition that he understands that language fluently. But if one prays in the sacred tongue, even if one does not understand it, he fulfills his obligation (ibid., 13). Even though in Ethiopia most of the congregants did not usually understand the prayer service, it is better that in Israel, they know and understand the liturgy.

Regarding playing the cymbals on holidays, as long as the prayer is in Ge'ez and the cymbals are an integral part of the service, they may continue. But this is only on condition that the service is conducted in Ge'ez – it is not permissible to use instruments when praying according to another liturgy.

Individual and Congregational Prayer

Ethiopian Halakhah

In Ethiopia there was no particular significance to prayer in a *minyan* (quorum of ten men), and there was no difference between individual and congregational prayer. In effect, most of the religious ceremonies took place in public, and usually involved more than ten men, not as an obligation but as a cultural conception, in the spirit of the verse "In the multitude of people is the King's glory" (Proverbs 14:28). The mitzvot were fulfilled by the collective congregation. Thus there was no reason to speak of the individual as opposed to the congregation. For the Beta Israel, public prayer continues as was practiced in biblical times. An illiterate person can also pray in public.

Past and Present in Talmudic Halakhah

According to the Sages, public prayer has greater power and influence than individual prayer. They also defined "public" as ten men gathered in one place. They found biblical support for this in the verse "I will be hallowed among the children of Israel" (Leviticus 22:32). Further, certain sections of the prayer service may be said only in a *minyan*: "No one may pass before the Ark, nor may they 'lift up their hands,' nor may they read the Torah…nor mention the name of God in the Grace after Meals when fewer than ten are present."[26] Regarding the importance of prayer in a *minyan*, the Sages said, "'But as for me, let my prayer be to You, O Lord, in an acceptable time' (Psalms 69:14); What is an 'acceptable time'? While the congregation is praying."[27]

---

26. Mishnah, *Megillah* 4:3.
27. Babylonian Talmud, *Berakhot* 8a.

The Rambam writes, "Public prayer is always heard, and even if there are sinners among the congregation, the Holy One, blessed be He, does not reject public prayer. Therefore a person should participate in the congregation, and should not pray alone, whenever he has the opportunity to pray with a congregation."[28] The *Shulhan Arukh* rules that "If a person is unable to come to the synagogue, he should try to pray at the same time that the congregation is praying."[29] The Rema adds to this: "This is the ruling for people who live in towns where there is no *minyan* – they should pray Shaharit and Arvit at the same time that the public prays."[30] "Prayer" in this case refers to the Amidah prayer, so the importance of praying in a *minyan* applies to the Amidah alone.[31]

The Recommended Custom in Israel

A priori, one should pray in a *minyan*, as is the practice in Israel today, and as was practiced in Ethiopia. Still, one who is subject to extenuating circumstances or difficulties (personal or family reasons) that prevent him from participating in public prayer should not conclude that he is exempt from praying – rather, he should pray alone. Prayer is like food for the soul. Prayer is not only a religious issue, but a spiritual and existential need. The world is incomplete, and needs repair, and thus prayer is always needed. A person may suffer any number of travails throughout his life, and at that time, he needs the warm embrace of his Creator. We may compare prayer to fire. A person does not need fire constantly, but when he does need it, if he does not have coals or matches at hand, he will find himself in serious distress. This is the moment for which a person must keep the coals lit, so that prayer will come easily to him. A fitting example of each individual's need for prayer can be found in this testimony from a soldier in Israel's War of Independence:

> During the War of Independence, I was a division commander. One day, I arranged my division facing the front lines of the Egyptian army, which had reached Ashdod. The division was wretched and inferior, with a few Sten guns and grenades. It was almost ridiculous to think we could stop the Egyptian tanks.... Usually I wasn't afraid, but this time I felt fear that was deathly, paralyzing. At one point, I felt the strong urge to pray, but I did not know how, as I

---

28. Hilkhot Tefillah 8a.
29. *Orah Haim*, ch. 90, par. 9.
30. Rema, ibid.
31. Herman, *Ma'agal hayei ha-yom*.

did not know any prayer by heart. But still, I prayed. My prayer was in simple language, as I was able. Actually, I recall my desire to recite a prayer that all the Jews throughout history had said – but I did not know any such prayer.[32]

Thus a person who is used to praying in Ge'ez, as the Beta Israel did in Ethiopia, should continue his custom and pray with a congregation. Those who are used to praying in Hebrew from the *siddur* should do so with a congregation in a *minyan*.

Shaliah Tzibbur (Prayer Leader)

Ethiopian Halakhah

In Ethiopia, the prayer services were led by a prayer leader or *hazzan*, but this role was not formally defined. A large number of the congregants did not know how to read or write, and so they followed the prayers of the spiritual leaders, the *kesim*. The *kesim* served as prayer leaders regularly and naturally, and thus friction was absent among the congregants as to who was worthy or unworthy of this honor. The *kesim* were worthy and essential.

Past and Present in Talmudic Halakhah

During the time of the Mishnah and the Talmud, when prayer was conducted orally, the prayer leader conducted the entire service out loud, and everyone listened to him.[33] The Tannaim were divided on the question of whether the prayer leader fulfills the obligation of those who are well versed in the prayers.[34] The Rambam rules the halakhah as follows:

> How does a prayer leader fulfill the obligation of the public? When he prays and they listen and answer *Amen* after each blessing – it is as if they are praying. To what does this refer? If a person does not know how to pray. But if he does know [how to pray] – his obligation is fulfilled only through his own prayer. When does this apply? On all days of the year except for Rosh Hashanah and Yom Kippur.... On these two days, the prayer leader fulfills the obligation of one who knows the prayers, just as he fulfills the obligation of one who does not know them, because [the Amidah recited on these days contains] long blessings and most people do not know them [to the extent] that they can

---

32. Mordecai Braun, "Emunato shel bilti ma'amin," *Petahim* (Jerusalem, 5728/1968), 3–10.
33. Herman, *Ma'agal hayei ha-yom*.
34. Mishnah, *Rosh Hashanah* 4:9.

have the same intention as the leader. Therefore, if he so desires, on these two days even a person who knows [how to pray] is permitted to rely on the leader's prayer to fulfill his obligation.[35]

In today's practice, the prayer leader repeats the Amidah out loud. In Sephardic, Edot ha-Mizrah, and Yemenite congregations, the prayer leader recites the entire Amidah out loud. The Talmud specifies the characteristics required by a prayer leader: "One whose youth was unblemished, who is meek and is acceptable to the people; who is skilled in chanting, who has a pleasant voice, and possesses a thorough knowledge of the Torah."[36] The Rambam expands on this:

> Only a person of great stature within the community in both wisdom and deed should be appointed as the leader of the congregation. If he is an older man, it is very praiseworthy. An effort should be made to appoint as the leader of the congregation, someone who has a pleasant voice and is familiar with reading [Biblical verses].
>
> A person who does not have a full beard should not be appointed as the leader of the congregation even if he be a wise man of great stature, as a gesture of respect to the congregation....
>
> Similarly, the inarticulate who pronounce an *alef* as an *ayin* or an *ayin* as an *alef* or one who cannot articulate the letters in the proper manner should not be appointed as the leader of a congregation.[37]

On this, the *Shulhan Arukh* adds:

> If one cannot find a person who has all these qualities, one should choose the best person among the congregation who studies Torah and performs good deeds. A Torah-observant person who studies Torah regularly is preferable, because he can ask for mercy. If there is a person who is Torah observant but who has not yet reached the age of thirty and is not married, as opposed to a simple person who is married and over thirty, the Torah-observant person has precedence.[38]

In the responsa literature from the Middle Ages, we find mention of the phenomenon of choosing a prayer leader according to the quality of his voice, while

---

35. Rambam, *Mishneh Torah*, Hilkhot Tefillah 8:9–10.
36. Babylonian Talmud, *Ta'anit* 16a.
37. Rambam, *Mishneh Torah*, Hilkhot Tefillah 8:11–12.
38. Kitzur *Shulhan Arukh*, *Yalkut Yosef*, ch. 53, par. 2, p. 66.

ignoring the halakhic specifications for his qualities. The *Shulhan Arukh* comments on this:

> Regarding a prayer leader who extends his prayers so that his beautiful voice will be heard – if he does so out of joy that he is giving thanks to God with his sweet voice, he should be praised, as long as he prays with a serious approach, with fear and awe. If, however, his intent is to make his voice heard and he is excited by his voice, it is shameful. Nevertheless, if he stretches out his prayer, this is not good, since it burdens the public.[39]

The Recommended Custom in Israel

The *kesim* and anyone who wishes to continue according to the classical Ethiopian liturgy is permitted to do so. Children who are learning to pray in Ge'ez, as those learning in Ashkelon today with Kes Azariah, should lead the prayer service, even though in Ethiopia, it was not the custom for children to lead the services. But where Ethiopian Jews pray according to the Israeli liturgy, everyone should be included. Whoever considers himself appropriate to serve as prayer leader is worthy. "Man looks at the outward appearance, but the Lord sees into the heart" (1 Samuel 16:7).

❧ The Number of Prayers

Ethiopian Halakhah

On weekdays, the Jews in Ethiopia followed the practice of praying twice daily – once in the morning (Shaharit), and once in the afternoon (Minhah). These prayers were usually attended by the *kesim*, the *shmaglotz* (respected elderly sages), and individuals who were not working. On Shabbat, the entire community assembled in the synagogue. Children also came, but they were not allowed to enter the building, as a sign of respect for the synagogue. Because custom held that one should not come to the synagogue empty-handed, the women brought food, drinks, or other items as gifts for the synagogue.

Past and Present in Talmudic Halakhah

The Torah does not specify the number of prayers one should recite daily. The book of Psalms contains the first record of prayer three times a day – "Evening, and morning, and at noon, will I complain, and moan; and He has heard my voice (55:18)." The book of Daniel records that this prophet prayed three times a day:

---

39. *Orah Haim*, ch. 53, par. 11.

"And when Daniel knew that the writing was signed, he went into his house – now his windows were open in his upper chamber toward Jerusalem – and he kneeled upon his knees three times a day, and prayed, and gave thanks before his God just as he had done before" (6:11). Yet I Chronicles records only two daily prayers: "And to stand every morning to give thanks and praise the Lord, and likewise in the evening" (23:30). In literary sources from the Second Temple period, some mention two daily prayers, while others mention three.

The Recommended Custom in Israel

In ancient times, the Jews prayed twice daily, while in Temple times, some prayed three times. Rabbi Gamliel of Yavne determined three daily prayers, stating that the evening prayer (Arvit) was also required. Rabbi Joshua ruled that Arvit was optional, thus questioning Rabbi Gamliel's authority. This controversy developed into a severe crisis, until finally Rabbi Gamliel was temporarily removed from his position as Nasi.[40] In Eretz Yisrael during the Amoraic period, the Sages had determined that Arvit was obligatory.[41] The Rambam, however, wrote that "the Arvit prayer is not obligatory as are Shaharit and Minhah. However, all Jews in all their places of residence followed the practice of praying Arvit, and took it upon themselves as an obligatory prayer."[42] In light of this, we should permit the first generation of Ethiopian Jews to follow their custom and recite two daily prayers, Shaharit and Minhah, for as we have seen, according to halakhah Arvit is discretionary. But the second generation should be encouraged to take upon themselves the Arvit prayer as well.

❧ Swaying during Prayer

Ethiopian Halakhah

Swaying was not practiced at all. Further, swaying was considered a frivolous practice, far from an expression of respect or awe. Swaying during prayer was comparable to the actions of one who was mentally unstable, or of a drunk who could not stand up straight.

---

40. Babylonian Talmud, *Berakhot* 27b.
41. Jerusalem Talmud, *Berakhot*, chapter 3, *heh vav* (7a in *daled vav*).
42. *Mishneh Torah*, Hilkhot Tefillah 1:6.

Past and Present in Talmudic Halakhah

The Mishnah and the Talmud provide no evidence of swaying during prayer.[43] This issue is first mentioned by the medieval sages, under the influence of the hassidic thinkers of Ashkenaz. The source of this custom is found in the Kabbalistic Heikhalot literature. From Ashkenaz, the custom spread throughout Europe, and following the exile from Spain, it moved to other locations as well. The Rema establishes this custom as halakhah: "Those who were exacting in their observance would sway while reading the Torah, as the Torah was given [while the Israelites were] shaking, and when praying as well, as in 'All my bones shall say, Lord, who is like You' (Psalms 35:10)."[44] But Rabbi Yeshayahu Horowitz (the Shelah) supported standing quietly without movement. In *Shnei Luhot ha-Brit*, he writes:

> Standing without swaying at all helps with intent [*kavanah*]. Regarding the verse "All my bones shall say," this refers to songs, praises, blessings, Shema, and studying Torah, but not to prayer. If a person argues that this applies to prayer as well, I think we need not agree with his statement, as experience has proven that standing without swaying leads to intent. Do you think it is appropriate for a person to make requests of a human king with his body swaying like a tree in the forest blowing in the wind?

Despite the widespread influence of the Shelah's book on the hassidic movement, this opinion was not accepted.[45]

The Recommended Custom in Israel

There is no obligation to sway during prayer, and some even say it is preferable not to do so. Thus one who feels that swaying reflects lack of respect – as in the Ethiopian understanding – should not sway. Still, one who does sway has support for this practice. If swaying during prayer helps a person to feel closer to God,

---

43. Herman, *Ma'agal hayei ha-yom*.
44. *Orah Haim*, ch. 48, gloss at the beginning of the chapter.
45. The hassidic movement strongly emphasized the importance of swaying during prayer due to the writings of the Ba'al Shem Tov on this issue in his will. He explained that "when a person is drowning in a river and he makes movements in the water in order to extract himself from the water that is washing him away, onlookers will certainly not mock him and his movements. Similarly, one should not mock a person who prays and makes movements, for he is saving himself from the evil waters, which are the spiritual veils [*klippot*] and unwanted thoughts that attempt to distract him from concentrating on his prayer" (*Likutim yekarim, Keter shem tov*, in Shai Agnon, *Sefer yamim noraim*, 67).

then he has achieved the goal, as King David said, "But as for me, the nearness of God is my good" (Psalms 73:28).

✺ Facing Jerusalem during Prayer

Ethiopian Halakhah

Throughout the bitter history of the Diaspora, the Jews never stopped longing for Jerusalem. "I sleep, but my heart is awake" (Song of Songs 5:2) – I am in Ethiopia, but my soul is in Jerusalem. The Jews waited in anticipation for the day when they could go there. Jerusalem occupied a central position in their daily lives. Their prayers are full of praise for Jerusalem and the hope for redemption, as in this prayer:

> Hallelujah, praise God, Jerusalem will be raised up.
> Your walls will be rebuilt, O Jerusalem, the gates of Jerusalem.
> Prayers will be addressed to You in Jerusalem.
> The ways of Jerusalem are in Your judgments, Jerusalem.
> In the midst of Jerusalem, raise the horn of Jerusalem.
> Return to Jerusalem and spill their blood around Jerusalem.
> Listen, Jerusalem.[46]

The hope was passed from one generation to the next. Some fasted for nine days over the defeat of Jerusalem and the destruction of the First Temple, and in the month of Av some fasted for seventeen days – from Rosh Hodesh until 17 Av – also in mourning for the destruction of the Temple. Many customs are related to Jerusalem. To give only several examples: during prayers the congregants faced Jerusalem; when slaughtering an animal, the Beta Israel pointed the animal's head toward Jerusalem; one of the central reasons for the Sigd holiday was the longing and hope for Jerusalem. Interesting evidence of the importance of Jerusalem among the Beta Israel is found in the story of Yosef Halevi. When he reached the Beta Israel, he was unable to convince them that he was a Jew like them, until he mentioned Jerusalem. He describes the meeting:

> My mention of the word *Jerusalem*, which I uttered coincidentally, immediately annulled any doubt the Falashas may have had regarding my words. Like lightning in the dark of night, the word *Jerusalem* lit up the eyes and hearts of my lost brothers.... I had a big job to do in answering all their questions, and

---

46. Translation based on Eshkoli, *Sefer ha-Falashim*.

they did not grow tired of asking and crying when remembering our beautiful Temple of ancient times. These moments are very dear to me, and I will never forget them as long as I live. I can hardly describe with my lips and express the excitement I felt at that moment, and at this wonderful sight, when I saw the faces of my brothers and fellow believers, lit up with powerful emotion when recalling the history of our people! I told them that when I had first set out for Ethiopia, I had been in Jerusalem. I told them that although in ancient times the city was crowned with beauty, now its dignity and beauty had faded, and it stood destroyed and desolate. I told them that on the site where our Temple, the hall of our glory, stood in the past, now stood an Arab house of prayer. When they heard this, they were greatly distressed and cried bitterly, until they were exhausted from weeping, and I cried along with them. These far-flung brothers believed that our Temple was still standing in all its glory, and that our honored people living there were great among the nations. They did not even know about the present situation in the Holy Land. They did not know that the [Turkish] sultan ruled over them. After I spoke with them, most of them believed that I was a Jew, but still some of them found it difficult to believe.[47]

Past and Present in Talmudic Halakhah

In the Torah, prayer was not related to any specific location.[48] The first mention of prayer that is connected to a specific place is in the story of Hannah, who chose to pray for a child in the temple at Shiloh, when she went there in accordance with her long-standing custom (1 Samuel 1:1–2, 10). Later, during the period of King Solomon, the Tanakh emphasizes the connection between prayer and the Temple. When King Solomon dedicated the First Temple, he prayed to God and recalled the Temple as the place through which prayers pass on their way to Heaven. Following are the relevant verses in his prayer (1 Kings 8:22–45):

> 22. And Solomon stood before the altar of the Lord in the presence of all the congregation of Israel, and spread forth his hands toward Heaven...

> 29. That Your eyes may be open toward this house night and day, even toward the place whereof You have said, 'My Name will be there;' to hearken to the prayer which Your servant shall pray toward this place.

---

47. Waldman, *Me-Etiopiah*, 161.
48. Herman, *Ma'agal hayei ha-yom*.

30. And You shall hearken to the supplication of Your servant, and of Your people Israel, when they shall pray toward this place; and You shall hear in Heaven Your dwelling place, and when You hear, forgive.

35. When Heaven is shut up, and there is no rain, when they do sin against You; if they pray toward this place…

36. then You shall hear in Heaven, and forgive the sin of Your servants…

38. whatever prayer and supplication will be made by any man of all Your people Israel, who shall know every man the plague of his own heart, and spread forth his hands toward this house;

39. then You shall hear in Heaven Your dwelling place, and forgive, and do, and give to every man according to all his ways, whose heart You know, for You, and You only, know the hearts of all the children of men.

41. Moreover concerning the stranger that is not of Your people Israel…

42. … when he shall come and pray toward this house.

43. You shall hear in Heaven Your dwelling place, and do according to all that the stranger calls to You for…

44. If Your people go out to battle against their enemy, by what way You send them, and pray to the Lord toward the city that You have chosen, and (toward) the house that I have built for Your name.

45. And you shall hear in Heaven their prayer and supplication, and maintain their cause.

The Tanakh also notes that King Hezekiah prayed in the Temple (II Kings 19:15–19). The first mention of the custom of facing Jerusalem when praying appears during the Persian period, in the book of Daniel. The windows of the prophet's house faced Jerusalem, and three times a day he kneeled in prayer (Daniel 6:11). Additional evidence for prayer in the direction of Jerusalem is found in the pseudepigraphic (apocryphal) works from the Second Temple period. The book of Esdras writes, "When the youth went [outside], he lifted his face to Heaven toward Jerusalem, and he blessed the King of Heaven, and said" (1 Esdras 4:58). Thus after the destruction of the Temple, when the Sages determined obligatory prayers, they taught that while reciting the Amidah, people should direct their bodies as well as their minds toward Jerusalem. But if one was unable to direct the body, it was sufficient to focus the mind on Jerusalem. These *halakhot* are reflected in Tannaitic literature. The Mishnah states, "If one was riding a donkey, he should dismount from it [while he prays]. If he is unable to dismount, he should turn his face [toward Jerusalem]. And if he is unable to turn his face, he should focus his heart toward the Holy of Holies."[49] Based on this, we learn that it is preferable to dismount from the donkey and turn the body toward Jerusalem, and if this is not possible, intention is sufficient. This halakhah is based on the halakhah in the Tosefta, which emphasizes the importance of focusing the mind on Jerusalem, at the same time as turning the body in that direction. The Tosefta specifies (*Berakhot* 3, 15–16):

> Those outside the Land of Israel should focus their minds on the Land of Israel, as in the verse, "If they … pray toward their land" (II Chronicles 6:38). Those who are in the Land of Israel should focus on Jerusalem when they pray, as in the verse "and they pray to You toward this city" (ibid., 34). Those in Jerusalem should focus their minds on the Temple, as in the verse "when they shall come and pray toward this house" (ibid., 32). Those in the Temple should focus on the Holy of Holies when they pray, as in the verse, "when they shall pray toward this place" (1 Kings 8:30). When standing in the north, they should face the south; when standing in the south, they should face the north; when standing in the east, they should face the west; and when standing in the west, they should face the east, so that all of Israel prays toward one place.

In this context, we note that prayer in the direction of Jerusalem characterizes synagogues that were built beginning in the late Second Temple period in Israel and the Diaspora. In connection with this, the *Shulhan Arukh* rules:

> When preparing to pray, if one is outside the Land of Israel, one should face in the direction of the Land of Israel. One should also focus one's thoughts toward Jerusalem, the Temple, and the Holy of Holies. If one is in the Land of Israel, he should face Jerusalem, and focus his thoughts on the Temple and the Holy of Holies. If he is in Jerusalem, he should face the Temple, and also focus on the Holy of Holies.… One who cannot face in the proper direction should focus his mind on his Father in Heaven.[50]

---

49. Mishnah, *Berakhot* 4:5.
50. *Orah Haim* 94:1–4.

In the laws pertaining to synagogue worship, the *Shulhan Arukh* specifies that the synagogue should have "doors or windows opening toward Jerusalem, in order to pray facing them, and ideally, the synagogue should have twelve windows."[51]

The Recommended Custom in Israel

Once there was a Jew who made aliyah from Ethiopia. While he was traveling from Afula to Jerusalem, he asked, "Why should I go up to Jerusalem, if I already live in Jerusalem?" In the first days of the Ethiopian aliyah, the Ethiopian Jews did not distinguish between Eretz Yisrael and the city of Jerusalem. In their world, Jerusalem included the entire Land of Israel. The longings of the Ethiopian Jews for Jerusalem should be expressed through living in Jerusalem, or at least pilgrimage three times a year, as written in the Torah, and on Jerusalem Day. Jerusalem Day was appointed in 2003 by the Knesset Committee for Immigration, Absorption, and the Diaspora as a day of commemoration for the approximately four thousand Ethiopian Jews who fell on their way from Ethiopia to Israel, and it is a fitting opportunity for pilgrimage to Jerusalem. This is in addition to directing one's body as well as one's mind toward Jerusalem during prayer.

ꙮ *Nefilat Apayim* (Prostration)

Ethiopian Halakhah

In every prayer service, the participants prostrated themselves before God, as other Jewish communities do on Yom Kippur. In prayers that included specific requests for forgiveness, the congregants performed a full prostration – that is, lying on the stomach while placing the hands on the ground. Avraham Yardai, however, noted that he never saw anyone in the prostrate position.

Past and Present in Talmudic Halakhah

In ancient times, the Jews performed *nefilat apayim* by either *hishtahvayah* (full prostration) or *kidah* (bowing to the ground). In prostration, they lay face down on the ground with hands and feet outstretched.[52] In bowing to the ground, they bent down on their knees and touched the ground with the head.[53] For several reasons, both prostration and bowing were annulled – due to the prohibition against prostration on a stone floor, and the prohibition against an important person prostrating himself in public without assurance that his prayer would be

---

51. *Orah Haim* 90:4.
52. Herman, *Ma'agal hayei ha-yom*.
53. Babylonian Talmud, *Berakhot* 34b; Rambam, *Mishneh Torah*, Hilkhot Tefillah 5:13–14.

answered, as in the biblical case of Joshua. But the main reason for annulment of this custom was the *Zohar*'s inflation of its importance.[54] The *Zohar* specified that the person praying had to give up his soul to God, and consider himself as if he had died, and thus his sins would be forgiven:

> This prayer should be made with full intention, and then God will have mercy on him and forgive his sins. Contented is the man who knows to cajole and worship his Lord with good intention. Woe to he who tries to cajole his Creator with a distant mind and unwillingly. As the verse says (Psalms 78:36–37): "They beguiled Him with their mouth, and lied to Him with their tongue. For their heart was not steadfast with Him..." He recites, "To You, O Lord, do I lift up my soul" (Psalms 25:1), but he speaks with a distant mind, and this causes him to leave the world before his time.

Because we suspect our intent is imperfect and we are undeserving, we refrain from bowing or prostrating ourselves. In actuality, all Ashkenazic Jews and some Sephardic Jews follow the practice of bending the upper body and resting the head on the forearm. This is a type of *nefilat apayim* that resembles a *kidah*, but not a full *kidah*, and does not bear the suspicion of prostrating oneself on a stone floor.[55] Perhaps so as to avoid the danger mentioned in the *Zohar*, Ashkenazic Jews did not recite the Psalm "To You, O Lord, do I lift up my soul," which the *Zohar* interprets as meaning giving up one's soul. Instead, they recite Psalm 6.[56] Those who follow the custom of the Ben Ish Hai are careful not to prostrate themselves face down, and many Eastern communities follow this practice as well.

The Recommended Custom in Israel

Clearly, Ethiopian Jews may continue their custom of prostrating themselves, either full prostration or bowing to the ground. In prostration, the individual lies face down on the ground with hands and feet outstretched. In bowing to the ground, one should bend down on knees and touch the head to the ground. One need not heed the *Zohar*'s specifications regarding this practice, as this is the Ethiopian custom. Still, I recommend that the first and second generation in Israel should not lie on their stomachs on the floor of the synagogue with hands and legs outstretched, as I have seen in a prayer service. This is not due to the

---

54. Numbers 121:1.
55. *Shulhan Arukh, Orah Haim* 131:1.
56. *Orah Haim* 41, 131:5.

Zohar's warning, but rather because in the Western culture in which we live, such prostration is likely to damage an individual's image in the public eye. We aspire to stand before God not as submissive individuals, but as people who carry the image of God within them. Still, a person who wishes to follow this practice out of tradition and a feeling of closeness to God may do so, as in the verse "But as for me, the nearness of God is my good" (Psalms 73:28).

Tefillat ha-Derekh (The Traveler's Prayer)

Ethiopian Halakhah

In Ethiopia, going on a trip entailed serious danger. Travelers, who journeyed on foot of course, made a spontaneous personal prayer, and then received a prayer for the journey from a relative or spiritual leader. Some even made vows.

Past and Present in Talmudic Halakhah

The traveler's prayer was instituted by the Sages in a special text recited when leaving to go on a journey. The traveler's prayer is first mentioned in the writings of the Amoraim.[57] The text of the prayer, as it appears in the Talmud, was accepted by the various communities, with slight changes. Rabbi Shlomo Goren, former chief rabbi of the Israel Defense Forces, composed a special version of the traveler's journey for the pilot, parachutist, submariner, and any soldier going out to battle.[58]

The Recommended Custom in Israel

Ethiopian Jews are permitted to continue their custom of saying a personal prayer. There is no need for them to visit a spiritual leader before every journey, even a boat trip or flight. Nevertheless, it is important to recite the traveler's prayer before each car trip. The dangers of the road are comparable to the dangers of lions or robbers in Ethiopia. Prayer has an influence on the individual's state, and can cause a change or transformation of fate. In addition, prayer can influence the conscience of the person praying. When a car passenger asks God to "lead us toward peace" with full intent, he will try to be more careful and avoid endangering himself and others. Fear of God in this sense is understood as personal responsibility.

---

57. Babylonian Talmud, *Berakhot* 29a–b.
58. Herman, *Ma'agal hayei ha-yom*.

2. Blessings

❧ Introduction

Ethiopian Halakhah

In the world of the Ethiopian community, as opposed to halakhic tradition, there is no regular text for blessings – rather, each person says a blessing as he feels appropriate. Some say a few words, while others prolong their versions. The *kesim* also did not use a regular text for blessings. They did, however, use a regular introduction for blessings recited before performing a mitzvah, and the general content of these blessings was also regular. For blessings recited after performing a mitzvah, there was no regular text at all. (In Ethiopia, the Beta Israel recited blessings after performing a mitzvah, thanking God for helping them to complete it.)

Past and Present in Talmudic Halakhah

In a process similar to the reinforcement of the nation's conceptual unity that took place following the destruction of the First Temple, the world of the Sages during the Yavne generation experienced similar compensation.[1] For the first time, the need arose to determine a normative halakhah that would apply to the entire nation.[2] On the basis of this trend in the world of the Sages, rules were established for blessings – regular texts, specific times, types of blessings, how to recite them, and what one should do in case of doubt. The shared components of the blessings, without which the blessing has no significance, are the mention of God's Name (*shem*) and the words "King of the universe" (*malkhut*). Thus the *Shulhan Arukh* determines: "Any blessing without the Name and 'King of the universe' is not a proper blessing, and if one inadvertently omits the Name or 'King of the universe,' he should repeat the blessing. Even if he only omits the

---

1. Herman, *Ma'agal hayei ha-yom*.
2. Gafni, From Jerusalem to Jabneh, 29.

word *universe*, he should repeat the blessing, as 'King' alone is not *malkhut*."[3] It is important to note in this context that all the blessings are rabbinically ordained, except for Grace after Meals, which is biblically ordained. According to tradition, the text of the blessings was determined by Ezra and his court, and must not be changed – neither additions nor deletions are permitted. The Babylonian Talmud specifies, "Anyone who changes the format that the Sages determined for the blessings is committing an error."[4]

The Recommended Custom in Israel

While in Ethiopia the blessings were said spontaneously, in the Talmudic world they are characterized by clear rules and *halakhot* that leave no room for the personal aspect. Thus we must find a path that integrates the two worlds. The first generation in Israel who are used to reciting spontaneous blessings may continue their custom, and it is even preferable for them to do so. The second generation may find it difficult to follow this practice, and thus they should learn the blessings according to the common practice today.

❧ Reciting Modeh Ani

Ethiopian Halakhah

In Beta Israel custom, there is no regular text for prayer upon awakening, like Modeh Ani. Rather, the custom was that upon rising from nightly sleep, the individual praises God for the past night and requests His protection for the coming day. Some would say a lengthy prayer, others a short one – each individual according to his expressive ability, with the main purpose being to pray with intent.

Past and Present in Talmudic Halakhah

As soon as the individual awakens, he should recall the mercies that God has done for him. We give up our soul to God when weary, and He returns our soul to our bodies renewed and calm, in order that we may worship Him to the best of our ability and serve him all day long. Thus we must thank Him with all our heart. While still lying in bed, we recite: *"Modeh ani lefanekha…,"* (I offer thanks before you, living and eternal King, for You have mercifully restored my soul within me; Your faithfulness is great).[5] The text of this prayer is based on an interpretation by Rabbi Alexandri, an Eretz Yisrael Amora, of the verse in Lamentations, "They

---

3. *Orah Haim* 214:1.
4. Babylonian Talmud, *Berakhot* 40b.
5. *Kitzur Shulhan Arukh*, ch. 1, par. 2.

are new every morning; great is Your faithfulness " (3:23). Said Rabbi Alexandri: "Because You renew us each morning, we know that Your faithfulness for the resurrection of the dead is great."[6] Rabbi Alexandri does not determine a fixed text, and so we assume that the prayer accepted today was written in a later period. We find the first evidence of this version in the writings of Rabbi Moshe ben Machir (sixteenth-century kabbalist of Safed). This text spread throughout the Jewish communities and eventually entered the prayer service.[7]

The Recommended Custom in Israel

First of all, as we saw, the Ethiopian community is upholding an ancient custom that was accepted among all Jewish communities. Still, we ask, what practice should the Ethiopian Jews follow in Israel today? In my opinion, there is no need for them to change their custom, and they have no obligation to follow Rabbi Moshe ben Machir's version. Each individual is free to follow the ancient practice of his ancestors. In fact, the spontaneous, personal prayer even surpasses the fixed text. As a personal example, when Kes Rachamim Nega, of blessed memory, slept in our home, immediately upon awakening in the morning he recited his usual personal prayer, and then the accepted text of Modeh Ani.

Birkhot ha-Shahar (Morning Blessings)

Ethiopian Halakhah

The Beta Israel were accustomed to recite a full blessing invoking God's name for every act performed after awakening. Each individual recited the blessings in Ge'ez or in his spoken language, either Amharic or Tigrinya. These blessings also did not have a regular text – rather, each person expressed himself according to his ability or as he heard in his home.

Past and Present in Talmudic Halakhah

In most Jewish communities today, the morning blessings (Birkhot ha-Shahar) are recited in the synagogue, and they form an integral part of the daily prayer book. In Talmudic times, however, the individual recited these blessings while performing daily activities. The name of God was included in the blessing. In later periods, Jews cease to follow this custom, and the Geonim wrote that this was perhaps due to the possibility that the hands might be ritually unclean. Instead,

---

6. *Lamentations Rabbati* 3:8.
7. Herman, *Ma'agal hayei ha-yom*, 43.

individuals would recite the morning blessings at the beginning of the morning service in the synagogue.

The Recommended Custom in Israel

I find no need to change the custom of Beta Israel – each individual should follow his ancestral custom. Those who followed the custom of reciting the blessing and then immediately performing the action as described in the blessing should continue this practice, and to invoke God's name. If possible, one should perform *netilat yadaim*, ritual washing of the hands, beforehand.

Birkat Asher Yatzar (The Blessing after Using the Bathroom)

Ethiopian Halakhah

This blessing was not known in Ethiopia.

Past and Present in Talmudic Halakhah

"Each time a person defecates or urinates, even just one drop, he should wash his hands with water and recite *Asher yatzar*."[8] The accepted text used today is "Blessed are You, Lord our God, King of the universe, Who has fashioned humans with wisdom and created within them many openings and many cavities. It is obvious and known before Your throne of glory that if but one of them were to be ruptured or but one of them were to be blocked, it would be impossible to survive and to stand before You. Blessed are You, God, Who heals all flesh and performs wonders" (from *Tefillat Kol Peh* prayer book).

The Recommended Custom in Israel

We may understand why the Beta Israel did not recite this blessing, as in Ethiopia, bodily elimination is considered a bestial act, completely disconnected from all that is sacred. However, the basis of the *Asher yatzar* blessing is proper functioning of the bodily systems, and clearly, we should bless and thank God for every drop. Thus Jews should recite this blessing each time we use the bathroom. As Rabbi Yitzhak Yosef writes:

> After a person eliminates, either urination or defecation, he should wash his hands and recite *Asher yatzar*. He should consider the wondrous wisdom of the Holy One, blessed be He, the manner in which He has fashioned

---

8. *Shulhan arukh ha-mekutzar*, *Orah Haim*, ch. 1, par. 27, Laws of washing the hands before a meal.

humans with all their physical systems that are formed of many cells, with each cell functioning in an exact manner. Many cells protect the body from the thousands of bacteria that enter the body each moment. For all this, we must thank God with joy for His favor. We must thank Him for our digestive system, which saves our body from various diseases and enables it to survive. In this blessing, we pray before "God's throne of glory," to refute the opinion of heretics who say that God does not oversee the material world. "Performs wonders" – beccause He preserves the spirit within the human body, thus connecting the spiritual element with the material element. This is because He "heals all flesh," He keeps the individual healthy and preserves the soul within the body.[9]

❧ *Birkhot ha-Nehenin* (Blessings of Praise)

Ethiopian Halakah
These blessings were unknown in Ethiopia.

Past and Present in Talmudic Halakhah
Blessings over food and scents are called *birkhot ha-nehenin* (literally, "blessings over things we enjoy").[10] The blessings over food are:

- For bread: *ha-motzi lehem min ha-aretz* (Who brings forth bread from the earth)
- For other prepared grain-based foods (such as cakes, crackers, pasta, and so on): *Borei minei mezonot* (Creator of varieties of nourishment)
- For wine and grape juice: *Borei pri ha-gefen* (Creator of the fruit of the vine)
- For tree fruit and nuts: *Borei pri ha-etz* (Creator of the fruit of the tree)
- For vegetables, as well as fruits picked directly from the ground: *Borei pri ha-adamah* (Creator of the fruit of the earth)
- For other foods and drinks: *she-ha-kol nihiyah bi-dvaro* (by Whose word all things came to be)

These blessings are also called "introductory blessings," because they are recited prior to eating. The blessings after eating are called "concluding blessings," and they are:

- After a meal: Birkat ha-Mazon (Grace after Meals)

---

9. *Yalkut Yosef*, "Awakening in the Morning," 481.
10. Herman, *Ma'agal hayei ha-yom*.

- After *mezonot* foods, and, with variations, after consuming foods from the seven special species of the Land of Israel: *al ha-mihiyah* (for the produce of the field), also called Birkat me-ein Shalosh
- After other foods and drinks: *Borei nefashot* (Creator of many kinds of living beings)

(See further information below in the "Grace after Meals" section.)

The blessings over scents are *Borei shemen arev* (Creator of pleasant oil), *ha-noten rei'ah tov ba-peirot* (Who gives fruits a pleasant smell), *Borei atzei besamim* (Creator of scented trees), *Borei isvei besamim* (Creator of scented grasses), *Borei minei besamim* (Creator of many types of fragrances). We do not recite a concluding blessing over scents, because a scent does not satisfy us as food does.

As noted, the blessings of praise were instituted by the Sages. The Talmud explains: "Rabbi Yehudah said in the name of Samuel: To enjoy anything of this world without a benediction is like making personal use of things consecrated to Heaven, since it says, 'The earth is the Lord's, and the fullness thereof' (Psalms 24:1)."[11] A blessing is a request of God to enjoy this world, and thus after the blessing, the end of this same verse is fulfilled – "and the world was given to human beings."

The Recommended Custom in Israel

The first generation in Israel who are used to reciting spontaneous blessings may continue their custom, and it is even preferable for them to do so. The second generation may find it difficult to follow this practice, and thus they should learn the blessings according to the common practice today.

Itbarech Israel Blessing

Ethiopian Halakhah

Members of the Beta Israel community followed the practice of reciting *Itbarech Egziabher amlake Israel* (With blessings to the King of Israel) before performing a mitzvah, and before eating any food, without distinguishing between different types of foods. This blessing was known to most and recited from memory, such that one who could not recite it smoothly was considered ignorant. The content of the blessing is as follows:

---

11. Babylonian Talmud, *Berakhot* 35a.

God is One and He is the God of Israel, He is responsible for the Exodus from Egypt and revelation on Mount Sinai, He is the first and the last, may He be blessed and His Name be blessed, in Heaven above and on the earth below, there is no other.

It is like a detailed version of *she-ha-kol*. The theological concept at the basis of this text carries supreme meaning. The major demand incumbent on the Jew – who is surrounded by a pagan environment – is to recognize the oneness of God. In such a reality, it is important to mention God's unity at every opportunity.

Past and Present in Talmudic Halakhah

According to tradition, the text of the blessings was determined by Ezra and his court, as explained above.

The Recommended Custom in Israel

Those who are accustomed to reciting the Ethiopian blessing *Itbarech Egziabher* may continue using this text, and there is no need to require them to learn Hebrew blessings. If the person also knows the Hebrew blessing, he may recite both. The order of the blessings is not important, and there is no suspicion of a *berakhah le-vatalah*, a blessing recited in vain. One who is not familiar with *Itbarech Egziabher* (usually the youth) is not required to find someone to teach it to him, and he should use the Hebrew blessings. But a person who searches out a teacher for the Ethiopian blessing due to his connection with his past and sense of identity is deserving of praise.

❦ Blessing for Washing Hands

Ethiopian Halakhah

According to Beta Israel custom, a person should not eat without washing the hands, if there is water nearby. If not, one may eat without washing hands. Before a meal, everyone sits down, and a child hands the washing cup to each person, beginning with the oldest and ending with the youngest. There is no obligation to dry the hands. Avraham Yardai has noted that one must distinguish between a practice based on halakhah and one based on culture and technology, such as drying the hands with a towel after washing them. In Ethiopia, the Beta Israel did not dry their hands, due to the technical fact that there were no towels. Thus they do not have the obligation of drying.

Washing the hands was in preparation for the main act of eating, and thus the

Beta Israel did not recite a blessing for this. After washing the hands, they began to eat. If there was a *kes* present among the diners, the *kes* recited a blessing. If there was no *kes*, the oldest diner recited a blessing. After the honored person took the first bite, everyone else could begin. The meal continued for some time – yet the length was not important, rather what the participants did during this time. Following the meal, a child once again handed the washing cup to each diner so they might wash their hands. Some wiped their hands dry after this washing, perhaps because they had eaten with their hands, and washing alone was not sufficient to clean them.

Past and Present in Talmudic Halakhah

In order to understand the source of the Sages' ruling about washing hands before eating bread, we should explain several principles about ritual impurity of the body. According to the Torah, the entire body is considered one unit for the purposes of ritual purity and impurity – either the entire body is pure, or it is entirely impure. In other words, if any one part of the body touches an impure item, the entire body becomes impure. For example, if one touches a dead body with his foot, one's entire body is rendered impure. Purification must be performed for the entire body. Thus when a person immerses himself in the *mikveh* in order to purify himself, he must immerse his entire body in the water all at once, as the *kohanim* did in biblical times. But the Sages determined that hands had a special status. Because they are involved in a plethora of activities and touch a wide variety of materials, they get dirtier than the rest of the body, and a person is likely to touch impure items without noticing. Thus the Sages ruled that the hands are considered impure, and they are purified by washing with water.[12]

This ruling underwent several stages. During the First Temple period, King Solomon ruled that hands should be washed before sacrifices (*kodashim*) – any person who intended to touch the sacrificial animal must first wash his hands, and if he touched it without washing, the meat was rendered impure and could not be eaten. During the Second Temple period, the followers of Shammai and Hillel ruled that hands were impure for *terumah* (tithe) as well. A person who touched a *terumah* without first washing the hands rendered it unfit for consumption, and in order to avoid the possibility of it being consumed in error, it had to be burned.[13] At the time of the destruction of the Second Temple, the

---

12. Rashi, Babylonian Talmud, *Shabbat* 14a.
13. Babylonian Talmud, *Shabbat* 14.

Sages broadened the scope of this mitzvah, and ruled that it was forbidden to eat bread without washing the hands beforehand.[14]

The Recommended Custom in Israel

Due to the similarity between customs, the Beta Israel may continue with the practice they followed in Ethiopia. Because in Ethiopia they washed hands before every mitzvah, on Shabbat and holidays they should wash hands before saying Kiddush over wine, and immediately following Kiddush, they should say *ha-motzi*, the blessing over bread. After washing the hands, one is permitted to talk about things related to the meal.

Grace after Meals

Ethiopian Halakhah

After washing the hands following the meal, the *kes* recites a blessing of thanks to God. The content of this blessing is very similar to the mainstream Birkat ha-Mazon (Grace after Meals). He says: "May what we have eaten satisfy us; may what we have drunk heal us; and may what we have left be given to the children." He adds a request that God continue to provide with His grace, that they want for nothing, and that He enable success in all their endeavors. The other diners listen to the blessing and answer "Amen." After the blessing, each individual adds his own personal blessing, and then the central plate is passed to the circle of the young children.

Past and Present in Talmudic Halakhah

Three concluding blessings are recited after eating: Grace after Meals, *al ha-mihiyah* (for the produce of the field, also called Birkat me-ein Shalosh), and *Borei nefashot* (Creator of many kinds of living beings).[15] The Grace after Meals, recited after eating bread, is a commandment of biblical origin, as the verse specifies: "And you will eat and be satisfied, and bless the Lord your God" (Deuteronomy 8:10). According to the Sages' interpretation, the exact number of blessings contained within is also derived from the Torah: "'And you will eat and be satisfied, and bless – this is the blessing of 'Who feeds'; 'the Lord your God' – this is the *zimmun* (invitation to bless); 'for the land' – this is the blessing for the land; 'the good' – this is 'Who builds Jerusalem.'"[16] The fourth blessing, *ha-tov ve-ha-meitiv*

---

14. Babylonian Talmud, *Hullin* 106a; Herman, *Ma'agal hayei ha-yom*.
15. Herman, *Ma'agal hayei ha-yom*.
16. Babylonian Talmud, *Berakhot* 48b.

(Who is good and does good to all) was added after the Bar Kochba revolt. The *me-ein shalosh* blessing is recited after eating grain-based foods and any of the *shivat ha-minim* (seven species that are special to the Land of Israel). It is called *me-ein shalosh* (like the three") because it is similar to Grace after Meals, which originally contained three blessings. *Borei nefashot* is recited after eating fruits and vegetables that are not included in the seven species, and after eating foods that do not grow from the earth, such as meat, milk, water, and eggs. It was instituted by the Sages. These blessings also have rules and quantities that determine in which cases we should recite the blessing, and which blessing we should recite.

The Recommended Custom in Israel

The first generation of Beta Israel is permitted to continue their custom. The second generation and those of the first generation who are able to do so should recite the blessing formulated by the Sages. Each person is permitted to choose the variant he feels comfortable with – Ashkenazic, Yemenite, or Sephardic – because in the final analysis, the goal of the blessing is to worship God.

The Blessing over Injera

Ethiopian Halakhah

Before we explain what blessing the Beta Israel recited over injera in Ethiopia, we must explain what injera is. Injera is the "bread" of Ethiopia, without which a meal is not a meal. It is made of flour and water only. As opposed to Western bread, injera is not baked, but cooked. The dough is poured into a large pan, covered with a thin cover. After a few minutes of cooking, the cover is removed and the injera is ready. The dough is made of a soft batter that is very liquid. As with all other foods, the Beta Israel recite *Itbarech Egziabher* over it and then begin eating.

Past and Present in Talmudic Halakhah

Bread is the basic food, and thus it has a special blessing – *ha-motzi lehem min ha-aretz* (Who brings forth bread from the earth) – even though technically it is made of a grain that grows in the earth, and thus we might think we should recite over it *borei pri ha-adamah* (Creator of the fruit of the earth). We recite *ha-motzi* only over bread made from flour of the five principal types of grain (wheat, barley, spelt, rye, and oats). The Sages defined "bread" carefully, distinguishing between it and *pat ha-ba'ah be-kisnin*, over which we recite *borei minei mezonot*. Because the definitions of these terms were based on methods of baking and eating in Talmudic times, they underwent adaptation as reality changed.[17]

The Rishonim debated the exact definition of *pat ha-ba'ah be-kisnin*. Some thought it was bread baked with fruit juice, sugar, and oil, as the taste was not like regular bread baked only with water. Others thought it was bread baked with water, and then filled with fillings such as nuts or almonds, and because its taste was different than regular bread, the proper blessing for it was *mezonot*. Still others considered it to be a dry, crunchy cracker. The *Shulhan Arukh* explains these three interpretations.[18] According to all opinions, however, for flour mixed with water only and then baked, one should recite *ha-motzi*.

The Recommended Custom in Israel

One who wishes to recite the blessing as done in Ethiopia may continue this custom. One who wishes to add to this custom and recite the special blessing according to the tradition of the Sages is permitted to recite both blessings. However, scholars debate which blessing should be recited over injera. Some prefer *mezonot*, since injera is not baked. Others maintain that the injera flour is not made of the five main grains and therefore one should recite *she-ha-kol*. Still others argue that in order to fulfill the mitzvah beyond a doubt, one should first recite *ha-motzi* over true bread, and then eat the injera. In my opinion, because the halakhic definitions were determined during the period of the Sages, it is possible that they are based on the fact that in their time, bread was made from the five principal grains. In Ethiopian culture, however, injera is a crucial component of the diet, and thus it is appropriate to accord it the blessing over bread – *ha-motzi*. I believe that if teff (the plant from which injera flour is made) had been present in the Sages' environment, it would have been granted the status of one of the principal grains. The reason that it is not counted as one of them is only technical. Furthermore, today the Ethiopians add regular wheat flour to the injera batter, and thus I believe that when eating injera, we should recite *ha-motzi* and Grace after Meals.

---

17. Herman, *Ma'agal hayei ha-yom*.
18. *Orah Haim* 168:7.

3. Shabbat

❧ The Sanctity of Shabbat

Ethiopian Halakhah

According to the sacred books of the Ethiopian Jewish community, the sanctity of Shabbat is very great, and exceeds that of all other mitzvot and the holidays. According to Ethiopian tradition, the angel responsible for Shabbat is named Sanbat, and he was created before the creation of the world. He rules over the sun and the rain, and guards all those who take shelter in his shadow. Thousands of angels submit to his authority, and he will show us the way to Jerusalem when the time of redemption arrives. Shabbat is not one of the days of the week – it is beyond time.

Past and Present in Talmudic Halakhah

The list of sacred dates in the book of Leviticus begins with the commandment of Shabbat,[1] and among all these, Shabbat is the only one that is included in the Ten Commandments.[2] The prophets connect observance of Shabbat to the fate of the children of Israel, the kingship of the House of David, and the rebuilding of Jerusalem.[3] "The Torah, the Prophets, and the Writings state that Shabbat is equivalent to all the other mitzvot in the Torah."[4] The sanctity of Shabbat exceeds that of all other sacred acts, its blessing exceeds that of all others, and thus it was sanctified and blessed at the beginning of Creation.[5] It is the source of blessing for the other days of the week, and thus Israel was commanded to keep the Shabbat in seven of the weekly Torah portions: Be-shalah, Yitro, Mishpatim, Ki

---

1. Leviticus 23:1–3.
2. Exodus 20:8–11.
3. Isaiah 55:2–6; Jeremiah 17:21–27; Ezekiel 20:12–24; Nehemiah 9:14.
4. *Midrash Tanhuma*, Parashat Metzora.
5. Herman, *Ma'agal ha-hagim* (Prolog, 2005).

Tisa, Va-yak'hel, Emor, and Va-ethanan. This is to teach us that all seven days of the week depend on Shabbat. We recall Shabbat daily when we introduce the Psalm of the day by declaring, *Ha-yom yom rishon be-Shabbat* (meaning "Today is the first day of the week" – literally, "Today is the first day of Shabbat"), *yom sheni be-Shabbat* (the second day of Shabbat), and so forth. Shabbat is the basic principle of faith in God, that He created the world in six days and rested on the seventh. A person who does not keep the Shabbat has no faith, and so the Sages compared one who violates Shabbat to an idol worshipper and heretic who denies the entire Torah.[6]

The Torah gives three reasons for observing Shabbat:

1. Commemoration of the Exodus – "Observe the Sabbath day to keep it holy, as the Lord your God commanded you.... And you shall remember that you were a slave in the land of Egypt, and the Lord your God bought you out from there by a mighty hand and by an outstretched arm; therefore, the Lord your God commanded you to keep the Sabbath day" (Deuteronomy 5:11, 14).
2. Commemoration of the creation of the world – "Remember the Sabbath day, to keep it holy.... For in six days, the Lord made heaven and earth, the sea, and all that is in them, and rested on the seventh day, wherefore the Lord blessed the Sabbath day, and hallowed it" (Exodus 20:7–11).
3. Social purpose – "Six days you shall do your work, but on the seventh day you shall rest, in order that your ox and your donkey shall rest, and the son of your handmaid, and the stranger, may be refreshed" (Exodus 23:12).

These reasons have a modern educational message: negating dependence on the material, and placing the life of the spirit at the center of human aspiration. Thus both the Beta Israel and Talmudic Judaism grant Shabbat a special status. But we may identify significant differences between Ethiopian halakhah of Shabbat and Talmudic halakhah – for example, in the laws of heating food on Shabbat and saving lives on Shabbat. For the Beta Israel, these two acts are completely forbidden. Shabbat is absolute, and cannot be overridden for any other mitzvah in the Torah. But in Talmudic law, both saving lives and circumcision must be performed on Shabbat.

---

6. *Arukh ha-Shulhan, Orah Haim* 242.

The Recommended Custom in Israel

As we have seen, the two communities both relate to Shabbat equally – the sanctity of Shabbat and its importance are equivalent for the Beta Israel and Talmudic Judaism.

✥ Erev Shabbat – Friday Afternoon

Ethiopian Halakhah

In Ethiopia, preparations for Shabbat began on Thursday – the Beta Israel washed clothes, cleaned house, ground flour for baking *dabu* (challah), and cooked food. On Friday afternoon, the family ceased all housework and outside work, and everyone went down to the river to wash their clothes and themselves. They dressed in white and returned to their villages. They did not leave any fires lit in the house. After sundown, everyone gathered in the synagogue for Shabbat services. The *kohanim* arrived at the synagogue first, before the rest of the community. After the Shabbat service ended, the participants returned home and recited blessings. They did not recite Kiddush on Shabbat eve – this was done only in the morning. They ate the Shabbat meal and went to bed. The *kohanim* woke up when they were called to prayer, and then the rest of the community joined them.

Past and Present in Talmudic Halakhah

The Sages limited work on Fridays so that individuals would be free to prepare for Shabbat, and not begin Shabbat at the last minute.[7] This was based on the verse regarding the manna, "And it shall come to pass on the sixth day that they shall prepare that which they bring in, and it shall be twice as much as they gather daily" (Exodus 16:5) – from this the Sages derived that it is a mitzvah to prepare on Friday everything that is needed for Shabbat. "Even if one has many retainers at his service, one should try to prepare personally something of the Shabbat needs, so as to thereby honor it.... One should not say 'I will not compromise my dignity' where preparations for Shabbat are involved, for it is to one's privilege to honor Shabbat."[8] Even a Torah scholar who has other people to prepare Shabbat for him should make a personal effort to prepare something for Shabbat. The Talmud names several great scholars who participated in Shabbat

---

7. Herman, *Ma'agal ha-hagim*.
8. *Shulhan Arukh* 250:1.

preparations.[9] Rabba salted fish; Rabbi Hisda chopped vegetables finely; Rabbah and Rav Yosef chopped wood for the fire in the oven; Rabbi Abbahu and Rabbi Zeira kindled the fire for cooking. Rabbi Hunah and Rabbi Pappa prepared the Shabbat candles, and Rabbi Nahman cleaned the house, cleared away the weekday items, and brought in the Shabbat items.

The Recommended Custom in Israel
No matter where we live, Shabbat has a special sanctity. For this reason, everyone prepares for Shabbat in advance.

❧ Beginning of Shabbat
Ethiopian Halakhah
In Ethiopia, there was no defined time for beginning Shabbat, as most people did not own clocks. Preparations began in the morning and continued until dusk. People began Shabbat at sunset.

Past and Present in Talmudic Halakhah
According to the Sages, the Jewish day begins on the preceding evening, in accordance with the verse "And there was evening and there was morning, one day" (Genesis 1:5). This means that Shabbat begins on Friday evening. Some say that it is a mitzvah to add time from the weekday to Shabbat, at the beginning and at the conclusion. This mitzvah is called *tosefet Shabbat* (addition to Shabbat). The book of Nehemiah documents Shabbat as beginning before the onset of darkness: "And it came to pass that, when the gates of Jerusalem began to be dark before the Sabbath, I commanded that the doors should be shut, and commanded that they should not be opened till after the Sabbath" (Nehemiah 13:19). We find additional documentation of this in the writings of Josephus, who states that Caesar Augustus commanded the provincial governor not to require the Jews to appear in court on Shabbat or on Friday afternoon after the ninth hour.[10] During the Tannaitic period, *tosefet Shabbat* was limited to the time immediately preceding sunset, and was defined as any additional period.

The custom practiced by the majority today in Israel regarding the time when Shabbat begins is as follows: in Tel Aviv and most other cities in Israel, twenty-two minutes before sunset; in Haifa, thirty minutes before sunset; and in Jerusalem,

---

9. Babylonian Talmud, *Shabbat* 119a.
10. *Antiquities* 16:6:2.

forty minutes before sunset. According to Rabbi Ovadia Yosef, *ztz"l*, in Jerusalem as well, one should begin Shabbat twenty minutes before sunset, and no earlier, as specified by the Sephardic sages of Jerusalem of previous generations. According to Rabbi Ovadia Yosef, the custom of welcoming Shabbat forty minutes before sunset is a later custom practiced following the arrival of Ashkenazic Jews in Jerusalem. The earliest time at which one may welcome the Shabbat is *plag ha-Minhah* (seventy-five minutes before sunset), and the latest time is just before sunset. In many cities in Israel, a siren is sounded before Shabbat begins. This custom commemorates the ancient practice of blowing the shofar in the Temple to declare the beginning of Shabbat. In Israel, the Shabbat times are publicized in calendars and newspapers.[11]

The Recommended Custom in Israel

The Ethiopian Jews should follow the times practiced throughout the Jewish world. In all matters related to observing sacred times and related issues, they should follow the practice of the general Jewish community.

Lighting Candles

Ethiopian Halakhah

On Friday before Shabbat, the Beta Israel did not light fires or candles for Shabbat (before Shabbat began, they did not begin any labor that was forbidden on Shabbat, so that it would not end after Shabbat had begun). Further, they did not make use of fire on Shabbat, even if it was lit before Shabbat. Still, in several locations in Ethiopia, people left a candle or fire lit for the purpose of light only. After this fire went out, it was forbidden to touch it. But they did not light candles to welcome Shabbat.

Past and Present in Talmudic Halakhah

This issue became one of the well-known points of contention between the Pharisees and the Karaites, based on their differing interpretations of the verse "You shall kindle no fire throughout your habitations upon the Sabbath day" (Exodus 35:3). According to the Sages, it was forbidden to kindle fire on Shabbat, but it was permitted to leave a fire lit if it had been kindled before Shabbat.[12] The Karaites, by contrast, asserted that the verse meant it was forbidden to leave any fire lit

---

11. Herman, *Ma'agal ha-hagim*.
12. Ibid.

during Shabbat, whether candle, fire in the oven, or on a gas hob. The Karaites thus sat in complete darkness on Shabbat eve, they had no fire lit for warmth in the winter, and they ate only cold food. The rabbinic world did not stop at verbal debates with the Karaites, but instituted decrees and customs "to restrain the Karaites."[13] Two mitzvot are based on this approach: the blessing over lighting the candles, and the custom of eating hot food on Shabbat. The Talmud even states that we must light candles for Shabbat, although it does not specify the blessing to recite.

The Geonim debated whether one should recite a blessing over candle lighting. Possibly, rejection of Karaite practice was one of the reasons for requiring the blessing. Today, the custom is to light candles in order to honor Shabbat and also for enjoyment of Shabbat. Preparing the candles and lighting them before Shabbat are to "honor Shabbat," while eating and other activities done by their light are considered "enjoyment of Shabbat." In ancient times, on weekdays the Jews ate their evening meal before dark, and afterwards the members of the household went to sleep until dawn, so there was no need for nighttime illumination. But on Shabbat the situation was different, because they had to eat the Shabbat meal after dark. Today, since we use electricity for lighting, most rabbis permit the use of electricity instead of candles. It is preferable to light candles, since this serves as a special sign that the lights were lit in honor of Shabbat. But if candles are not available, one may recite the blessing over electric lights. This mitzvah is a requirement for each household, and it does not matter which person in the house lights. But the custom is for the husband to prepare the candles while the wife lights them, since she is busy with preparations, and the candles are part of "honoring Shabbat."[14]

The Recommended Custom in Israel

Lighting Shabbat candles has become a very special mitzvah for the Jewish people, one that is much loved by those who perform it. The candles bring calm and peace to the home, create a special spiritual atmosphere, and lead to family togetherness. Lighting candles is a clear sign of a Jewish home. Thus Ethiopian

---

13. See, for example, Babylonian Talmud, *Yoma* 2a.
14. Another explanation is that the woman was responsible for "extinguishing the light of the world [Eve caused Adam's death], as in the verse 'the spirit of man is the lamp of the Lord' (Proverbs 20:27). Thus the woman is the one who should keep the mitzvah of candle lighting" (Jerusalem Talmud, *Shabbat* 2:6). Every woman who lights Shabbat candles atones for this sin, as women's souls are all part of Eve's soul (*Genesis Rabbah* 7:8).

Jews who find it very difficult to light Shabbat candles may continue the custom of not lighting, but those who understand that this practice has special import, particularly the younger generation, should light, especially since the actual lighting takes place before Shabbat begins.

❦ Electric Hot Plate

Ethiopian Halakhah

According to Ethiopian tradition, it was forbidden to leave a fire lit from Friday into Shabbat. This meant that in Ethiopia, the Beta Israel ate cold food on Shabbat. It was forbidden to heat food in any way. There were no electric hot plates in the villages, but even if there were, their use would have been forbidden. Thus when the *kesim* came to Israel, they were very surprised at the use of this appliance on Shabbat.

Past and Present in Talmudic Halakhah

As mentioned, according to the Sages' tradition, the verse "You shall not kindle fire in any of your dwelling places on the Sabbath day" does not forbid us from leaving a fire lit, and thus it is permitted to place cooked food on the fire on Shabbat eve. But if the food is not completely cooked, we must not place it directly on the fire, so that we are not tempted to "stir the coals" or hasten the cooking process, thus violating the biblical prohibition against kindling and cooking.[15]

Under certain circumstances, the Sages permitted placing cooked food directly on the fire. According to the Rif and the Rambam, we may place only a completely cooked dish on the fire – meaning that if it continues to cook, its taste will be ruined. In halakhic terminology, this is called "dried-up and ruined." This way, there is no fear that we will stir the coals, because doing so would heighten the flames and ruin the food even more. According to Rashi, we are permitted to place on an open fire even a partially cooked dish, which the halakhah calls "a Ben Drusa dish." (Ben Drusa was a well-known robber, who rushed to consume the meat he stole, and did not wait for it to be completely cooked. Some say he ate it when it was one-third cooked, others said half-cooked.) Rashi permits this even if the dish becomes "dried-up but tasty" on Shabbat.

The *Shulhan Arukh* gives these two opinions without giving a definite ruling. According to most commentators, the *Shulhan Arukh* rules according to Rashi's opinion, and this is the practice followed by Sephardic and Eastern communities.

---

15. Herman, *Ma'agal ha-hagim*.

The Rema, whose opinion is followed by the Ashkenazic communities, also ruled according to Rashi. But the *Mishnah Berurah* disagrees with the Rema, and rules that one should rely on his decision only when one has no choice. In contrast, the Hazon Ish and other contemporary commentators accepted the ruling of the Rema. When the fire is covered, there is no reason to suspect that one might "stir the coals," and all opinions permit placing a dish that is not completely cooked on a covered fire before Shabbat begins. Most rabbis do not consider the electric hot plate to be an open fire, and thus permit placing any kind of food on it on Friday afternoon, before Shabbat. Despite this, it is praiseworthy for all the foods to be completely cooked before Shabbat begins. On Shabbat, one may place on the hot plate only foods that are completely cooked, and some say that one should place a separation under the pot, such as a piece of aluminum foil or an empty vessel.

The Recommended Custom in Israel

One who considers use of the electric hot plate or any other source of heat as a violation of Shabbat, as was the case in Ethiopia, may continue to follow the ancestral custom. This should not be considered a Karaite practice, since their motivations are different, as the Ridbaz wrote.[16] In any case, the Ethiopian Jews consider use of the hot plate like use of real fire. In the world of Ethiopian Jewry, what counts is the end result, and not the method of warming – while for the Sages, debate on this issue focuses on the manner of warming the food. Still, the second generation of Ethiopian Jews, who have become accustomed to the reality in Israel, will consider eating cold food to be detrimental to the enjoyment of Shabbat, and thus they are permitted to use the warming methods accepted in mainstream halakhah. This should not be considered a violation of the proverb "Do not foresake the Torah of your mother" (Proverbs 1:8).

❊ Kiddush over *Meswait* (Bread)

Ethiopian Halakhah

In Ethiopia, every family who came to the synagogue brought a loaf of bread, called *dabo* in Amharic, *kitche* in Tigrinya, or *meswait* in Ge'ez, and some alcoholic beverage – "every man shall give as he is able" (Deuteronomy 16:17). Following the morning prayer, which began at sunrise (*sanvat*), members of the community brought their food, which they had prepared on Friday, and everyone

---

16. Responsa of Ridbaz, part 7:5.

ate together. First, the *kohen* recited the blessing: "May the Lord, God of Israel be blessed, Lord of all living things and souls … Who sanctifies the Shabbat." A younger *kohen* then divided the *dabo* and handed out *birkata nikra* (the central portion) to the congregants. Then they ate the rest of the bread, and the other food and drinks. My grandfather, *ztz"l*, recounted the custom of first removing a piece from the middle portion of the bread. They then cut the other two pieces into six pieces each, making twelve pieces total, to symbolize the twelve tribes.

Past and Present in Talmudic Halakhah

There is no record of this custom in Talmudic sources.

The Recommended Custom in Israel

The Beta Israel may continue to adhere to this custom in modern times.

🎕 Kiddush over Wine

Ethiopian Halakhah

Beta Israel custom forbids the use of wine for any reason, even for performing a mitzvah. Wine (as distinct from other alcoholic beverages) is considered to bear evil spirits. One who consumes wine is compared to an idol worshipper. The negative view of wine derives from the common use of wine for idol worship in Ethiopia. When communication with Jews in other parts of the world began, Jews from abroad brought wine to Ethiopia, and then the Ethiopian Jews began to recite Kiddush (the blessing over wine) on Shabbat.

Past and Present in Talmudic Halakhah

The Torah forbids drinking wine that was consecrated for idol worship.[17] The Sages ruled that we must not drink the wine of non-Jews, for two reasons: 1) as it might have been used in idol worship, and 2) "due to their daughters" – drinking the wine of a non-Jew might bring Jews in contact with non-Jews, and eventually lead to intermarriage.[18]

The Recommended Custom in Israel

The first generation of Ethiopian Jews in Israel, who denigrate wine as a symbol of idol worship, are not required to say the blessing over wine on Shabbat. But the second generation has undergone a transformation in the attitude toward wine

---

17. Rambam, *Mishneh Torah*, Hilkhot Ma'akhalot Assurot 11:1.
18. Herman, *Ma'agal ha-hagim*.

as a drink designated for idol worship. If they want to continue to say the blessing only over bread, they may do so. But Kiddush over wine has become a clearly recognized symbol of Shabbat for every Jew, and so they should say the blessing over kosher wine, as is the practice among the other Jewish communities.

❧ Reading the Torah on Shabbat

Ethiopian Halakhah

In Ethiopia, reading the Torah was not part of the prayer service. Following the service, the congregation went out to the synagogue courtyard, and they read from the Torah there. The *kohanim* opened the Orit (Torah) and taught the people. The *kes* read in Ge'ez, while another person, usually a young *kes* or someone studying to become a *kes*, translated into the spoken language. The listeners could ask questions during the reading, and the *kes* responded calmly. There was no defined section to be read – they began at the beginning of the book and read until the *kes* decided to stop. No one got up without the permission of the *kes*. Everyone sat respectfully and listened to the *kes* and the translator. All this took place on Shabbat only.

Past and Present in Talmudic Halakhah

When did the custom of reading the Torah in the synagogue begin?[19] The Torah commands the king to read from the Torah,[20] and mandates the Hak'hel ceremony in which the Torah is read before the entire nation,[21] but there is no specific command for the individual to read the Torah. The Sages asserted that the custom of reading from the Torah on Shabbat and holidays was derived from Moses: "Moses instituted the practice for the Israelites of reading from the Torah on Shabbat and holidays and Rosh Hodesh."[22] According to midrashic sources, the practice of reading the Torah on Mondays and Thursdays and during the Minhah service on Shabbat also originated in ancient times: "Thus the Prophets and the Elders instituted for them the custom of reading from the Torah on Shabbat, Mondays, and Thursdays."[23] A *baraita* in the Babylonian Talmud says it was instituted by the Prophets:

---

19. Herman, *Ma'agal ha-hagim*.
20. Deuteronomy 17:19.
21. Deuteronomy 31:11.
22. Jerusalem Talmud, *Megillah* 4, 1, 75a.
23. *Mekhilta de-Rabbi Ishmael*, ed. Horowitz-Rabin (Jerusalem, 5730), *Be-shalah*.

For it was taught: "And they went three days in the wilderness, and found no water" (Exodus 15:22), upon which those who expound verses metaphorically said: water means nothing but Torah, as it says: "Ho, every one that thirsts, come for water" (Isaiah 55:1). It thus means that as they went three days without Torah, they immediately became exhausted. The prophets among them rose and enacted that they should publicly read the law on Shabbat, make a break on Sunday, read again on Monday, make a break again on Tuesday and Wednesday, read again on Thursday and then make a break on Friday so that they should not go three days without Torah.[24]

Another *baraita* states that Ezra instituted the practice, apparently as part of his attempts during Second Temple times to expand knowledge of Torah among the people.[25] The Talmudic debate resolves the contradiction by stating that the Prophets decreed that one person should go up to the Torah on these days and read three verses, or three readers should go up and read one verse each, for the *kohanim*, Levites, and Israelites. Later, Ezra decreed that three readers should go up and read at least ten verses total, corresponding to "ten *batlanim*," meaning ten men who are *mevatel* their work (i.e., do not work) but who dedicate their time to Torah studies.[26]

The shared principle revealed in all these literary sources is that the ruling regarding reading the Torah on Mondays, Thursdays, and Minhah on Shabbat originated in ancient times. The Tosafot wrote that the Prophets ruled to read on Mondays and Thursdays because these were times for making petitions and asking forgiveness, since Moses had gone up to Mount Sinai to receive the two tablets on a Thursday, and descended forty days later, on a Monday.[27] The number of readers was apparently set in the Tannaitic period, just after the destruction of the Temple: "On Monday, and on Thursday, and on the Sabbath at the afternoon service, three persons read from the Torah; they must not reduce the number nor may they add to it.... On the first days of the months [*roshei hodashim*] and on the intermediate festival days [*hol ha-moed*], four read; they must not reduce the number nor add to it."[28]

As noted, in ancient times the Sages decreed that they should not go three days without a public Torah reading. One of the reasons for this was that reading

---

24. Babylonian Talmud, *Baba Kama* 82a.
25. See Nehemiah, chapter 8.
26. Baba Kama 82a.
27. Baba Kama 82a, s.v. "in order to."
28. Mishnah, *Megillah* 4:1–2.

the Torah reminds us of the giving of the Torah at Sinai, and each time we read, we renew our acceptance of it. The Midrash explains, "My children, if you read this Torah portion at its appointed time, every year, I will consider it as if you were standing before Me at Mount Sinai and receiving the Torah."[29]

The Recommended Custom in Israel

The first generation is permitted to continue their custom, but the second generation should accept the common Jewish practice.

❧ Weekly Portions

Ethiopian Halakhah

In Ethiopia, reading from the Torah was not part of the prayer service. After services, community members went out to the synagogue courtyard, and they read from the Torah there. The *kohanim* opened the Orit (Torah) and taught the people. The *kes* read in Ge'ez, while another person, usually a young *kes* or *kes* in training, translated into the spoken language. Listeners could ask questions during the reading, and the *kes* would respond patiently. The portion read was not predetermined; rather, the *kes* read topics he thought were important for the congregation to hear. He always began with the Ten Commandments and continued until he decided to stop. No one got up without permission from the *kes*. Everyone sat respectfully and listened to the *kes* and the translator. This custom of reading from the Torah was practiced only on Shabbat.

Past and Present in Talmudic Halakhah

The Babylonian Talmud notes that the Jews in Eretz Yisrael completed reading the entire Torah in three years, while in Babylonia, they completed it in one year. According to the Babylonian system, the Torah is divided into fifty-four sections called *sedarim*, and the reading ends on a regular date.[30] According to the method practiced in Eretz Yisrael, the Torah is divided into 154 *sedarim*. Some think that the three-and-a-half-year cycle had no relation to the yearly calendar, and apparently it was not uniform. Others assert that there were different customs for completing the three-and-a-half-year cycle, and the finishing point was not uniform. Still, the Jews united to complete the cycle together every seven

---

29. *Pesikta de-Rav Kahana* 12, s.v. "in the third month."
30. Herman, *Ma'agal ha-hagim*.

years, in order to complete the reading at the Hakhel gathering at the end of the Shemitah year on Sukkot.[31]

Some think that the annual cycle is the older custom, and was practiced in Eretz Yisrael until the time of Rabbi Yehudah ha-Nasi, and that the three-year cycle became widespread late in the Tannaitic period. The reason for the three-year custom was the long sermon that was added to the synagogue service, which limited the time available for reading the Torah. But in Babylonia, where the sermon in the synagogue was not as long as in Eretz Yisrael, there was enough time to read the long Torah portion, and so they finished the cycle in one year. Over the years, the sermon in the synagogue was shortened, both in Babylonia and in Eretz Yisrael, leaving more time available. In addition, the Babylonian influence in Eretz Yisrael was amplified, so that by the ninth century CE, the triennial cycle disappeared and was completely replaced by the annual cycle.

The Recommended Custom in Israel

Because reading the Torah is not an integral part of the service, and its significance is public learning, the *kesim* and Beta Israel community leaders may read the Torah as they did in Ethiopia. In other words, immediately after the service, they should recite the blessing over bread, then eat and drink, and then continue learning Torah. Second-generation Ethiopian Jews may prefer reading the Torah during the prayer service, as is the practice among the broader Jewish community.

❧ Marital Relations on Shabbat

Ethiopian Halakhah

According to Beta Israel tradition, it is absolutely forbidden to have marital relations on Shabbat, and the punishment for transgressing this prohibition is death. The book of Jubilees records a similar halakhah, which may be the source of the Beta Israel prohibition:

> Six days you will work, but the seventh day is the Sabbath of the Lord your God.... You will not do any work.... Every man who does any work on this day, who will lie with his wife...let him die. (50:7)

While Jubilees names the prohibition against marital relations as one of the forbidden labors on Shabbat, I think that this prohibition was accepted and

---

31. Deuteronomy 31:1–13.

preserved among the Ethiopian community until today as part of their zealousness regarding purity and impurity. Apparently, marital relations was forbidden because it was associated with impurity, as the Torah states: "And if the flow of seed go out from a man, then he shall bathe all his flesh in water, and be unclean until evening.... The woman also with whom a man shall lie carnally, they shall both bathe themselves in water, and be unclean until evening" (Leviticus 15:16, 18).

Past and Present in Talmudic Halakhah[32]

According to halakhah, having marital relations is not only permitted on Shabbat, it is a mitzvah. We may discern the general attitude of the Sages to marital relations from Rashi's commentary on the verse "You shall be holy" (Leviticus 19:2). Rashi writes that the requirement of the Jew to sanctify himself applies only to avoiding forbidden sexual relations – there is no requirement to avoid permitted relations: "Separate yourselves from sexual immorality and from sin, for wherever one finds a barrier against sexual immorality, one finds holiness."[33] From Rashi's comment, we learn that the sexual act itself is not innately sinful and does no damage to human sanctity. Therefore, there is no reason to forbid it on Shabbat. The Ramban's comment on this verse teaches that just as halakhically forbidden relations impede the attainment of sanctity, so does frequency and immersing oneself in permitted sexual relations:

> The Torah warns us regarding forbidden sexual partners and foods, and permitted sexual relations between man and wife, and the consumption of meat and wine. Still, one who has excessive desire may be consumed with having relations with his wife or his many wives, and to seek the company of gluttonous wine drinkers and meat eaters. He will speak as he wishes to these vile individuals, that there is no such prohibition in the Torah, and thus he will be a vile person within the delineations of the Torah. For this reason, after detailing the prohibitions that are explicitly forbidden, the Torah gives the general command that we should separate ourselves from the permitted. Thus one should limit sexual relations, as the Sages said, "So that Torah scholars

---

32. Rabbi Sharon Shalom, *Heter yehasei ishut be-Shabbat le-or iyun be-minhagei kehillat Beta Israel: Bein zurah le-mahut* [Permission for marital relations on Shabbat in light of the customs of the Beta Israel] (unpublished).
33. Rashi, Leviticus 19:2, s.v. "You shall be holy."

should not constantly be found with their wives like cocks,"³⁴ and should only have relations as needed to fulfill the mitzvah performed through it. He should sanctify himself through wine in limited quantity.³⁵

According to the Ramban, the mitzvah of "You shall be holy" demands that the individual also "limit sexual relations" that are permitted. The limitation of relations for Torah scholars to one day a week was designed to ensure that they would not be consumed with having relations with their wives. But his writing does not imply any significant positive or negative connection between the sanctity of Shabbat and sexual relations. If we had to decide on our own, we might assume that if such a connection exists, it is negative. Then what is the reason for the explanation in the Talmud that the Sages purposely had relations on Shabbat? In Tractate *Ketubot*, we read:

> How often are scholars to perform their marital duties? – Rabbi Judah in the name of Samuel replied: Every Friday night. "That bringeth forth its fruit in its season" (Psalms 1:3). Rabbi Judah, and some say Rabbi Huna, or again, as others say, Rabbi Nahman, stated: This [refers to the man] who performs his marital duty every Friday night. Judah the son of Rabbi Hiyya and son-in-law of Rabbi Jannai was always spending his time in the study hall but every Sabbath eve he came home. Whenever he arrived, the people saw a pillar of light moving before him. Once he was so attracted by his subject of study [that he forgot to return home]...Rabbi Jannai said to those [around him], "Lower his bed, for had Judah been alive he would not have neglected the performance of his marital duties."³⁶

The halakhah follows this vein: "Sexual relations are considered a dimension of Sabbath pleasure. Therefore, Torah scholars who are healthy set aside Friday night as the night when they fulfill their conjugal duties. At the outset, it is permitted to engage in sexual relations with a virgin on the Sabbath. It is not [forbidden because] one is creating a wound, nor because of the pain the woman [feels]."³⁷ The proper time for healthy Torah scholars³⁸ was expressly specified from one

---

34. Babylonian Talmud, *Berakhot* 22a.
35. Ramban, Leviticus 19:2.
36. Babylonian Talmud, *Ketubot* 62b.
37. Rambam, *Mishneh Torah*, Shabbat 30:14.
38. Although today the definition of Torah scholars does not apply, still, a person who studies Torah regularly may consider himself as such. This does not include a person who does not

Friday night to the next,[39] because sexual relations is part of the pleasure of Shabbat, part of an enjoyable evening of rest and physical pleasure.[40] The halakhah makes a direct connection between marital relations and Shabbat – there is a mitzvah of pleasure on Shabbat, and sexual relations is a physical pleasure.

The Recommended Custom in Israel

Because the prohibition is mentioned in the book of Jubilees, an early work, and its source is in an ancient custom practiced among Jewish groups in the Sages' time, I would like to propose a new reason for specifying that Torah scholars should have relations on Shabbat. In light of the sources we have examined, we may assume that the Sages recognized the existence of groups that completely prohibited sexual relations on Shabbat. Therefore, perhaps the Sages chose Shabbat purposely, as part of the struggle against these groups, and gave this instruction expressly to Torah scholars, in order to negate the opposite, prohibiting opinion.

In summary, we may say that strict observance of the laws of purity, which led the Beta Israel to prohibit this practice, was followed by certain sects during

---

study Torah at all (*Responsa Me'il Tzedakah* 51; *Mishnah Berurah* 240:6, citing *Peri Megadim*, and explanation of the halakhah given there. See *Magen Avraham* 240:3). One commentator writes that the definition of Torah scholar for this purpose is one who studies in depth throughout the day and at night. But one who studies only during the day, or those who teach children, are not considered Torah scholars for this purpose (*Responsa Tzitz Eliezer*, ch. 11, par. 18). Another commentator writes that every person should consider himself a Torah scholar, and have relations every Friday evening as well as on the evening of the wife's monthly immersion in the *mikveh* (*Sefer Mitzvot Katan*, mitzvah 285).

39. The expression in the Babylonian Talmud, *Ketubot* 62b, is *mi-erev Shabbat le-erev Shabbat*, literally "from one Friday eve to the next." Although this might be interpreted to mean Friday afternoon before Shabbat begins, the text of the halakhah here is very clear – it refers to Friday evening. A friend referred me to Rashi (Exodus 12:6, s.v. "in the afternoon"), who explains: "From six hours [after sunrise] and onward is called *bein ha-arbaim*, literally, 'between the two evenings,' for the sun is inclined toward the place where it sets to become darkened. It seems to me that the expression *bein ha-arbaim* denotes those hours between the darkening of the day and the darkening of the night. The darkening of the day is at the beginning of the seventh hour, when 'the shadows of the evening are stretched out' (Jeremiah 6:4), and the darkening of the night at the beginning of the night. *Erev* is an expression of evening and darkness, like 'all joy is darkened [*arvah*]' (Isaiah 24:11)." In this context, it is interesting to note that for the Beta Israel, Friday is called Arvi, meaning Shabbat eve, which refers to the entire sixth day. Thus Friday night is the time after dark, as Rashi explains, and then it is actually Shabbat.

40. If a Torah scholar is unable to have relations one Friday night, he should do so in the middle of the week instead (*Responsa Iggerot Moshe, Even ha-Ezer*, part 3, par. 28).

Second Temple times. Thus we should not disparage Ethiopian Jews who today continue to refrain from relations on Shabbat. The Sages' opposition should be understood in light of the struggle against the Karaites, but today it is not a heretical custom, and so we should permit those who prefer to follow their ancestral custom. On the other hand, those Ethiopian Jews who do not wish to follow the custom of abstaining on Shabbat are not erring against the precept of "Do not foresake the Torah of your mother," as the majority of the Jewish people do have sexual relations on Shabbat. Unity and the desire to become one people, such that each individual can realize his personal inclination in worshipping God, supersede ancestral customs.

Saving a Life on Shabbat

Ethiopian Halakhah

According to Ethiopian halakhah, saving a life does not take precedence over any mitzvah. Even if there is danger in fulfilling the mitzvah, we do not consider the danger, but rather the value of fulfilling the mitzvah. Thus saving a life is not defined as a mitzvah. In the religious world of the Ethiopian community, there is no hierarchical division of mitzvot – there is no distinction between a minor mitzvah and a major one. As my grandfather said, "God has commanded us to perform a mitzvah, and we will do what is written without further consideration, because God knows what He has commanded. If something bad happens to a baby, God forbid, then this is God's plan, and we do not question God's plan. If the baby dies during the circumcision, this is a great source of merit for the baby."

I once asked my grandfather, Abba Gideon (Dejen) Mengesha, of blessed memory, why they were not afraid to perform mitzvot without considering the danger involved. For example, a woman who was *niddah* went alone to the "house of impurity," where lions and wolves wandered freely – clearly this was dangerous for the woman. He replied by telling a story: two Jewish women who were *niddah*, who were staying in the "house of impurity," went to sleep, believing that God would protect them from wild animals. A non-Jewish woman came to sleep with them. The non-Jewish woman felt afraid, so she went to sleep in between the two Jewish women. That night a wolf came inside. He pulled her out from the middle and devoured her. My grandfather ended, "Whoever believes fully, God will protect him. We carry out God's mitzvot with full faith and trust." "For My thoughts are not your thoughts" (Isaiah 55:8) – God's "thoughts" are the mitzvot in the Torah, and the Jew must fulfill them with no exceptions or doubt.

Past and Present in Talmudic Halakhah

Apparently, during the early development of the Oral Law, the Sages thought that saving a life did not take precedence over Shabbat. We find this in historical descriptions from the time of the Hasmonean rebellion. Jerusalem fell into the hands of Ptolemy I Soter because its inhabitants refused to fight on Shabbat.[41] Antiochus Epiphanes entered Jerusalem with a large army on Shabbat because he knew that the Jews would not fight on Shabbat, and as a result, many Jews were killed.[42] Due to these bitter experiences, the Sages apparently offered a new interpretation of the halakhah that valued saving a life over almost all the mitzvot. They placed great importance on the value of life, considering it as belonging to God, God's gift to humanity.

Humans are responsible for life. Individuals must preserve their own lives and guard them from any danger, and also guard the lives of others from danger, protect them and save them from any harm. "For the blood of the murdered is not the property of the blood redeemer – it is the property of God."[43] "Our Sages forbade many matters because they involve a threat to life. Whenever a person transgresses these guidelines, saying: 'I will risk my life, what does this matter to others,' or 'I am not careful about these things,' he should be punished by whipping for rebelliousness."[44] This concept is clearly emphasized in the Torah itself: "I call heaven and earth to witness [that I have warned] you this day, that I have set before you life and death, the blessing and the curse; therefore choose life, that you may live, you and your offspring" (Deuteronomy 30:19); and "You shall therefore keep My statutes and My ordinances, which if a man do, he shall live by them. I am the Lord" (Leviticus 18:5). The Sages explained, "The mitzvot were given so that we would live by them, as it says, 'which if a man do, he shall live by them' – this means we should not die because of them."[45] The laws of saving a life were determined according to the Jewish principle "Saving a life takes precedence over the entire Torah." The Jerusalem Talmud states, "A person who [administers treatment] quickly is praiseworthy, and one who raises questions

---

41. *Antiquities* 12:6; Y. Gutman, *Ha-sifrut ha-Yehudit ha-hellenistit*, 1; II Maccabees 5; M.D. Herr, "La-ba'ayot milhamah be-Shabbat bi-yemei Bayit Sheni u-bi-tekufat ha-Mishnah ve-ha-Talmud," *Tarbiz* 30 (5721/1961).
42. I Maccabees 2:29–37, trans. Uriel Rappaport (Jerusalem, 5764/2004).
43. Rambam, *Mishneh Torah*, Hilkhot Rotzeah 1:4.
44. Ibid., 11:5.
45. Tosefta, *Shabbat* 15:17.

is considered as if he shed blood."[46] The Rambam, who usually writes succinctly, chose to comment at length on this source:

> It is forbidden to hesitate before transgressing the Sabbath [laws] on behalf of a person who is dangerously ill.... This teaches us that the judgments of the Torah do not [bring] vengeance to the world, but rather bring mercy, kindness, and peace to the world. Concerning those non-believers who say that [administering such treatment] constitutes a violation of the Sabbath and is forbidden, one may apply the verse [Ezekiel 20:25]: "[As punishment,] I gave them also statutes that were not good, and ordinances, whereby they cannot live."[47]

Explaining the Rambam, Rabbi Soloveitchik writes:

> The teachings of the Torah do not oppose the laws of life and reality, for were they to clash with this world and were they to negate the value of concrete, physiological-biological existence, then they would contain not mercy, loving-kindness, and peace but vengeance and wrath. Even if there is only a doubtful possibility that a person's life is in danger, one renders a lenient decision; and as long as one is able to discover some possible danger to life, one may use that doubt to render a lenient decision.... This law that saving a life overrides all the commandments and its far-reaching effects are indicative of the high value which the halakhic viewpoint attributes to one's earthly life – indeed they serve to confirm and nurture that value. Temporal life becomes transformed into eternal life; it becomes sanctified and elevated with eternal holiness.[48]

In summary, we may state that the authorization to violate Shabbat for purposes of war and healing developed throughout history, as the rabbis determined that even in questionable cases, the chance of saving a life takes precedence over Shabbat.[49]

---

46. Jerusalem Talmud, *Yoma* 8:5.
47. Rambam, *Mishneh Torah*, Shabbat 2:3.
48. Soloveitchik, *Halakhic Man*, 34–35.
49. Rabbi Sharon Shalom, "Brit milah be-kehillat Beta Israel" (Circumcision practices in the Beta Israel community), master's thesis, Bar-Ilan University, supervised by Professor D. Sperber, 2007.

The Recommended Custom in Israel

Although the Ethiopian custom is based on the ancient method, the Sages' writings on the value of life have penetrated the depths of Jewish consciousness. Thus it is absolutely forbidden to continue to follow the Ethiopian custom, and the Beta Israel must immediately adopt the general Jewish custom for all issues of saving a life.

Labors Forbidden on Shabbat

Ethiopian Halakhah

As noted, Ethiopian halakhah rules that the labors forbidden on Shabbat are absolute, and cannot be overruled. The source for this halakhah is apparently in the book of Jubilees,[50] from which the author of the *Tataza Sanvet* seems to have copied. The *Tataza Sanvet* states:

> I will now list the laws of Shabbat, all of its mitzvot and rules. On six days you will work, and the seventh will be for Hashem, your Lord, your God. You will do no labor on this day, neither you, nor your wives, nor your sons, nor your daughters, nor your mothers, nor your beasts, nor the foreigners, nor the horses that are with you. One who violates this day should die. One who lies with his wife on Shabbat should die.... Anyone who sells or purchases on Shabbat should die. One who draws water from a fresh water source, one who fights, one who curses or swears on this day should die. One who did not prepare his food or drink, and one who did not sanctify the Shabbat should die. One who carries something, one who takes something out of his tent, and one who takes something in from outside, should die. You should not do any work on Shabbat.... Any person who works on my Shabbatot, who travels on the road, who works in the field or at home, who lights a fire, or who stands in the sun should die.... One who rides a beast, one who sails on a boat should die.... As for women, do not clean, do not cook, do not draw water, do not grind in a mortar, do not shout.[51]

Thus it is forbidden to perform any labor on Shabbat that is considered housework or fieldwork. It is forbidden to go to war on Shabbat, even in defense. One must not light fire or candles for Shabbat, even on Friday afternoon (every labor forbidden on Shabbat must not be begun on Friday afternoon if it will carry over

---

50. Jubilees (ed. Kahane) 15:25–26, p. 254.
51. Eshkoli, *Ha-halakhah ve-ha-minhag*.

into Shabbat). We must not violate Shabbat, even for a sick person. We must not have sexual relations on Shabbat, nor sail in a boat on the ocean or on a river. Avraham Yardai recalls that there was a river near his village, and everyone knew that it was absolutely forbidden to cross it on Shabbat, even in a boat. We are careful not to drink milk that was milked on Shabbat. We do not carry from one domain to another on Shabbat, and we do not walk outside the village boundaries. We do not violate Shabbat in order to fulfill another time-based mitzvah, such as the fast of Yom Kippur or *brit milah*. In other words, the Beta Israel are forbidden to do any labor on Shabbat, whether it is one of the thirty-nine biblical labors forbidden on Shabbat or a rabbinic derivation, known as *shvut* in rabbinic terminology.

Past and Present in Talmudic Halakhah

It is a positive commandment to refrain from labor on Shabbat, as in the verse "On the seventh day you shall rest" (Exodus 23:12). The thirty-nine principal labors are those that a Jew is forbidden by biblical law from performing on Shabbat. The Torah gives only sparse detail, while the Oral Law provides lengthy explanations of all the labors, and explains how they were derived from the labors involved in constructing the Tabernacle. These were artisanal crafts that required special skill. Performing any of these labors was considered violation of Shabbat.[52] The Torah forbids doing work on Shabbat: "Six days you shall labor, and do all your work; but the seventh day is a Sabbath to the Lord your God, in it you shall not do any manner of work, you, nor your son, nor your daughter, nor your manservant, nor your maidservant, nor your cattle, nor your stranger who is within your gates." (Exodus 20:8–10)

As opposed to the popular assumption that the abstention from labor on Shabbat is designed to ensure rest from work and travail, and any labor associated with travail, the true understanding of the prohibition against labor on Shabbat is different. The labors forbidden by the Torah on Shabbat are only those that fit the definition of "skilled craftsmanship" or "artisanal craft" (like the labors of the Temple that the Torah defined as "skilled craftsmanship"). In the Torah, we do not find an exact definition of the term *melakhah* (labor), except for a small number of labors expressly mentioned there. These are lighting a fire, plowing and reaping, and carrying from one domain to another. The Sages noted the lack of proportion between the Torah and the Talmud on this issue, and remarked

---

52. Herman, *Ma'agal ha-hagim*.

that the Shabbat labors are "like mountains hanging from a hair – few verses but many laws."[53]

The Sages determined the definition of "labor": each of the thirty-nine activities required in the construction of the Tabernacle in the desert, and all activities derived from them. The Sages found an indication of this definition in the fact that the mitzvah of keeping Shabbat is recorded in the Torah directly following the command to build the Tabernacle: "See, I have called by name Bezalel.... According to all that I have commanded you they shall do.... 'Only keep My Sabbaths!'" (Exodus 31:2, 11, 13). The number thirty-nine is derived several ways: representing the number of times the word *melakhah* appears in the Torah, in its different forms (in fact, the word appears more than thirty-nine times, and the Talmud discusses which instances to include in the total); the number of times the words *melakhah* and *avodah* (work) appear in the description of construction of the Tabernacle; the number of times the words "These are the words" appear in the section containing the commandment of forbidden labor. These are the forbidden labors involved:

1. Sowing
2. Plowing
3. Reaping
4. Binding sheaves
5. Threshing
6. Winnowing
7. Selecting
8. Grinding
9. Sifting
10. Kneading
11. Baking
12. Shearing wool
13. Cleaning
14. Combing
15. Dyeing
16. Spinning
17. Stretching threads
18. Making loops

---

53. Babylonian Talmud, *Haggigah* 10a.

19. Weaving threads
20. Separating threads
21. Tying a knot
22. Untying a knot
23. Sewing
24. Tearing
25. Trapping
26. Slaughtering
27. Skinning
28. Salting
29. Tanning
30. Scraping
31. Cutting
32. Writing
33. Erasing
34. Building
35. Dismantling
36. Extinguishing a fire
37. Kindling a fire
38. Striking the final hammer blow
39. Carrying from one domain into another

The Recommended Custom in Israel

The first generation of Beta Israel should continue to follow their custom, but the second generation should adopt the mainstream practice.

Muktzeh on Shabbat

Ethiopian Halakhah

The term *muktzeh* (an object that may not be moved or handled on Shabbat because it is associated with weekday activities, or because its handling may result in a Shabbat violation) was not known to the Ethiopian Jews. However, they did not handle or move *muktzeh* item on Shabbat, because they avoided all forbidden labors on Shabbat. The related rabbinic prohibition against carrying items from one domain to another (which will be explained further below) was also unknown to the Ethiopian community; it was permitted to carry any item for the purpose of worshipping God.

Past and Present in Talmudic Halakhah

Muktzeh is an item we are forbidden to move or handle. The Sages defined various types of *muktzeh*.

1. Any item that is specifically designated for performing a forbidden labor cannot be moved or handled, since it may result in using the item for the forbidden labor. The Mishnah lists items whose primary use is for a forbidden labor, but that are nonetheless permitted to be moved or handled for the purpose of a permitted labor: "A man may take a hammer to split nuts, a chopper to cut [a round of] pressed figs."[54]
2. An item used for a specific mitzvah.[55] This would include a shofar, a *lulav* (used as one of the four species ritually waved on the holiday of Sukkot), and the like.
3. An item one would only touch on Shabbat in order to prevent material loss, i.e., an item of value that one usually uses only for its designated purpose. Such an item may not be used on Shabbat, even for a permitted purpose, and even if its main purpose is for a permitted act.
4. An item that is intrinsically useless on Shabbat and that has not been prepared or designated for any use on Shabbat, is not food for humans or animals, and is not a container nor does it have the form of a container. Included in this category are wooden beams, stones, dust, and dirt.

The Rambam and Ravad (Rabbi Avraham ben David of Posquières) disagreed over the reasoning for the prohibition against carrying on Shabbat. According to the Rambam, avoiding carrying objects aids in preserving the character of Shabbat:

> If the prophets warned that the manner in which a person walks on the Sabbath should not resemble the manner in which he walks during the week, and similarly, one's conversation on the Sabbath should not resemble one's conversation during the week, as it is written, "nor pursuing thy business, nor speaking thereof" (Isaiah 58:13) – surely the manner in which one carries on the Sabbath should not resemble the manner in which one carries during the week. In this manner, no one will regard [the Sabbath] as an ordinary weekday and lift up and repair articles, [carrying them] from room to room, or

---

54. Babylonian Talmud, *Shabbat* 122b.
55. See *Mishnah Berurah* 18.

from house to house, or set aside stones and the like. [These restrictions are necessary] for since the person is idle and sitting at home, [it is likely that] he will seek something with which to occupy himself. Thus, he will not have ceased activity and will have negated the motivating principle for the Torah's commandment, "Thus…will rest" (Deuteronomy 5:14).[56]

According to Rabad, the concept of *muktzeh* is derived from the forbidden labor of carrying from one domain to another – if a person handles objects as he does on a weekday, he might inadvertently take the item into another domain.

The Recommended Custom in Israel

The Ethiopian Jews, at least in the first generation, are permitted to continue following their custom. But in the second generation, they should follow the generally accepted practice regarding *muktzeh*. Those who wish to continue the past custom out of respect for tradition are permitted to do so and should not be criticized, as this desire is connected to worshipping God. Unity of the nation and acceptance of Ethiopian Jewry is a realization of God's will and the fact that we are different but equal.

❧ Money on Shabbat

Ethiopian Halakhah

The Ethiopian Jews are accustomed to use any item on Shabbat that is needed for serving God. In Ethiopia, the Beta Israel used to bring coins to the synagogue on Shabbat, following the verse "Every man shall give as he is able, according to the blessing of the Lord your God which He has given you" (Deuteronomy 16:17).

Past and Present in Talmudic Halakhah

Above we defined four types of *muktzeh*. Money comes under the category of an item whose use is forbidden. It may be used "for its space" – if a person needs the space that it occupies, he may pick it up and place it wherever he wants. One may also use it for a permitted activity on Shabbat, such as using a hammer to crack a nut, or using scissors to cut open a sealed bag of food.

The Recommended Custom in Israel

In various locations in Israel, in synagogues of the Ethiopian community, the congregants bring cash to the synagogue. Those who follow the custom of bringing

---

56. *Mishneh Torah*, Shabbat 22:12.

should continue to bring, as the money is designated for use on Shabbat. In the Ethiopian world, which is based on trust, we do not suspect that a person might use this money for other purposes on Shabbat. We believe that the individual wishes to serve God, and one who does not want to do so will not attend synagogue. In our world, "suspicion" is a foreign word.

ᛋ Umbrella on Shabbat

Ethiopian Halakhah

Another example of using objects for the purpose of worshipping God is use of the umbrella on Shabbat. In Ethiopia, the people, particularly the *kesim*, carried umbrellas on Shabbat on their way to synagogue. The umbrella was an important tool and formed part of the proper clothing for worshipping God.

Past and Present in Talmudic Halakhah

Erecting a "permanent tent" is a derivation of the labor of construction, and is biblically prohibited. The Sages forbade building a "temporary tent" out of concern that one might also build a permanent tent. According to some *poskim*, an umbrella is a temporary tent, and thus we are forbidden from opening one on Shabbat. We are also prohibited from using an umbrella opened before Shabbat, due to *marit ayin* (lit. "the way it looks," i.e., an observer might think the person has committed a violation of Shabbat) – an onlooker might think we opened it on Shabbat. According to several *poskim*, there is no prohibition against opening an umbrella on Shabbat.[57]

The Recommended Custom in Israel

The Ethiopian Jews are permitted to use an umbrella on Shabbat. They should be permitted to use the umbrella not only when walking to synagogue, but also for protection against rain, on condition they open the umbrella before Shabbat beings. As noted, in the Ethiopian world, there is no reason to suspect what others might think: "You shall be wholehearted with the Lord your God" (Deuteronomy 18:13).

---

[57]. *Responsa Hatam Sofer*, part 1, *Orah Haim* 72; Rabbi Israel Lipschitz, *Tiferet Yisrael, kalkalat ha-Shabbat, malekhet boneh*.

4. Holidays and Festivals

❧ Introduction

The Ethiopian Jews celebrated all the holidays mentioned in the Torah, which they call Orit ("light," from the Aramaic word *oraita*). The drastic changes that affected the Jewish people after the destruction of the Second Temple, and the development of the Mishnah and the Talmud, did not reach Ethiopia. The Jews there continued to follow their customs, which were firmly based on the biblical spirit. Thus we may observe among the Beta Israel customs that were preserved from the First Temple period. The community gave the holidays names in Amharic, their spoken language. The Ethiopian community uses its own calendar, which is based on the lunar cycles, like the Hebrew calendar, and so the dates of the holidays mostly coincide. Aside from the traditional holidays described in the Torah, the Beta Israel also have special holidays rooted in community tradition, such as Sigd, fasts, and various other traditions.

❧ Rosh Hodesh – Laws and Customs

Ethiopian Halakhah

The Beta Israel celebrated every Rosh Hodesh as a holiday. The most important of these was Rosh Hodesh Nissan, which is related to the date of the Exodus from Egypt. Rosh Hodesh was a joyous, festive day, on which they refrained from performing any labor outside the village. Unlike on biblical festivals, labor inside the village was permitted, and they went to the river to bathe and immerse themselves. (As noted above, in the world of the Beta Israel community, there are no rules or halakhic restrictions, definitions of permitted and forbidden. Members simply follow accepted custom.) On Rosh Hodesh, they recited special prayers in synagogue and ate festive meals. I think no other community emphasizes the sanctity of Rosh Hodesh as the Ethiopian Jews do.

Past and Present in Talmudic Halakhah

During biblical times, the Jews commemorated Rosh Hodesh by offering sacrifices and blowing trumpets (Numbers 10:10; 28:11–15). During First Temple times, they made pilgrimages to the Temple to offer sacrifices there (Isaiah 1:13–14). The gate of the inner courtyard was opened specially for the masses of pilgrims who came to prostrate themselves in its opening (Isaiah 46:1–3). On this day, the Jews went to visit prophets in order to hear God's word (II Kings 4:23), and refrained from labor (I Samuel 29:19; Amos 8:5). Apparently, the reason for refraining from labor was the Musaf (additional) sacrificial offering in the Temple, as work was proscribed on a day when this sacrifice was offered.[1] For this reason, in Second Temple times as well, the Jews did no work on Rosh Hodesh. After the destruction of the Second Temple, the Sages instituted the Musaf prayer service instead of the special additional sacrifice. But the men did not refrain from labor, although the women did.[2]

The Recommended Custom in Israel

Ethiopian Jews are permitted to continue their custom. However, it is difficult to completely refrain from labor on Rosh Hodesh, for various reasons, such as employment. Certainly one may recite the special prayers for Rosh Hodesh. One should go to the *mikveh* and wear a white shirt as was the practice in Ethiopia. One should also make efforts to hold a family meal and study Torah.

❧ Birkat ha-Levanah (Blessing over the New Moon)

Ethiopian Halakhah

This practice was not followed. Ethiopian Jews were surrounded by people who worshipped the sun and moon, and were thus very concerned about any prayer that might appear to be doing the same. It is expressly forbidden to pray to the heavenly bodies – one must pray only to God.

Past and Present in Talmudic Halakhah

The blessing over the new moon is an expression of thanks to God for creating the moon, as we benefit from its light at night. The blessing is recited at the beginning of the month, outside, in the presence of the moon. We should recite

---

1. Herman, *Ma'agal ha-hagim*.
2. *Shulhan Arukh, Orah Haim* 417.

it while dressed in festive clothing, thus it is customarily said on the night just after Shabbat or a holiday, in public.[3]

The Recommended Custom in Israel

One who views this blessing as conflicting with his world of belief, for whom focusing on the moon is comparable to idol worship, may avoid this blessing. However, the Ethiopian Jews must not view one who recites this important blessing as an idol worshipper. The Sages placed great importance on this blessing,[4] and so the second generation should recite it along with the general Jewish community.

Pasika (Passover)

Ethiopian Halakhah

THE MONTH OF NISSAN

The month of Nissan is called Lissan. In this month, the Israelites went out of Egypt with signs and wonders, and the Ethiopian Jews celebrate in a special manner. They began preparations at the beginning of the month for the holiday of Pasika (Passover), in an atmosphere of joy that permeated the entire community. On the fourteenth of the month, the entire community gathered at the *masgid* (synagogue), dressed in white. The *kesim* and community elders entered first, followed by the rest of the community – men, women, and children. The *kahin* (priest) stood and recited the blessing over the *dabu* (*kitche* in Tigrinya, *meswait* in Ge'ez) – challah baked especially for this day. The *kahin* led the service with blessings and prayers, and the congregation responded.

HAGALAH (IMMERSING UTENSILS)

Immediately after Rosh Hodesh, the women began preparing new vessels for Passover. They replaced all the old vessels with new ones, because most of them were made of clay. They began the process of cleaning and removing all *hametz* (leavened food) in the courtyard, and continued into the house.

PREPARING THE SACRIFICIAL OFFERING

At the beginning of the month, they chose a goat or a sheep. On the tenth of the month they brought it to the synagogue courtyard and tied it up there until the fourteenth day of Nissan, when they sacrificed it.

---

3. Herman, *Ma'agal ha-hagim*.
4. Babylonian Talmud, *Sanhedrin* 42a.

PROHIBITION AGAINST *HAMETZ*

Three days before offering the sacrifice, the house was clean of all *hametz*. New clay vessels had been brought to replace the old, broken ones, and any food that had come into contact with water was removed from the home. Three days before Passover, they ate only roasted chickpeas, "so as to begin Passover with no *hametz* in our intestines" (Kes Barhan Yeheis). The preparations were performed in the joy of doing a mitzvah, with expectation that soon they would merit full redemption by the Messiah. The definition of *hametz* for the Beta Israel is very different from the mainstream definition. To them, every kind of food can be *hametz*, and so all foods, including meat, milk, peas, and corn, must be eaten while fresh.

The reason for not eating *hametz* is that on the eve of the Israelites' departure from Egypt, due to their haste, they did not have time to allow the dough to rise. In Ethiopian halakhah, *hametz* is not determined by the raw materials of the food, but rather the time of preparation. Food must be eaten on the same day that it is prepared. After one night has passed, the food becomes *hametz*. For example, milk must be drunk immediately following milking, or on the same day. Any milk left over on the day after milking is *hametz*. Similarly, any food that requires lengthy preparation time is *hametz*. This includes, for example, carbonated drinks and yellow cheese. If the Israelites did not have enough time to make *rugelach*, the thinking goes, then how would they have time to make Coca Cola or hard cheese?

Dry food, however, is not subject to these restrictions, so for Shabbat Chol Hamoed Pesah, the Ethiopian community would eat dry foods such as Ethiopian matzot or seeds, which could be left overnight without becoming *hametz*. Wet foods, however, were forbidden on Shabbat during Passover (as they could not be prepared on Shabbat nor could they be left overnight from the day before lest they become *hametz*). And, as on any Shabbat in the Beta Israel community, no foods could be heated.

PASSOVER EVE

Early on the fourteenth day of Nissan, the entire community went to immerse themselves in the river closest to their village. After immersion, they returned to the village and dressed in holiday clothing. The mothers changed into holiday clothing after they finished baking *kita* (*matzot*). Baking the *matzot* was done swiftly. Some of the community, particularly the *shmagla* (elders) or the *kohanim* (rabbis), fasted on the fourteenth. In the evening, everyone gathered in the synagogue courtyard, feeling that something special was about to happen. The *kahin* approached the sheep or goat that had been prepared on the tenth of the month, and slaughtered it. He then carried it to a stone altar that was erected in the synagogue courtyard, where the Passover sacrifice was offered. After roasting the meat of the offering, the *kohanim* recited prayers and sang songs. This was an exciting and uplifting moment. Then each family was given a piece of meat and some *kita* that had been prepared in advance. While they ate the offering, silence reigned.

While eating, the *shmagla* held sticks in their hands, wore belts around their waists, and carried sacks on their backs. Then the *kohanim* recited special prayers. After the prayers, one of them read a section of the Torah about the Exodus from Egypt. Another rabbi translated it into Amharic or Tigrinya, and everyone listened raptly, as if diamonds were coming out of his mouth. After the eating and prayers, the remains of the offering were collected and burned. Some of the people went home, while others remained in the synagogue all night long to listen to the *kohanim* tell stories about the Exodus. The next day, which was the first day of Passover, was a holiday on which labor in the villages was forbidden. Basic labors such as preparing food and minor work in the villages was permitted. Throughout the holiday, they were very careful to avoid *hametz*. Labor was permitted in all locations, but not for commercial purposes.

SEVENTH DAY OF PASSOVER

On the seventh day of Passover, they did not work, as on the first day. On the eve of the seventh day, they congregated in the synagogue to read the section of the Torah with the Ten Commandments. At the end of the seventh day, they did not eat *hametz* right away, but waited until the morning of the eighth day. The *kahin* recited the blessing, then everyone ate injera and beer (*tela* in Amharic, *swa* in Tigrinya). The beautiful moments of the holiday inspired the people with faith that this year, they would finally see Jerusalem.[5]

Past and Present in Talmudic Halakhah

We celebrate Passover to commemorate the Exodus of the Israelites from Egypt after 210 years of slavery. Pharaoh, king of Egypt, refused to accede to God's demand (as communicated by Moses and Aaron) to free the Israelites. God punished Pharaoh and his people with ten plagues, and then He sent the Israelites out of Egypt (Exodus chapters 1–12). The last plague, the slaying of the firstborn, was the harshest. God slayed every firstborn male in Egypt, both man and beast.

---

5. Sperber, *Minhagei Yisrael*, vol. 4, *Yemei ha-Pesah ha-rishonim etzel Yehudei Luv* [The first days of Passover among Libyan Jews], 57.

On the tenth of Nissan, God commanded the Israelites to take a sheep or goat, guard it until the fourteenth of the month (Exodus 12:6), then slaughter it and place the blood on the lintel and the two doorposts of the house. On the night of the fifteenth of the month, each household had to be dressed and ready to leave, and to eat the meat in haste, roasted in the fire together with *matzot* and bitter herbs. Any meat that was not eaten by morning was burned.

This holiday was called *hag ha-Pesah*. *Hag* means sacrifice, and so the name recalls the sacrifice made on that day. *Pesah* is derived from the Hebrew root *p.s.h.*, which is repeated three times in the Torah portion. The Sages gave several interpretations for this: some thought it meant "to skip" or "pass over" (hence the name Passover in English), while others thought it meant "to take pity on," as in the verse "As birds hovering, so will the Lord of hosts protect Jerusalem; He will deliver it as he protects it, He will rescue it as He passes over" (Isaiah 31:5). The slaying of the firstborn took place on the eve of 15 Nissan, in the year 2448 after the creation of the world (according to the Jewish calendar). Pharaoh rose from his bed in the middle of the night, summoned Moses and Aaron, and informed them that he would permit the Israelites to leave Egypt. The next morning, 15 Nissan, the Israelites went out of Egypt with a mighty hand, in the light of day, for all to see. The Egyptians, led by Pharaoh king of Egypt, chased after them to bring them back. According to the Midrash, the Egyptians caught up to the Israelites after seven days, on the seventh night of Passover, on the shore of the Red Sea. God made a miracle happen and parted the waters of the Red Sea, and the Israelites walked through. The Egyptians went in after them, and then the waters rejoined, drowning the Egyptians (Exodus 13:17–22; 15:1–22). In commemoration of these events, the Torah gives five positive commandments and six negative ones.[6]

The Recommended Custom in Israel

Members of the community may continue the Ethiopian custom of ceasing the consumption of *hametz* three days before Passover. If a person wishes to eat injera on Passover eve, he should be certain to finish eating before midnight. Individuals may follow the strict Ethiopian definition of *hametz*. Those who wish to continue the practice of refraining from *hametz* until the day after the last day of Passover may do so, and this should not be considered as adding to the law (which is forbidden). Second-generation Ethiopian Jews who find it difficult

---

6. Herman, *Ma'agal ha-hayim*.

to follow the Ethiopian customs of Passover are permitted to make their own decision. As for the Passover sacrifice, the classic sacrificial offering as practiced in Ethiopia must not be performed. However, Beta Israel Jews may slaughter on Passover eve, as they do today, not as a ritual sacrifice but as a reminder of that practice. On Seder eve, parents who made aliyah should tell their children the story of the community's journey to Israel, as an integral part of the Maggid section of the Haggadah.

When Does the Prohibition against Eating *Hametz* Begin?

Ethiopian Halakhah

The Beta Israel would stop eating *hametz* three days before Passover. As mentioned, the definition of *hametz* in Ethiopia did not correspond to the rabbinic definition.

Past and Present in Talmudic Halakhah

The prohibition against eating *hametz* began at noon on 14 Nissan, from the appropriate time to sacrifice the Passover offering, about which the Torah says, "You shall not eat *hametz* with it" (Deuteronomy 16:3). Eating *hametz* after this time is a prohibition punishable by thirty-nine lashes, while eating *hametz* beginning on the night of 15 Nissan is punishable with excommunication. The Sages forbade eating *hametz* beginning in the fifth hour of the day, but permitted using it for benefit (such as earning a profit from selling it) until the sixth hour, to prevent people from possible error. Thus in actuality, the end time for eating *hametz* is until the end of the fourth hour of the day. In the fifth hour, *hametz* is forbidden for eating but permitted for benefit, and at the end of the fifth hour, it must be burned. These hours are determined according to halakhic principles, and the exact clock times are published in Jewish calendars and newspapers.[7]

The Recommended Custom in Israel

Regarding the time to stop eating *hametz*, the Beta Israel may stop three days before Passover, as was the practice in Ethiopia. A person who wishes to eat injera on Passover eve should stop before midday. They may define *hametz* according to the strict Ethiopian definition, and a person who wishes to continue the prohibition against *hametz* until the day after the seventh day of Passover may do so, and this should not be considered *bal tosif* (lit. "do not add" – prohibition

---

7. Ibid.

against adding to the mitzvot). Members of the second generation who find it difficult to keep the Ethiopian customs are permitted to follow their own preference. Regarding offering the sacrifice, the people should no longer perform the classical sacrifice as done in Ethiopia. But they may slaughter on the eve of the holiday, as done today, not as a sacrifice but as a commemoration of it. On Seder night, parents who experienced aliyah to Israel should recount to their children the story of the Ethiopian Jews' journey as an integral part of the Maggid section of the Haggadah.[8]

Sefirat ha-Omer (Counting the Omer)

Ethiopian Halakhah

The custom in the Ethiopian community was to begin counting the Omer from the last *yom tov* (festival day) of the week-long Passover holiday. The Torah commands *sefirat ha-Omer* (the counting of the Omer) from the day after Shabbat, and uses the phrase "*mi-maharat ha-Shabbat*" (Leviticus 23:15). The Beta Israel community understood the term *Shabbat* in this biblical phrase to refer to *yom tov* (as did rabbinic Judaism). But the Beta Israel interpreted *yom tov* to refer to the last *yom tov* festival of Passover (and not the first *yom tov*, which was the rabbinic interpretation). Given that in Ethiopia the counting of the Omer began at the end of Passover, the Shavuot festival consequently always fell on the twelfth day of Sivan. When I asked one of the *kesim* about the reason for this custom, he answered me, "This is something we received from our forefathers over many generations. It may be that the counting of the Omer was postponed to the end of Passover so as to avoid mingling the precepts of Passover with the precept of counting the Omer." Therefore, only when the Passover holiday was over did the Jews in Ethiopia begin the new mitzvah.

Past and Present in Talmudic Halakhah

The phrase in the Torah that established the date for beginning the counting of the Omer is *mi-maharat ha-Shabbat*, and this led to a tremendous controversy during Second Temple times. According to the followers of Baithos (a Sadducee), who rejected the Oral Torah, the word *Shabbat* in this phrase meant the weekly Shabbat, so that the phrase *mi-maharat ha-Shabbat* would refer to the day after the intermediary Shabbat of Hol ha-Moed Passover, which means that the day

---

8. A recommended Haggadah is *Haggadat Etiopiah*, ed. Menachem Waldman (Jerusalem, 5771/2011).

of the Omer offering would always be on a Sunday. In contrast, the Pharisees (or Rabbanites), who relied on the Oral Law, interpreted *mi-maharat ha-Shabbat* to refer to the day after the first *yom tov*, since *yom tov* is also called a Shabbat, a day of *shvitah* (rest from work). Therefore, for them the Counting of the Omer began after the first *yom tov* of Passover.[9]

Some explained the reason for this as follows. The Shabbat was sanctified by the Holy One, blessed be He, after the creation of the world, before the people of Israel became a nation. Other than Passover, the holidays were fixed by the people of Israel based on Kiddush ha-Hodesh (sanctification of the new month). However, with respect to the first Passover holiday, the people of Israel did not yet exist as a nation in order to sanctify the new month. This means that the very first Passover was instituted by the Holy One Himself, as was the Sabbath. In order to remind us of this and to memorialize this, the Torah specifically calls Passover a "Shabbat" in the biblical phrase *mi-maharat ha-Shabbat*. Thus it follows that that *mi-maharat ha-Shabbat* means the day after the first *yom tov* of Passover, which is always the sixteenth day of Nissan.

The controversy during the Second Temple era was quite acerbic, and therefore the harvesting of the Omer and its offering were purposely performed publicly in an impressive ceremony that emphasized the interpretation of the Pharisees. In those years when it fell on Shabbat, the ceremony even entailed the setting aside of Shabbat prohibitions in order that the full ceremony could take place. The reason for this was to ensure that the rabbinic interpretation and the importance of following the Oral Law would take root among the people.

The reason for the Omer offering was that the grain harvest ripens around Passover, and God judges the world. This is reflected in the abundance, or lack thereof, of the grain harvest, as it says in the Talmud: "The Holy One, blessed be He, said: 'Set before Me Omer on Passover so that I can bless you with a good harvest in your fields.'"[10]

The Recommended Custom in Israel

Even though in Ethiopia the community started *sefirat ha-Omer* on the last day of Passover, the community today should keep the tradition of the rest of the Jewish people, in order to promote unity. Those of the first generation from Ethiopia who wish to observe Shavuot on the twelfth of Sivan may do so, but they

---

9. Herman, *Ma'agal ha-hagim*.
10. Babylonian Talmud, *Rosh Hashanah* 16a.

should also observe Shavuot on the universally accepted date according to *sefirat ha-Omer* as it is practiced in Israel. About the matter of abstaining from shaving, this is a very late custom which is not mentioned in the Talmud, nor even in the Rambam's writings. Thus the men in the Yemenite community, which adheres closely to the Rambam's rulings, do not follow the custom of abstaining from shaving during *sefirat ha-Omer*, and by the same token, Ethiopian immigrants do not have to keep the customs related to shaving (according to Rabbi Nachum Rabinowitz). However, immigrants from Ethiopia who identify with this custom, or who were educated in religious schools and institutions where this custom was kept, may certainly abstain from shaving. In any case, one should shave on Fridays in preparation for Shabbat, since the status of Shabbat in Ethiopia was extremely high. Shabbat takes precedence over many customs, especially customs such as this, which were not practiced in Ethiopia. In addition, it should be emphasized that during the *sefirah* period we should be especially concerned with acting respectfully toward each other.

Shavuot

Ethiopian Halakhah

Shavuot is called Bale Merr. The holiday began on 12 Sivan, immediately following the counting of the Omer. On the eve of the holiday, everyone went to immerse in the river, wore new clothes, and prepared themselves to receive the Torah (Orit) anew. Everyone gathered in the synagogue, and the *kohanim* began a special prayer for Shavuot. On this holiday, the community emphasized two main themes. The first was the giving of the Torah – the *kohanim* read a portion from the Orit that was longer than the usual reading, mainly Parashat Yitro, the portion that describes the giving of the Torah on Mount Sinai. The community also emphasized the mitzvah of bringing first fruits. This mitzvah is divided into two periods: the month of Sivan and the month of Kislev. This was in accordance with the seasons in Ethiopia, as the wheat harvest in Ethiopia begins in Kislev, not Sivan. On Shavuot, there was no harvest or new fruits. Thus the community's main celebration of this holiday was in Kislev, when they recited prayers and petitions, baked bread from the newly harvested wheat, and harvested new fruits.

They brought the bread and the new fruits to the synagogue as offerings. At the synagogue, they placed the fruits before the *kohanim*, who recited blessings over them. The fruits were considered holy, and they were designated for consumption only by the *kohanim*, the poor, and orphans. After the *kohanim* said the blessing, the congregants blessed each other, then everyone went home. They enjoyed a holiday meal with relatives and friends, and served injera made from new grain, together with lamb. Following the meal, they sat together and told stories about times gone by. In these moments, their faces glowed with happiness, contentment, and thanks to the Creator for every mouthful, for having brought them to that day and gracing them with His bounty. This joy can only be fully comprehended when we consider the years of drought that plagued Ethiopia – "They that sow in tears shall reap in joy" (Psalms 126:5).[11]

Past and Present in Talmudic Halakhah

In the Bible, the holiday has several names. It is called "the feast of weeks" (Exodus 34:22), because it begins seven weeks after the beginning of the counting of the Omer; "the festival of the harvest" (Exodus 23:16) because it falls at the time of the wheat harvest; and "the day of the first fruits" (Numbers 28:26), because on this day, the Israelites offered two breads made of grain from the first wheat harvest, and after that, the new produce of that year was permitted for use in the Temple (outside the Temple, the new produce was permitted for use following the offering of the Omer on 16 Nissan). In the Mishnah, this holiday is called Atzeret (lit., "stopping"), as it falls after the end of seven weeks, like Shemini Atzeret which falls the day after the final (seventh) day of Sukkot; and also because on that day, the Israelites stopped all labor, like on the seventh and concluding day of Passover (also called Atzeret in the Torah – Deuteronomy 16:8). According to one explanation, the Torah uses the name Shemini Atzeret because on that day, the Israelites were commanded only to stop work, while on Shavuot, they had the commandment of the two breads and first fruits. After the destruction of the Second Temple, these mitzvot were annulled, and Shavuot became characterized by the abstention from labor. Thus the Sages called it Atzeret. They also added another important name – "the time of the giving of the Torah," because on that day, God gave us the Torah.[12]

The Recommended Custom in Israel

The Beta Israel should follow the general Jewish custom. Those who wish to celebrate Shavuot as in Ethiopia are permitted to do so with no restraints, on condition that they also follow the general custom.

---

11. Sperber, *Minhagei Yisrael*, vol. 1, *Shtihat asavim be-beit ha-knesset be-Shavuot*, 118.
12. Herman, *Ma'agal ha-hagim*.

࿓ Labor on Holidays

Ethiopian Halakhah

A *yom tov* (holiday) is truly a special day. Each one has special prayers that are unique to that holiday, and labor is forbidden, except for labors related to preparing food, including kindling a fire, and everything related to worshipping God, such as using cymbals during the prayer service.

Past and Present in Talmudic Halakhah

Holidays are days on which the Torah forbade labor (*malekhet avodah*). They include the first and seventh days of Passover, Shavuot, Rosh Hashanah, the first day of Sukkot, and Shemini Atzeret. In the Prophets and the Writings, the term *yom tov* (holiday) means a day of celebration, and it maintained this meaning in certain locations mentioned in Tannaitic literature. Simultaneously, the Tannaitic literature began to use this term to indicate days of rest on which labor was forbidden. From the Talmudic period and later, the term was applied only to days on which labor was forbidden, and this is the meaning that applies today as well.[13]

The Torah forbids the Jews from performing labor on holidays. The definition of "labor" is found in the Torah in relation to the first and seventh days of Passover: "And in the first day there shall be to you a holy convocation, no manner of work shall be done in them, save that which every man must eat, that only may be done by you" (Exodus 12:16). From this we learn that the work of preparing "that which every man must eat" is permitted on holidays, and not considered labor. In light of this, the Sages defined the halakhic principle: "There is no difference between a holiday and Shabbat except for that which every man must eat."[14] According to the Rambam and most of the Rishonim, this meant that out of the thirty-nine labors prohibited on Shabbat, the labors that could be permitted on holidays were those related to preparing food: reaping, binding sheaves, threshing, winnowing, selecting, grinding, sifting, kneading, baking, slaughtering, and kindling fire. But the binding halakhic opinion permitted only kneading, baking, cooking, and slaughtering. The rabbis forbade the other labors related to preparing food, because these labors could be performed on the eve of the holiday, and doing them later did not lead to any loss or inferior taste of the food. The Rambam specifies:

---

13. Ibid.
14. Mishnah, *Megillah* 1:5; *Beitzah* 5:6.

We may, however, knead, bake, slaughter, and cook on a holiday, since if these activities had been performed on the previous day, the taste would be adversely affected. For warm bread or food that is cooked today does not [taste] the same as bread or food that was cooked the day before. Similarly, meat that is slaughtered today does not [taste] the same as meat slaughtered on the previous day.[15]

But according to Ravad, the labors for preparing food that precede kneading are biblically prohibited, since the Torah's phrase "that which every man must eat" indicated only food that would be eaten immediately, which the soul would enjoy at once. Today, the Jews are no longer accustomed to slaughter on holidays.

The Recommended Custom in Israel

Members of the first generation who wish to light a fire on the holiday for the purpose of preparing food for the holiday should do so in private. Members of the second generation should refrain from kindling fire, as most opinions hold that this is biblically forbidden, but they may kindle fire from a flame that had been lit before the holiday, as is the general Jewish practice. Regarding turning on an electric light, we may rule leniently, based on the ruling of Rabbi Shalom Mashash.[16] Those who follow the general Jewish custom should be encouraged.

Tisha be-Av and Other Fasts

Ethiopian Halakhah

First of all, there is a basic error in the question of what the Ethiopian Jews knew about the destruction of the Second Temple. Some say that they did not know about it at all. In other words, throughout their history, they thought that the Temple was still standing in all its glory. For this reason, when they came to Israel and realized that the Temple had been destroyed, they felt deep disappointment, and experienced a profound crisis.[17] This conception has proof in the description given by Yosef Halevi. In the nineteenth century, the Alliance Israélite sent him to visit the Ethiopian Jews in order to strengthen ties with the community. His report of their reaction is described above in the chapter "A Short History of Ethiopian Jewry." According to Halevi, the community was convinced that the Temple still stood.

---

15. Rambam, *Mishneh Torah*, Hilkhot Yom Tov 1:8.
16. *Responsa Shemesh u-magen*, vol. 3, *Orah Haim* 57:11; vol. 4, 78:4.
17. Sperber, *Minhagei Yisrael*, vol. 1, p. 138.

But according to my grandfather, Abba Gideon (Dejen) Mengesha, of blessed memory, and according to the *kohanim* and *shmaglotz*, the Beta Israel had heard of the destruction of both the First and Second Temples. Still, they continued to believe that Jerusalem was enveloped in sanctity. Any individual could achieve sanctity of body as well as mind. Every Jew who came to Jerusalem could immediately sense the spiritual abundance that was expressed even in material ways.

We may accuse the community of naiveté, but not blindness. The following story illustrates this innocence. During the aliyah period, the new immigrants in the absorption center in Kiryat Gat used to go out to an orange grove nearby and fill sacks with fruit. They returned to the absorption center and thanked God for providing them with a land of abundance. This continued until one day, the owner of the grove happened to see them. When he asked them for an explanation, they replied that they had merely come to enjoy the plentiful produce of the Land of Israel, which yielded fruit without effort or travail. The owner was sorry to disappoint them, but replied regretfully that the grove belonged to him, not to the State of Israel. Similar stories are told of the Yemenite Jews in Israel.

Further, the Ethiopian Jews even commemorated the destruction of the Temple with fasts and prayer. The fifth fast, in the month of Av, was observed by the elders and spiritual leaders. They began this fast after Rosh Hodesh Av and fasted every day until the Shabbat preceding Rosh Hodesh Elul, not including Fridays and Shabbatot. The last Shabbat was called Zebrube Senbet. The fast began in the morning and ended in the evening. At night they ate only enough to maintain strength. In addition, the elders fasted every Monday and Thursday throughout the year. According to tradition, these fasts were begun by Ezra the Scribe, who gathered the people on those days to teach them Torah. Further, they fasted on the twenty-ninth of each month, so as not to forget the new moon. In Tammuz, they fasted during the day from the first until the tenth of the month, and ate and drank at night. The children did not fast on any of these days except for Yom Kippur, which was mandatory from age seven.

Past and Present in Talmudic Halakhah

The days between 17 Tammuz and Tisha be-Av are called *bein ha-metzarim* (between the boundaries), after the verse "Judah is gone into exile because of affliction, and because of great servitude; she dwells among the nations, she finds no rest; all her pursuers overtook her between the boundaries" (Lamentations 1:3). This is considered a period of woe and calamity, and thus the Sages advised us to be especially carefully during this time. On Shabbatot during this period, the Sages selected special *haftarot* that speak of disaster. The general Jewish community follow various mourning customs during this period, such as prohibition against marriage, prohibition against shaving and cutting hair, avoiding dancing, and some also avoid playing and listening to music. Beginning on Rosh Hodesh Av, the mourning intensifies, and some avoid meat and wine until after Tisha be-Av, because these foods are associated with joy. The Sages enjoined, "When Av begins, we limit enjoyment."[18]

The Recommended Custom in Israel

Jerusalem occupies a significant space in the faith of Ethiopian Jewry. Thus the Beta Israel should follow all the mourning customs practiced by the general Jewish community.[19] That said, weddings should be permitted until Rosh Hodesh Av, as every wedding adds another brick to the rebuilding of Jerusalem, our holy city.

The Month of Elul

Ethiopian Halakhah

The period from Rosh Hodesh Elul to Yom Kippur, and especially the ten days between Rosh Hashanah and Yom Kippur, is considered a time of repentance and atonement. The *kesim* and the elders fasted during this period. Some fasted the first ten days of Elul and on Rosh Hashanah eve. The tenth of Elul was considered Yom Kippur Katan ("little" Yom Kippur). They fasted for half the day, recited some of the Yom Kippur prayers, and reminded the congregants that Yom Kippur fell in one month. From 10 Elul until 10 Tishrei, they fasted half the day. On 18 Elul they commemorated the death of the patriarchs Abraham, Isaac, and Jacob, by reading books about their greatness.

Past and Present in Talmudic Halakhah

Elul marks the beginning of spiritual preparations for the High Holidays. The sixth month was named Elul during the Babylonian Exile, when Babylonian Jewry began to give Babylonian-Assyrian names to the months. But Jewish commentators transformed the meaning of this name, to fit the spirit of the period. Some say that Elul means introspection and self-searching, based on Onkelos's translation of the verse about the spies Moses sent: "Send out for yourself men,

---

18. Mishnah, *Ta'anit* 4:6; see also Rav Eliezer Melamed, "Tisha'at ha-Yamim" (The Nine Days), http://www.yeshiva.org.il/midrash/Shiur.asp?id=3812.
19. As for shaving, I do not shave from 17 Tammuz to Tisha be-Av.

that they may spy out [*vi'alelun*] the land of Canaan" (Numbers 13:2). Some interpreted Elul – *aleph lamed vav lamed* – as an acrostic for the phrase in Song of Songs 6:3, *ani le-dodi ve-dodi li* ("I am my beloved's, and my beloved is mine"). In this month, the commentators wrote, the Jewish people become closer to their "beloved," who is God, and He accepts their repentance. The Lubavitcher Rebbe explained that through "I am my beloved's," our awakening to God by intensifying our study of Torah and performance of mitzvot, "my beloved is mine" takes place – God gives us an abundance of blessings and success.

Some found a hint at the name Elul in the verse "And the Lord your God, will circumcise your heart, and the heart of your offspring" (Deuteronomy 30:6) – *et levavkha ve-et levav zarekha* (also an acrostic for Elul). They interpret this as meaning that in this month, God assists the individual to repent. Others found an acrostic in the verse from the book of Esther, "sending portions one to another, and gifts to the poor" (9:22) – *ish le-re'ehu u-matanot la-evyonim*, because as the Sages said, "Prayer and charity and repentance commute the evil decree."

Between Elul and Yom Kippur, God is closer to us than ever. In hassidic thought, these days are metaphorically compared to a period when "the king is in the field" – the king leaves his palace to tour around his kingdom, and all citizens are invited to approach him and present their requests. In hassidic thought, this month is called "the month of reckoning," as it is a time of personal reckoning about our worship of God in the past year, in order to repair and complete it, and also a period of preparation for the upcoming year.[20]

The Recommended Custom in Israel

The Beta Israel are permitted to follow their customs.

❧ Rosh Hashanah

Ethiopian Halakhah

Rosh Hashanah is called Brhan Sereke or Sereke Brhan, meaning in Ge'ez "shining light" – the light of the New Year. My grandfather said that this was the shining of the first light that God created in the story of Genesis. According to custom, the year began in Nissan, as specified in the Torah. Rosh Hodesh Nissan is the first day of the year. The community also held that the creation of the world and of human beings was in Tishrei, not Nissan. Another name for Rosh Hashanah is Tizkor Avraham (remember Abraham), since according to tradition, the Binding

---

20. Herman, *Ma'agal ha-hagim*.

of Isaac took place on this date. On the eve of the holiday, everyone went to the river to bathe, immerse, and purify themselves. After immersion, they donned white clothing or other new, clean clothing, and welcomed the holiday. They walked to the synagogue in joy and trembling. Early the next morning, they gathered in the synagogue in the village center and began the morning services. On that day, the *kohanim* read a special book, called *Gedele Avraham*. This book recounts the death of Abraham. After the morning service, they went to the synagogue courtyard, where the *kohanim* recited the blessing over *meswait* (special bread baked for Rosh Hashanah). The *kohanim* then broke the bread and distributed it to the congregation. After the ceremony, everyone went home to eat the holiday meal. Rosh Hashanah was passed in prayer, eating the festive meal, and studying Torah with the *kohanim*. On Rosh Hashanah, field labor was forbidden, but labor related to the home was permitted, such as preparing food and lighting fire for cooking. After the holiday ended, everyone began preparations for the Ten Days of Repentance.

Past and Present in Talmudic Halakhah

The Torah does not specify the first day of the seventh month as Rosh Hashanah, the first day of the year, or as the Day of Judgment, but calls it Zikhron Teruah, "a memorial proclaimed with the [shofar] blast" (Leviticus 23:24) and as "a day of [shofar] blasts" (Numbers 29:1). According to the book of Exodus, the month of spring – Nissan, according to the Babylonian name – was the first month of the year (Numbers 12:2). But in two places, the Torah says that the holiday of Sukkot falls at the end of the year (Exodus 23:16; 34:22). The book of Ezekiel mentions Rosh Hashanah on the tenth of the month (40:1), apparently meaning the seventh month. But Yom Kippur falls on the tenth of this month – thus the prophet seems to have considered the entire period from 1 Tishrei until Yom Kippur as one unit, which he called Rosh Hashanah. The latest biblical mention of Rosh Hashanah is from the book of Nehemiah, during the time of Ezra, at the beginning of the Second Temple. This book describes an event that took place "on the first day of the seventh month" – this day was characterized by reading the Torah and joyous celebration (Nehemiah 8:1–12).[21]

Two approaches appear in Second Temple literature. One is found in the writings of Yonatan ben Uziel, a student of Hillel, in his translation of I Kings (8:2). The other is in Josephus's *Antiquities* (1:3:3). These both consider Tishrei

---

21. Ibid.

as the first month of the original year, until the commandment "This month shall be to you the beginning of months; it shall be the first month of the year to you" (Exodus 12:2). But these sources do not associate this date with the Day of Judgment. Another approach appears in Philo of Alexandria, who views the month of Nissan as primary, considering Tishrei to be secondary. He also does not mention this day as the Day of Judgment. We may conclude that the Sages' designation of 1 Tishrei as the first day of the year[22] is based on the biblical text.

Explicit association of this day with the Day of Judgment is found in Tannaitic literature: "The world is judged at four intervals [of the year].... On the New Year, all who have entered the earth pass before Him, one by one, like young sheep."[23] Talmudic tradition ascribes this statement to Rabbi Eliezer, who related the creation of the world with the month of Tishrei. According to him, the world was created on 25 Elul, and 1 Tishrei was the sixth day of creation, on which human beings were created. On that day, man sinned and was judged, and God said, "This is a sign for your children. Just as you come before me in judgment and I granted you an exemption, so do your children come before me in judgment, and I grant them an exemption. When? On Rosh Hashanah, in the seventh month, on the first of the month."[24] One of the well-known Babylonian Amoraim composed the introductions to the special prayers for the day, known as *malkhuyot* (kingships), *zikhronot* (remembrances), and *shofarot* (shofar blowings). In the fourteenth century, increasing emphasis was placed on prayer for the Day of Judgment. Still, Rosh Hashanah was considered a holiday, and as Ezra and Nechemiah instructed the people when they gathered in Jerusalem on the first day of the seventh month: "And he said to them, 'Go, eat fat foods and drink sweet drinks and send portions to whoever has nothing prepared, for the day is holy to our Lord, and do not be sad, for the joy of the Lord is your strength'" (Nehemiah 8:10).

The Recommended Custom in Israel

The first generation is permitted to continue the Ethiopian custom. The second generation should follow the mainstream Jewish practice, since unity overcomes separation. Those of the second generation who insist on continuing the Ethiopian practices should not be criticized.

---

22. Mishnah, *Rosh Hashanah* 1:1.
23. Ibid., 1:2.
24. *Leviticus Rabbah* 29:1.

꣸ Blowing the Shofar

Ethiopian Halakhah

Blowing the shofar on Rosh Hashanah was not practiced in Ethiopia, prompting us to ask why, as this is an explicit commandment in the Torah. A significant number of sages of the community assert that they did not know of this custom. My grandfather told me that "Although we did not blow the shofar, we knew about this mitzvah and its reason. But unfortunately, during our exile in Ethiopia, they ceased performing this important mitzvah, and it was forgotten, as we had no choice. Blowing the shofar could have been interpreted as a rebellion against the authorities, and risked inciting the anger of the non-Jews against us." (Tradition holds that there was a period of forty years during which the community was not permitted to observe the mitzvot. During this period, many mitzvot were forgotten, and afterwards, the community sages were unable to reconstruct them.)

But a story I heard from a Beta Israel member puts the absence of this custom in another light. A few years after Operation Moses, the *shmaglotz* and *kohanim* were invited to Jerusalem for a meeting with members of the Chief Rabbinate of Israel. The Ethiopian representatives were asked if they knew about the mitzvah of blowing the shofar and the reason behind it. Silence filled the room. Then my grandfather began to speak, and he gave comprehensive explanations that no one had ever heard. The members of the rabbinate were amazed at his knowledge, and asked him, "Did you hear all this from your ancestors in Ethiopia?" My grandfather answered, "Yes."[25]

Past and Present in Talmudic Halakhah

The Torah states that Rosh Hashanah is Yom Teruah, "a day of blasts," but does not specify how these blasts should be sounded. The Sages recognized the tradition that they should be sounded on the shofar, as in the jubilee year (Leviticus 25:9). The Karaites, who do not accept the Oral Torah, interpreted *teruah* to mean reciting prayers out load. Jewish philosophers have given various reasons for blowing the shofar. Philo of Alexandria ascribes two meanings to this mitzvah. The first is for the Jewish people – it recalls the giving of the Torah so that we awaken to renew faith in God. The second is for all of humanity, in that the sounds the shofar make recall war among nations and the battle of humanity against the powers of nature. These wars endanger humanity, and the blasts on Rosh Hashanah are to petition God to prevent such disasters from affecting

---

25. Kaplan, *Hamesh he-arot metodologiyot*.

humanity. Rabbi Sa'adia Gaon lists ten reasons for this mitzvah. These include crowning God as King on the day creation was finished, awakening us to repent before Yom Kippur, recalling the giving of the Torah on Mount Sinai, recalling the destruction of the Temple, the ingathering of Israel's scattered, and the resurrection of the dead.[26] The Rambam writes that this is a biblical command whose meaning is hidden, but he identifies a hint:

> Wake up, you sleepy ones, from your sleep, and you who slumber, arise. Inspect your deeds, repent, remember your Creator. Those who forget the truth in the vanities of time and throughout the entire year devote their energies to vanity and emptiness which will not benefit or save: Look to your souls. Improve your ways and your deeds and let every one of you abandon his evil path and thoughts.[27]

The Recommended Custom in Israel

The mitzvah of blowing the shofar is a biblical injunction, and so everyone must fulfill it as the general Jewish population does.

🎺 Rosh Hashanah – One or Two Days?

Ethiopian Halakhah

This holiday lasts only one day, as written in the Torah: "In the seventh month, on the first day of the month."

Past and Present in Talmudic Halakhah

When the Jews sanctified the month according to the viewing of the new moon, they celebrated in Jerusalem either one or two days. If the witnesses who had seen the moon arrived on 30 Elul and the *beit din* sanctified the new month of Tishrei on that day, then this day was declared the first of Tishrei, the next day was an ordinary weekday, and Elul was a short month. If, however, the *beit din* did not sanctify the month of Tishrei on that day, then Rosh Hodesh began on the next day, making Elul a full month. Because the residents of Jerusalem could not be certain whether 30 Elul would be sanctified as the first of Tishrei, they began to observe Rosh Hashanah on the eve of 30 Elul. If the new month was declared, then they had retroactively observed the holiday at the right time. If, however, the new month was not declared, then they had to observe the next

---

26. Herman, *Ma'agal ha-hagim*.
27. Rambam, *Mishneh Torah*, Hilkhot Teshuvah 3:4.

day as Rosh Hashanah. Outside Jerusalem, the Jews always observed two days, because there was no way to inform them whether 30 Elul had been sanctified.

Eventually, the practice of sanctifying the month through witnesses was annulled, and Hillel the Second set the calendar with predetermined months and years. In the mid-fourth century, the doubt about the date was removed, and the Jews everywhere celebrated Rosh Hashanah on one day only. This was the case for several hundred years, but the Sages of Provence, followed by the major medieval rabbis – the Rif, Ramban, and Rosh – ruled that they must observe two days, because we must not stray from ancestral tradition. So in the thirteenth and fourteenth centuries, Jews in the Land of Israel observed two days for Rosh Hashanah, and the *Shulhan Arukh* also followed this ruling. Commentators were divided as to whether the second day stands as a separate unit, or whether it is a continuation of the first day. The final ruling was that the two days are one sacred unit, one long day.[28] Yet we still recite *sheheheyanu* on the second day as well as the first, and in order to remove any doubt about the propriety of saying this blessing (which sanctifies something new and should therefore not be said twice over the same thing), we place a new fruit on the table or wear a new article of clothing. Furthermore, it is forbidden to prepare anything on the first day for use on the second.

The Recommended Custom in Israel

The Ethiopian community may continue the ancient custom of celebrating one day of Rosh Hashanah. Still, on the second day they should not behave as on a weekday in public. Members of the second generation who live in other communities that observe two days of Rosh Hashanah should follow local custom, without fear of "forsaking the Torah of your mother." Unity takes precedence over ancient customs.

Tashlikh

Ethiopian Halakhah

This custom was not observed in Ethiopia.

Past and Present in Talmudic Halakhah

In the afternoon of the first day of Rosh Hashanah, the Jews customarily went to the seaside or to a river populated with fish, and recited the special prayer of

---

28. Herman, *Ma'agal ha-hagim*.

Tashlikh. This prayer is a request to throw our sins into the depths of the ocean, as in the verse "And You will cast [*ve-tashlikh*] all their sins into the depths of the sea" (Micah 7:19). In some Sephardic congregations, the prayer is called *ve-Tashlikh*, with the addition of the *vav*, reproducing the word in the verse. The reason for going to a body of water with fish is that the Jews are compared to fish – just as the fish are judged by the fisherman and his net, so the Jews are judged by God on Rosh Hashanah. Another reason for visiting a location with fish is the Sages' opinion that "The evil eye does not rule over them," and on Rosh Hashanah, we ask that God make us "be fruitful and multiply like fish." The book of customs *Hemdat Yamim* (Rabbi Yisrael Ya'akov Elgazi) gives a kabbalistic interpretation – that this custom serves to mitigate the judgment of Rosh Hashanah through an act of kindness, as water symbolizes kindness.

The Jews of Kurdistan had a custom of reciting Tashlikh and then jumping into the water wearing their clothes. In communities without a body of water nearby, they prepare a special pit or fountain in the synagogue courtyard for the purpose of this ritual. In other locations, Jews go up to a high place from which they can see water. If necessary, one may merely turn on a water faucet over a sink in the synagogue and recite the prayer over this water. We shake out the pockets of our clothing, symbolizing the removal of our sins. If the first day of Rosh Hashanah falls on Shabbat, Ashkenazic communities and some Sephardic communities (in Georgia, for example) postpone this prayer until the second day, to avoid the possibility of erring by carrying prayer books outside the *eruv*. But most of the Sephardic communities recited the prayer even on Shabbat.

This custom originated among the Ashkenazic communities, apparently in the fourteenth century. Beginning in the sixteenth century, the custom was accepted in almost all Sephardic communities, following the influence of Rabbi Haim Vital, who praised it. The Portuguese synagogue in Amsterdam has a special pit for reciting Tashlikh. This synagogue was built in 1675, which shows that at that time, the custom was known among Sephardic Jews. A small number of Sephardic communities did not accept this custom, nor did some Yemenite Jews. In addition, a small minority of Ashkenazic Jews, who belong to an extremist group that follows opinions of the Gaon of Vilna, object to this custom.[29]

---

29. Ibid.

The Recommended Custom in Israel

Praying together with the rest of the public is important. Tashlikh is a symbolic act that expresses our desire to remove our sins and to take responsibility for improving our deeds.

Ten Days of Repentance

Ethiopian Halakhah

In Ethiopia, the Ten Days of Repentance between Rosh Hashanah and Yom Kippur are called Aseru Inzh Kdus. During this period, the Ethiopian Jews intensified their prayers and petitions and giving to charity. They also tried to resolve interpersonal conflicts, with the assistance of the *kohanim* and *shmaglotz*. But as opposed to the atmosphere of this period in the Talmudic world, in Ethiopia this was a time of feasting and joy. The Beta Israel anticipated the arrival of Yom Kippur, instead of waiting for it to be over.

Past and Present in Talmudic Halakhah

During the Ten Days of Repentance, human beings are asked to evaluate themselves and repent, as during the month of Elul, but with greater intensity. The Sages interpreted the verse in Isaiah, "Seek the Lord while He may be found, call upon Him while He is near" (55:6) as referring to the Ten Days. According to the Talmud, on Rosh Hashanah three books of judgment are opened: the righteous are inscribed for life, the wicked for death, while the judgment of those in the middle is suspended until Yom Kippur.[30] The Rambam defines the Ten Days in his *Yad ha-Hazakah*: "Even though repentance and calling out [to God] are desirable at all times, during the ten days between Rosh Hashanah and Yom Kippur, they are even more desirable and will be accepted immediately, as it is said: 'Seek the Lord while He may be found' (Isaiah 55:6)."[31]

The Ten Days are also called Yamim Nora'im (Days of Awe). The period is also known as *bein keseh le-asor*: *keseh*, "hidden," refers to Rosh Hashanah, because it falls on the first day of the month when the moon is hidden; *keseh* is also based on the verse "Blow the shofar on the new moon, *ba-keseh* [when the moon is hidden] for our feast day" (Psalms 81:4); and *asor* [tenth] refers to Yom Kippur, which falls on 10 Tishrei. The Talmud specifies that during the Amidah prayers on these days, we emphasize God's kingship over the world. At the conclusion

---

30. Ibid.
31. *Mishneh Torah*, Hilkhot Teshuvah 2:8.

of the third blessing, we say "the holy King" instead of "the holy God," and at the end of the eleventh blessing, we say "the King of judgment" instead of "the King Who loves justice and judgment."

During the Geonic period, four sentences were added to the prayers, in which the individual asks for a favorable judgment for Israel. In the first blessing, which recalls the forefathers, we say: "Remember us for life, King Who desires life, and inscribe us in the book of life, for Your sake, living God." In the second blessing, recalling God's powers, we add, "Who is like You, merciful Father, Who remembers His creatures for life, in mercy?" In the eighteenth blessing, which mentions thanksgiving, we add, "Inscribe all children of Your covenant for a good life." In the nineteenth blessing, which focuses on peace, we add, "In the book of life, blessing, peace, and good livelihood (and favorable decrees, salvation, and consolation), may we be remembered and inscribed before You, we and all of Your people Israel, for a good life and for peace."

According to the Rishonim, the Rambam, and other commentators, the custom of reciting Selichot, penitential prayers, was particularly meant for this period, in which we recite penitential prayers at length, and many communities recite longer Selichot during the Ten Days than before Rosh Hashanah. On 3 Tishrei, the Fast of Gedaliah is observed, and some fasted on the other days as well. The Shabbat between Rosh Hashanah and Yom Kippur is known as Shabbat Shuvah, recalling the first word in the special *haftarah* read on this Shabbat, which begins "Return, O Israel, to the Lord your God, for you have stumbled in your iniquity" (Hosea 14:2).

The Recommended Custom in Israel
There is no significant difference between the practices of the Beta Israel and those of the general Jewish population.

Yom Kippur – Introduction
Ethiopian Halakhah
Yom Kippur is called Asterey (the festival of sighting) or Ba'al Yosef (the festival of Joseph), because on this day, Joseph saw his father, after a period of separation. We find support for this in a midrash in Jubilees:

> For this reason it is ordained for the children of Israel that they should afflict themselves on the tenth of the seventh month – on the day that the news which made him weep for Joseph came to Jacob his father. On that day they

should make atonement for themselves with a young goat, on the tenth of the seventh month, once a year, for their sins; for they had aggrieved the affection of their father regarding Joseph his son. And this day has been ordained that they should grieve for their sins, and for all their transgressions and for all their errors, so that they might cleanse themselves on that day once a year. (34:18–19)

Preparations for the holiday began on the morning of the ninth of Tishrei. They walked to the river to wash their clothes, bathe, and immerse themselves.

SELECTION FROM THE ETHIOPIAN YOM KIPPUR SERVICE

> Blessed is the Lord, God of Israel…
> Blessed is the Lord, God of Adam and Seth.
> Blessed is the Lord, God of Noah and Shem.
> Blessed is the Lord, God of Abraham and Isaac.
> Blessed is the Lord, God of Jacob and Israel…
> Blessed is the Lord, God of Zedek and Azariah.
> Blessed is the Lord, God of Dvar Barukh[32] and Avimelekh.
> Blessed is the Lord, God of Hananiah, Azariah, and Mishael.
> Blessed is the Lord, God of Zabra Sega Amlak.[33]
> Blessed is the Lord, God of Zion and Jerusalem.
> Blessed is the Lord, God of the *kohanim* and the prophets.
> Blessed is the Lord, God of the first and last generations.
> Blessed is the Lord, God of the righteous and the pure.
> Hallelujah, praise the Lord.[34]

Past and Present in Talmudic Halakhah

The holiday of Yom ha-Kippurim is usually known as Yom Kippur, or just Kippur.[35] Falling on 10 Tishrei, it is considered the holiest day of the year, and the Torah calls it Shabbat Shabbaton, "a Shabbat day of rest" (although the severity of punishment for violation of this day is less than that of Shabbat). The focus of the day is *teshuvah* (repentance) and atonement, and the Torah commands us to

---

32. Barukh ben Neriah, writer and student of the Prophet Jeremiah.
33. Zabra Sega Amlak was an Ethiopian Jewish nazirite who lived and worked in the fifteenth century.
34. From translation into Hebrew in Eshkoli, *Sefer ha-Falashim*.
35. Herman, *Ma'agal ha-hagim*.

afflict ourselves on this day, which is understood as fasting. This is the only fast that takes precedence over Shabbat. According to the Sages, on Yom Kippur, after Moses had been on Mount Sinai for forty days beginning on Rosh Hodesh Elul, God forgave the Israelites for the sin of the Golden Calf, and Moses descended from Sinai with the second set of tablets. The Rambam defines Yom Kippur as "a time of repentance": "Yom Kippur is the time of repentance for all, both individuals and the community at large. It is the apex of forgiveness and pardon for Israel. Accordingly, everyone is obligated to repent and confess on Yom Kippur."[36]

The concept of repentance is mentioned in the Torah in several places, and in many verses in the books of Prophets. In the Sages' view, Yom Kippur is the main day for forgiveness, and purification – on this day God forgives the sins of the Jewish people. Because forgiveness cannot occur without repentance, this day is dedicated to erasing our sins and starting a new page of behavior. Many philosophers have discussed the important question of repentance, of how a sin that an individual has committed can be annulled and disappear, despite the fact that the act has been done and that it sometimes has results and effects in the world. But clearly, the concept of repentance is a fundamental idea in Judaism, and it is related to this holiday.

The nature of Yom Kippur in ancient times is unclear. The ancient nature of the holiday mainly surrounded worship in the Temple. Some differentiate between the fast and the day of purification of the Temple. In the Temple Scroll (one of the Dead Sea scrolls), Yom Kippur is considered the day of purification of the Temple, but in rabbinic sources, Yom Kippur is also considered the day of dedication of the Temple and the *kohen gadol* (high priest). In effect, the Torah presents this day as one of atonement in the Temple for the Israelites' impurity. The atonement of the Israelites was intended to "cleanse" them, and thus enable a reality in which God's presence was in continuous habitation, among a people that by nature committed sins. On this day, worship in the Temple followed a special order, at the center of which stood the *kohen gadol*. On this day only, he entered the Holy of Holies (*kodesh ha-kodashim*), the holiest place in the Temple. He was the only person permitted to enter that space, and only on this day. The Yom Kippur service included special sacrificial offerings: a bull for a sin offering, a ram for an *olah* offering, and two goats, over which the lottery was drawn. One goat was sent to Azazel, while the other was sacrificed. The blood of the bull and the goats was sprinkled in front of the Ark of the Covenant in the Holy of Holies,

---

36. *Mishneh Torah*, Hilkhot Teshuvah 2:7.

and on the curtain in the *heikhal* (Holy). The *kohen gadol* recited confession over the goat and bull, for his sins, those of the other priests, and those of the entire Israelite congregation.

On Yom Kippur, the *kohen gadol* wore white clothing – four simple cloth garments, as opposed to his usual raiment of golden garments. Worship in white clothing expressed the cleansing of atonement for sins, and complete self-annihilation before God.

The Torah commands us to afflict ourselves on this day: "And [all this] shall be a statute forever to you; in the seventh month, on the tenth day, you shall afflict yourselves, and you shall do no manner of work, neither the native nor the stranger who dwells among you" (Leviticus 16:29). The Sages of the Mishnah interpreted this affliction to mean refraining from five acts: eating and drinking, anointing the body with oil, bathing, wearing leather shoes, and marital relations.[37] According to some opinions, only eating and drinking are Torah-based prohibitions, while the others are rabbinic prohibitions. Yom Kippur atones for sins between the individual and God, but not for sins between the individual and fellow human beings. For these, the Sages required the individual to ask his fellow for forgiveness. For this reason, Jews customarily ask others for forgiveness in the days preceding this holiday. In Mishnah times, on this day and on the holiday of Tu be-Av (the fifteenth day of the month of Av), young men customarily went out to the vineyards to where the young women danced, to look for potential wives. The Mishnah specifies: "Israel had no greater days of joy than the fifteenth of Av and Yom Kippur. On these days the daughters of Israel would go out dressed in white … and dance in the vineyards.… A man who was not married would go there."[38] Some explained that this custom was because on that day people were particularly pure and happy, and so this day was most appropriate to look for a wife.

Recommended Custom in Israel

Ethiopian Jews may continue their tradition and observe Yom Kippur as practiced in Ethiopia. As mentioned, in Ethiopia this holiday was not a day of awe, but rather a celebration on which they recited prayers, danced, and sang before God. It was also a day of personal introspection. One who prays in a Beta Israel *minyan* is not required to pray again in another *minyan* – he fulfills his prayer

---

37. *Yoma* 8:1.
38. Babylonian Talmud, *Ta'anit* 31:1.

From What Age Should Children Fast?

Ethiopian Halakhah
In Ethiopia, everyone over the age of seven fasted.

Past and Present in Talmudic Halakhah
Boys and girls who reach two years before the age of bar or bat mitzvah are permitted to fast the entire day, on condition that fasting will not harm their health. This fast is a rabbinically ordained mitzvah for educational purposes. From four to two years before the age of bar/bat mitzvah, we postpone their meals until later than usual, and they are forbidden from fasting a whole day. For younger children, we do not postpone their meals. Some *poskim* rule stringently on this, and specify that it is even forbidden to do so.[39]

The Recommended Custom in Israel
The Beta Israel should follow the general Jewish practice, that individuals are required to fast from age thirteen. They should not require younger children to fast, as was done in Ethiopia. Still, if a child of school age or older wishes to fast, we should not prevent him from doing so.

Yom Kippur – Joyous or Fearful?

Ethiopian Halakhah
In Ethiopia, Yom Kippur had two opposite implications. On one hand, it was a day of fasting, atonement, and forgiveness. On the other, it was a supremely joyous day, which everyone awaited in great anticipation.

Past and Present in Talmudic Halakhah
In Talmudic tradition as well, Yom Kippur had a dual meaning. On one hand, it was a day of fasting and special service by the *kohen gadol* in the Temple; on the other, it was a day of rejoicing and dancing in the vineyards, as we learn from the Mishnah. The reason for this joy was that on Yom Kippur, Moses was given the second set of two tablets, and God forgave the Israelites for the sin of the

---

39. Herman, *Ma'agal ha-hagim*.

Golden Calf. Therefore on this day, He forgives all of Israel's sins. Another reason is that during this period, including Yom Kippur, Solomon dedicated the Temple that he built (II Chronicles 7:8–10). After the destruction of the First Temple, the motif of rejoicing was restricted, and the motif of the Day of Judgment was emphasized and took on greater significance.

The Recommended Custom in Israel

The Beta Israel should continue the practices they followed in Ethiopia. This is a holiday filled with rejoicing. Those who pray according to the Ethiopian service with *kesim* are permitted to use the musical instruments that the spiritual leaders traditionally used on this day (such as drums, cymbals, stick, and *chira* [horsehair instrument]). However, those who follow a different service should not do so.

࿓ Yom Kippur on Shabbat

Ethiopian Halakhah

When Yom Kippur falls on Shabbat, according to custom the Beta Israel recited Kiddush and ate a small amount, so as not to reduce the sanctity of Shabbat. They then continued the fast, so as not to reduce the sanctity of Yom Kippur.

Past and Present in Talmudic Halakhah

In contrast to the Ethiopian community, which chose to observe both sacred days simultaneously, Talmudic halakhah rules that when Yom Kippur falls on Shabbat, we must fast.[40]

The Recommended Custom in Israel

Apparently, the Ethiopian interpretation of preserving both sacred days at once is based on an ancient tradition. Thus we recommend that when Yom Kippur falls on Shabbat, the Ethiopian community should continue their custom. Even on Shabbat, they should recite Kiddush over bread or wine, but they should only give food or drinks to the children under age seven (as for a *brit milah* that falls on Yom Kippur). Adults should not eat or drink anything, not even a small taste. Some propose following the custom of the Rambam, to recite Kiddush at the time of the afternoon prayer service, before Yom Kippur actually begins, during the final meal.[41] In this manner, they can continue observing their tradition, but without violating the laws of Yom Kippur.

---

40. Ibid.
41. Rabbi Nachum Rabinowitz, *shlita*.

꙳ Sukkot

Ethiopian Halakhah

Sukkot is called Bale Meselet, and is celebrated according to the biblical injunction "in the seventh month, on the fifteenth day of the month," meaning on 15 Tishrei. People from the village volunteered to build a *sukkah* in the synagogue courtyard. They built a very large *sukkah* for the whole village. The *sukkah* was built of wood, never of metal – not for halakhic reasons, but because wood was more readily available, or perhaps they did not think of the idea of using metal. On the eve of Sukkot, everyone gathered in the synagogue courtyard. The *kohanim* recited a special prayer in honor of the holiday. The first day of Sukkot was a holy day, on which labor was forbidden, as written in the Torah of Moses the prophet. On the other days, they performed labors in the home, such as cooking, gathering the harvest in the field, and even walking or riding donkeys to go shopping. On the eighth day, all labor was forbidden. This day was sacred, like the first day. In practice, they sat in the *sukkah* only on the first day, but not on the other days.

Past and Present in Talmudic Halakhah

The command to celebrate the holiday of Sukkot, also called *hag ha-asif*, "festival of the ingathering," is given in several locations in the Torah (Exodus 23:16; Exodus 34:22; Leviticus 23:33–43; Deuteronomy 16:13–17), in the Prophets (1 Kings 8:2; Ezekiel 45:25), and in ancient rabbinic texts. In the Prophets, it is called simply *hag* (1 Kings 8:2; Nehemiah 8:14). The commandment to build the *sukkah* is to commemorate the booths that God provided for the Israelites when He took them out of Egypt. The Tanna Rabbi Eliezer comments that these *sukkot* were the clouds of glory that protected the Israelites as they were walking in the desert. The Gaon of Vilna supports this interpretation, saying that on Yom Kippur, 10 Tishrei, Moses descended from Sinai with the second set of tablets, and on the next day, 11 Tishrei, he gathered the nation and commanded them: "'Take from among you an offering to the Lord; whoever is of a willing heart, let him bring it, [namely] the Lord's offering: gold, and silver, and copper' (Exodus 35:5)."

The Torah then specifies, "So they took from before Moses all the offering[s], which the children of Israel had brought for the work of the service of the sanctuary, to make it. And they brought him more gifts every morning [*ba-boker ba-boker*]" (Exodus 36:3). The word *boker* (morning) appears twice, meaning that the Israelites brought their offerings for two days, on 12 and 13 Tishrei. The next day, 14 Tishrei, the craftsmen received the offerings, and then on 15 Tishrei they began to build the Tabernacle. At this point, the clouds of glory, which had disappeared due to the sin of the Golden Calf, returned to protect the people – thus we build *sukkot* on 15 Tishrei, in commemoration of those clouds of glory. The Tanna Rabbi Akiva offers another explanation, that the commandment of *sukkah* is designed to remind us of the *sukkot* that the Israelites constructed when they camped in the desert.[42]

The Recommended Custom in Israel

The Beta Israel should follow the general custom. Each individual should try to construct his own private *sukkah* for his family. In addition, they should also build a large *sukkah* in the synagogue courtyard and hold at least two meals inside it.

Arba'at ha-Minim (The Four Species)

Ethiopian Halakhah

The mitzvah of the four species was not practiced in Ethiopia. Although the Beta Israel were aware of the biblical verses regarding the taking of the four species, they did not follow the practice as was done in the Talmudic world. They did place willow or date branches on top of the *sukkah* that was built in the synagogue courtyard. I asked the community priests about the meaning of this custom, but they did not have a clear, uniform answer. They also used to bring several types of vegetables to the *sukkah* – corn, peppers, and peas. The priests recited a blessing over these, and only after this blessing were members of the community permitted to eat from the new harvest, even in their own homes.

Past and Present in Talmudic Halakhah

The Torah commands us to take "four species" on Sukkot, as the verse specifies: "And you shall take for yourselves on the first day the fruit of goodly trees [*pri etz hadar* – the *etrog*], branches of palm trees [*lulav*], and boughs of thick trees [*hadas* – myrtle], and willows of the brook [*arvei nahal*, known commonly today as *aravot*], and you shall rejoice before the Lord your God for seven days" (Leviticus 23:40). In rabbinic literature, this mitzvah is called the "mitzvah of the *lulav*," as the *lulav* is the tallest and most conspicuous of the four species.

According to Pharisaic tradition, this mitzvah is not related to the mitzvah of constructing the *sukkah*. But for the Samaritans and the Karaites, these species are used to cover the *sukkah*. We find evidence for this in Ezra's instruction to

---

42. Ibid.

the people: "Go forth to the mountain, and fetch olive branches, and branches of wild olive, and myrtle branches, and palm branches, and branches of thick trees, to make booths, as it is written" (Nehemiah 8:15). According to the Rambam, the reason for this mitzvah was that the four species symbolized the joy of entry into the Land of Israel, which was flowering and green, and had both fruit trees and non-fruit-bearing trees, after life in the treeless desert. In addition, apparently the four species were more common in the Land of Israel at that time. Others explain that during the festival of ingathering, an individual might mistakenly think that he attained his wealth due to his own strength and talents. Therefore he must take from the crops that grew and wave them before God, in order to express thanks for the abundant yield.[43]

Another reason for this mitzvah was that the four species symbolize the four most important parts of the body: the *etrog* symbolizes the heart, the *lulav* the spine, the *hadas* the eyes, and the willow the mouth. Particularly in times of joy, a person must stand watch over these body parts, to ensure they do not tempt him to deviate from the straight path. Taking the four species thus reminds an individual that he must use these body parts for faith in God.

The Midrash views the four species as a metaphor for the Jewish people. The *etrog*, which has both taste and smell, represents the righteous, who have both Torah (taste) and good deeds (smell). The *lulav* has no taste, but it has taste in its fruit – the date – and it represents those who have Torah, but no good deeds. The *hadas* has only smell, and so it represents those Jews who have only good deeds; while the willow has neither taste nor smell, and so it represents the wicked. Binding them together in one cluster teaches us of the aspiration for unity of our nation, and has the power to atone for the people, as the Midrash says: "Bind them together in one cluster, and one atones for the other."[44]

The Recommended Custom in Israel

The first generation is permitted to continue the custom from Ethiopia. But the second generation is advised to adopt the custom practiced in the majority of Jewish communities. There is no preference for a specific practice in this area – one may adopt any variation one wants.

---

43. Ibid.
44. *Leviticus Rabbah* 30:12.

ꙮ Shemini Atzeret–Simhat Torah

Ethiopian Halakhah

This holiday was not observed in Ethiopia. According to the testimony of several *kesim*, however, on the eighth day of Sukkot, one of the young *kohanim* would hold the Orit and pass before the congregation. The *kohanim* recited songs of joy, to a special beat played on cymbals and drum, similar to that of Yom Kippur. Everyone danced a special dance in front of the Torah. Here we should note that once a year, on the Sigd festival, they took the Torah scrolls out of the synagogue and carried the Orit up a hill.

Past and Present in Talmudic Halakhah

Shemini Atzeret is a biblical holiday that falls on 22 Tishrei. The Torah mentions this holiday after the laws of Sukkot: "And on the fifteenth day of the seventh month you shall have a holy convocation: you shall do no manner of servile work, and you shall celebrate a festival to the Lord for seven days.... On the eighth day you shall have a solemn assembly [*atzeret*]: you shall do no manner of servile work" (Numbers 29:12, 35). Although the Torah mentions it as the eighth day of Sukkot, we do not practice the mitzvot of Sukkot on this day, and it is considered a separate holiday. This day has no characteristic symbols, in contrast to Passover and Sukkot. According to a midrash, the significance of this holiday lies in its biblical name, Atzeret, which implies that God asks His children, the Israelites, to stop and stay with Him for another day, instead of rushing to return home. He asks the pilgrims who have come to Jerusalem to remain another day, the eighth day of Sukkot.[45]

In Israel, the Jews celebrate this day as Simhat Torah (the [day of] rejoicing over the Torah), and this is the most well-known name for the holiday. But this is not the same holiday. Shemini Atzeret is a biblical holiday, while Simhat Torah was declared later, during the Geonic period.

Further, holidays in the Torah have an agricultural aspect, in addition to their religious nature. Sukkot is also known as "the feast of ingathering, at the end of the year, when you gather in [the products of] your labors out of the field" (Exodus 23:16). This period is the beginning of the rainy season in Israel, and so on Shemini Atzeret we recite the prayer for rain, which marks the beginning of the rainy season, and in which we ask God to bless the year with rain. During Second Temple times, the Jews followed other customs related to water, such as

---

45. Herman, *Ma'agal ha-hagim*.

the water libation ceremony, Simhat Beit ha-Shoevah, and recitation of *hoshanot* prayers. Apparently, these customs are of ancient origin.

The Recommended Custom in Israel

The first generation should continue to follow the custom from Ethiopia. For the second generation, we recommend adopting the general Jewish custom.

The Sigd Festival (Mahlele)

Ethiopian Halakhah

SOURCE OF THE FESTIVAL

The biblical source for the Sigd[46] holiday is in the book of Nehemiah:

> And Ezra opened the book in the sight of all the people – for he was above all the people – and when he opened it, all the people stood up. And Ezra blessed the Lord, the great God. And all the people answered, "Amen, Amen," with the lifting up of their hands; and they bowed their heads, and fell down before the Lord with their faces to the ground. (Nehemiah 8:5–6)
>
> And they stood up in their place, and read in the book of the Law of the Lord their God a fourth of the day; and another fourth part they confessed, and prostrated themselves before the Lord their God. (Nehemiah 9:3)

DATE

For many generations, this holiday was celebrated on 29 Heshvan, fifty days after Yom Kippur.[47]

The Sigd holiday connects between the individual's spiritual self-accounting, which takes place on Yom Kippur, and the central disaster of the Jewish people – exile to the Diaspora, which took place due to the breakdown of proper interpersonal relations. The basic assumption is that in order to be deserving of pilgrimage to Jerusalem, fasting on Yom Kippur and personal improvement are not enough. The individual must count seven weeks during which the days are enlightened with the bright light of the individual repentance and atonement of Yom Kippur. On the fiftieth day, the circle of this counting is closed, and we

---

46. The exact transliteration of the Ge'ez word is "Sgd," but Western texts usually use "Sigd" for ease of pronunciation. The alternate name Mahelele is parallel to the Hebrew word *mehalelah*, "supplication," derived from the Hebrew word Hallel, "praise" (of God).
47. This is similar to Shavuot, which falls fifty days after Passover. Shoshanah Ben-Dor, *Ha-Sigd shel Beta Yisrael: Hag hidush ha-brit* [Sigd: the festival of the renewal of the covenant] (Hebrew University, 5745).

must return to the experience of Yom Kippur, but this time as a collective that has undergone a reparative experience and heightening of moral, individual, and social awareness.

MEANING OF THE HOLIDAY

This holiday has several meanings:

1. Sigd recalls the giving of the Torah on Mount Sinai as the foundation of the covenant with God.
2. On this day, we commemorate the renewal of the covenant by the exiled Jews who returned to Jerusalem in the days of the Return to Zion.
3. Sigd serves as an opportunity to remind the Beta Israel, who are distant from the rest of the Jewish people, of the need to be faithful to the mitzvot, the Torah, and Jerusalem, despite the difficulty this may involve.
4. This holiday is an opportunity for the Beta Israel to recognize their repentance, to demonstrate their faithfulness to the covenant, and to address their heavenly Father through fasting and prayer.
5. Sigd leads to reconciliation between individuals. It creates a feeling of unity and security.

PREPARATIONS FOR SIGD

The day before Sigd, everyone, from children to the elderly, prepared with great anticipation for the next day. It was customary to prepare one's holiday clothes and launder them.[48] The *kohanim* slaughtered cows and sheep and prepared the meat for a celebratory meal at the end of the Sigd holiday, and everyone gathered in the central villages, where the festival was held. In order to reach the villages on time, sometimes they had to travel long distances over several days.[49] On the eve of the festival, it was customary to recite special prayers.

LOCATION OF SIGD

The Sigd celebration was always held on a high hill. Two reasons are given for this practice:

---

48. Similar to the preparations made by the Israelites for the giving of the Torah at Mount Sinai, which included laundering their clothes: "And the Lord said to Moses: 'Go to the people, and sanctify them today and tomorrow, and let them wash their garments" (Exodus 19:10).
49. In ancient times, the pilgrimage to Jerusalem took a long time as well.

1. To reenact Moses' ascent to Mount Sinai on the day of the giving of the Torah.
2. A high place was considered sacred.

Before beginning prayers, the *kohanim* or elders of the community ascended the hill to the prayer site, in order to ascertain that everything was clean and pure, and to reinforce the fence that surrounded the site. They prepared a place for the Orit at the front part of the fence.

ON THE DAY OF SIGD

Early in the morning, the residents of the village and guests who had arrived went to the river to immerse themselves, and put on their clean holiday garments. Everyone gathered together, and the *kohanim* took out the Orit and sang while the women emitted joyous sounds. Then they marched up the hill, carrying the Orit at the head of the procession. Some of the climbers carried stones on their backs or heads, to symbolize submission and surrender before God. When they reached the prayer site, the *kohanim* began the prayers for the day. Prayer was accompanied by hand movements.[50]

Below is the order of prayers:

1. Prayer for Jerusalem and the desire to bow down before God in Jerusalem.
2. The high priest enjoins the congregation to observe the laws of the Torah.
3. Reading from the Orit:
    - The story of God's revelation on Mount Sinai.
    - Reading from chapter 9 of the book of Nehemiah: renewal of the covenant between the people and God at the time of the Return to Zion.
    - Reading the sections on blessings and curses – Leviticus 26 and Deuteronomy 28–29.

The *kohanim* translated everything from Ge'ez to the spoken language – either Amharic or Tigrinya.

Toward the end, everyone asked for forgiveness for their sins. They went down on their knees and prostrated themselves on the ground while spreading their palms to Heaven. Then the shofar was blown, and they said, "Just as we have merited celebrating the holiday this year, so may we merit celebrating it next year in Jerusalem." The day concludes with everyone descending the mountain

---

50. Sperber, *Minhagei Yisrael*, vol. 4, *Tefillat Moshe ve-inyan prisat ha-yadayim ba-tefillah* [Moses' prayer and the topic of spreading the hands during prayer], 71.

in joy and dancing to the *tzelot* building (house of prayer), where they hold a festive meal.

Excerpts from the prayer for Jerusalem:

Hallelujah, praise God	Rise up, Jerusalem
May your walls be rebuilt, Jerusalem	Gates of Jerusalem
We direct our prayer to You in Jerusalem	Roads of Jerusalem
Within the justice of Jerusalem	In the midst of Jerusalem
Lift the horn of Jerusalem	Return, Jerusalem
And pour out your blood around Jerusalem	Listen, Jerusalem.[51]

Past and Present in Talmudic Halakhah

Some assert that Sigd is a particular, local holiday that developed in Ethiopia, and that it was never known in any other Jewish community. But I would like to argue that in ancient times, Sigd was known among the entire Jewish people, and that due to historical circumstances, it was forgotten, while in Ethiopia it was preserved. A Talmudic source indicates the existence of this custom in the past throughout the Jewish world:

> Rabbi Yehoshua ben Levi said, By rights, the Eighth Day of Assembly (Shemini Atzeret) should have followed Sukkot after an interval of fifty days, as Shavuot follows Passover. But since at the Eighth Day of Assembly summer passes into autumn, the time is not suitable for traveling. To what may this be compared? A king had several married daughters, some living nearby, while others were a long way away. One day they all came to visit their father, the king. Said the king: "Those who are living nearby are able to travel at any time. But those who live at a distance are not able to travel at any time. So while they are all here with me, let us make one feast for all of them and rejoice with them." So with regard to Shavuot, which comes when winter is passing into summer, God says, "The season is fit for traveling." But the Eighth Day of Assembly comes when summer is passing into autumn, and the roads are dusty and hard for walking; hence it is not separated by an interval of fifty days. Said the Holy One, blessed be He: "These are not days for traveling; so while they are here, let us make of all of them one festival and rejoice." Therefore Moses admonishes Israel, saying to them, "On the eighth day you shall have

---

51. Translation based on Eshkoli, *Sefer ha-Falashim*.

a solemn assembly" (Numbers 29:35). Thus we may say, "How beautiful are your steps in sandals" (Song of Songs 7:2).[52]

This midrash indicates that the counting began from the first day of Sukkot, as opposed to the Ethiopian custom, which began from Yom Kippur. Still, I think it is strong evidence of the existence of this custom among the general Jewish community.[53]

The Recommended Custom in Israel

The Ethiopian Jews should continue to celebrate Sigd, which is an ancient holiday that may have been celebrated by the entire Jewish people. Further, the Jews living in their homeland today are very much in need of the messages and focus of the Sigd holiday in Ethiopia, which have eternal relevance: fraternal love, unity, and the formation of the covenant with the God of Israel and Jerusalem.

Extra-Biblical Holidays

Ethiopian Halakhah

These holidays were not known in Ethiopia, since they were established after the Tanakh was canonized.

Past and Present in Talmudic Halakhah

The extra-biblical holidays include Hanukkah and Purim, which were instituted after the destruction of the First Temple. Additional dates are mentioned in ancient rabbinic literature, and while they have no specific mitzvot associated with them, they do have customs that were also listed in the *Shulhan Arukh*. These are Tu bi-Shvat, Lag ba-Omer, and Tu be-Av. Further, specific communities have popular days of rejoicing that are not mentioned in rabbinic literature, such as the Moroccan Mimouna festival that marks the end of Passover.[54]

There are also a number of holidays instituted by the modern State of Israel, including Yom ha-Atzma'ut (Israel Independence Day) and Yom Yerushalayim (Liberation of Jerusalem Day). Yom ha-Atzma'ut was established following the creation of the state on 5 Iyyar 5708 (1948), and Yom Yerushalayim was established following the liberation of Jerusalem during the Six-Day War, on 28 Iyyar 5727 (1967). Other days of Israeli national commemoration and mourning are

---

52. *Songs Rabbah* (Vilna ed.) 7:4, s.v. "another explanation."
53. I thank Rabbi Re'em Zafri for pointing out this *midrash* to me.
54. Herman, *Ma'agal ha-hagim*.

Yom ha-Shoah (Holocaust and Heroism Remembrance Day) on 27 Nissan, and Yom ha-Zikaron (Memorial Day for Fallen Soldiers of the IDF) on 4 Iyyar.

Contemporary rabbis disagree over whether to consider these Israeli national days as religious holidays. The national-religious camp, led by the Chief Rabbinate of Israel, views them as such. In contrast, the ultra-Orthodox, led by the Council of Torah Sages of the Agudat Yisrael, the Beit Din Zedek (religious high court) of the ultra-Orthodox community, and the Sephardic Moetzet Hakhmei ha-Torah, among other groups and leaders, asserts that these holidays have no religious significance, and should not be included in the list of holidays.

The Recommended Custom in Israel

The second generation should accept all the extra-biblical holidays that were decreed by the Sages, and it is advisable for the first generation to do so as well.

Hanukkah

Ethiopian Halakhah

This holiday was unknown in Ethiopia. The custom of Hannukah was brought to the villages only recently.

Past and Present in Talmudic Halakhah

The eight days of Hanukkah begin on 25 Kislev. The holiday is a time of rejoicing over the purification of the Temple and rededication of the Altar by Judah Maccabee in 164 BCE, after he vanquished the Greeks and their allies, the Hellenizing Jews.[55] In order to understand the background for the struggle against the Greeks, we must go back in time to 333 BCE. In this year, Alexander Macedon conquered the Middle East, including the Land of Israel. This began a process of integrating the cultures of East and West into what became known as "Hellenistic culture." Its outstanding characteristics were the development of a shared language, blurring of national differences, and encouragement of individualism, and change in the concept of the state – in other words, a worldview that placed the individual at the center of society. Dozens of Jewish towns became city-states, following the pattern of the Greek city, which was called *polis*. The *polis* was led by a people's council and elected officials. Security was maintained by a civilian army, and the towns supported a Greek cultural lifestyle: theaters

---

55. Herman, *Ma'agal ha-hagim*.

were built, sports competitions were held, and Greek-style civil education was provided to the inhabitants.

The Jews of ancient Palestine from the wealthy, well-connected strata of society, and mainly the priestly families, adopted the characteristics of this culture, thus acquiring the confidence of the Hellenistic rulers, who gave them authority over the Temple service. The Jewish populace, however, viewed this trend as assimilation and a desecration of Judaism. Disputes broke out between the Hellenistic priestly nobility and the masses. The tension reached its peak during the reign of Antiochus Epiphanes, who ruled from 175 to 164 BCE. The priests participated in sports competitions in Jerusalem, which had recently become a Greek *polis*, and neglected their duties in the Temple, as described in the book of Maccabees: "Even the priests lost all interest in their sacred duties. They lost interest in the Temple services and neglected the sacrifices. Just as soon as the signal was given, they would rush off to take part in the games that were forbidden by our Law. They did not care about anything their ancestors had valued; they prized only Greek honors."[56]

Resentment toward the Hellenizers simmered until eventually it ignited into rebellion. In 167 BCE, Antiochus Epiphanes passed anti-religious decrees. He forbade the Jews from observing the mitzvot, and forced them to participate in idol worship and to eat forbidden foods. For example, any Jew who circumcised his son or kept Shabbat was executed. The Temple was desecrated and renamed after the Greek god Zeus. Jews gave their lives for sanctifying God's name. The rebellion spread under the leadership of Matathias the Hasmonean and his sons. Following his death, leadership passed to his son Judah, called "the Maccabee," and on 25 Kislev, 164 BCE, he conquered Jerusalem. He purified the Temple and transferred its service to the anti-Hellenizers. The rebels celebrated the purification of the Temple and the rededication of the Altar for eight days. In commemoration of this, a holiday was decreed, to be celebrated by praising and thanking God and by lighting candles each day.[57]

The first evidence of lighting candles in a *hanukkiyah* (an eight-branched candelabra or menorah) is from the medieval period. The Jews adorned these with a variety of decorative elements, and they were made of different types of metal,

---

56. II Maccabees 4:14–15.
57. Sperber, *Minhagei Yisrael*, vol. 5, *Mai Hanukkah?* [What is Hanukkah?], 1–19; vol. 1, *Hadlakat nerot Hanukkah be-minhag Yehudei Paras* [Lighting Hanukkah candles in Persian Jewish custom], 167.

according to financial resources of the period. After lighting the first candle, we recite the blessing *ha-nerot ha-lalu*, which is mentioned in Tractate Sofrim, in order to publicize the halakhah that it is forbidden to use the candles for any specific purpose, including a sacred act such as studying Torah.

The Recommended Custom in Israel

The Beta Israel should follow the general Jewish custom. Today, the entire community has adopted the beautiful custom of Hanukkah, and so we observe Hanukkah candles lit in Ethiopian homes as well. This phenomenon proves the distinction that the Ridbaz made between the Ethiopian Jews and the Karaites in his well-known halakhic ruling accepting the Ethiopian Jews as part of the Jewish people.[58] In other words, when the Ethiopian Jews return to the Land of Israel, they certainly will not object to accepting the mitzvot that were handed down orally through the Mishnah and the Talmud. The mitzvah of Hanukkah is a good example of this willingness.

Purim

Ethiopian Halakhah

The Beta Israel community did not recognize the holiday of Purim as it is celebrated today in the Jewish world. But it did celebrate this holiday in its own way. The complete Megillat Esther (Scroll of Esther) appears in Ge'ez. The Ethiopian Jews observed the Fast of Esther in the daytime for three days, eating only a small amount at night for sustenance. This was the extent of their observance of this holiday. When I asked why they did not celebrate with rejoicing or feasting, as is recorded in the Megillah, I was given several answers.

1. The community wished to rejoice and feast, but did not do so because true joy was in Jerusalem, not in the Diaspora.
2. The first missives declaring the destruction of the Jews reached Ethiopia, but the second batch informing them of the change of fortune did not reach their country.
3. My grandfather's answer: "We were aware of the good fortune that God bestowed on us, but we did not rejoice due to fear of the non-Jews. We did not want to provoke them." He then added, "We lived in distress and hardship for years. Were we to suddenly break into rejoicing in our village, this

---

58. Responsa of the Ridbaz, part 7, par. 5.

would have aroused the curiosity of our Christian neighbors, with adverse results." He continued, "The joy of Purim was internal; deep in our hearts we felt intense happiness.... The heart of our community is able to contain the joy of Purim inside, even with no external expression. We can rejoice and dance in elation, but quietly."

Past and Present in Talmudic Halakhah

Although Esther asked King Ahasuerus to annul the decree of destruction of the Jews that he had sealed with his ring (Esther ch. 3), he was unable to fulfill her request, because according to Persian law, "the writing that is written in the king's name, and sealed with the king's ring, no man may reverse" (Esther 8:8). Thus the king's servants rushed to send out new orders with their runners. The mounted couriers rode out hastily (8:13) to distribute the missives, which said that on 13 Adar, the Jews were permitted to gather in self-defense, kill their enemies, and take the spoils (8:11). When the Jews received the dispatches, they feasted and rejoiced (8:17). On 13 Adar, they fought and killed their enemies, but did not take the spoils of battle (9:10), and on 14 Adar, they again feasted and rejoiced.

The Sages consider that the three days of fasting to annul the decree were at Passover, after Haman wrote the first dispatches on 13 Nissan (3:12; 4:16). In literary sources dated after Megillat Esther, we find that Jews in the Land of Israel fasted on different dates than the Jews in Babylonia. The custom of fasting on 13 Adar did not become widespread until the Geonic period (see below). Rabbinic literature reveals that Purim was not easily accepted by the Jewish people. Some objected to its observance, fearing that it would arouse the animosity of the non-Jews. During the Hellenistic period and at the beginning of the Roman period, it was not widely recognized.[59] It was finally accepted by the majority of Jews in the late Second Temple period, as evidenced by Josephus: "Thus today all the Jews also celebrate ... these days, and send portions, each to his friend."[60]

The Recommended Practice in Israel

The Beta Israel should follow the general Jewish practice. Most of the community already celebrates Purim as it is done in Israel. Members of the first generation, however, who wish to fast for three days, may do so, as long as this does not cause bodily harm – saving a life supersedes all customs. In general, we should limit fasting. The second generation should adopt the widespread customs of Purim.

---

59. Herman, *Ma'agal ha-hagim*.
60. *Antiquities* 11:292.

❧ Date of the Fast of Esther

Ethiopian Halakhah
The three days of fasting fell during Passover.

Past and Present in Talmudic Halakhah
The Fast of Esther was observed on 13 Adar. Before Esther went in to King Ahasuerus to ask him to annul Haman's decree of destruction for the Jews, Esther fasted for three days, and asked her people to join her. According to rabbinic tradition, these three days of fasting fell during Passover. The custom in ancient Palestine was to fast for three non-contiguous days after Purim: Monday, Thursday, and the next Monday. This was because one should not fast during the month of Nissan, since the Temple was constructed then, and also due to the conflict with Passover. But the Babylonian custom was to fast for three non-contiguous days before Purim, and one of these days was apparently 13 Adar. In Palestine, however, the Jews did not do so, for two reasons: (1) Commemoration of sorrows should not be pushed forward in time. (2) Later, in Second Temple times, 13 Adar became a day of rejoicing over Judah Maccabee's victory over Nicanor and the Greeks in 161 BCE (I Maccabees 7:43–49). Thus it was forbidden to fast on this date. This date appears on the list of days of rejoicing in the Second Temple period, and is mentioned in Megillat Ta'anit as a day when fasting and mourning are forbidden. Following the destruction of the Temple, Megillat Ta'anit was annulled, and fasting was again permitted on 13 Adar, in Palestine as well.[61]

Apparently, in the first few centuries BCE, the majority of the Jewish people stopped fasting for three days due to the difficulty of such a fast, and they accepted 13 Adar as the day of commemoration of the Fast of Esther. By the Geonic period, the custom of fasting on 13 Adar had become widespread. Some explain that even during the time in which the Megillah was written, the Jews fasted on 13 Adar, on the day they battled their enemies. The Fast of Esther was established in commemoration of this fast. Even though the Megillah does not specify this fast, we may assume that the Jews fasted and prayed on this day, as we find that they fasted and prayed in other times of war.[62]

The Recommended Custom in Israel
The Beta Israel should follow the general Jewish custom.

---

61. Herman, *Ma'agal ha-hagim*.
62. *Mishnah Berurah* 686:2.

❧ Additional Holidays

Ethiopian Halakhah

- The tenth day of each month is a special day. The main expression of this is in the prayer service. On that day, we recite special prayers that recall Yom Kippur, which falls on 10 Tishrei.
- The twelfth day of each month is observed with special prayers in commemoration of Shavuot, which falls on 12 Sivan.
- The fifteenth day of each month is observed in commemoration of Passover, which falls on this day in the month of Nissan.
- 18 Elul commemorates the anniversary of the death of the patriarchs.
- The seventh Shabbat after Rosh Hodesh Nissan is called Yesenvet Senvet (Shabbat of Shabbatot).

These holidays were mainly observed by the spiritual leaders and the *shmaglotz*.

Past and Present in Talmudic Halakhah

17 TAMMUZ

According to tradition, this day commemorates five events:[63]

1. Moses broke the Tablets of the Law after the sin of the Golden Calf. Moses ascended Mount Sinai on Shavuot. Forty days later was 17 Tammuz, the date when the Israelites realized that Moses was delayed, and they strayed and committed this sin.
2. The *tamid* offering in the Temple was annulled, at the morning and afternoon service. Rabbinic sources document that this took place during the Babylonians' siege of the First Temple, and again during the Hellenistic regime during the Second Temple.
3. In 70 CE, the Romans besieged Jerusalem, and on this date they breached the walls of the city and began their destruction of the Second Temple. According to the Jerusalem Talmud, the walls were breached on this date during First Temple times as well. The prophet Jeremiah notes 9 Tammuz as the day of the breaching (52:6–7), but this is apparently a mistake due to the crisis situation.
4. On this date, Apostomus burned the Torah. The identity of this man is unknown. Some say this took place in the Hellenistic period, during the reign of Antiochus Epiphanes, as the books of Maccabees relate that he and

---

63. Ibid.

his cohorts tore and burned Torah scrolls. Some relate this event to a later period, in Roman times, sixteen years before the Jewish Revolt, during the rule of the Roman procurator Ventidius Cumanus.
5. An idol was placed in the Temple, apparently by Apostomus, but some say that it was erected by King Menashe, son of Hizkiyahu, in the seventh century BCE.

9 AV

Traditionally, five events occurred on this date:

1. God punished the Israelites who participated in the sin of the spies, decreeing that they would not enter the Land of Israel.
2. In 586 BCE, the First Temple was destroyed by the soldiers of Nebuchadnezzar, king of Babylon.
3. In 70 CE, the Second Temple was destroyed by the Romans, under Titus.
4. The city of Beitar was destroyed following the failure of the Bar Kochba Revolt, in 135 CE.
5. The Romans plowed over the city of Jerusalem after the Bar Kochba Revolt, to prepare the ground to build a temple honoring the god Jupiter on the site of the Jewish Temple.

3 TISHREI – FAST OF GEDALIA

On this date in 582 BCE, Gedalia son of Ahikam was assassinated in Mitzpe. Four years after the destruction of the First Temple, Gedalia was appointed by the Babylonian king to govern the remaining Jewish community in Judah, as they began to return to their usual way of life. But a group of extremists led by Ishmael son of Natanya viewed Gedalia as a traitor and collaborator, and they assassinated him. The remaining community dispersed, and the hope of rebuilding Judah and Jerusalem was lost.

10 TEVET

This date marked the beginning of the siege of Jerusalem by the Babylonian king Nebuchadnezzar in 588 BCE. One source holds that the siege lasted for two years, until 9 Tammuz in 586 BCE, while another source says it lasted until 17 Tammuz of that year. In 5715/1956, the Chief Rabbinate of Israel decided to set this date for the commemoration of the deaths of the six million Jews who were killed in the Holocaust, and whose actual death anniversaries are unknown. On this day, we pray for the ascent of their souls, light memorial candles, recite the Kaddish (mourner's prayer), and hold memorial ceremonies. The Chief Rabbinate chose this day because the harm to the Jews began on 10 Tevet and reached its peak in the events of the Holocaust. Thus 10 Tevet is also known "the general Kaddish day."[64]

The Recommended Custom in Israel

Regarding fasts (except for Tisha be-Av), Rabbi Nachum Rabinowitz recommends that the Ethiopian Jews follow their original custom. A group that did not take the fasts upon itself does not have to adopt them now after returning to the Holy Land. The Talmud and the Rishonim indicate that the fasts depend on public acceptance.[65] We should also discuss the status of these fasts in modern times, when Israel is no longer under foreign rule, considering the Rambam's statement that the fasts will be annulled in the messianic era.[66] Thus the Ethiopian Jews should continue their original custom with regard to fasts. But members of the second generation may change their custom, for educational or personal reasons.

---

64. Ibid.
65. Babylonian Talmud, *Rosh Hashanah* 18.
66. *Mishneh Torah*, Hilkhot Ta'anit, end of section.

5. Bride, Groom, and Family

❧ Engagement and Marriage

Ethiopian Halakhah

Under Ethiopian custom, a man does not approach a woman on his own to propose a connection that leads to marriage. If he did this, he would be suspected of enticing her into prostitution, and would not be answered at all. Rather, the parents of the groom take the initiative for making a match. The parents of the bride wait for proposals. When parents think the time has come for their son to start his own household, they begin to consult with relatives about appropriate women.

The family usually helps with the search. When they identify a young woman of appropriate age, they check several details. First, they make sure she is not a relative, as in Ethiopia it is forbidden to marry a relative for seven generations back. They then investigate the potential bride's family, for observance of tradition, interpersonal behavior, financial status, or any rumors about the family. The investigations are done in secret, within the family.

After they have decided on the appropriate bride, the father of the groom and a close friend visit the home of the bride's parents, and ask to be their guests, with no advance notice. The prospective bride's parents do not know the reason for the visit. After the guests eat and drink, one of them stands before the parents and says, "We have come here today because we would very much like to become your relatives, we wish to ask for your daughter's hand in marriage to our son." The bride's parents ask the guests to sit. They ask for time to consult with their relatives, and promise them an answer soon.

Then it is the turn of the bride's parents to investigate the groom's parents, their family connections, and their financial status. If they decide to give a negative answer, the connection is terminated. If the answer is positive, the parents of the bride and groom fix a time for the engagement.

The engagement is held in the home of the bride's parents. At this event, the groom's parents give them a small sum of money to validate their agreement. The groom's father and his friend stand before the bride's parents wearing special clothing, and they say, "As you have agreed, we have come to engage your daughter to our son." After agreement is officially given, the groom's father gives money to the bride's father. Then a festive meal is eaten, together with guests who come in honor of the event. Throughout the ceremony, the bride is forbidden to show her face to the guests, so she does not leave her room. The groom will not see or meet with the bride until the wedding. The period of engagement can continue for one to three years.

In the period before the wedding, the family builds a large shelter and prepares the meat that will be served at the wedding. The day of the wedding begins with a preliminary ceremony called *keshera* (see below), in the groom's home. The groom's family then go to the bride's home and take her to the home of the groom. The bride goes without any jewelry (her jewelry is sent with her in a box), and she adorns herself in the groom's home after the blessing of the *kesim*. Following the blessings, bride and groom go into a separate room, where they have marital relations. After relations, two witnesses enter the room to check that the bride was a virgin. (My grandfather related that the witnesses almost always found blood indicating that the bride was a virgin.) After the *kesim* authorize their testimony, they congratulate the bride's parents on her proper moral education and modesty, and for keeping her virginity. Then the true rejoicing begins, and lasts for seven days and even longer.

If the witnesses do not find blood, they go with the groom to the *kesim* and community elders and remove the groom's *keshera*, thus declaring that they did not find any blood. The *kesim* ask the witnesses a number of questions in order to verify their testimony. They then indicate to the bride's mother that she should investigate what happened. Finally, they ask the bride herself. If there is proof that she is not a virgin, the bride and her parents are sent home in shame. The groom's parents recommence their search, while the bride must wait for proposals from people who lack family status or other qualities.

Past and Present in Talmudic Halakhah

The Sages viewed the act of marriage as a framework for spiritual completeness, in which man and woman become complete individuals, as in the verse "Therefore shall a man leave his father and his mother, and shall cleave to his wife, and they shall be one flesh" (Genesis 2:24).[1] Marriage unites their shared soul, which before that time was temporarily divided into two bodies – his and hers. According to the Sages, before marriage, life is incomplete: "A man who has no wife exists without happiness, without blessing, without goodness…without peace."[2] Marriage represents the perfect framework for bringing children into the world, raising them and educating them; the couple become partners with God in creating the world, and continue the act of creation. Marital life also serves to prevent sinful thoughts and guards the individual from the sin of prohibited sexual relations.

During the time of the Mishnah and the Talmud, marriage took place at a young age, in order to prevent sexual impropriety and sinful thoughts. According to halakhah, a boy over the age of thirteen may legally marry. The Babylonian Talmud relates that some Amoraim married at age thirteen. But the widely accepted age for a man to marry during that period was between eighteen and twenty, by which time the young man was able to develop mature thinking, study Torah, Mishnah, and Talmud, find a profession. The issue of a place to live was not such a serious issue as it is today, because the usual custom was for the son to bring his wife to his father's house. The father gave them a room in his house, or else he built them a "wedding house" on the roof or in the yard.

It was not accepted to postpone marriage beyond the age of twenty, except for those who wished to continue Torah studies, who could wait longer. In periods of severe economic hardship, such as during the Roman regime in ancient Palestine in the third century CE, men did get married until thirty or even forty. This was reported by Rabbi Levi, who was a teacher in the *beit midrash* of Rabbi Yochanan in Tiberias: "Rabbi Levi said, the usual custom is for a man to marry a woman at age thirty or forty."[3] The reason for marriage at such an advanced age was that young men could not meet the commitments specified in the *ketubah* (marriage contract). In medieval times, Jewish men customarily married at a young age.

Social and economic changes that took place beginning in the sixteenth century in central Europe gradually led to an increase in the marriage age of the general population there, and later in Eastern Europe as well. These changes

---

1. See also *Genesis Rabbah* 17:2.
2. Babylonian Talmud, *Yevamot* 62b–63a.
3. *Songs Rabbah* 7:3.

influenced the Jews as well. In various countries, limitations placed on the marriage age also led to an increase in the average age.[4]

As for women, in biblical times the custom was to marry at a young age. According to Jewish law, a girl is considered the responsibility of her father when she is a child and an adolescent. In ancient times, a girl was considered a child until age twelve, and then, when she showed signs of physical maturity, she was defined as an adolescent. The period of adolescence lasted for six months, after which she became an adult. While she was still in the child or adolescent stage, her father could arrange her marriage, even without her agreement. If the father did not arrange marriage for her during this period, he could not do so without her agreement after she became an adult, because at that age she was responsible for herself.

In the third century CE, a change of opinion is documented among the Babylonian sages. They protested the practice of the father arranging his daughter's marriage while still a child or adolescent, and preferred that he wait until she reached adulthood, and could state her own preference. In Jewish communities in medieval times, the custom was to arrange marriage during childhood and adolescence, out of fear for sudden economic hardship, assimilation, or kidnapping. The latter was common in various periods in certain locations under Islamic rule. Beginning in the sixteenth century, the age of marriage for women rose, first in central Europe and then in Eastern Europe. Eastern European literature from the late nineteenth century reveals that women married after age twenty.

In ancient times, the custom for Jews, as in other cultures, was for the parents to choose a spouse for their grown child based on objective considerations, such as the biblical choice of Rebecca for Isaac.[5] Romantic love developed between the partners only after marriage. Parents initiated the wedding, and ideally, they chose a partner from a family of good reputation, whose members were all accepted as Jews. Another consideration was the financial status of the family. In choosing a wife, her beauty and physical perfection were also weighed – she should have no physical defects, whether visible or hidden. Sometimes the choice was made when the partners were children, and even before they were born. During Mishnah times, if a man married a woman who was not of equivalent family status, the family performed a ceremony called *ketzatzah* (cutting). They opened casks of nuts and roasted seeds, distributed them to the participants, and declared: "Our

---

4. Herman, *Ma'agal hayei ha-yom*.
5. Ibid.

fellow Jews have heard that our brother So-and-so has married a woman who is not his equal. We fear that his seed will mingle with ours. Come and take an example for future generations, that his seed should not mingle with ours."[6]

But there were some cases in which marriage took place following acquaintance between the partners. In Tannaitic sources, we find descriptions of popular celebrations on Tu be-Av and Yom Kippur, in which the young women went out to dance in the vineyards, and unmarried men were sent there to search for partners. Judges 21 mentions a similar popular festival, although without a date. This text describes a holiday for God that was celebrated in Shiloh, and to which the sons of Benjamin were sent to take wives. Talmudic sages emphasized the importance of acquaintance between partners. Rav, a respected Babylonian Amora, decreed that a father must not arrange marriage for his daughter until she grew up and could say, "I want So-and-so." One who arranged marriage for his daughter without first introducing her to the intended groom was liable for punishment with lashes. Thus some understood the word *shiduchin* (matchmaking) as referring to acquaintance and communication between the partners. Others interpreted *shiduchin* as the result of acquaintance and communication, since in Palestinian Aramaic, the word *shadech* means "quiet," and the couple enjoyed emotional quiet or calm when they knew their intended spouse. In medieval Europe, romantic love became the dominant factor in choosing a spouse. This concept gradually influenced other cultures, including European Jewry, and is reflected in Jewish literature from the nineteenth century.

The primary "matchmaker" is God, who created Eve as a wife for Adam. Abraham's servant Eliezer also acted as a matchmaker. But the concept of matchmaker as a profession is a relatively late phenomenon in Judaism, mentioned in medieval Ashkenazic halakhic literature from the twelfth and thirteenth century. In the fourteenth century, matchmaking became a source of income for rabbis, thus transforming the matchmaker's social status. In Sephardic communities, we have no evidence of matchmakers until the exile from Spain in the fifteenth century. This custom spread to Sephardic communities only in the sixteenth century.[7]

The Recommended Custom in Israel

We see that the customs of the Ethiopian community are consistently grounded in ancient tradition. The separation from global civilization and the Jewish world

---

6. Babylonian Talmud, *Ketubot* 28b.
7. Herman, *Ma'agal hayei ha-yom*.

led to a static state in their cultural and halakhic world. After aliyah to Israel, we note significant changes. In the State of Israel, the average age of marriage for a man is now almost twenty-eight, and for a woman almost twenty-six.[8] This is partially due to the fact that after high school, most men serve in the army and then study a profession. Contemporary *poskim* encourage them not to postpone marriage for too long. On one hand, today there is no need to marry at a young age, but on the other, one should not put off marriage for too long. Establishing a home is a very important step, symbolic of the creation of the world. Marriage is not a burden, but a Jewish spiritual value and an inherent need of the individual, as the Torah declares about the creation of man: "It is not good that man is alone" (Genesis 2:18). Still, one who has not yet found his spouse should not feel that he is a failure, and may it be God's will that his deepest wishes be fulfilled for good purpose.

The *Keshera* Ceremony

Ethiopian Halakhah

My grandfather, of blessed memory, told me that up until the 1930s, when Christian influences began to penetrate into the Jewish world, such as tattoos and the word *kes* instead of *kahin*, they used to make the *keshera* out of a gold or silver chain. Later, they made it out of woolen threads that were woven by the mothers of the bride and groom. These threads were made in two colors, red and white, and arranged in the following order: white, red, white, red, white. The *keshera* looks like a rainbow made of two colors that were connected and interwoven. In Israel, the Ethiopian Jews continue to use these two colors, but make only two rows of red and white. The colors are symbolic: red symbolizes the purity of the bride, who is a virgin and permitted to her husband, while white symbolizes the purity of the groom, who is of good character, has a kind heart, and is free of sin.

In the ceremony, the guests enter the shelter of the bride and groom. The groom is dressed like a king. One of the spiritual leaders takes the *keshera* in his hand and blesses the groom:

> Praise and thanks to the Lord of Lords, and praise to the guardian angels, for granting us life and bringing us to this day, and not forgetting us to this day.

---

8. *Israel in Figures 2013*, Israel's Central Bureau of Statistics.

Who has seen such joy, and who has enjoyed such years of life? We have no King but You, You are His merciful Name.[9]

After this blessing, everyone responds "Amen," and the *kes* places the *keshera* on the groom in this order: first on the two big toes, representing a human being who is born into this world; then he places it on both knees, symbolizing the *brit milah*; then on the chest, symbolizing the joy of marriage; and last on the forehead, symbolizing God's kingship in this world and the world to come. After this blessing, the congregation performs special songs and dances for bride and groom. Then the groom goes out on a horse and is accompanied by leaders of the community to the bride's parents' home.[10]

Past and Present in Talmudic Halakhah

It seems that the custom of crowning the groom is an ancient custom. The *ateret hatanim* (groom's crown) is an ornament that encircles the head, like a royal crown.[11] This is a symbol of honor, mentioned in these verses: "You shall be a crown of glory in the hand of the Lord, and a royal diadem in the open hand of your God" (Isaiah 62:3); "And I put a ring on your nose, and earrings in your ears, and a crown of glory on your head" (Ezekiel 16:12); "And Mordecai went forth from the presence of the king in royal apparel of blue and white, and with a great crown of gold, and with a robe of fine linen and purple; and the city of Shushan shouted and was glad" (Esther 8:15).

In relation to weddings, the crown is mentioned regarding King Solomon: "Go forth, O daughters of Zion, and gaze upon King Solomon, even upon the crown with which his mother crowned him on the day of his nuptials and on the day of the gladness of his heart" (Song of Songs 3:11). The Jerusalem Talmud cites Lamentations 5:16 – "The crown has fallen from our head; woe to us! for we have sinned" – in relation to different types of crowns worn by grooms.[12] The Mishnah also mentions various kinds of crowns for grooms, including salt, ashes, roses, and myrtle.[13] The crown was traditionally woven of branches of various plants, particularly myrtle, which was considered protection against harm.

After the destruction of the Second Temple, the Sages forbade the use of the

---

9. From translation into Hebrew by David Yosef, a leading philosopher of the Ethiopian community.
10. Based on report of David Yosef.
11. Herman, *Ma'agal hayei ha-yom*.
12. Jerusalem Talmud, *Sotah* 89, 24b–c.
13. Mishnah, *Sotah* 15:8.

groom's crown, both in memory of the destruction[14] and as a reaction against the Roman's custom of placing wreaths on the heads of victors. In Amoraic times, it was customary for the groom to place ashes on his head, and the Amoraim considered this as a commemoration of the destruction of Jerusalem. In the medieval period, other customs developed: some placed a black cloth on the heads of the bride and the groom, while others placed a white cloth over a black cloth on their heads. In another custom, bride and groom wore white clothing, symbolizing purity, atonement, and the day of death, to mitigate the joy.

Recalling the day of death brought other related customs: the groom did not dress himself, but rather others dressed him, just as others dress the dead in burial wraps. The groom stood under the *chuppah* (wedding canopy) without money or jewelry, and wearing no knots, such as a necktie, just as a dead person is buried (to symbolize that the person is taking nothing with him to the grave except for Torah study and good deeds).

Before the destruction of the Second Temple, the bride wore a golden crown in the shape of the city of Jerusalem. But after the destruction, the Sages forbade this custom. During Mishnah times, the bride went out in her "veil" – this term was subject to various interpretations. Some thought this should be interpreted as a headscarf covering her eyes, and others referred to a canopy made of braided myrtle branches.

The Recommended Custom in Israel

In view of the development of the *ateret hatanim* ceremony in Talmudic halakhah, we learn that this custom is very ancient, like most of the community's traditions, and so it is important to continue it. However, it is the subject of controversy within the community due to its symbolic meaning. Objectors argue that we can have no responsibility for the virginal status of the bride or groom. But in my opinion, we should reach an understanding with the couple and the family that this is a symbolic act, not a reflection of the couple's premarital relations. I encourage the couple to follow the custom, and I can assert that is the most emotional moment of the wedding ceremony, in which the community feels at home and rejoices.

---

14. Mishnah, *Sotah* 9:14.

❧ Henna Ceremony

Ethiopian Halakhah

The wedding celebration begins the night before. On this night, Ethiopian Jews held a ceremony similar to the henna ceremony practiced in the Sephardic community. The ceremony included painting the bride's fingernails (but not her palm or fingers) with a red solution made of the roots of a potato-like vegetable. A festive meal was held, with mutton as a main dish.

Past and Present in Talmudic Halakhah

Today the henna ceremony is held in many Jewish communities of Eastern origin, including Yemen and Morocco. The henna ceremony has changed over time, and today is only a symbol of the original custom. The bride wears makeup according to modern fashion. The ceremony is held on the night before the wedding. The henna itself is a paste made of the leaves of the henna plant with white or yellow leaves, mentioned in the Song of Songs: "My beloved is to me as a cluster of henna in the vineyards of Ein-Gedi" (Song of Songs 1:14). This plant grows in North Africa, Egypt, and India. The leaves are ground and mixed in a special ceremony, and the resulting red paste is spread on the bride's fingertips, hands, legs, and fingernails. Candles are lit and placed at both sides of her face. Some also spread the paste on the groom's palm, in the form of a coin-sized circle, with small dots around it.

Underlying this custom is a popular folk belief that spreading the henna brings good luck to the couple and banishes evil spirits that threaten to harm them and disturb them in establishing their household. The origin of the custom is unclear, but it seems to have penetrated into Judaism under the influence of Arab culture. Popular belief "converted" this ceremony and even identified in the word *henna* (חנה or *h.n.h*), a suggestion of the three mitzvot that are unique to women: challah, *niddah*, and *hadlakah* (ritually separating challah dough, observing the laws of marital purity, and lighting Shabbat candles). Others understand *henna* as related to the word *hen*, "beauty."[15]

The Recommended Custom in Israel

In Sephardic communities today, the henna ceremony is held a few days before the wedding. In Ethiopia and in Israel, at the beginning of the Ethiopian aliyah, the henna was a modest ceremony limited to close family members. Today, people

---

15. Herman, *Ma'agal ha-hayim*.

often hold a large ceremony involving extensive preparation and expense. Many resources are directed to the henna ceremony, when it would be preferable to use them for more important purposes, such as life after the wedding. We must remember that the henna ceremony is not obligatory, and involves no mitzvah. Thus it is preferable for the couple to dispense with it, and if due to family obligation they cannot, they should try to keep it very modest.

Between Man and Wife

Ethiopian Halakhah

Marriage in Beta Israel tradition is built on a patriarchal structure, with the husband at the center. He rules the roost, from the decision to marry to the decision to divorce. Public displays of affection are not acceptable, and private displays are also discouraged (even if not seen by others), as they could be interpreted as an expression of the woman's control, which is contrary to Ethiopian culture. The members of the couple do not volunteer information about such things as feelings or plans for the future. There are no discussions; they decide and carry out the decision. The world of the couple is expressed more in action, in carrying out tasks, and less on the emotional side. The woman must obtain her husband's permission before doing anything. The husband is permitted to take a second wife, even without consulting his first wife, and he may divorce his wife for various reasons, such as dissatisfaction with her cooking. In most cases of divorce, the woman is blamed, not the man.

Past and Present in Talmudic Halakhah

According to the Torah, a man is permitted to marry an unlimited number of women, on condition that he can support them financially and satisfy their sexual needs, as obligated by marriage. But the woman may marry only one man, so that all will know the identity of her children's father. From biblical descriptions of the creation of one woman for Adam and the patriarchs who married one wife (with the exception of Abraham's marriage to Hagar due to Sarah's barrenness, and Jacob's marriage to Rachel and Leah due to Laban's trickery), the spirit of the Torah seems to express the ideal of one wife per man. Still, biblical sources show that some took several wives.

About one thousand years ago, polygamy was forbidden. This decree is credited to Rabbenu Gershom Ma'or ha-Golah, "Light of the Exile," who lived from 965 to 1028 (some sources indicate 1040), and it is known as "Rabbenu Gershom's ban." The original text of the ban was not found, but appears in the thirteenth century in a text by Rabbi Meir of Rottenburg: "The ban of the decree of communities, instituted by Rabbenu Gershom, Light of the Exile, that one must not marry two wives, and this may not be permitted except by one hundred men in three countries and from three communities, and they should not do so until they find good reason to permit it."[16] Several reasons were given for the ban:

1. Concern over arguments among the wives;
2. Concern that the husband would not be able to provide for the needs of all his wives, which would damage their honor and status;
3. To prevent animosity between Jews and Christians, who practiced monogamy.

The ban spread and was accepted among all Ashkenazic communities, and was considered as a decree of a higher religious court. In later generations, some questioned this ban, and said that it applied only until the end of the fifth millennium (1240 CE), but others considered it permanently valid, and this was the final decision. In fact, Sephardic and Eastern communities also limited the man to marrying only one wife, not because of the ban, but rather due to the obligations of the marriage contract (*ketubah*). The purpose of Rabbenu Gershom's ban and the Sephardic and Eastern limitation in the *ketubah* to one wife was not to negate the legal power of the husband to take a second wife, but rather to forbid this practice. Thus if a man did take a second wife, this marriage was legal.[17] In modern times, polygamy is almost nonexistent among Jews, except for a few Eastern communities.[18]

The Recommended Custom in Israel

According to the Ethiopian model of marriage, the areas of responsibility within the family are very clear. Each partner knows his or her place, and thus the stability of the marriage is usually preserved. The low level of divorce in the community bears witness to this. By contrast, in Western culture the areas of responsibility are usually not separated, and roles can even be reversed, such that the woman develops a career and may bear primary responsibility for earning the family's income, while the husband takes care of the children and the home. This reality can cause tensions in marital life and a rise in the level of divorce, as we see in

---

16. Responsa of Maharam of Rottenburg, part 4, par. 1:22.
17. Ibid.
18. Ibid.

reality. Thus marriage should be based on respect and responsibility, and both partners should remember that they are not marrying an angel – no one is perfect. They should learn "human" behavior from God – just as God is able to accept the human, both as we are in reality and in the potential He wants and expects us to live up to as humans, so must we accept the other partner in our marriages.

Partnership based on the value of mutual respect, a listening ear, warmth, love, feelings, empathy, encouragement, empowerment, and emphasizing the positive can lead to a long-lasting relationship. We must listen carefully to our partners in order to understand, not out of defensiveness but out of a desire for true communication. We must also eliminate any act that harms. When people keep issues inside themselves, an argument can turn into quiet animosity and a cold war.

Divorce

Ethiopian Halakhah

If the couple does not get along, the *kesim* and the *shmaglotz* try to lead to a peaceful resolution. If attempts at compromise are unsuccessful, the couple can get divorced. The divorce process is short and simple – the *kes* tears the *ketubah*. In several locations (according to the testimony of David Yosef), the husband would write out a *get* (bill of divorce), in which he expressed his desire to divorce his wife, thereby permitting her to any man. The exact text of the *get* varied slightly in the different villages, but the principle was the same. After the divorce ceremony, the woman returned to her parents' home. The man could marry another woman, or continue his marriage to his second wife, if he had one. The woman was also permitted to remarry, but she faced a steep challenge since most men preferred a virgin. In addition, a *kes* could not marry a divorced woman.

Past and Present in Talmudic Halakhah

Delivering the *get* was usually carried out in the presence of the *dayanim* (religious judges), the husband, wife, two halakhically valid witnesses, and the court scribe. First, the court checked whether the partners had reached an agreement regarding all the financial arrangements between them. Then the judges explained to those present all the stages in the process, and the witnesses were asked to pay close attention to every detail. The husband had to declare that the *get* was given of his free will, and not through force. Then the *get* was written. It had to be the property of the husband, and so before writing it, the scribe sold the paper, the ink, and the writing instrument to the husband in a legal sale. He had to address the *get* to himself – [his name], son of [his father's name], and to his wife for the purpose of her divorce. In the text, he orders the witnesses to sign the *get*. Scribe and witnesses must express their explicit agreement to this.

When the scribe completed the writing, the witnesses read the *get* and signed it in front of each other. The court reread the *get* and verified that there were no errors. Then the court asked the woman if she accepted the *get* of her own free will and knowledge. If she replied that the *get* was given to her of her own free will and to her knowledge, they informed her that after receiving the *get* from the husband, she was permitted to marry any person she wanted, except for a *kohen*. The woman extended her hands and brought them together. The religious judge asked the husband to recite after him: "This is your *get*, accept your *get*. Through it, you are now divorced from me from now on, and you are permitted to any man." The man placed the *get* into the woman's outstretched hands. The court informed the woman that she was not permitted to remarry until ninety-two days had passed (this was in order to definitely establish paternity should she turn out to be pregnant), and that she could never marry a *kohen*. Finally, the judge tore the *get*, put it away for safekeeping, and wished the man and woman "*get*" – an abbreviation for *gmar tov* (a good conclusion). The man and woman went to the court secretary to get a temporary confirmation of their divorce, and a few days later they received the divorce certificate.[19]

The Recommended Custom in Israel

The differences in wedding and divorce practices, as summarized above, create thorny problems and much friction. The problem stems from the differences in the manner of delivering the *get* to the woman. While in Ethiopia, in some places tearing the *ketubah* was sufficient, rabbinic law specifies that the *get* must be written and delivered to the woman. Thus from now on, these issues must be resolved. In case of divorce, the couple must go to a religious court.

A husband may not take more than one wife at a time, following today's practice under Israeli law. It is very important to be aware of changes in the status of women and men, whose respective roles today are not defined by gender but rather egalitarian.[20] They are equal, and no one is of higher status. The couple must find a way of life that will lead to a happy and fruitful marriage. There is no one model that is appropriate for everyone. The partners should divide roles in

---

19. Ibid.
20. D. Sperber, *Minhagei Yisrael*, vol. 1, *Ha-hashpa'ah ha-hevratit shel minhag: Al hashka'at ha-yayin ba-brit milah u-ma'amadah shel ha-ishah ba-hevrah* [The social status of custom: On giving wine to drink at the circumcision ceremony, and the status of women in society].

a manner appropriate to each person, out of respect and esteem. Avraham Yardai has noted that incidents of extreme violence, such as murder of the wife or suicide, were foreign to the Jewish world in Ethiopia. Such incidents began in Israel, with the first suicide taking place in Ashdod in 1983.

Modesty

Ethiopian Halakhah

According to Ethiopian halakhah, a married woman must cover her head with a scarf. If a woman committed a sexual impropriety or exceeded the boundaries of modesty, her head was permanently uncovered. A single woman did not have to cover her head. Some explained that uncovered hair was not considered immodest as uncovered arms and legs, and that a woman should cover her hair for other women. The hair represented the woman's honor, as evidenced by the fact that women take great care in styling and cutting it. A woman feels that attractive hair honors her and presents her to the public in a respectable manner. As long as a woman is not set aside for a particular man, this is acceptable. But when a woman is married, it is as if she becomes part of his very flesh, and her honor should be concealed inside the house and reserved for her husband alone. This does not mean that the woman should go outside in a disrespectable fashion, but rather that she should reserve her most special appearance for her husband. It is a special sign that makes her unique only to him. It is also a sign to others that she is married. An unmarried woman does not need such a sign – on the contrary, if she does not cover her head, everyone will know that she is available for marriage proposals.

Past and Present in Talmudic Halakhah

The Torah gives no specific instruction that commands a married woman to cover her hair, nor does it mention a woman who covered her hair. Covering with a scarf or shawl is mentioned regarding Rebecca (Genesis 24:65) and Tamar (Genesis 38:14), and this apparently refers to covering the face, as was common in those times. The Torah mentions hair in the context of the adulterous wife whose husband suspects her of being unfaithful. He must take her to the *kohen*, "and the priest [*kohen*] shall set the woman before the Lord, and let the hair of the woman's head go loose" (Numbers 5:18). According to the plain meaning of the text, the *kohen* unbinds the woman's gathered hair.

In later times, married Jewish women covered their heads in public, as evidenced by the Mishnah, which refers to head covering as part of *da'at Yehudit* (traditional Jewish practice). "These are to be divorced without receiving their *ketubah*: a wife who transgresses the law of Moshe or [one who transgresses] Jewish practice.... What is [regarded as a wife's transgression against] Jewish practice? One who goes out with an uncovered head."[21] Accordingly, a Tannaitic midrash interpreted the unbinding of the hair of the adulterous woman: "'He uncovered the woman's head – this is to teach us that the daughters of Israel cover their hair, and although there is no evidence of this, we do find mention of this in 'And Tamar took *afar*' (understood as meaning "a scarf" – see I Kings 20:38; II Samuel 13:19) upon her head."[22] In Babylon, in the Amoraic period, covering the hair for a married woman became *da'at Moshe* (biblical law). We learn this from the Talmud's questioning of the Mishnah's understanding that covering the hair is *da'at Yehudit*: "The prohibition against going out with the head uncovered is biblical, as it is written, '[He] let the hair of the woman's head go loose' (Numbers 5:18). The school of Rabbi Ishmael taught that this is a warning to the daughters of Israel that they should not go out with the head uncovered."[23]

The Talmud asks how the Mishnah can state that unbinding the hair is *da'at Yehudit*, while according to Rabbi Ishmael, it is *da'at Moshe* and not *da'at Yehudit*. From this point on, in the literature of the Geonim and Rishonim, they used the term "unbinding the hair" to mean uncovered hair, continuing the interpretation given in Talmudic literature of the prohibition against "unbinding the woman's hair." We learn from this that during Talmudic times, covering the hair was such a well-accepted custom for women that it was considered *da'at Moshe*. The Talmud explains the seeming conflict between the Mishnah and Rabbi Ishmael as follows: "Biblically, it is quite satisfactory [if her head is covered by] her work-basket; according to traditional Jewish practice, however, she is forbidden [to go out uncovered] even with her basket [on her head]."[24] In other words, the Torah obligates a woman who goes out into the public domain to cover her hair with a *kaltah*. This was a braided basket with many holes, which did not cover the hair completely, and seems to have been only a symbolic covering. But based on *da'at Yehudit*, a woman is obligated to fully cover all of her hair.

In contrast to the situation in Babylonia, where they ruled strictly and forbade the woman to go out in public wearing a *kaltah*, in Eretz Yisrael they were

---

21. Mishnah, *Ketubot* 7:6.
22. Sifri, Naso, ch. 19.
23. Babylonian Talmud, *Ketubot* 72a.
24. Ibid.

more lenient, as we learn in the name of the Amora Rabbi Yochanan: "*Kaltah* is not unbinding the hair." The Amoraim of Babylonia, in an attempt to avoid controversy, said Rabbi Yochanan was referring to a place less public than the public domain, such as when a woman is in her private courtyard – in such a location, covering the hair with a *kaltah* was sufficient. According to several Rishonim, the conclusion derived from the Talmudic passages is that in her own courtyard, or her own home, a woman is not required to cover her hair: "In the courtyard, a *kaltah* is sufficient."[25] In this case, if she does not wear the *kaltah*, she is violating *da'at Yehudit*, but in the public domain, she is obligated to wear a full head covering, and if she does not do so, she violates *da'at Moshe*, a biblical prohibition.

Other Rishonim, including the Rambam, did not reach this conclusion from the Talmudic passages. In their opinion, the prohibition against uncovering the head in the public domain is only *da'at Yehudit* (agreeing with Rabbi Yochanan in the Jerusalem Talmud). The Rambam writes: "Daughters of Israel should not walk in the marketplace with their hair uncovered."[26] Rabbi Yisrael Isserlin, a fifteenth-century European rabbi, follows this ruling in his *Responsa Terumat ha-Deshen*: "The Rambam writes that covering the hair is merely taking care regarding a rabbinic prohibition, as evidenced by his words, and although the Talmud interprets it as biblical, the Torah only hints at it."[27]

The conclusion of these interpretations of the Rishonim is that there is an obligation for the married woman to cover her hair in the public domain and in entryways, but not in her own courtyard or house, when in the presence of her immediate family members. But in the seventeenth century, Rabbi Joel Sirkis wrote in his commentary on the Tur: "Uncovering the hair is completely forbidden, even if the woman remains in her own home.... This is the practice in all Jewish homes, that even before the members of her household she does not appear with her head uncovered without a scarf or cap on her head."[28]

These discussions influenced later *poskim*, such as the Hatam Sofer and the *Mishnah Berurah*, to rule that covering the hair is obligatory for a married woman, even in her own home in the presence of the members of her household. Rabbi Moshe Feinstein ruled: "The halakhah is, even though it is preferable for women to follow the strict practice of covering their hair, following the opinion of the

---

25. See also Tosafot, ibid., s.v. "*Ve-elah ba-hatzer*."
26. *Mishneh Torah*, Hilkhot Issurei Bi'ah 21:17.
27. Herman, *Ma'agal ha-hayim*.
28. *Bayit Hadash*, Tur, *Even ha-Ezer*, par. 115.

Hatam Sofer, as this is the opinion of such a great Torah scholar as he.... But those who wish to follow the lenient practice should not be considered as violating *da'at Yehudit*, God forbid."[29]

The Recommended Practice in Israel

Today, in the Western world, for the very reason of its fascinating openness, its myriad possibilities and opinions, we recommend following this beautiful custom starting immediately after the wedding. A woman's beauty is dedicated and sanctified to her husband. Outside the house, complete strangers, both men and women, give us compliments. No matter what the compliment, there is no substitute for one that comes from a person who is close to us. Still, there is no need to cover the entire head, nor should a woman appear slovenly due to this. The book of Proverbs asserts, "Charm is deceitful, and beauty is vain" (Proverbs 31:30). We need not take this dictum literally. Rather, as the verse in Proverbs continues, "a woman who fears the Lord, she shall be praised." Beauty takes on deep meaning when it comes together with fear of God. A woman who knows how to combine fear of God and beauty is certainly deserving of praise and admiration.

ॐ Strict Conversion and the Status of *Mamzer*

Ethiopian Halakhah

As is known, the aliyah of Ethiopian Jewry was made possible due to the halakhic ruling of Rabbi Ovadia Yosef, chief rabbi of Israel in 1973, who recognized the Jewish status of the community. Following his decision, in 1975, the State of Israel decided to apply the Law of Return to the Ethiopian Jews. However, even in the period following aliyah, a shadow of doubt still hovers over the community and each of its members.

Rabbi Nachum Ben Yehuda relates: "I encountered members of the community here in Jerusalem, and this led to halakhic questions. A student of mine at Machon Meir did not have tefillin, and I had a pair that was not being used. So it was natural for me to give him the tefillin. But I asked myself if this was permitted. I asked a Torah scholar, but he did not know the answer, and he referred the question to a greater scholar. This one refused to answer, and referred me to Rabbi Ovadia Yosef. I was not able to reach Rabbi Ovadia Yosef, but I understood from his published writings that it was possible to permit the Ethiopian Jews to wear tefillin." Rabbi Nachum concluded, "The student was very pleased."

---

29. *Responsa Iggerot Moshe, Even ha-Ezer* 1, par. 58.

But the Chief Rabbinate of Israel did not agree with Rabbi Yosef. They decided that in order to remove any suspicion of intermarriage with non-Jews and with children of forbidden marriages, the Ethiopian Jews should immerse themselves in the *mikveh* and accept the mitzvot. In addition, at the beginning the community was asked to undergo *hatafat dam brit* (a symbolic circumcision ceremony in which a drop of blood is drawn). *Brit milah* (religious circumcision specifically for the sake of the mitzvah) is a basic requirement of any male convert to Judaism, and *hatafat dam brit* is done whenever a male convert has already been circumcised, as the overwhelming majority of the Beta Israel were. This demand was annulled only after a large demonstration was held in Jerusalem in front of the Chief Rabbinate building. Some think that the requirement was withdrawn without relation to the demonstration, and that the reason was halakhic and not political. Rabbi Yisraeli commented on this process:

> We find that on the issue of the Ethiopian immigrants, there are two kinds of doubt ... and because we have two doubts, we may rule leniently and permit them to join the community, as in any case of a doubt on top of a doubt. Even if we suspected them of *mamzerut* [illegitimate birth, as defined in halakhah], there is another kind of doubt, as the individual might not even be a Jew.

In other words, if there was only one doubt, of *mamzerut*, then there would be no way to resolve the issue. But because there was doubt over whether they were Jews, they could be accepted after conversion. Rabbi Yisraeli then asks:

> How should we perform the conversion of the Ethiopian Jews? ... The most pleasant way to do so, and this was the instruction, is to draw blood from the circumcised area and have them immerse after formal acceptance of the mitzvot before a recognized religious court. But the public raised a great outcry, as if we were declaring that they were not Jews. Retrospectively we found room to rule leniently and require only immersion. This was because they performed circumcision properly and they were circumcised as a sign of Judaism, and even though they do not know what true Judaism is, still they were circumcised for the purpose of Judaism.

Rabbi Yisraeli then concludes:

> But regarding immersion for the purpose of conversion when they accept the mitzvot, we cannot rule leniently. Even though there are some who would argue that because it is their custom to immerse themselves regularly, there

is no need for a special immersion for the purpose of conversion, and they can be accepted into the Jewish people without any act of conversion – we must not rule leniently on this, and they must immerse for the purpose of conversion. I must emphasize that this halakhah is accepted by the majority of rabbis in Israel.[30]

In fact, this decision of the Chief Rabbinate, according to which the Ethiopian Jews were required to immerse and declare acceptance of the mitzvot, remains valid to this day. I have been approached numerous times by yeshiva students of Ethiopian origin who related that others refused to permit them to join a prayer quorum. Such rejection, to feel that you do not exist, that you do not count, harms the individual to the depths of the soul. In other cases, this frustration appears among couples who are about to marry. They wonder why they need to obtain authorization of their Judaism. Avraham Yardai asserts that the community should not focus on the question of whether they are accepted by others as Jews, but rather they should live and behave as Jews, and this should be their main concern.

Past and Present in Talmudic Halakhah

There is some confusion about the meaning of the status of *mamzerut*, which is generally translated as "illegitimacy." The halakhic concept of *mamzerut* is not at all the same thing as the secular legal definition. A child who is born through a halakhically forbidden union, meaning relations between certain family members or relations between a married woman and a Jewish man who is not her husband, is called a *mamzer*.[31] The child of a *mamzer* is also considered a *mamzer*. Thus it is a serious error to ascribe *mamzer* status to a child born out of wedlock. In addition, in the following cases, a child born out of forbidden relations should not be considered a *mamzer*:

1. A child born as a result of sexual relations with a woman who is *niddah* (during her menstrual period and for seven days afterward) without performing the proper stages of purification (see chapter 5, "Bride, Groom, and Family"). Such a child is not a *mamzer*, because the prohibition of *niddah* is temporary, as opposed to other forbidden relations in this category, which are permanent.

---

30. Rabbi Shaul Yisraeli, "Birur hilkhati be-she'elat Yehadut Etiopiah" [Halakhic clarification on the question of Ethiopian Jewry], *Al madin*, ed. Yitzhak Heckelman (Jerusalem, 5752/1992), 107–15.
31. Herman, *Ma'agal hayei ha-yom*.

Spiritually, the child is considered faulty, and is called "a child of *niddah*," but this has no effect on his/her legal status, and s/he is not considered a *mamzer*, nor is the mother considered a *zonah* (harlot).

2. A child born as a result of relations between a married Jewish woman and a non-Jew. The reason for this is that the status of *mamzerut* exists only within the Jewish people, when both man and woman are Jews. The fact of having relations with a non-Jew is considered defective, but it does not mean the child is a *mamzer*. Still, such an act is considered improper sexual relations punishable by death for both partners.

The halakhic principle explained here appears in the Mishnah: "Any [woman] for whom there is no betrothal to him [a particular man], but there is betrothal to others, the child [born of their union] is a *mamzer*."[32] In other words, the status of *mamzer* for a child whose parent is not a *mamzer* is only when a child is born to a man and woman to whom the halakhic category of Kiddushin should apply, but there has been no Kiddushin between them. Such a situation can take place only between a Jewish man and woman between whom Kiddushin cannot be valid, even if they have contracted Kiddushin according to the principles of halakhah. Such a situation can take place only for a man and woman between whom relations are forbidden, but who are halakhically permitted to contract Kiddushin with other Jews.

One concern that was raised among the rabbinic community of Israel concerning the Beta Israel was the possibility that they might have the halakhic status of *mamzerim*. Halakhah defines "a state of doubt regarding a *mamzer*," which is explained as "the offspring of partners who are suspected of improper relations, such as a man who has relations with a woman whose Kiddushin with another man might be invalid, or a divorcee whose divorce might be invalid."[33] Halakhah also defines a status known as the *asufi*: "Similarly, a child who is found in the marketplace is called an *asufi*, and he is considered as a *mamzer* whose status is questionable, for we do not know his [lineage]."[34] Consideration of the *asufi* as a Jew who might be a *mamzer* is only on condition that he was found in a town whose inhabitants are all Jews. But in a town with even a minority of non-Jews,

---

32. Mishnah, *Kiddushin* 3:12.
33. Rambam, *Mishneh Torah*, Hilkhot Issurei Bi'ah 15:10.
34. Ibid., 15:13.

he is considered "as gentile of indefinite status with regard to his lineage – if he consecrates a woman, she needs a bill of divorce because of the doubt."[35]

The implication that the Beta Israel might have *mamzer* status could carry grave halakhic consequences. A person who is defined as a possible *mamzer* may not marry a *mamzer* or another possible *mamzer*, "for perhaps the other is definitely a *mamzer* [and therefore not eligible to marry a Jew who is not a *mamzer*].... Similarly, in any other instance [where a person is forbidden to marry] because of a doubt, one person of this status may not marry another.... Individuals of indefinite status such as this have no option except to marry converts. The status of their offspring follows their blemish."[36] The import of the halakhah that "the offspring follows their blemish" is that the offspring will have the same status of the "blemished" parents, either *asufi* or *shtuki* (one who knows the identity of his mother, but does not definitely know the identity of his father).

The Recommended Practice in Israel

It should be amply clear that the Beta Israel do not have the status of *mamzerim* and are fully eligible to marry other Jews. This is on condition that the individual is recognized as a Beta Israel Jew and not a non-Jew, per Rabbi Ovadia Yosef's ruling. In any case, whoever claims to be an Ethiopian Jew must bring proof of such.

Ba'al Keri (Seminal Emission)

Ethiopian Halakhah

A man who senses a nocturnal emission gets out of bed and lies on the floor. Early in the morning he goes to immerse himself, and immediately returns home with no ceremony. A man who has a nocturnal emission on Shabbat sits to the side, by himself, and may not be touched, and on Sunday morning he immerses himself.

Past and Present in Talmudic Halakhah

A man who has any kind of seminal emission (such as a nocturnal emission) is called *ba'al keri* (from the word *mikreh*, "incident," based on Deuteronomy 23:11, "a nocturnal incident"). He is considered impure, and he may immerse himself on the same day and purify himself. According to the Torah, a man who has an

---

35. Ibid., 15:25.
36. Ibid., 15:22–23.

emission is not required to immerse himself, unless he wishes to enter the Temple or touch consecrated items. But because an emission is considered related to levity, and in order to encourage men to exercise control over their sexual desire, Ezra the Scribe decreed that a man who had an emission was forbidden from studying Torah or praying until he immersed himself in a river or *mikveh*. Over time, beginning in the Tannaitic period, the Sages ruled that "Torah matters are not affected by impurity," and they annulled the need for immersion in such a case.[37] The *Shulhan Arukh* rules:

> Anyone who is impure may read from the Torah, recite the Shema, and pray, except for one who has had an emission, whom Ezra differentiated from the other impurities. He forbade such a person from studying Torah and from reciting the Shema and prayer until he immersed himself, so that they should not cohabit with their wives like roosters. Later this decree was annulled, and they ruled that even one who had an emission was permitted to study Torah and to recite the Shema and pray, without immersing himself and without washing himself with nine *kab* of water, and this custom became widespread.[38]

Still, a man who has had an emission should first cleanse himself of the semen before putting on tefillin.[39]

The Recommended Custom in Israel

In all matters of purity and impurity, the practice of the Ethiopian Jews was uniquely careful. In Ethiopia, they had the means to preserve practices of purity and impurity. Every Jewish village had its *beit tum'ah* (house of impurity) where the impure men stayed. The villages were purposely built next to rivers, and the family living arrangements permitted the absence of one family member for a long period, when someone went to stay outside the village due to a status of impurity. Unfortunately, it is very difficult to continue these practices in Israel. Israel is a Western country, and usually the extended family does not live together, and rivers are not easily accessible to all. Thus in Israel, the Ethiopian Jews should follow the usual practices of Israeli Jews. Still, in the first and second generations, those who wish to continue the Ethiopian custom may do so, without suspicion

---

37. Babylonian Talmud, *Berakhot* 21.
38. *Shulhan Arukh*, *Orah Haim* 88.
39. Herman, *Ma'agal ha-hayim*.

of following a futile custom. Yet they must remember that in any case, family unity and education of children are more important than customs of the past.

Menstrual Impurity

Ethiopian Halakhah

The laws of purity and impurity, as in other Jewish communities, were at the focus of Jewish family life in Ethiopia. In general, the Beta Israel avoided contact with anything considered *tamei*, "impure." Jewish villages in Ethiopia were located near sources of flowing water, and their immersion practices were so frequent that one of the names given to the group by their neighbors was related to the scent of the water that lingered on their bodies. Their careful observance of purity laws served as a way of keeping the community separate from their non-Jewish neighbors, ensuring their uniqueness and distinction.

The laws of purity and impurity have several aspects: purity of family life and sexual relations, daily contact with non-Jews, contact with food (including slaughter), and contact with the dead. A woman was considered impure during her monthly menstrual period and after childbirth. All the Jewish villages in Ethiopia had a separate hut called the "house of blood" or *marjam gogo* (hut of the curse). It was located at the edge of the Jewish village, or on the margins of the area of Jewish huts in mixed villages. The Beta Israel women lived there during menstruation and after childbirth.

The laws of *niddah* were kept very strictly in accordance with the laws of the Torah, which obligated separation for seven days. A stone fence was erected around the "house of blood," marking the border between the impure and pure areas. Only women who were *niddah* and nursing babies sat inside the hut. The family or women friends brought them food in special dishes that they placed on the stone fence, behind the circle of red stones that surrounded the *niddah* hut. After childbirth, the women stayed in the *niddah* hut for forty days following the birth of a boy, or eighty days following the birth of a girl. During their menstrual period, the women sat in the hut for seven days. At the end of the seventh day, they went out to immerse themselves in the river and purify themselves, and then returned home. The "houses of blood" and the *niddah* customs were so marked that non-Jews viewed them as the principal external sign of the existence of Jews in a mixed village.

Ethiopian custom, based on ancient custom, does not include the stringent ruling of Rabbi Zeira (see below). The discussion about "white days" and seven clean days was not known to them at all. As soon as a woman saw blood, she left her home and immediately went to the *niddah* hut. She waited seven days, and then immersed herself. For a stain, she waited until evening of that day, and then immersed herself.

Past and Present in Talmudic Halakhah

Sexual relations between husband and wife are permitted only when a woman is not *niddah*. The Sages explained that the Torah forbade relations when a woman was *niddah*, so that afterward she would return to her husband and be as attractive to him as on the day of their wedding. However, the Sages explained that the proposed "reason" for a mitzvah is not the main purpose of the mitzvot in general, and that we should perform them solely because they are God's commandments. The proposed reason is merely an attempt at providing an explanation that can encourage a person to keep the mitzvah.[40] During the period when a woman is *niddah*, the spiritual connection between the partners is strengthened. Their lives are managed on the basis of mutual support and assistance, building the home, educating the children, and giving to each other. The *niddah* period is a time of distance for the purpose of coming closer, and reinforces the connection between the partners for the long term.

Sexual relations with a *niddah* is an improper sexual act, and both partners are liable for the punishment of *karet* (divine punishment by untimely death or eternal excommunication). Today, the strict ruling of Rabbi Zeira, which adds to the biblical commandment, is accepted in all Jewish communities. What is this strict ruling? The Talmud relates, "Rabbi Zeira said: The daughters of Israel have imposed on themselves the restriction that even if they observe a drop of blood the size of a mustard seed, they wait seven days."[41] He did not state this on his own authority, but rather that the daughters of Israel took this stringency upon themselves. Possibly, the stringent trends in the observance of *niddah* were part of a general trend of asceticism that spread after the destruction of the Second Temple, as part of the mourning and desire to find a substitute for the sacrificial rituals. In any case, for two thousand years, Jewish communities in all their variety have observed this additional restriction of stains.

Most Jewish women also took upon themselves an ancient custom of waiting seven days after observing "a drop of blood the size of a mustard seed" – the

---

40. Herman, *Ma'agal hayei ha-yom*.
41. Babylonian Talmud, *Niddah* 66a.

moment she sees blood, she waits until it stops, and then (after four to five days) she performs a *hefsek taharah* ("pause [to initiate] purity") and begins to count seven days. These laws are summarized in Kehati's commentary on mishnah 4:4 in Tractate Niddah, and in great detail in the Rambam's *Mishneh Torah, Sefer Kedushah*, Hilkhot Issurei Bi'ah. We have evidence that the Sages did not unanimously accept Rabbi Zeira's ruling. For example, on the same page in Tractate Niddah, Rabbi Papa cites Rabbi Zeira's statement to Raba as an answer to a different problem that they were discussing. Raba, the great Amora, answers Rabbi Joseph: "I am speaking to you of a prohibition, and you talk of a custom. Where one must restrict, we restrict, and where there is no reason to restrict, we do not restrict." Rabbi Zeira's decree citing the daughters of Israel demanded that the Sages confront resulting halakhic problems. In any case, the ruling spread throughout the Jewish communities, except for the Beta Israel, who continued to follow the biblical commandment.

The Recommended Custom in Israel

The women of the Ethiopian community should continue to immerse themselves on the seventh day, after sunset. In the final analysis, this is the biblical commandment, and the community did not take the Talmudic stringency upon itself. The second generation may adopt it – the goal of marital harmony and national unity has great value, which supersedes other values such as preserving past customs. As Rabbi Meir Simcha Hacohen of Dvinsk taught in his commentary on the Mekhilta, *Meshekh Hokhmah*:

> "The waters were a wall [*homah*] to them on their right and on their left" (Exodus 14:29): This teaches that Samael [the prosecuting angel] stood up and said, "Master of the universe! Did Israel not worship idols in Egypt, and you are doing miracles for them?!"…[God] became angry at them and wanted to swallow them up. (This explains why the text has *homah* without a *vav*, as if it means *hemah*, "anger")…God did not regret the miracles that He did for them when He took them out of Egypt, because even though they were corrupt, practiced idol worship, and did not perform *brit milah*, still they demonstrated good character qualities – they did not engage in gossip, and treated each other well.… Thus for the public, God performed miracles. But in the water, they were divided into four groups, and some said, "Let us go back to Egypt." [Samael] argued that God should judge them as individuals, and that for idol worship they should be punished with *karet*, so how could God

perform miracles for them?... When the community is united, even though there may be many sinners, Israel does not fall in war, as we have been taught in the Jerusalem Talmud, "The people of David's generation were all righteous individuals, but since they had informers among them, they suffered losses when they went to war.... In Ahav's generation, on the other hand, the people were idol worshippers, but since there were no informers among them, they went to war and were victorious" (*Pe'ah* 1:1).

❧ Forbidden Behavior during the *Niddah* Period

Ethiopian Halakhah

When she is *niddah*, a woman leaves her house and goes to the *niddah* hut, and does not leave. Anyone who enters the hut for any reason becomes immediately impure, and may not return home until after immersing in the river. The husband must not approach the area of the hut.

Past and Present in Talmudic Halakhah

The custom of the *niddah* residing away from her home has ancient roots. We learn this, for example, from the Mishnah in Tractate *Niddah* (4:4), which refers to *beit ha-tum'ot* (house of the impure women), and Rashi explains that this is a "room that women use during their time of *niddah*." The Mishnah seems to imply that this may have been a separate house. Concentrating the impurity in a defined area enabled the rest of the household to continue their daily routine while preserving a state of purity.[42] Today, the laws of purity and impurity are not practiced in this manner, and a *niddah* does not leave her home. Further, the man and woman sleep in the same room, albeit in separate beds. They may not have any physical contact with each other whatsoever. Additionally, the halakhah mandates *harhakot*, limitations in all forms of intimate connection between husband and wife during her period of *niddah*. These include a ban on indirect contact such as handing an object to each other, as well as restrictions on communication or behavior that may be construed as intimate.

The Recommended Custom in Israel

The Beta Israel may continue to follow the ancient custom. However, they should realize that the reality in Israel is different from the reality that enabled the practice of this custom. Today, it is almost impossible for a mother of a family to

---

42. Yedidya Adoniya-Adiv and Yikhat Rosen, *Ad alot ha-shahar* (Merkaz Shapira, 5763/2003).

leave the home for an extended period. Therefore, it is preferable not to remove the woman from the home, for educational and familial reasons. As an alternative, we may propose sleeping in separate beds, and in this manner the custom is preserved, while family unity is unharmed. If the family/educational situation and marital harmony permit, we may even propose sleeping in separate rooms. In general, the Ethiopian Jews are permitted to follow their custom, and this is not problematic – on the contrary, they are preserving the ancient traditions. However, if differences of opinion arise between husband and wife due to the changes that accompanied aliyah, we must find a way that enables preservation of the tradition together with marital accord – such as adopting the general Jewish custom.

❧ Purification Rituals

Ethiopian Halakhah

On the seventh day, the woman immerses herself in the river, accompanied by her husband or relatives. It is customary for the woman to fast from morning until evening. At the river, she cleans herself well, combs her hair, trims her fingernails, and launders her clothes. When she immerses, her female escorts verify that her hair is completely submerged. When she gets out of the water, they tap her lightly with bunches of soft grass. After sunset on the seventh day, she returns home, where she is greeted with a meal with bread baked especially for the occasion.

Past and Present in Talmudic Halakhah

In order to purify herself, the *niddah* must immerse in a *mikveh* – a natural source of water that is not pumped from the earth, in which a person can completely immerse the body in order to purify him- or herself from various states of impurity. In halakhah, the *mikveh* serves for immersion of individuals (both men and women) who became impure and want to purify themselves, as well as for purifying utensils and clothes that have become impure. The Torah lists many instances of impurity that require immersion as part of the process of purification. These include *niddah*, a man who had an emission of ejaculate, a convert, and a person who touched a corpse.[43]

Today, most of the laws of purity are no longer in practice because we cannot purify most of the cases without the ashes of the red heifer, as specified in the Torah. In Ethiopia, however, the Jews practiced all the purification laws until they

---

43. Herman, *Ma'agal hayei ha-yom*.

came to Israel. But after the Second Temple was destroyed, the general Jewish community practiced only the following immersions: a woman who was *niddah* or who was forbidden to her husband as part of the family purity laws, immersion of men, and immersion of new utensils that were purchased from a non-Jew (some say this law is biblically based). Further, in the State of Israel, marriage is permitted between Jews only according to halakhah, and so before a wedding, the bride is required to present a certificate of immersion to the rabbinate.

According to halakhah, today there is only one case of biblical obligation for individuals to immerse in the *mikveh* for the purpose of purification, because the Temple no longer stands and we no longer perform the sacrificial offerings. The one exception is women who are *niddah*, and so every settlement where Jews live must have a women's *mikveh*. Men may immerse themselves in any source of fresh water that is not pumped and contains at least forty *se'ah* (a biblical measurement that is equivalent to about 572 liters), such as an ocean or river.

The main source for the laws of the *mikveh* is the verse "But a spring or a cistern wherein is a gathering of water shall be clean" (Leviticus 11:36). The Sages explain this verse in Sifra: just as a spring is fashioned by God without human intervention, so a *mikveh* must be a natural source that is not pumped. Water from a naturally flowing source of any quantity can purify, but a *mikveh* of standing water that is not from a flowing source can purify only in a quantity of forty *se'ah*. The water in a *mikveh* comes from rain. In order to preserve the cleanliness of the water, it must be changed often. Today we use a regular store of rainwater that is connected to pumped water and changed on occasion. The collection of rainwater is usually accomplished by draining it from the roof of the *mikveh* into the storage container, which is attached to the *mikveh*. In rainy areas, this water is enough to supply the need. Another detail that must be ensured when building a *mikveh* is to avoid any water seeping out into the ground. Thus when constructing the pit, the builders must take great care to completely seal the floor and the walls.

In Israel, the state is responsible for such construction as part of the religious services. Today, almost every Jewish settlement in Israel maintains a *mikveh*. Most collect a small sum to cover expenses. Some improved *mikva'ot* offer private immersion, with additional services such as spa services, hair removal, and other beauty treatments, and the price is more expensive.

The Recommended Custom in Israel

The Beta Israel may continue to follow their custom, which requires immersion in a source of flowing water, but forbids use of standing water. For this reason, many

Ethiopian Jews in Israel do not keep this mitzvah. For many reasons, the mitzvah of immersion, once beloved to the Ethiopian community, became unappreciated in Israel – unfortunately. Thus we must explain the *mikveh* to the *kesim*. We must also propose that they immerse in a source of flowing water, such as the ocean.

Pregnancy, Birth, and Purity

Ethiopian Halakhah

From her third month of pregnancy, the woman receives support from a professional called a *bale tet* ("wise woman"). She advises the pregnant woman on what she should and should not eat, and other advice to ease the pregnancy. She also helps with housework. During pregnancy, the woman wore a necklace made of conch shell around her neck, which was a charm against miscarriage, and she also carried an amulet to protect her from harm.

When signs of labor begin, the "wise woman" instructs the pregnant woman to get down on her knees, and birth takes place in this position.[44] The wise woman who accompanied her throughout the pregnancy acts as the midwife. If the mother-to-be does not feel well and the birth process is delayed, others join them in order to assist. The impurity of birth begins at the moment the new mother sees blood – at this moment, the new mother and the assistants become impure for three days. The birth takes place beside the entrance to the home. After the baby is born, they declare the sex. The midwife is responsible for the joyous announcement, and it is declared by signaling through ululation. If the child is a boy, she utters twelve staccato ululations of joy, while if it is a girl, she gives nine ululations.[45] Why did they use ululation instead of words? This was to express joy, and so as not to tempt Satan. After birth, mother and baby were taken to the *niddah* hut.

On the seventh day after birth, the woman may immerse herself. After shaving her hair and trimming her fingernails (as was also done for the regular monthly purification following menstruation), she goes to the river, accompanied by another woman. If the baby is a boy, they immerse it as well, in preparation for the

---

44. My mother related that in Israel, when it was time to go to the hospital to give birth, the staff asked her to lie down on the bed, and she thought this was very strange. She also said that she knew of cases in which Ethiopian women in Israel ran away from the hospital, or decided to give birth at home in the absorption center, without access to medical assistance.
45. Nine is for nine months of pregnancy, as documented in the book *Awede Ngist* (*Respect for the kings: The Ethiopian national epic*, translated with an introduction and notes by Dr. Ran Cohen, Tel Aviv University).

brit milah, which is held on the eighth day. After the *milah*, the woman remains in the *niddah* hut for an additional thirty-three days. After forty days have passed, she goes to the river and immerses herself again.[46] After immersion she returns to the village and waits until nightfall. She picks forty long branches, like sticks, and ties them together into a bunch. If the baby is a girl, she immerses herself on the eightieth day, and prepares eighty sticks. After nightfall, she goes to the synagogue, where a ceremony is held commemorating the completion of her impure days. In the ceremony, the mother gives the branches she has gathered to the *kes* and lies on her stomach. The *kes* takes the bunch of branches and gently taps her on her head and foot.[47] The forty branches are a sign that she was impure for forty days. While tapping, the *kes* recites a prayer from the book *Ardat*.[48]

Following is a selection of a prayer from *Ardat* in translation:

> Blessed is the Lord, God of Israel, You are God, Amen, Hallelujah.
> You are righteous, God, Amen, Hallelujah.
> You are pure, God, Amen, Hallelujah.
> You have no impurity of sin, Amen, Hallelujah.
> You are praiseworthy, God, Amen, Hallelujah.
> You are extolled, Amen, Hallelujah.
> You are magnificent, Amen, Hallelujah.
> You are awesome, Amen, Hallelujah.
> You are blessed, Amen, Hallelujah.
> You are supreme, Amen, Hallelujah.
> You are mighty, Amen, Hallelujah.
> You are faithful, Amen, Hallelujah.
> You sustain us, Amen, Hallelujah.
> You lift us up, Amen, Hallelujah.
> You are wise, Amen, Hallelujah.
> You are the King of kings, Amen, Hallelujah.
> You are the Judge of judges, Amen, Hallelujah.
> You are the Minister of ministers, Amen, Hallelujah.

---

46. She waits forty full days, so immersion is on the forty-first day.
47. In this context, see also Sir James George Frazer, *The Golden Bough: A Study in Magic and Religion*, abridged edition (London: Macmillan, 1950).
48. The book title *Ardat* is related etymologically to "helpers, assistants," and also "students." The full title of the book is *Shemot ha-kodesh asher masar Hashem le-Moshe* [The holy names that God taught Moses]. See Eshkoli, *Sefer ha-Falashim*, 116–19.

You are the Lord of lords, Amen, Hallelujah.
Praises is fitting for You for all time, Amen.[49]

At this point, the baby is given a name.

Following the ceremony, a festive meal is held in the mother's home.

Past and Present in Talmudic Halakhah

A woman who has given birth to a boy is considered impure for one week. After this time, she immerses herself, and immediately begins a period known as *yemei tohar*, "days of purity," which lasts for thirty-three days. If she gives birth to a girl, she is impure for two weeks, then immerses herself and observes sixty-six days of purity. What happens if she observes bloody discharge during the days of purity? According to the Talmud, if she observes bloody discharge during these days of purity, whether after the birth of a boy or a girl, she is permitted to her husband. However, she is still impure according to the laws of *tumah kalah* (minor impurity) – that is, she does not transmit impurity to other people or to vessels she touches, but until she brings the required sacrifice, she cannot enter the Temple or eat meat from sacrifices. On the fortieth day after birth of a boy, or eighty days after birth of a girl, the mother brings a sacrifice to the Temple: a sheep and a chicken, or if she is poor, she may bring only a chicken. However, today the Temple no longer stands and we are all considered impure (on account of being unable to purify ourselves after contact with a human corpse, using the ashes of the red heifer). Thus in rabbinic law, the days of impurity no longer have significance.[50] Those who follow Ethiopian halakhah, however, follow the laws of the days of impurity strictly. According to Beta Israel tradition, the woman is forbidden to have relations with her husband for forty days after birth of a boy and eighty days after birth of a girl.

The Recommended Custom in Israel

The Ethiopian Jews are permitted to continue the customs of purity and impurity as practiced in Ethiopia. According to their tradition, although the Temple was destroyed, these laws were not annulled. However, we cannot ignore the changes and transformations that the community and its families underwent with aliyah, and so a precondition for preservation of the old customs must be interpersonal

---

49. Eshkoli, ibid.
50. Babylonian Talmud, *Niddah* 29b; *Shulhan Arukh, Yoreh De'ah* 194:14.

harmony. If a certain custom leads to strife within the community or family, the path that leads to agreement should be preferred.

First and Last Names

Ethiopian Halakhah

In Ethiopia, there were no last names. An individual was known by his first name, his father's name, and his grandfather's name, as was the custom in biblical times. When the Ethiopian Jews came to Israel, they had to adopt last names, following the Israeli practice. Most of them took their grandfather's name as the last name. If the grandfather was still alive, they used the great-grandfather's name. If the father of the family was no longer alive, they used his name as the last name. Furthermore, the Beta Israel also changed their first names to Hebrew names, as part of the "melting pot" assimilation policy. Today, the situation has changed, and Ethiopian immigrants keep their Ethiopian names. Still, when they arrive at the absorption centers, they are given Hebrew names. Some individuals have many names, given by parents, teachers, and friends. Among many youth, this situation may lead to a feeling of discomfort and damage to identity. Thus today we note a phenomenon of youth who return to their original Ethiopian first names.

Past and Present in Talmudic Halakhah[51]

In ancient times, people usually used their father's name, such as Joshua son of Nun, or a longer genealogical string, such as "Noah son of Lamekh, son of Methuselah, son of Hanokh." In the Bible, the last name is the name of the father, not a name specific to the nuclear family. A person was identified by his first name and his father's or grandfather's name.

Applying a last name to the nuclear family developed in Greek and Roman culture. Since the Middle Ages, this has been the accepted norm in Europe and throughout the world, including among the Jews. The first people to adopt last names in the Middle Ages were the nobility, who adopted the name of their property or its location as their last name. Other citizens followed this practice. People added last names according to their profession or their family's profession. In addition, some last names are identified with or belong to a certain ethnic group. In Ashkenazic communities, last names were adopted only in the eighteenth century. Until then, they used the father's name or nicknames taken from the father's profession, physical qualities, or personality characteristics. Government decrees

---

51. Herman, *Ma'agal hayei ha-yom*.

required the Jews to choose last names such as we use today. Some upper class Jewish families adopted last names in the manner of the non-Jewish nobility.

Regarding changing a name, the Sages specify that four things determine an individual's final judgment: charity, prayer, changing one's name, and changing one's actions. In the past, people would change the name of a sick person, but later the practice became to add a name so that the new name became the principal one used, instead of changing it.

The Recommended Custom in Israel

Most of the Ethiopian Jews came to Israel with Ethiopian names. The question they face is what to do with this name – should they change it to a Hebrew name, or leave the Ethiopian one? On one hand, a person's name has significant value. A name is not only a way of addressing a person, but has meaning, as in the verse, "Whatever the man would call every living creature, that was to be its name" (Genesis 2:19). The name is given to a person by his parents. Whatever an individual's name is, it is his most precious possession. On the other hand, a Hebrew name is also valuable. The Sages relate that Israel was redeemed from Egypt in return for doing four things, including not changing their names and not changing their language.[52]

In my opinion, this is a decision that must be made by the individual. One who feels that his Ethiopian name gives him security and personal and national identity should keep it. But one who feels uncomfortable with his Ethiopian name for any reason should try to translate it into a Hebrew name. This method involves no difficulties, because the person is switching to a Hebrew name that has the same meaning as his previous name. The ideal option is to add a Hebrew name to the original Ethiopian one.

---

52. *Exodus Rabbah* 1:1.

6. Foundations of the Jewish Home

❧ Educating the Children

Ethiopian Halakhah

Ethiopian Jewish education is unique in its content as well as the method of instruction. Education was informal and given by the adults, based on practical application. What characterizes the educated child? He is introverted, speaks politely, works hard around the house and at any task, does not speak to adults, and when an adult speaks to him, he looks down at the ground. The father was responsible for educating the sons, while the mother was in charge of teaching the daughters. In actuality, however, most fathers found it difficult to find time for educating their sons. But the children always respected their father, even when he was absent for long periods. According to the Ethiopian method, at age seven a child is considered an adult. One of the main things the older child had to do was participate in earning a living. Boys went out to the fields with their fathers every day and helped with any task. If the family owned sheep, a child was in charge of guarding them throughout the day.

The *amhary* (children's teacher) usually received teaching fees from the pupil's father on a weekly basis. This fee was given as charity, so that a person would not make a living from teaching Torah. In some locations, the teacher received his fee in the form of meals at the pupils' homes.

Past and Present in Talmudic Halakhah

The Torah commands the father: "And you shall teach them diligently to your children, and shall talk of them when you sit in your house, and when you walk on the path, and when you lie down, and when you rise up" (Deuteronomy 6:7). In other words, you must teach your children and speak of the commandments. But how? By personal example, in all your behavior, both at home and on the road. It does not say you should teach your children and speak of the commandments when *they* (the children) are at home and on the road, but rather when *you* are at home. This means that if you behave at home with patience and are not too strict, the children learn proper behavior from you.

Some people are polite, restrained, and patient toward others, but at home they have no patience, they are severe, and the children observe this and learn from it. Rabbi Zeira was asked, "How did you live for so long?" One of his answers was, "I was never strict inside my home." In other words, a person is not measured outside the home, where others observe him, but rather in his own home, where one has no reason to make pretenses. If you worship God within yourself with your whole heart, your children see this and learn from it.

"When you walk on the path" – traveling can be a valuable lesson for children of how their parents cope with tension and stress. "When you lie down, and when you rise up" – the children see you in the morning and at night. There is no vacation for a parent as an educator. If you want your children to be *bnei Torah*, God-fearing Torah-observant Jews, and well educated, you should follow the advice of the Talmud: "Raba said, he who loves scholars will have sons that are scholars."[1] One who appreciates scholars will have sons and sons-in-law who are scholars, and one who respects scholars will himself become a scholar. Even if he is not worthy of scholarship, others will respect him in the manner of a Torah scholar, and they will listen to him.

The work of education demands effort and thought, and parents should not pressure their children to push for fleeting external achievements. Rather, they should try to envision long-term results, as if not, they will obtain the opposite of their goal. For this purpose they should use the services of educators who are Torah scholars with proven experience.

In this context, we note the beautiful custom of blessing the children every Friday evening with the priestly blessing. For sons one begins with "May God make you like Ephraim and Menashe." For daughters one begins, "May God make you like Sarah, Rebecca, Rachel, and Leah." For both sons and daughters one then proceeds to say, "May God bless you and protect you. May God shine His countenance on you and show you favor. May God be favorably disposed toward you, and may He grant you peace." This blessing expresses the parents' love, appreciation, and respect for their children, and encourages communication between them.

---

1. Babylonian Talmud, *Shabbat* 23b.

The Recommended Custom in Israel

The Beta Israel face the challenge of integrating two worlds. Education in Ethiopia is very intense. The child has almost no autonomy, and discipline is extraordinary. This method has led to great success in Ethiopia, and undoubtedly, the present generation needs some discipline. At the same time, parents must give their children the opportunity to talk and discuss things. They must not educate through humiliation, but through mutual respect and interpersonal esteem, without hierarchy.

Brit Milah – Introduction

Ethiopian Halakhah

Regarding the day of circumcision, there are conflicting reports. Some say that the Beta Israel performed the ceremony on the seventh day, while others insisted that this was done on the eight day. They did the circumcision in the afternoon so that the woman circumciser would be able to immerse after the ceremony and return to the village close to sunset, and would not have to wait a long time until sunset. Jews who lived in the Amhara district report that the circumcision was done on the eighth day.

The ceremony followed this order: in the afternoon, the woman circumciser entered the impurity hut with the circumcision tools – razor blade, *shimpa* (healing herb), and thread. The mother held the baby, and the circumciser tied the foreskin with thread and cut it. After cutting, the circumciser removed the skin and applied the healing herb to the wound. If other women of *niddah* status were present in the hut, they assisted, but otherwise other women were not allowed to enter. After the ceremony, the circumciser went to the river, washed her clothes, immersed herself, and immediately returned to the village, but not her own home. Only after the stars appeared did she enter her home. After three days had passed, the circumciser came to check the baby, but she did not go inside the impurity hut.

Past and Present in Talmudic Halakhah

Circumcision is the first commandment given to Abraham (Genesis 17:12), although we perform the mitzvot because they were given to us on Mount Sinai. The mitzvah of circumcision is repeated in the chapter on the new mother's sacrifice: "And in the eighth day the flesh of his foreskin shall be circumcised" (Leviticus 12:3). The Torah defines this as a covenant between God and Abraham and his descendants "for their generations" (Genesis 17:7). This covenant is not only with the people, but with the land as well: "And I will give you and your seed after you the land of your sojournings...for an everlasting possession.... This is My covenant...every male among you shall be circumcised" (Genesis 17:8–10). Whether a person is a Jew does not depend on performing circumcision, but rather on birth to a Jewish mother. But a Jew who is not circumcised is punished by *karet* (being cut off from one's people). Abraham's acceptance of this covenant marks the beginning of the Jewish people, and since then, it has served as a central symbol of Jewish identity and consciousness for the nation,[2] for which Jews have given their lives during periods of anti-Jewish decrees and persecution.

Circumcision occupies a leading position in the Jewish system of mitzvot. It is unique in that it is the only mitzvah that changes the body from the form in which it was born. The pages of Jewish history in Israel and around the world are saturated with the blood of those who kept this mitzvah, as recorded in Jewish chronicles from Hellenistic times, the Bar Kochba Revolt, the Spanish Inquisition, and under the communist regime. The book of Maccabees describes the punishment of Jewish mothers who kept this mitzvah: "Two women were arrested for having circumcised their children. They were publicly paraded about the city with their babies hanging at their breasts, and then thrown down from the top of the city wall" (II Maccabees 6:11). This dedication served as a credit to our forefathers and ourselves. It is the secret of the eternal existence of the Jewish people – "I said to you, 'In your blood, live'" (Ezekiel 16:6).

The Recommended Custom in Israel

This mitzvah was precious to the Ethiopian Jews, and they lost thousands of babies who died due to circumcision. In Israel, Ethiopian Jews may continue their custom as practiced in Ethiopia.

❧ Female Circumcision

Ethiopian Halakhah

Circumcision of women is not required by halakhah. It seems to have been adopted during times of anti-Jewish decrees and persecution, when Jewish parents were threatened that their daughters might be forcibly taken away. Parents who circumcised their daughters were trying to postpone the date of marriage and prevent their daughters from being taken, thinking that circumcision reduced

---

2. Nissan Rubin, *Reshit ha-hayim* (Israel, 2005).

a woman's sexual attractiveness. Girls were circumcised on the eighth day after birth, reminiscent of circumcision of males. The ceremony was performed by a woman. Birth and infant care in general was the woman's domain.

Past and Present in Talmudic Halakhah

Jewish sources have no evidence of female circumcision, even though this custom existed in the surrounding cultures. One source about this practice among Jews was documented by the ancient historian and geographer Strabo of Amaseia (first century BCE). He observed this custom among certain Jewish communities in Egypt: "One of the customs most zealously observed among the Egyptians is this, that they rear every child that is born, and circumcise the males, and excise the females, as is also customary for the Jews, who are also Egyptian in origin, as I have already stated in my account of them."[3] In another source, Strabo says that apparently it was the descendants of Moses who were responsible for bringing the custom of female circumcision to Egypt. He adds that this custom was also practiced among Jewish women in Ethiopia, although it was done in a Jewish manner. He concludes that the Jews as well as the Egyptians circumcised both males and females.

Circumcision of females among the Beta Israel may be proof of the ancient origin of this custom; however, possibly the Jews were influenced by their surroundings, and their practice may not actually be ancient. In addition, we should note that Strabo did not directly mention the Beta Israel, and his statement is unproven. In conclusion, his reference is inexact, and Strabo, although he was a geographer, historian, and anthropologist, did not distinguish between Jews and Egyptians.

The Recommended Custom in Israel

Apparently, the custom of circumcision of females is not a custom that originated among the Beta Israel, and seems to have penetrated the community from the surrounding Ethiopian environment. Evidence from six hundred years ago reveals that the Beta Israel did not perform this practice.[4] Thus there is no reason to maintain this foreign and cruel custom.

---

3. Cited in Shaye J.D. Cohen, *Why Aren't Jewish Women Circumcised? Gender and Covenant in Judaism* (Berkeley, CA: University of California Press, 2005), p. 59n23.
4. Edward Ullendorff, "The Confessio Fidei of King Claudius of Ethiopia," *Journal of Semitic Studies* 32, no. 1 (1987): 159–76.

⁂ Circumcision on Shabbat

Ethiopian Halakhah

From interviews I have conducted with representatives of the Beta Israel community, I found that they never performed *milah* on Shabbat. When the eighth day after birth fell on Shabbat, they postponed the ceremony until the following Sunday. However, rabbinic sources state that Shabbat is equal in importance to all the other mitzvot in the Torah, yet *milah* takes precedence over Shabbat. What is the source of the Beta Israel's custom? According to the author of *Tataza Sanvet* (Laws of Shabbat), the Jews were forbidden from performing any labor on Shabbat, and this included the thirty-nine biblically forbidden labors as well as rabbinic prohibitions. Thus the mitzvah of *milah* does not supersede Shabbat in any circumstance. According to the book of Jubilees, from which the author of *Tataza Sanvet* apparently copied, circumcision on Shabbat is forbidden. But this halakhah conflicts with another halakhah in Jubilees that the circumcision must not be postponed after the eighth day for any reason (even if the baby is not healthy and it might endanger his life).

In order to resolve the conflict between these laws, I spoke with several *kesim*. They asserted that Shabbat is not an ordinary day, but rather above time – it is not considered one of the days of the week. Thus when the eighth day after birth falls on Shabbat and the circumcision is postponed until Sunday, essentially it is taking place on the "eighth day" after birth, since Shabbat is not included in the days counted. In light of this, we may understand the Sages' statement about *milah* on Shabbat against the background of a contentious battle among various groups within the Jewish people.

The simple meaning of the verses does not indicate that it should be permitted to circumcise on Shabbat. But the Mishnah specifies that "Circumcision is great, for it supersedes the severity of Shabbat."[5] The Sages of the Talmud were pressed to prove the source for this halakhah. Possibly, then, the custom of the Beta Israel not to circumcise on Shabbat for any reason originated in an ancient practice to which Pharisaic-rabbinic halakhah objected, and due to the break between the Beta Israel and the rest of Jewry, this ancient tradition was preserved. Therefore, the Beta Israel do not circumcise on Shabbat for any reason, but they also do not postpone the *milah* for other reasons, such as disease. An infant boy who dies before the *milah* ceremony is circumcised. But if the baby is a girl and

---

5. Mishnah, *Nedarim* 3:11.

she dies before circumcision, they do not circumcise her. A male who was not circumcised is considered a non-Jew – he cannot participate in religious ceremonies and cannot eat with Jews.

Past and Present in Talmudic Halakhah

As we have discussed, the Beta Israel did not set rules to govern the mitzvot, nor did they discuss which mitzvah should take precedence over another. By contrast, rabbinic literature outlines rules and definitions that regulate the validity of the mitzvot. One of these rules specifies that *brit milah* takes precedence over Shabbat.

The Recommended Custom in Israel

If the eighth day falls on Shabbat, the parents should consult with a rabbi as well as a *kes*, and the halakhah should follow the decision of the *kes* on this issue.

Male and Female Circumcisers

Ethiopian Halakhah

Among the Beta Israel, the custom was that women circumcised the infants. A man circumcised only if the community had no woman who knew how to do so. Moses' son was circumcised by a woman – his mother Zipporah, and so clearly there is no problem for a woman to circumcise.[6] According to tradition, any contact with a non-Jew was forbidden due to laws of purity, and so clearly there was no authorization for a non-Jew to circumcise a Jewish baby.

Past and Present in Talmudic Halakhah

The Sages of the Talmud were divided over the question of whether a woman was permitted to circumcise, despite the story of Zipporah who circumcised her son (Exodus 4:24–26). The medieval scholars also debated this question: the Rif and the Rambam permitted it, and following them, the *Shulhan Arukh* also ruled to permit it. The Tosafot, however, forbade women circumcisers, as did the Rema.[7]

Second Temple literature documents circumcision by women:

---

6. Sperber, *Minhagei Yisrael*, vol. 4, *Shnei inyanei nashim: Nashim mohalot, nashim shohtot* [Two women's issues: Women circumcisers, women butchers].
7. *Yoreh De'ah* 264a.

> No one could keep the Sabbath or celebrate the traditional feasts, nor even admit to being a Jew.... It was obvious, therefore, that disaster had come upon them. Two women were arrested for having circumcised their children. They were publicly paraded about the city with their babies hanging at their breasts, and then thrown down from the top of the city wall.[8]

Rabbinic literature, however, has no clear evidence that circumcision was performed by women. In later periods, we find that this role was taken from women and passed into the men's area of responsibility – for cultural, social, and economic reasons. Women apparently served as circumcisers until the thirteenth century, just as they served in the honored position of *sandak* (holder of the baby) at the *brit*. We may assume that when the custom ended for women to serve as *sandak*, they also stopped serving as circumcisers, for the reason recorded by the Maharam of Rothenburg: "It is not the way of the land for a woman who is adorned to be present among men and before the Divine Presence." In fact, halakhah specifies that if there is no Jewish man present who knows how to circumcise, and there is a Jewish woman who does know, then she is permitted to do so. A non-Jew is forbidden from acting as circumciser, and the rabbis debated whether a Jew had to subsequently perform *hatafat dam brit* (a symbolic drawing of a drop of blood) if a non-Jew had performed the circumcision. Under ordinary circumstances women do not serve as circumcisers today.[9]

The Recommended Custom in Israel

This custom is apparently ancient and unique among the Beta Israel, and for reasons specifically related to their community, the mitzvah of *milah* was performed by women throughout their history. In locations where an eligible and qualified woman is present, they may uphold this custom, and *le-khathilah* (as a first choice), this woman is permitted to circumcise.

Bar Mitzvah

Ethiopian Halakhah

The age at which a child is obligated in the *mitzvot* in Ethiopia was seven, lower than the usually accepted age in other Jewish communities of twelve for girls and

---

8. II Maccabees 6:8, 11.
9. There is a well-known story of a woman cirumcizing her newborn in a concentration camp during World War II; obviously this is an extreme situation.

thirteen for boys. In Ethiopia, they did not commemorate this occasion with a special celebration.

Past and Present in Talmudic Halakhah

The Written Torah (Tanakh) does not specify the age at which a boy becomes obligated in the mitzvot. However, the Oral Torah tradition specifies that a boy becomes an adult when he has reached the age of thirteen full years, and at that point he is obligated in all the mitzvot of the Torah. We count the years according to the Hebrew calendar. Some found a hint at this in the verse "The people which I formed for Myself, that they might tell of My praise" (Isaiah 43:21) – "this" in *gematriah* (Hebrew numerology) is equivalent to the number thirteen, and so a boy who reaches this age must begin to "recite God's praises" by keeping the mitzvot.

There is no need for a ceremony or special blessing – when the boy reaches thirteen, he is obligated in the mizvot, like an adult. We have no evidence of a bar mitzvah ceremony until the Geonic period. At that time, the custom was for a boy who turned thirteen to have an aliyah to the Torah in order to publicize his acceptance of the mitzvot, and to announce that he was qualified to join a prayer quorum and to perform other religious duties. According to today's custom, the boy has an aliyah to the Torah at the time of the bar mitzvah and on the following Shabbat as well. In some communities, he reads both the weekly Torah portion and the portion from the Prophets.

The Recommended Custom in Israel

The Beta Israel should follow the general practice.

✣ Bat Mitzvah

Ethiopian Halakhah

In Ethiopia there was no ceremony held for the bat mitzvah, and the transition took place without formality.

Past and Present in Talmudic Halakhah

Rabbinic authorities of recent times have debated over the question of the bat mitzvah celebration. According to Rabbi Moshe Feinstein, bat mitzvah parties should not be held, because they are an imitation of the practices of Reform and Conservative Jews. But if a family has already decided to hold a celebration, it may be done at home, as long as it is not done in the synagogue, because the synagogue should not be used for an optional ceremony. By contrast, Rabbi Y. Weinberg, who was a Holocaust survivor and one of the major rabbinic authorities of the generation that followed, ruled that the bat mitzvah ceremony should be held, and that girls should not be discriminated against in this, especially considering that today girls go to school and participate in many activities just like boys. In modern times, the practice of holding bat mitzvah celebrations has spread among many circles. At the celebration, the girl often gives a speech on Torah-related topics. The celebration encourages and strengthens her in her religious observance, in light of the responsibilities and challenges of Israeli society. According to Rabbi Ovadia Yosef, of blessed memory, at a bat mitzvah celebration the girl's father should recite the same blessing he does for a boy.

The Recommended Custom in Israel

Today, members of the Beta Israel community in Israel hold formal celebrations that can be ostentatious. In Ethiopia, family celebrations were modest, attended by relatives, fellow villagers and neighbors, and in accordance with the family's financial means. Today, the well-developed transportation system in Israel and social influences have led to celebrations attended by many guests, some of whom come from afar, and the celebrations are sometimes grandiose. The feeling of communal participation has become a burden, as the bar and bat mitzvah, which were not celebrated at all in Ethiopia, have become mass events. Further, in Israel, the expenses can be very high. Many agree that the present situation is undesirable. People focus on the celebration instead of on the significance of the event, which is acceptance of the mitzvot; the unfortunate emphasis is on doing what is socially acceptable, not on a decision made of free will. Thus we must consider how to transform these events into occasions that encourage advancement instead of holding back; occasions planned with careful thought and in accordance with the family's financial status, without getting carried away, and out of the desire to focus on the meaning of the event and not merely waste money on halls, catering, and photography.

Modesty

Ethiopian Halakhah

In Ethiopian culture, greeting a man or woman includes shaking hands and kissing the cheek. People who see each other often only need to shake hands, but if they have not seen each other for some time, the custom for women and men is to kiss the other's person's cheek, to show that one has missed him or her. Because the kiss is to express missing the other, in the Ethiopian conception this is not a question of modesty. In Ethiopia, the issue of modesty has much broader significance, as it represents ethical behavior, as in the words of the prophet Micah: "It has been told you, O man, what is good, and what the Lord demands of you; only to do justly, and to love mercy, and to walk modestly with your God" (6:8). Modesty in the sexual sense was not a recognized concept in Ethiopia, and thus the leaders of the Beta Israel had no problem with natural human social contact between men and women. Guarding against sexual impropriety was a natural act, not halakhically imposed.

Past and Present in Talmudic Halakhah

In recent years, the sexual aspect has come to occupy center stage in the subject of modesty, both in halakhah and in philosophy, and the significance and weight of sexual modesty has multiplied in the kabbalistic and ethical literature. Here we will offer a short summary of prohibited sexual practices, beginning in the Torah and ending with modern rabbinic authorities. The book of Leviticus specifies: "None of you shall approach to any that is near of kin to him, to uncover their nakedness. I am the Lord" (18:6). The Sages of the Talmud were divided over the question of whether this prohibition included physical proximity to individuals with whom sexual contact was forbidden. Rabbi Pedat, for example, did not consider this proximity as biblically forbidden. He thought that the Sages were the ones who forbade this in order to strenghten the biblical prohibition.[10] This Talmudic controversy over the status of modesty regulations continued among the Rishonim, and was expressed in a debate between the Rambam and Ramban. In his enumeration of the 613 mitzvot, the Rambam counted the extended regulation of modesty. In his words,

> We are forbidden from deriving pleasure from any forbidden partner, even without sexual relations, through kissing, hugging, and the like. The source of this prohibition is God's statement, "To a close relative, do not approach to have forbidden sexual relations," as if to say, "Do not come close to them in any type of closeness that could lead to sexual relations."[11]

---

10. Babylonian Talmud, *Shabbat* 13a.
11. *Sefer ha-Mitzvot*, negative commandment 353.

By contrast, Ramban considers that "physical proximity to a forbidden partner" means the act of sexual relations, and in his opinion, even the Talmudic sages permitted close but non-sexual contact.[12]

Another consequence of proximity to forbidden partners that is difficult to measure clearly is forbidden thoughts. This prohibition differs from other prohibitions in that it applies only to acts and not to thoughts. The Sages recognized the difficulty involved in controlling one's thoughts, yet did not minimize the severity of a failure to do so. Sinful thoughts are among the three sins for which "an individual is not saved from them on a daily basis";[13] and "forbidden thoughts are worse than the sin itself."[14]

Another law related to sexual morality that is derived from the prohibition is the issue of a woman's voice. Rabbinic authorities have varying opinions on the conditions of this prohibition. Some believe that it is only seeing a woman singing or seeing a woman singer whom the observer knows. Others differentiate between live listening and listening through digital means. The prohibition against looking at women is also based on the above verse. As the Talmud specifies, "Anyone who looks at women will eventually commit a sin."[15] Touching, including shaking hands in greeting, and even hugging and kissing without affection, are subject to controversy among the later rabbinic authorities. Most of the authorities forbid it, but a number of major authorities permit it, such as the Shach: "Even the Rambam did not forbid this, except for hugging and kissing with sexual desire, as we find in the Talmud in several places that the Amoraim hugged and kissed their daughters and sisters."[16]

In various Jewish communities in Europe in the Middle Ages, they engaged in mixed dancing. This even became an institution in Ashkenazic communities, and public buildings were built expressly for this purpose. The mixed dances invited severe critique throughout their history, including repeated attempts by rabbis to ban them, as they viewed them as trespassing most of the boundaries of modesty: sinful thoughts, looking at women, touching, and hearing a woman's singing voice. In the early twentieth century, it was customary among the religious Zionist youth groups and the religious kibbutz movement to dance mixed circle dances. During the late twentieth century, the tide of public opinion swelled

---

12. *Hasagot ha-Ramban le-Sefer ha-Mitzvot*, negative commandment 353.
13. Babylonian Talmud, *Baba Batra* 164b.
14. Babylonian Talmud, *Yoma* 29a.
15. Babylonian Talmud, *Nedarim* 20a.
16. *Yoreh De'ah* 157:10.

against these dances, and they were significantly limited. Today we are witness to increasing stringencies among many religious groups. Numerous schools in which both boys and girls studied together in the past are today completely separated. Separation between the sexes affects all ages, and some even separate at preschool age. The background for this is to protect against forbidden touching or sexual relations, looking at women, sinful thoughts, immodest dress, wearing clothing of the opposite sex, and imitating gentile forms of dress. However, it seems that those who rule severely on these issues are not satisfied with the Sages' rulings, and attempt to completely suppress human desire.

The Recommended Custom in Israel

Today the halakhic issue that a non-emotional act is not included in the prohibition is no longer a consideration. Today it is difficult to understand how the Rambam could ever have allowed friendly hugging and kissing as a greeting; why Rabbi Moshe Feinstein permitted travel on the subway, although it is difficult to avoid touching women there, as he argued that this is not an act of sexual desire; and how boys and girls ever learned together in the same classroom. Today we hear the demand that parents of pupils should dress according to this or that code, as a requirement for their children's acceptance. It seems that the massive attention to the laws of modesty in their sexual meaning has led to starving the human sex drive instead of conquering it.

We ask whether this is the proper path, in light of the permissive reality of society. The Sages indeed felt it was precisely the proper path, as they said, "If you starve it – it becomes satisfied; if you satisfy it – it grows hungry"[17] – the more a person tries to satisfy his sexual needs, so his sexual desire will grow. When his desire is fulfilled, it expands. On the other hand, if a person limits sexual satisfaction, he can reduce it to an appropriate level.

It is not my role to decide on this issue. Further, in light of the statements of my teacher Rabbi Yehuda Amital, of blessed memory, I think the decision is not easy. Rabbi Amital often recalled the Sages' saying, "If the despicable one [i.e., the Evil Inclination] harms you, drag it to the study hall"[18]; in other words, you can certainly enter the study hall, but another despicable one will await you there. Beta Israel leaders do not understand the high separations that divide men and women. In their opinion, this separation takes place naturally, without unnatural

---

17. Babylonian Talmud, *Sukkah* 72b.
18. Babylonian Talmud, *Kiddushin* 30b.

barriers, but the barrier itself tempts sexual desire. Today people are occupied all day long with desire and thus it only increases. Thus many parents have difficulty adapting to the practices of their children who become newly religious and refuse to greet women, even girls in the family. Further, they disparage these customs and view them as a result of improper education. It is contrary to the cultural world of the parents, and even contrary to the path of Torah – "Its ways are ways of pleasantness, and all its paths are peace" (Proverbs 3:17). Thus the Ethiopian Jews should continue their custom to greet members of the opposite sex, shake hands, and even kiss on the cheek. However, they must preserve the barriers of modesty that existed in Ethiopia (modest dress, no relations before marriage, separate seating in the synagogue, etc.).

Tattoos

Ethiopian Halakhah

In Ethiopia, girls customarily had images tattooed on their faces, on the forehead or neck. Some even chose the sign of the cross. To the outside observer, this phenomenon seems particularly contemptible, as it is forbidden in the Torah. The *kesim* also viewed this as a biblical prohibition, and warned against it. Still, the women continued to do it. Why? And why was the issue of tattoos so important in Ethiopian culture? I have found several explanations for this:

1. Protection from the evil eye: people believed that the tattoo had the power to deflect evil spirits.
2. Esthetics: lighter skin signified higher social status. Having a tattoo made the skin look lighter.
3. Cross symbol: religious and cultural reasons.

Some say that the Ethiopian Jews did this out of awareness and intent, in order to make it difficult to distinguish them from the Christian population. Some, however, say it is a matter of interpretation, and that the biblical commandment "You shall not make any cuttings in your flesh for the dead, nor imprint any marks upon yourselves" (Leviticus 19:28) was intended only for men. I do not intend to rule on this issue. But it is interesting to note that this custom was more prevalent in larger numbers among recent immigrants, and less among the first immigrants to Israel, apparently because the first immigrants were less exposed to the Christian world.

Past and Present in Talmudic Halakhah

A tattoo is a design made using ink or another form of dye that is permanently inserted under the skin, for decoration or marking. From the fact that the Torah expressly forbids tattooing, we may assume that this was a common practice among the Canaanite peoples, and biblical commentators have remarked on this. The Rambam notes that the gentiles tattooed themselves to indicate loyalty to their gods.[19] Rabbi Avraham Ibn Ezra writes that non-Jews tattooed themselves in memory of the dead, and this is why the prohibition against tattoos appears in the same verse with the prohibition against cutting oneself to honor the dead.

Jewish law forbids making a tattoo on the body. This prohibition is one of the 613 mitzvot. The Rambam writes:

> The tattooing which the Torah forbids involves making a cut in one's flesh and filling the slit with eye-color, ink, or with any other dye that leaves an imprint. This was the custom of the idolaters, who would make marks on their bodies for the sake of their idols, as if to say that they are like servants sold to the idol and designated for its service. When a person makes a mark with one of the substances that leave an imprint after making a slit in any place on his body, he is [liable for] lashes. [This prohibition is binding on] both men and women.[20]

The prohibition against tattoos applies to any part of the body, whether it is usually revealed or covered. One of the reasons given for this prohibition is that the Jews belong to an important people, and thus it is disrespectful for them to deface their bodies. The biblical commentator Hizkuni gives the explanation that it is inappropriate for a Jew to make any other mark on his body other than the *brit milah*. Another reason given in *Sefer ha-Hinukh* is the need to differentiate ourselves from the customs of idol worship.

The Recommended Custom in Israel

In Israel, the Ethiopian women suffer from their tattoos, especially those who have the tattoo of a cross on their forehead, which is particularly difficult to hide. These women are subject to humiliation and shame. Indeed it is very strange for an Israeli to see a Jewish woman with a tattoo in the shape of a cross, and the negative reactions are completely understandable. Today there are volunteers,

---

19. *Mishneh Torah*, Hilkhot Avodat Kokhavim 12:11.
20. Ibid.

including physicians and people of means, who help the girls erase the tattoos with laser procedures. The question is, if they are not able to remove the tattoo of the cross on the forehead, whether it is halakhically acceptable to add additional lines so as to blur the shape of the cross? Here we confront a conflict between a biblical prohibition and respect for fellow human beings. I have heard that there are some rabbis who permit blurring the cross mark, based on respect for humans. But I do know that today, technology offers creative solutions in order to erase these marks, thus enabling Beta Israel girls to feel at home in Israel.

Honoring Parents

Ethiopian Halakhah

Honoring parents was one of the most important mitzvot in Ethiopia, to the point of complete self-negation in the face of parental authority. Honoring parents demanded educating the child for discipline and obedience. Saying no to parents was unthinkable, and boys and girls were taught total submission to parental authority.

Past and Present in Talmudic Halakhah

The Sages said, "There are three partners in man: the Holy One, blessed be He, the father, and the mother. When a man honors his father and his mother, the Holy One, blessed be He, says: 'I ascribe [merit] to them as though I had dwelt among them and they had honored Me.'... When a man vexes his father and his mother, the Holy One, blessed be He, says: 'I did right in not dwelling among them, for had I dwelt among them, they would have vexed Me.'"[21] Others said, "The Torah tells us, 'Every man shall fear his mother and his father' (Leviticus 19:3), and 'You shall fear the Lord your God' (Deuteronomy 6:13) – the Torah compares the fear of father and mother to fear of God."[22] Talmudic commentators explained that one who honors his parents becomes accustomed to act kindly to one who does good to him, as his parents have given him his every need. Fulfilling this mitzvah in its entirety is practically impossible, and some explain that for this reason, we do not recite a blessing over it, so as to avoid an unfulfilled blessing. A son is obligated to honor his parents even if they commit sins. A convert is required to honor his gentile parents, at least through rabbinic interpretation,

---

21. *Kiddushin* 30b.
22. *Kiddushin* 31a.

and after their deaths, according to some opinions he is permitted to recite the Mourners' Kaddish for them and to pray for the ascension of their souls.

The Recommended Custom in Israel

The custom of honoring parents as practiced in Ethiopia is quite important. Therefore, the second generation of Ethiopian Jews in Israel should make every effort to learn from their parents and be respectful toward them. However, they must be aware that excessive honoring of parents may lead to complete self-abnegation. The child's independence should be preserved. In this case, as in many others, it is all a matter of balance.

Studying Torah

Ethiopian Halakhah

The way of life in Ethiopia preserved the biblical model, in which the majority of the people worked the land for their living, and spiritual matters such as Torah study were reserved for the spiritual leaders. On holidays, Rosh Hodesh, and Shabbat, everyone gathered in the synagogue to hear a Torah lesson from the *kesim*. Study focused on practical application of halakhah, and was not given any spiritual significance in and of itself. The concept of *Torah lishmah*, "studying Torah for its own sake" did not exist in their world.

Past and Present in Talmudic Halakhah

The study of Torah is a mitzvah like any other. The principle of this commandment, as apparent in the text, is designed to teach the individual how to fulfill this commandment. The Torah repeats the commandment to study in several places, as the Rambam specifies in *Sefer ha-Mitzvot*,[23] citing the biblical text: "And these words, which I command you this day, shall be upon your heart. And you shall teach them diligently to your children, and shall talk of them when you sit in your house, and when you walk on the path, and when you lie down, and when you rise up" (Deuteronomy 6:6–7); "…that you may learn them, and observe to do them" (Deuteronomy 5:1); "…that they may learn" (Deuteronomy 31:12). The book of Joshua states, "You shall meditate therein day and night, that you may observe to do according to all that is written therein" (1:8). Shimon ha-Tzaddik, a member of the Great Assembly, reveals the value and importance of the Torah in his statement: "The world is based on three things – Torah, divine service, and

---

23. Positive commandment 11.

the practice of kindliness."[24] After the destruction of the Second Temple, when the Torah was construed as the only supreme value, the Sages determined that "The study of Torah outweighs them all."[25]

"Torah" means the Written Torah and the Oral Torah, which interprets the written text. This is one of the principles of Jewish belief, that the Written and Oral Torah both originate in divine revelation on Mount Sinai. The main purpose of study is for human beings to know how to behave, because "Study is not the most important thing, but actions"[26]; and "An uncultured person does not fear sin, nor is the ignorant person pious."[27] Another purpose of study is to reach closeness to God: "Because through it, you will know God and follow His ways."[28] The commentator Bayit Hadash adds to this and writes, "It seems that God always intended for us to be occupied with Torah so that our souls would be strengthened with physical power, spirituality, and the sanctity of the source of the Torah.... So that our souls and bodies cleave to the mitzvot, with all 248 bones and 365 tendons, with 248 positive commandments and 365 negative commandments in the Torah."[29]

In biblical times, those who studied the Torah were the descendants of the tribe of Levi, and they performed the service in the Tabernacle and taught Torah to the people, as Moses instructed them: "They shall teach Jacob Your ordinances, and Israel Your Torah; they shall put incense before You, and burnt offerings upon Your altar" (Deuteronomy 33:10). They kept this role throughout the First Temple period, as we learn from the deeds of King Jehoshaphat, who sends the Levites and priests to teach Torah in the cities of Judah (II Chronicles 17:8–9). In the early Second Temple period, we learn from the prophet Malachi: "For the priest's lips shall guard knowledge, and teaching should be sought from his mouth, for he is the messenger of the Lord of Hosts" (2:7). In the mass gathering for Torah study that took place in Ezra's time, the *kohanim* played a central role, and they were the ones who "caused the people to understand the Torah" (Nehemiah 8:7). Over the years, and especially after Second Temple times, Torah study came to occupy a central position in the Jewish world, and expanded among the nation.

---

24. Mishnah, *Avot* 1:2.
25. Mishnah, *Pe'ah* 1:1.
26. Mishnah, *Avot* 1:17.
27. Ibid., 2:5.
28. Sifri, Deuteronomy, par. 33.
29. *Bayit Hadash, Orah Haim*, par. 47.

The Recommended Custom in Israel

I do not know what the significance of Torah study is in Heaven. However, I do know what influence it has on a person's soul. In Ethiopia, the Jews did not study Torah because they worked in the fields, and many of them were illiterate. But in Israel, there are many opportunities to study Torah with relative ease – every house has basic religious books, the synagogue libraries are full, and Torah classes are held at all hours. Thus everyone should use his free time to study Torah. Of course, he should not do so in the workplace – "If there is no flour [i.e., earning a living], there is no Torah."[30] As Jews, we must preserve the flame of Torah and continue to transfer Torah knowledge to the next generation. At the same time, the Jewish people needs individuals who dedicate most of their time to Torah study, people who make Torah their profession. This mission is reserved for the top students. This role is not for all who desire it. The state should decide the conditions under which the Torah student may join the company of scholars and be relieved of other duties such as military service. This has been the situation in the past, and should remain the case today as well.

Dedication of a New House

Ethiopian Halakhah

The construction of a house for a newly married couple is considered an exciting and important event. After the wedding, the couple lives with the parents for a long period, and at a later date, they move into their own home and live independently. In Ethiopia, there is no need to take a mortgage, look for a real estate agent or contractor, or finance construction of a house on their own. When the time for building the house arrives, the relatives all help with construction. After construction is completed, they set a moving date. A sheep is slaughtered in honor of the occasion. At the festive meal, the *kes* offers a special prayer for the success of the couple in their new home.

Past and Present in Talmudic Halakhah

Purchasing a home is one of the most joyful events of a person's life; when he does so, he should thank God and recite the *sheheheyanu* blessing. If he has a wife and children, he should not recite *sheheheyanu*, but rather *ha-tov ve-ha-meitiv* ("Blessed are You…Who is good and Who bestows good"), thanking God for bestowing good on the members of his family as well as himself. He should recite

---

30. Mishnah, *Avot* 3:17.

the blessing when he makes the purchase, while some say that he should recite it after affixing the mezuzah.[31] If he has purchased a house that is not yet constructed, he should recite the blessing only when going to live there.

Buying a home in Israel is an important mitzvah, as it means fulfilling the mitzvah of settling the Land, which is considered equal in importance to all the rest of the mitzvot together. Thus it is customary to hold a festive meal in honor of the occasion, and this meal is considered a mitzvah. We invite relatives and friends, and read special prayers that emphasize love for the Land of Israel, its sanctity, and the value of settling it. Some think that a meal honoring the purchase of a house outside of Israel is also a mitzvah. It is most appropriate to hold the celebration immediately upon entering the new house, and not to put it off. However, if it was not held right away, one may do so within one year of entering the house.

The Recommended Custom in Israel

It is appropriate to mark the occasion of entering a new house with a family celebration. One should and may invite a *kes* or rabbi to bless the celebrants on their new path. At any rate, one should not go to undue expense for this occasion – drinks and baked goods are sufficient.

❧ Mezuzah

Ethiopian Halakhah

This mitzvah was not known in Ethiopia.

Past and Present in Talmudic Halakhah

It is a biblical commandment to affix a mezuzah on the doorpost of the house. The mezuzah is made of parchment and contains two sections from the Torah, which are basic elements of Jewish faith. One is the first paragraph of the Shema (Deuteronomy 6:4–9), which contains the belief in one God. The second is the second paragraph of the Shema, "If you listen" (Deuteronomy 11:13–21), which contains a commitment to keep the mitzvot, and connects observance of the mitzvot to events in the life of the individual and the nation.

---

31. Sperber, *Mo'adei Yisrael*, vol. 1, *Al kivun hanhatah shel ha-mezuzah* [On the direction of affixing the mezuzah], 46.

The Recommended Custom in Israel

For some reason, the mezuzah mentioned in the Torah was not practiced in Ethiopia. Today almost every Jewish home has a mezuzah, and all recognize its importance. Thus the Beta Israel should certainly observe this mitzvah.

Living Outside Israel

Ethiopian Halakhah

In the days before Ethiopian aliyah, of course this was not a relevant issue to the community. Today, however, we are witness to the phenomenon of Ethiopian Jews from the second generation in Israel who leave to live abroad, whether in the United States or Ethiopia, for various reasons. How can it be that after two thousand years of longing to return, young people are leaving Israel? What do the *kesim* think about this? Before we answer this question, we will give a short summary of the halakhah on this matter.

Past and Present in Talmudic Halakhah

Halakhic literature contains a discussion over whether living in the Land of Israel is included in the 613 mitzvot. In the commentary of the Tosafot, we find an interesting debate on this question. Some say that this is a mitzvah, "but we do not practice it now, due to danger on the roads." Rabbenu Chaim writes, "Now living in the Land of Israel is not a mitzvah, because there are several mitzvot that depend on the Land, and several punishments, and we cannot observe them carefully or fulfill them."[32] Rabbi Yeshayahu Halevi Horowitz (the Holy Shelah) wrote on this topic in the seventeenth century:

> Rabbi Chaim's statement is but the opinion of a single individual, and his justifications are not reasonable.... Certainly one who lives in the Land of Israel and does not observe what he is supposed to is committing a sin. But if one sanctifies himself and observes the tithes and the sabbatical year as he is obligated, then he is praiseworthy. As for his statement that we cannot observe them carefully, I cannot understand this – who prevents us from doing so?[33]

---

32. Tosafot, *Ketubot* 110b, s.v. "*Hu omer la'alot.*"
33. *Sefer ha-Shelah, Sha'ar ha-otiyot*, "*Kedushah.*"

Interestingly, the Rambam did not count settlement of the Land of Israel as a mitzvah, and it does not appear in his *Mishneh Torah*, although he praises living there and does note the prohibition against leaving it:

> It is forbidden to leave Eretz Yisrael for the Diaspora at all times except to study Torah, to marry, or to save one's property from the gentiles. After accomplishing these objectives, one must return to Eretz Yisrael.
>
> Similarly, one may leave Eretz Yisrael to conduct commercial enterprises. However, it is forbidden to leave with the intent of settling permanently in the Diaspora unless the famine in Eretz Yisrael is severe.... Though it is permitted to leave Eretz Yisrael under these circumstances, it is not pious behavior. Behold, Mahlon and Khilyon were two of the great men of the generation and they left Eretz Yisrael only out of great distress. Nevertheless, they were found worthy of death by God.[34]

The Ramban thought that the Rambam did not consider living in the Land of Israel to be a mitzvah. He thus responded and wrote that settling the Land was a positive mitzvah that applied to all generations, obligating every individual even during the Diaspora. Rabbi Yitzhak DeLeon, one of the leading Italian sages, a descendant of the Jews banished from Spain during the sixteenth century, defended the Rambam's position against the Ramban, and argued that the Rambam did consider settling the Land as a mitzvah, but not in those times, meaning during the Diaspora. In his book, entitled *Megillat Esther*, on the Rambam's *Sefer ha-Mitzvot*, he specifies:

> It seems to me that the Rambam did not count [this mitzvah as one of the mitzvot], because the mitzvah of inheriting the Land and settling it was only practiced in the time of Moses, Joshua, and David, and as long as the Jews lived in their Land. But after they were banished from their territory, this mitzvah was not practiced [and will not be practiced] by subsequent generations, until the Messiah comes. On the contrary, we were commanded in this, as the Sages said at the end of Tractate *Ketubot*,[35] that we should not rebel against the nations to conquer the Land with force. They supported this with the verse, "I adjure you, O daughters of Jerusalem: Why should you awaken, or stir up love, until it please?" (Song of Songs 8:3). The Sages interpreted this

---

34. Rambam, *Mishneh Torah*, Hilkhot Malakhim 5:9.
35. 111a.

to mean that Israel should not breach the wall [i.e., they should not attempt to organize against the non-Jews to go to Israel by force].... What he [the Rambam] also said, that the Sages abundantly praised living in the Land, this actually refers to the period when the Temple was standing. But at present, there is no mitzvah to live there.[36]

Rabbi Kook addresses the Rambam's reasoning. He explains that the Rambam removed this mitzvah from the list in *Sefer ha-Mitzvot* not because he thought this was not a biblically based mitzvah. On the contrary, he said the Rambam also thought that settling the Land was a biblically based commandment for all time. But the Rambam determined principles for this book, one of which was that he would not count a general mitzvah that including many mitzvot within it. Under this principle, the mitzvah of settling the Land of Israel should not be included in the count, as it forms the basis for many other mitzvot. By contrast, Rabbi Moshe Feinstein writes that in modern times, the mitzvah is only for those who already live in the Land of Israel, but that there is no obligation for a Jew from abroad to go live in Israel:

> Regarding your question of whether it is a mitzvah at this time to live in the Land of Israel, according to the Ramban, or [whether to follow] Rabbi Chaim in Tosafot on folio 110, that it is not a mitzvah at the present time, most rabbinic authorities think that it is a mitzvah. But at this time, it is simply not a positive mitzvah that one must fulfill with one's body, for if so, it would be prohibited to live abroad, because one would be violating a positive mitzvah. This is like one who wears a four-cornered garment without *tzitzit* [fringes] – it is forbidden to wear such a garment, so as not to violate the positive mitzvah of *tzitzit*. No such prohibition is mentioned [regarding going to live in the Land of Israel], rather, one who lives in Israel may not leave in order to reside abroad (Rambam, Hilkhot Melakhim, 5:9). Certainly [living abroad] is not a negative commandment, for if it were prohibited for people abroad, the Rambam would have written simply, "It is forbidden to live abroad, unless there is a severe famine in the Land of Israel." In other words, the only prohibition is for those living in the Land, as the Sages specified, but there is no positive commandment. But one who lives there is performing a mitzvah.[37]

---

36. According to Rabbi Nachum Rabinowitz, this was not the Rambam's opinion.
37. *Responsa Iggerot Moshe, Even ha-Ezer* 1, par. 102.

The Zionist movement, particularly religious Zionism, viewed these halakhic opinions as justification and support for the Zionist project. However, well-known rabbis opposed it, including Rabbi Shalom Dov-Ber Schneersohn, the fifth Admor of Chabad, and Rabbi Chaim Elazar Spira, the Admor of Munkacs. They objected in principle to the Zionist idea, because they considered this to be "forcing the end," an act opposing the vow that God demanded from Israel, that they refrain from "forcing the end." According to this viewpoint, only God will take the Jewish people out of exile, when He sends the Messiah to redeem Israel and rebuild the Temple. Harsh criticism of Zionism was voiced by Rabbi Yoel Teitelbaum, the Admor of Satmar, who headed the anti-Zionist and anti-state movement. In his book *Va-Yo'el Moshe*, he argues the Zionist movement and the establishment of the State of Israel were acts of provocation and heresy against God. He writes that the Holocaust was a punishment for the Zionist idea and movement, for "daring to force the end, and for attracting Jewish support for this impure idea.... Even if all the members of the government were beloved and pure, like Tannaim and Amoraim, if we establish a government and freedom on our own before the time has come, this is pushing the end, which is heresy against the holy Torah and faith."[38] After establishment of the state, Rabbi Yitzhak Isaac Halevi Herzog (1889–1959), first chief rabbi of the State of Israel, commented on the vow:

> When there is a chance to succeed, there is no obstacle to the vow, as its validity has already expired. At any rate, there is no doubt regarding the vow, because the gentile nations are giving us a Jewish state, and so there is no rebellion or "ascending the wall."[39]

In this spirit, Rabbi Shaul Yisrael (1909–1995), head of Yeshivat Merkaz ha-Rav and a member of the supreme rabbinical court, wrote as follows:

> The recognition of the gentile nations of Israel's right [to exist] is certainly sufficient to be considered not by "a mighty hand," even though the neighboring Arab countries and Arabs living in the Land of Israel objected to it. For the rulers of a country are considered to be those who acquired it by military victory, and these were the British, who conquered Palestine and continued to rule it by mandate of the other nations, to whom Britain gave its right of

---

38. *Va-Yo'el Moshe*, 5, 7, 93.
39. Responsa of Rabbi Herzog, *Orah Haim*, par. 115.

ownership, and in whose name it accepted the mandate in the past. If so, the decision of these nations, which were owners of the Land, is valid. The Arab nations have no right to the Land.... The objection of these nations in the United Nations to the establishment of the State was invalidated by UN procedure. Because the UN made a legal decision, the establishment of the state by the Jewish people, since we occupied this place, had the validity of acquisition by agreement and free will of the owners of the Land. In any case, the State is legal from the point of view of the Torah, and from now on, even if the nations cancelled their decision, they would not have the power to do so, as we have already earned the territory. Again, preservation of our rights is not "ascending the wall," as we are merely guarding what we already own.[40]

The Recommended Custom in Israel

As we have seen, the obligation to settle the Land of Israel is the subject of controversy. However, most rabbinic authorities believe that this is a mitzvah, and so there is room for subjective expression. This means that one who feels that his soul cannot stand the atmosphere of the Diaspora, and who is constantly longing for Zion, must go live in Israel. By contrast, one whose soul is not in Israel or who has other reasons that make living there difficult – family, income, language, mentality, or other factors – he should wait until circumstances have changed, or until he feels that the desire to make aliyah outweighs these challenges. A story is told about the Zemach Zedek: once a hassid visited him and asked permission to make aliyah to the Land of Israel, because he thought that there he could study and pray better than while abroad. The Rebbe told him, "Make here the Land of Israel." In other words, every individual is a messenger of God, and the question is where he should perform his mission.

A Jew who lives in Israel cannot claim to be more righteous than one who lives abroad, and vice versa. Further, Herman (Yechezkel) Cohen, a Jewish philosopher, has said that one of the greatest contributions of the Jewish people to the world is the messianic concept, because this is the greatest expression of hope for a better world. Thus this philosopher objects to Zionism. He considers Zionism to be derived from the abandonment of religion, as it means giving up on the concept of messianic hope. What, then, should a Jew do? He should continue to live in the Diaspora, and aspire to work for a better world under the Kingship of God. Even if we disagree with his ideas, in reality the presence of Jews among

---

40. Rabbi S. Yisraeli, *Eretz hemda*, vol. 1, 35.

the gentile nations has a direct influence on the security of the Jews who live in Israel. Political considerations justify the presence of Jews abroad. Many Jews who live among non-Jews succeed in their own way at serving as a "light unto the nations," and to spread God's Name and the reign of Heaven. It seems to me that living abroad is not merely justifiable after the fact, once we are already there, but is valid as a preliminary choice. As said, of course, this is a personal decision.

As for Ethiopian Jews living abroad, it is difficult to accept a situation in which Jews who gave their lives on the long journey to Jerusalem immigrate to other countries. According to the Rambam's ruling, there is no permission for Jews who came to Israel from Ethiopia, and those who were born in Israel, to leave Israel (according to Rabbi Nachum Rabinovitch's interpretation). Still, if they feel a sense of mission and through this, they feel they can find themselves as Jews and as representatives in the world of God, the King of Israel, this is admirable. They should go out with this feeling and merit serving as faithful representatives of the Jewish people. But, fellow children of Israel, you should recall that everywhere you go, you are going to the Land of Israel. "The mountain of the Lord's house shall be established as the top of the mountains," (Isaiah 2:2); "For out of Zion shall go forth the Torah, and the word of the Lord from Jerusalem" (Isaiah 2:3); "They shall come that were lost in the land of Assyria, and they that were dispersed in the land of Egypt, and they shall worship the the Lord in the holy mountain at Jerusalem" (Isaiah 27:13).

7. Dietary Laws

֍ Table Manners

Ethiopian Halakhah

According to an Ethiopian saying in the Tigrinya dialect, "Food is greater than the person." Food sustains human beings – if there is no food, humans cannot exist – and thus we must show great respect for food. We must not scorn food; we must conserve it. The character of a meal is also formed and influenced by our special attitude toward food. The Western concept of the family meal, for example, is not a part of the Ethiopian culture; rather, in Ethiopia, first the adults eat, and only afterwards the children. Food is not apportioned among the diners, but rather placed in a central dish from which everyone partakes. The diners begin their meal together. During the meal, they do not talk at all, nor do they interrupt the meal for unrelated matters. It is forbidden to eat while walking. Leftovers from the adults' meal are given to the children – no food is thrown away. Diners always leave something on their plates so as not to appear greedy. In summary, we respect our food, for one who scorns food harms his soul as well as his body.

Past and Present in Talmudic Halakhah

> Proper manners at a meal: one should not eat while standing, nor drink while standing, nor talk during the meal, nor wipe the plate, nor lick one's fingers. One should know before whom one may recline, and should not recline before one's elders. One who eats radishes and onions should grasp them by the leaves. One should not eat food, then pick remains from between one's teeth and place them on the plate or on the table. One who drinks in public should turn his head to one side and then drink. One should not eat part of a slice of bread, then replace the remains on the plate, for this is fatal. Rabbi Elazar said, one who does not leave morsels of bread on the table sees no blessings

in this world. One should not hold a slice of bread as if holding an egg in his hand, and one who does so is greedy. One should not gather crumbs and place them on the table. One should not cut a slice of bread and replace it on the dish. Two people should wait for each other when dining. One who eats in the marketplace is considered like a dog, and is unfit to serve as a witness.[1]

The Recommended Custom in Israel

Today there is no need to eat from a central dish, but the other rules of table manners practiced in Ethiopia should be followed, as the Sages have instructed. We must respect our food, we must begin to eat together. It is preferable to eat in a group, together, but each person with a separate plate. In particular, a man and wife should serve each other their food. We must make sincere efforts to eat together – the entire family, including the children, even though this was not the custom in Ethiopia.

Laws of Forbidden Foods

Ethiopian Halakhah

The Jews of Ethiopia were very careful in their observance of the laws of kosher foods. They learned these laws from the Torah and from the oral tradition. They were extremely careful not to eat meat from non-kosher animals. They did not even touch these animals, and one who touched a non-kosher animal was considered impure and remained outside the village until he or she could immerse in the river. Avraham Yardai notes that it was absolutely forbidden to touch a *nevelah* (carcass of a kosher animal not killed in accordance with Jewish law and therefore forbidden for consumption). It was not forbidden to touch a dead animal that was not kosher, but if one stepped on the feces of a carnivore, it was customary to immerse oneself. Slaughtering of kosher animals was performed by cutting the animal's neck, and they were careful that during slaughter, the animal's head was pointed toward Jerusalem. The *kes* or other experienced person performed the slaughter. In fact, because the Written Torah does not define the exact method of slaughter, the custom in Ethiopia was that the head of every observant family slaughtered for his family.

They then dug a pit at the location of the slaughter, and the blood spilled after killing the animal or bird was poured straight into this pit. Then they covered the pit with dirt.

---

1. *Sefer ha-Rokeah*, Laws of meals, 229; see also Herman, *Ma'agal hayei ha-yom*.

Past and Present in Talmudic Halakhah

The Torah commands us to cover the blood of an animal or bird immediately after slaughter: "And any man of the children of Israel or of the strangers who sojourn among them, who traps a quarry of a wild animal or bird that may be eaten, and sheds its blood, he shall cover it [the blood] with dust" (Leviticus 17:3). *Sefer ha-Hinukh* explains why the mitzvah of covering the blood is only for wild animals and birds, and not for domesticated animals:

> We were not commanded to do this for domesticated animals, as the blood of these animals was given in sacrifice to atone for our souls, and so cannot be covered. Another reason is that the Torah did not want to divide the animals into sanctified ones and non-sanctified ones. If there is a difference among birds, since some were sacrificed on the altar [turtledoves and pigeons], it is a small difference, and the Torah does not distinguish where there is a small difference. Thus we are required to cover the blood for all types of birds.[2]

The Recommended Custom in Israel

In all aspects of *kashrut*, the Beta Israel should follow the contemporary Jewish practice, and they should follow the instructions of the Chief Rabbinate. Any strict ruling above and beyond the generally accepted law is not recommended. If different forms of *kashrut* are still in practice, this is never hierarchical, but spiritual in nature. In my opinion, we should avoid definitions that approach creation of a hierarchy of *kashrut*, but rather recognize different modes of *kashrut* that are of equal levels.

Nikkur

Ethiopian Halakhah

The usual practice is to conduct the slaughtering as a group. Afterwards, two or three people remove the parts that are not eaten. Some families do not eat the heart. According to the testimony of Kes Mentosnot Eli Wende and of Avraham Yarai, they removed the *gid ha-nasheh* (sciatic nerve) and disposed of it. Some parts of the *helev* (fat) were forbidden, while other parts were permitted. According to the *kes*, the difference between Talmudic halakhah and Ethiopian halakhah on this issue was not significant.

---

2. Mitzvah 187.

Past and Present in Talmudic Halakhah

The practice of *nikkur* means removing the parts that are forbidden from consumption: the *helev* with the forbidden tendons, blood vessels, and the sciatic nerve. *Nikkur* demands special expertise and detailed knowledge of the *halakhot*. Thus it should be performed only by a God-fearing person who has been authorized to perform this procedure.[3]

The Recommended Custom in Israel

For all *kashrut*-related issues, the Beta Israel should follow the general Jewish practice and the instructions of the Chief Rabbinate.

❧ Salting

Ethiopian Halakhah

In Ethiopia, the Jews did not salt the meat, but cut it into small pieces, washed it, and hung it on a rope to dry.

Past and Present in Talmudic Halakhah

Consumption of blood is biblically forbidden. In order to avoid cooking the meat in its blood, we must remove the blood before cooking. This is done by salting the meat. As the Amora Samuel said, "The meat is not separated from its blood unless it has been well salted and well rinsed."[4] The *kashrut* procedure includes these stages: rinsing, soaking for half an hour, and rinsing again. The *Shulhan Arukh* rules that one should rinse the meat before salting it.[5] This means washing it in a basin filled with water – not just rinsing. The Rema says that as a preliminary step, one should soak the meat in water for half an hour. Why must one rinse the meat before salting it? The Rishonim were divided on the explanation for this. Some said the purpose was to soften the meat, so that the blood would be better removed by the salt. Others said that the salt removed only the blood that had penetrated into the meat, not the external blood, and that after the blood was drawn out from the meat, the salt would absorb the external blood into the meat, and this would not drain out.

In all Jewish communities, the accepted custom is to rinse the meat and clean it well from any remains of blood, and then to soak it for half an hour in

---

3. Herman, *Ma'agal hayei ha-yom*.
4. Babylonian Talmud, *Hullin* 113a.
5. Yoreh De'ah 69:1.

a bowl with water. Then one must remove the meat and rinse it until the water has dripped off, so that one can salt it without the salt rinsing off in the water or dissolving. But when pressed for time, such as when guests are expected or on Shabbat eve, one may act leniently and follow the *Shulhan Arukh*, which requires only rinsing, and does not require soaking for half an hour. One should salt the meat with dry, medium-ground salt, not coarse salt that falls off the meat without sticking to it, but not fine salt like table salt, as this dissolves and does not draw out the blood. One should sprinkle the salt on all sides, and use a quantity such that the piece could not be eaten with that salt still on it. To rinse the meat – after salting, rinse the meat twice. Some do this three times. Rinsing should be done in a bowl filled with water, by rubbing the meat so that the salt and the blood wash away. One should change the water and rinse the bowl thoroughly between each rinse. Some Yemenite Jews place the meat in boiling water before cooking it.

As mentioned, in Ethiopia the Jews knew they had to rinse the meat thoroughly, but without any formal procedure. Possibly, this is evidence of the ancient nature of their custom – the formal process described in halakhah is apparently a later development.[6]

The Recommended Custom in Israel

Without entering the complex issue of the *kashrut* laws practiced in Ethiopia, the question of which practice is "more kosher" applies to all Jewish communities, and not just the Ethiopian Jews. I would like to suggest that in all questions of *kashrut* and meat, individuals should accept the practice followed in Israel according to the instructions of the Chief Rabbinate. Still, one should take care not to disparage those who continue to slaughter according to the Ethiopian custom. I believe that with a positive attitude, we can create a world of respect and understanding – "As in water, face answers to face, so the heart of man to man" (Proverbs 27:19).

Laws of Meat and Dairy

Ethiopian Halakhah

Some have said that Ethiopian Jews were careful not to eat meat and milk together, and certainly they did not cook them together, as the Torah expressly specifies. But they did not have a custom of waiting between eating meat and milk. On

---

6. Babylonian Talmud, *Hullin* 113a.

the other hand, many said they did cook meat and milk together, but they did not cook meat in the milk of the animal's mother.

Past and Present in Talmudic Halakhah

The Torah does not specify that meat and milk should be separated, aside from cooking. But in order to ensure this biblical prohibition, the Sages forbade eating a mixture of meat and dairy, such as a sausage dish with a glass of milk. An Amora relates that his father waited a whole day after eating meat, and then he would eat dairy, and that he himself waited from one meal to another.[7] The Rambam, the Rishba, and the Rosh, who lived in medieval Spain, determined that one should wait six hours between one kind of meal and the next:

> When a person ate meat first – whether the meat of an animal or the meat of a fowl – he should not partake of dairy afterwards unless he waits the time for another meal, approximately six hours. This stringency is required because of meat that becomes stuck between teeth and is not removed by cleaning.[8]

The *Shulhan Arukh* gives the same ruling.[9] Other Rishonim who lived in Ashkenaz, such as the authors of the Tosafot, the Mordekhai (Mordekhai ben Hillel) and the Ra'avyah (Eliezer ben Yoel Halevi), interpreted the expression according to the plain meaning of the text – to separate between a meat meal and a milk one. Thus after reciting Grace after Meals, cleaning the table, and removing the meat, one could eat dairy right away. Some said one should wait one hour. Thus we find that the Jews of Holland wait one hour, while German Jews wait three hours. In the Rema's town, "The custom was to wait one hour," but he relies on the *Shulhan Arukh*:

> Some say that one need not wait six hours, but that after one has removed the meat and recited Grace after Meals, it is permissible by wiping and rinsing the mouth. The simple custom in these states is to wait one hour after eating meat and then eat afterwards cheese…. And there are careful people who wait six hours between eating meat and cheese, and it is proper to do.[10]

---

7. Babylonian Talmud, *Hullin* 105a.
8. Rambam, *Mishneh Torah*, Hilkhot Ma'akhalot Assurot 9:28.
9. *Yoreh De'ah* 89:1.
10. Ibid.

Rabbi Shlomo Zalman Auerbach is cited as saying that today, even Dutch and German Jews should wait six hours.[11] According to Rabbi Yosef Shalom Elyashiv, in principle one must wait just over five hours, following the Rambam, who wrote in the source cited above that one should wait "approximately six hours," but that many followed the strict practice of waiting six hours. Rabbi Ovadia Yosef wrote that one may follow the lenient practice and eat dairy after waiting five and a half hours in a situation of great need, such as when one is visiting important people, and if one does not taste a dairy dish, the hosts might be offended. A sick person or a woman who has just given birth may eat dairy after waiting one hour, for thirty days after she has given birth.[12] At any rate, the wait begins after one has finished eating meat, even if one has not yet recited Grace after Meals. One should wait for this period of time even after eating a dish in which meat was cooked and then removed, such as a meat-based soup.

According to the *Shulhan Arukh*, one who has eaten soft dairy products, such as sour cream, or derivatives such as heavy cream, yogurt, or pudding, and wants to eat meat, must wash his hands – even if he ate with silverware, rinse his mouth, and wipe it by eating solid food, or else brush his teeth thoroughly, and this is the custom in the Eastern Jewish communities.[13] According to the *Zohar* (Parashat Mishpatim), one must wait one hour in this case as well. The Rema writes that after eating hard cheeses, one must wait six hours. One who has eaten a spicy food that was cut with a meat knife may eat dairy products immediately afterward. But if one has eaten meat, one must not eat a spicy food that was cut with a dairy knife – rather, he must wait the amount of time one usually waits between meat and dairy.

The Recommended Custom in Israel

Unity is more important than custom. One should carefully observe the waiting period between meat and milk, but there is no need to accept the ruling of the *Shulhan Arukh* for six hours. In my opinion, the Ethiopian Jews should wait for the minimum amount of time – after meat one should wait one hour, and after milk there is no need to wait at all.

---

11. Rabbi Aharon Pfoifer, *Kitzur Shulhan Arukh* 1, 10, 16.
12. *Shu"t yabia omer* 1:4.
13. *Yoreh De'ah* 89:2.

❦ Eating Chicken with Dairy

Ethiopian Halakhah

Eating chicken with dairy was permitted. The Ethiopian Jews did not consider this to be prohibited, because this prohibition does not appear in the Written Torah at all.

Past and Present in Talmudic Halakhah

The Torah prohibits only cooking the meat of a domesticated animal in the milk of a domesticated animal. Other kinds of meat and milk are permitted under biblical law. The Rambam writes:

> According to Scriptural Law, the prohibition involves only [a mixture of] meat from a kosher domesticated animal and milk from a kosher domesticated animal, as implied by the verse "You shall not seethe a kid in its mother's milk" (Exodus 23:19, 34:26; Deuteronomy 14:21). The term *a kid* includes the offspring of an ox, the offspring of a sheep, and the offspring of a goat, unless the verse states explicitly "a goat kid." The term "a kid in its mother's milk" [does not exclude all other situations]. Instead, the Torah is speaking regarding the commonplace circumstance. With regard to the meat of a kosher animal that was cooked in the milk of a non-kosher animal, or the meat of a non-kosher animal that was cooked in the milk of a kosher animal, by contrast, cooking is permitted, and deriving benefit is permitted. One is not liable for [transgressing the prohibition against partaking of] meat and milk if one partakes of it.[14]

However, the Sages forbade eating chicken with dairy as well as the meat of a non-domesticated animal in order to enforce the biblical prohibition, but they did not prohibit cooking and enjoyment. Apparently, during the Tannaitic period the prohibition was not accepted by all the Sages, and the Talmud relates that Rabbi Yose ha-Gelili permitted eating chicken with dairy.

The Recommended Custom in Israel

Although there is no biblical prohibition against eating chicken with dairy, the Beta Israel should stop the practice of eating them together, in order to create a uniform halakhah. First-generation immigrants who wish to do so should do it only in private. Second-generation immigrants are not permitted to do so.

---

14. *Mishneh Torah*, Hilkhot Ma'akhalot Assurot 9:3.

8. Societal Relationships

❧ Separation between Women and Men

Ethiopian Halakhah

At every event or gathering, whether for mourning or celebration, the Ethiopian practice was to separate between women and men. The separation was not done through a *mehitzah* (partition), but naturally. The women sat together on one side, and the men sat together on the other side. In the synagogue, the women stood in the back and the men in the front, without a partition.

Past and Present in Talmudic Halakhah

Apparently, in ancient times, women were not accustomed to attending synagogue, and so there was no women's section or balcony in the synagogues. If women did come to the synagogue, they sat on separate benches, or at the edge of the hall.[1] In modern times, women began to attend, and the modern *poskim* had conflicts of opinion over the height of the *mehitzah*. Rabbi Moshe Feinstein ruled that a *mehitzah* at the height of the women's shoulders – eighteen *tefahim* – was sufficient.[2] In contrast, the Satmar Rebbe and Hungarian rabbis ruled that the *mehitzah* should hide the women completely from view and surpass the height of their heads.

The Temple was the first place for which a separation of the sexes is documented, as part of the partition that the Sages erected on Sukkot for the Simhat Beit ha-Shoeva celebration. The detailed descriptions about the structural changes made in the Temple make no mention of a partition, and apparently no partition existed. There may have been a railing for safety purposes, but there was

---

1. Herman, *Ma'agal hayei ha-yom*.
2. *Iggerot Moshe, Orah Haim* 1:41.

no partition.[3] We have no knowledge of a partition being erected in the Temple at other times. The partition is mentioned many times in classical rabbinic literature, mainly with regard to purification. But a partition in the synagogue is mentioned only with regard to separation of the leper from the rest of the congregants, to prevent the spreading of impurity.[4]

The Recommended Custom in Israel

The Ethiopian Jews may continue their custom, and there is no reason to require them to use a *mehitzah*. They should continue the practice they followed in Ethiopia, of men and women sitting separately, but without a partition. An additional condition is that the women should dress modestly, as was the practice in Ethiopia. There is no difference between gathering for the purpose of prayer or gathering for the purpose of any other event.

❧ Laws of Interpersonal Relationships

Ethiopian Halakhah

The world of faith of the Ethiopian community and its relationship to God are based on the concept of reward and punishment. If you do good, you will be rewarded, while if you do wrong, you will be severely punished. Relationships between people are based on respect. Respect is an absolute value; just as the believer is asked to demonstrate absolute submission toward God, so individuals must respect others for what they are. The believer may ask questions and weep over the bitterness of his fate, but he will always find an apologetic explanation that will relieve his frustration and calm his inner agitation. In relating to others, a person must always be respectful, despite difficulties and frustrations.

The *kesim* instructed their followers to behave respectfully, and with their authority, they formed a culture that is introverted, reserved, and undemanding. They do not say "no," nor do they rebel against authority. In Ethiopian culture, one does not use the first name of an important person, and when speaking to such a person, one does not look directly at his face. If he is elderly, one should kiss his knee, and only then commence speaking to him. There is a saying that the Jewish people were graced with three characteristics – bashfulness, mercy, and kindness to others. In Ethiopia, the Beta Israel, like Jews elsewhere, practiced

---

3. Mishnah, *Sukkah* 5:2; *Middot* 2:5; Tosefta, *Sukkah* 4:1; Jerusalem Talmud, *Sukkah* 20:2:5, halakhah 2; Babylonian Talmud, *Sukkah* 51b–55a.
4. Mishnah, *Nega'im* 13:12.

kindness to others. They assisted the weak, converts, and the sick. Their way of life in Ethiopia enabled significant social support for each individual. Communal life in family groups was based on mutual aid – I help you and you help me, you give to me and I give back to you. When one person plowed, the neighbors came to plow with him. When one person built a house, his friends came to assist him. In times of crisis, the individual was not left alone without support.

Past and Present in Talmudic Halakhah

"The foundation of all foundations and the pillar of wisdom is to know that there is a Primary Being Who brought into being all existence. All the beings of the heavens, the earth, and what is between them came into existence only from the truth of His being."[5] Yet, "Free will is granted to all men. If one desires to turn himself to the path of good and be righteous, the choice is his. Should he desire to turn to the path of evil and be wicked, the choice is his.... He can do what he desires. There is no one who can prevent him from doing good or bad."[6] Thus it is desirable that worship of God and faith be based on free will and choice.[7] Moreover,

> A person should love God with a very great and exceeding love until his soul is bound up in the love of God. Thus, he will always be obsessed with this love as if he is lovesick. [A lovesick person's] thoughts are never diverted from the love of that woman. He is always obsessed with her; when he sits down, when he stands up, when he eats and drinks. With an even greater [love], the love for God should be [implanted] in the hearts of those who love Him and are obsessed with Him at all times as we are commanded: "[Love God...] with all your heart, and with all your soul..." (Deuteronomy 6:5). This concept was implied by Solomon when he stated, as a metaphor: "I am lovesick" (Song of Songs 2:5). [Indeed,] all of the Song of Songs is a parable describing [this love].

Loving and knowing God also influences an individual's relationship to others, as the Sages expounded the verse "After the Lord your God shall you follow" (Deuteronomy 13:5):

---

5. Rambam, *Mishneh Torah*, Hilkhot Yesodei ha-Torah 1:1.
6. Ibid., Hilkhot Teshuvah 5:1.
7. Herman, *Ma'agal hayei ha-yom*.

Is it possible for a human being to walk after the Shechinah? For has it not been said: "For the Lord your God is a devouring fire" (Deuteronomy 4:24)? But [the meaning is] to walk after the attributes of the Holy One, blessed be He. As He clothes the naked, for it is written: "And the Lord God made for Adam and for his wife garments of skins, and clothed them" (Genesis 3:21), so shall you also clothe the naked. The Holy One, blessed be He, visited the sick, for it is written: "And the Lord appeared unto him by the terebinths of Mamre" (Genesis 18:1); so shall you also visit the sick.[8]

In his explication of the laws of mourning, the Rambam makes a relevant comment: "Although all these mitzvot are of rabbinic origin, they are included in the scriptural commandment 'Love your neighbor as yourself' (Leviticus 19:18). That charge implies that whatever you would like other people to do for you, you should do for your comrade in the Torah and mitzvot."[9]

The Recommended Custom in Israel

As we have seen, among the Beta Israel, the relationship between an individual and the Creator and between an individual and other human beings is based on obedience, awe, respect, and complete self-effacement. In the Talmudic world, relationships are based more on understanding, free choice, and self-awareness. In both environments, individuals aspired to worship God and respect others, but the methods are different. In my opinion, in Israel, the Beta Israel should adopt the method of the surrounding culture. The mode of behavior practiced in Ethiopia, as in the Diaspora in general, is inefficient and does not stand the test of reality. In order to instill faith and build a system of social relationships, the individual must speak to others eye to eye, without relation to hierarchy. One must remove any residue of pride and superiority, through patience and love. This is also true for the generation of adults who came from Ethiopia, who were used to acting with obedience and submission.

Kes or Kahin?

Ethiopian Halakhah

Since ancient times, the spiritual leaders of Ethiopian Jewry were called *kohanim* – but not because they were descendants of Aaron the high priest. None of the Beta Israel are descended from the families of *kohanim* or Levites – they are all

---

8. Babylonian Talmud, *Sotah* 14a.
9. *Mishneh Torah*, Hilkhot Avel 14:1.

considered Israelites. Instead, this is because they served the role of priests, like Aaron the high priest. Some eighty years ago, they began to use the title *kes*, which they borrowed from the Christian community, and since then, the title *kohen* fell into disuse, as my grandfather, of blessed memory, related.

Past and Present in Talmudic Halakhah

A *kohen* is a descendent of Aaron the high priest. Aaron was a descendant of the tribe of Levi, son of our forefather Jacob, and he and his sons were awarded the priestly role for all time, as the Torah specifies (Numbers 40:15). Any male descendant of the tribe of Levi through the line of Aaron is called a *kohen*, while a Levite who is not from the line of Aaron is called Levi.

The Recommended Custom in Israel

The spiritual leaders may be called by the original title of *kohen*. There is no reason to change the leadership for reasons of genealogy. Still, as the title *kes* is widespread today, its use should not be prohibited.

Interactions with Non-Jews

Ethiopian Halakhah

There is an expression in Amharic that means "Don't touch me." This expression originated with the well-known Beta Israel religious leader Abba Zabra, who avoided contact with Christians through fear of impurity. However, the Beta Israel wished to maintain friendly relations, so a varied system of customs developed to facilitate interactions with Christian neighbors. For example, the Beta Israel spread branches on the floor in order to permit non-Jews to enter their homes without touching the floor. When a Christian woman wanted to speak with a Jewish woman, she stood outside the house and called to her, and they conversed from either side of the window. When a Jew invited a non-Jew to drink coffee with her, they sat at a distance from each other, and the non-Jew was given a special cup. In certain cases, the Beta Israel kept a separate set of dishes for their non-Jewish neighbors, storing the dishes outside in a tree or bush.

The Christians also maintained a similar system toward their Jewish guests. At celebrations, the two groups followed agreed arrangements that enabled them to be present together. Each group slaughtered and cooked meat for itself in its own hut, and then the guests gathered in a central shelter to sing and dance together. After the celebration, the Jews immersed themselves in the river before entering their homes.

The Ethiopian Jews strictly separated themselves from the Christian environment, and according to custom, one who touched a non-Jew was impure and had to immerse himself in the river before returning to his home in the Jewish village. It was forbidden to eat any food that belonged to a non-Jew, and if a non-Jew touched foods belonging to a Jew, the foods became non-kosher and the Jew could not eat them. A Jew who ate food touched by a non-Jew for any reason had to eat chickpeas for one week in order to clean the digestive system and purify it of the non-kosher food.

Past and Present in Talmudic Halakhah

The Sages forbade participating in meals, celebrations, and weddings of non-Jews. The source of this prohibition was in a statement by the Tanna Rabbi Ishmael in a *baraita*:

> Rabbi Ishmael taught: Israelites who live outside the Land of Israel are idol worshippers in pure innocence. In what way? If an idol worshipper holds a feast for his son and invites all the Jews in his town, even if the Jews eat and drink their own food and their own attendant waits on them, the Torah considers them as if they have eaten of sacrifices to dead idols, as in the verse "Take heed to yourself lest you make a covenant with the inhabitants of the land into which you are going, lest they be for a snare in your midst...and they offer sacrifices to their gods, and they invite you, and you eat of their sacrifice, and you take of their daughters for your sons, and their daughters go astray after their gods, and make your sons go astray after their gods" (Exodus 34:12, 15–16).

Relying on this, the *Shulhan Arukh* ruled:

> When an idol worshipper makes a feast for the wedding of his son or daughter, the Jew is forbidden to eat there, even if he eats his own food and his attendant stands beside him and serves him. From what point does the prohibition begin? When he begins to prepare what is needed for the feast, and for thirty days following the feast. If the non-Jew specifies that he is inviting the Jew for the wedding, the prohibition holds for twelve months, and after twelve months it ends, unless he is an important person [in which case he should continue to observe the prohibition].[10]

---

10. *Yoreh De'ah* 152:1.

There are two areas of concern with regard to the *kashrut* of utensils: immersing utensils and kashering utensils. After the battle of the Israelites against the Midianites, the Torah specifies, "They took all the spoil and all the prey, both of man and of beast" (Numbers 31:11). Regarding the bounty of eating utensils, Eleazar the Cohen instructs the Israelites:

> This is the statute that the Lord commanded Moses. Only the gold, the silver, the copper, the iron, the tin, and the lead, whatever is used in fire you shall pass through fire and then it will be clean; it must, however, [also] be cleansed with sprinkling water, and whatever is not used in fire you shall pass through water. (Numbers 31:21–23)

Based on this, the Sages derived two conditions for use of eating utensils that were used by non-Jews: 1. kashering the utensils by "as it absorbs, so does it release" – a pot releases food and becomes kosher in the same way as food is absorbed in it; 2. immersing the utensils in a *mikveh*. According to most rabbinic authorities, the obligation of immersion is biblical, and is derived from the verse "nevertheless it shall [also] be purified with the water of sprinkling" (Numbers 31:23), but some believe that the obligation of immersing utensils is rabbinic, and that the verse serves only as a prooftext for this. One of the reasons given for immersion is that God appointed us as His chosen people, and differentiated us spiritually from the other nations, and this is expressed in dietary restrictions. By immersing utensils in the *mikveh*, we elevate the utensil to the level of Jewish sanctity. Similarly, the convert immerses himself, and by doing so enters the sanctity of Judaism.

The Sages forbade the consumption of cheese, bread, and oil that was prepared by non-Jews, even if they did not contain non-kosher ingredients. According to the Mishnah, these prohibitions were decreed at a gathering with Hananiah ben Hizkiyahu ben Gurion, who lived at the end of the Second Temple period: "They voted, and those of the School of Shammai outnumbered those of the School of Hillel, and they instituted eighteen rulings on that day."[11] A *baraita* remarks, "They instituted eighteen rulings on that day … regarding bread of gentiles, their cheese, their oil, and their daughters."[12]

---

11. *Shabbat* 1:4.
12. Jerusalem Talmud, *Shabbat* 1:3, 3.

The Recommended Custom in Israel

Today there is no reason to observe stringencies related to impurity from non-Jews as was practiced in the past. One of God's names is peace, and peace is a supreme value. The Sages said, "Human beings are beloved, as they were created in the Divine image, and they are particularly loved because they were created in His image, as in the verse 'in the image of God created He him'" (Genesis 1:27). On the other hand, we must preserve the uniqueness of the Jewish people. The Ethiopian Jews demonstrated loyalty to the Jewish people despite many trials and a long period of exile. Through this extreme practice, the community was able to preserve its uniqueness and avoided mingling with the Christian neighbors. This commitment has enabled us to be accepted today within the Jewish people and in the State of Israel. We must work to eliminate the phenomenon of intermarriage between Jews and non-Jews. We also must erect an iron wall against the missionaries that are attempting to destroy the camp of Israel.

I emphasize that I am not claiming any kind of superiority over non-Jews. The Jewish people has a special mission and purpose, and each individual must fulfill his mission according to his national or religious identification.

Conversion for Adults

Ethiopian Halakhah

One of the first procedures that a non-Jew must perform in order to convert to Judaism is to purify the body from the impure foods he has ingested. To do so, he must eat only chickpeas for an entire week. According to the testimony of Kes Mentosnot, a Jew who had become estranged from Judaism (a Jew who had converted to Christianity) and wanted to be reaccepted into the Jewish community had to eat only chickpeas for two weeks, twice the required time for a non-Jew who had converted. Still, a male convert to Judaism had to undergo circumcision, no matter his age, as accepted under Talmudic halakhah. Circumcision is a difficult procedure at an adult age; the community had the custom to place ground leaves on the wound in order to stop the bleeding.

Past and Present in Talmudic Halakhah

While the Temple was standing, a non-Jew who wanted to convert would offer a sacrifice (Babylonian Talmud, *Yevamot* 47). After the destruction of the Second Temple and during the Talmudic period, sacrifices were no longer a necessary part of the conversion process, and circumcision was the only required act for a male. The Rambam described the process as follows: "We inform him about some of the easy mitzvot and some of the more severe ones. We do not elaborate, nor are we punctilious on this matter. If he replies, 'I know, and I am unworthy,' we accept him. After he is accepted, we circumcise him immediately.... After he has healed, we immerse him. After he immerses, he is a Jew on all accounts" (*Hilkhot Issurei Bi'ah* 14).

During the period of the Rishonim, an additional step was included in the conversion process: acceptance of the mitzvot. For this reason, today the process of becoming a Jew requires participation in a conversion ceremony held before a *beit din*. The formal conditions of conversion include accepting belief in one God, learning *halakhot* and Jewish customs, immersion in water, and for men, circumcision.

Today, there are many conversion programs throughout Israel. Due to immigration to Israel from the former Soviet Union and Ethiopia, the existence of converts from other countries, and the large number of mixed marriages around the world, two approaches have developed within the Israeli rabbinic world – one stringent, the other more lenient. Today, rabbis debate the question of the proper attitude toward converts. Some rabbis push for more flexibility in the conversion process, for families who consider themselves part of the Jewish people and who want to become integrated. There are those who assert that the rabbis of the conversion courts are unnecessarily strict, that they impose excessive bureaucratic barriers, thereby adopting the stringent approach of Shammai instead of the more flexible approach of Hillel. This topic has led to vocal arguments, which have influenced the IDF rabbinate to operate its own conversion program within the framework of the army.

This program permits soldiers to undergo the conversion process during their army service. Surprisingly, rabbis in the religious Zionist camp are also attempting to establish an independent conversion program, separate from the Chief Rabbinate of Israel. We thus find that the topic of conversion is complex, and we may anticipate unexpected developments in this area in the near future. Personally, I tend to support the opinion that we must take this complexity into consideration. We must find creative solutions within the framework of halakhah, in order to cope with the sensitive situation in Israel and around the world. We need to approach this issue from a human point of view, yet without compromising on the halakhah.

The Recommended Custom in Israel

In light of the community's situation in Israel, the Chief Rabbinate must show tolerance and find a way, within halakhah, to solve the problem of conversion that the Jewish people are facing today. They must provide a general solution that places the entire Jewish people, in all its variety, under one umbrella: immigrants from Ethiopia and the former Soviet Union, the Ten Tribes, Reform and Conservative Jews. All Jews stood at Mount Sinai. The history of the Jewish people has taught us that the attempt to build a homogenous society and one-dimensional halakhic reality leads to destruction and questioning of our existence as a sovereign people. As for circumcision of adult men, I think that the rabbinate should find a more humane solution for individuals undergoing this method of conversion, a pleasant manner of questioning how – rather than whether – men were circumcised, based on a respectful and genuine inquiry into a person's background, without suspicions. In all matters related to circumcision in general and to circumcision of adults in particular, the community should follow the instructions of the Chief Rabbinate.

9. Laws of Mourning

❧ Visiting the Sick

Ethiopian Halakhah
The mitzvah of visiting the sick was observed strictly by the Ethiopian Jews. A person who heard that a friend or relative was sick stopped work and went to visit, sometimes traveling a long distance to do so. This enthusiasm was not based on any halakhah written in a book, but rather out of natural emotion and a sense of shared human fate.

Past and Present in Talmudic Halakhah
In Jewish tradition, visiting the sick is an especially important mitzvah. This mitzvah is one of the acts whose merit is considered beyond measure. The Babylonian Talmud states that one who visits the sick reaps the benefits in this world as well as the next, and that one who performs this mitzvah often is deserving of praise (*Shabbat* 127b). Why is this mitzvah so important? There are several opinions. Some say that the purpose of the visit is to strengthen the spirit of the sick person, to comfort him, and to ease his distress. Others assert that the main purpose of the mitzvah is to pray for the sick person and ask God to have mercy on him. Either way, the focus of the mitzvah is the ill person, not the visitor. Thus the halakhah specifies instances when one should not visit, such as when the ill person is embarrassed by his illness, or when the visit may cause him discomfort. In such cases, the visitor may go to the ill person's home, ask after his welfare and check if he can help, but not enter the sickroom.

The rabbis specified the laws of behavior in these circumstances. For example, for the sake of preserving good relations, one should first visit a non-Jewish patient, and visit the Jewish patient afterward. Visiting a poor patient takes precedence over going to a rich one, who usually has many visitors. When one goes to visit, the visitor should not sit on a high chair above the patient, nor above his head. He should speak encouragingly to the ill person, and ask him if he has enough money for his health needs, and help him to pray for mercy. In some cases, making a phone call is enough to fulfill the requirement of visiting the sick, but still, one should make the effort to visit the person and not rely only on a phone call. May all enjoy a speedy recovery.

The Recommended Custom in Israel

There is no difference between the mitzvah of visiting the sick in Ethiopia and the Talmudic law. Beta Israel and second-generation Ethiopian Jews may continue their custom of visiting the sick. It is an important mitzvah, and they should make every effort to fulfill it.

Laws of *Aninut* (before Burial)

Ethiopian Halakhah

Ethiopian Jewish customs of burying the dead and comforting mourners are fundamentally different from the customs of the communities in which they lived.[1] However, many mourning practices have a parallel among their Christian neighbors. For example, the Christians bury their dead on the day of death or the next day; they have a custom of visiting the sick and comforting mourners, including a special meal after the funeral (known in Jewish practice as the *seudat havra'ah*).

When a member of the community died, word spread rapidly among the villages. Family members and friends gathered and stood in a circle surrounding the deceased's relatives. They wept and lamented until the funeral began. Usually, the funeral was conducted on the day of death, so as not to delay burial. The relatives of the deceased did not need any special halakhah to absolve them of performing the mitzvot, as they were busy burying their loved one, and naturally were not free to perform mitzvot. Who was capable of ignoring such a tragic event and performing mitzvot?

Past and Present in Talmudic Halakhah

After someone dies, the deceased's relatives who are required to mourn him are called *onanim* (the singular form is *onen*, as in "Ben Oni" [Benjamin], Genesis 35:18). *Aninut* is the time period between death and burial. After the burial is

---

1. Sperber, *Minhagei Yisrael*, vol. 1, *Minhagei avelut be-tekufat sefirat ha-Omer* [Mourning customs during the period of counting the Omer], 101; vol. 4, p. 65.

completed, *aninut* is over and the period of mourning (*avelut*) begins. The *onen* is exempt from all mitzvot, such as prayer, blessings, and laying tefillin; he is forbidden from sexual relations, bathing, anointing himself, rejoicing, eating meat, drinking wine, business dealings, and studying Torah. The reason for this is so that the *onen* will not be distracted from the mourning process, and may focus on the burial requirements for the deceased. The *onen* is permitted to recite Psalms for the dead. During the time of the Mishnah and Talmud, the Jews fasted on the day a parent died in order to rouse themselves to repentance, but over time this custom disappeared.[2]

The Recommended Custom in Israel

In all matters of burial and laws of *onen* (a mourner before the deceased is buried), Ethiopian Jews are permitted to continue their custom. In Ethiopia, the *onen* bears no halakhic obligations, as is the case in mainstream halakhah.

Kri'ah (Tearing)

Ethiopian Halakhah

Kri'ah (tearing one's clothing as a sign of mourning) is forbidden. According to Ethiopian tradition, tearing was forbidden, as the *kesim* considered it an evil practice that had elements of idol worship.

Past and Present in Talmudic Halakhah

Tearing the clothes is an expression of pain and sorrow. The Torah relates the stories of several individuals who tore their clothes after hearing bad news – for example, Jacob tore his clothes when he heard that Joseph was killed (Genesis 37:34), and the Israelites tore their clothes when they were vanquished by the Ai (Joshua 7:6). The source for this obligation is derived from the death of the sons of Aaron. Aaron and his remaining sons were commanded not to act as mourners, and they were told: "Let not the hair of your heads go loose, neither rend your clothes" (Leviticus 10:6). The Sages learned from this that the mourner should uncover his head and tear his clothing. Tearing represents the rent caused between body and soul.[3]

The halakhah specifies that anyone who is present when the soul leaves the body is required to perform *kri'ah*, as are relatives of the seven categories

---

2. Herman, *Ma'agal hayei ha-yom*.
3. Ibid.

listed above, when they hear the news of death. This is the practice followed by Yemenite Jewry. Ashkenazic Jews perform *kri'ah* before burial, while Sephardic Jews and Eastern communities do so after burial, at the cemetery or in the house of mourning, before the *havra'ah* meal. The mourner tears for his or her father or mother on the left side above the heart, because there is no substitute for a parent. For other relations, the mourner tears on the right side. After sleeping, there is no need to tear again. For one's father or mother, the mourner tears until he uncovers the heart, and for other relatives, he tears a *tefah* (a biblical measurement equivalent to a handbreadth, approximately three to four inches) across the length of the article of clothing. The Yemenites tear across the width of the clothing. For a parent, the mourner should tear all his clothes, but some authorities rule leniently on this, and do not require tearing an upper garment, sweater, *tallit katan*, or undershirt. For other relatives, the mourner tears only his or her shirt. The usual custom is for a member of the burial society to make a small cut in the mourner's lapel. The mourner then grasps the cut edges, stands, and recites the blessing "Blessed are You…the True Judge." He or she then tears the shirt. During Tannaitic times, the Jews also practiced the custom of *halitzat katef* (revealing the shoulder) – they removed the shoulder and arm from the shirt and exposed it. This custom was also common in the ancient world, but it gradually died out until it was completely annulled during the Amoraic period, apparently due to changes in mode of dress. We do have one text that evidences that practice of this custom in Jerusalem during the eighteenth century.[4]

The Recommended Custom in Israel

Since Ethiopian tradition forbids tearing, we must not oblige Ethiopian Jews to perform *kri'ah*.

The Funeral

Ethiopian Halakhah

The focal point of the funeral was the prayers of the *kesim*, and they integrated selections from the holy writings into the ceremony. These prayers were designed to atone for the dead person's soul, and to accompany him in peace.

When burying a corpse in the grave, the Beta Israel followed a unique practice – a man was positioned on his right side, a woman on her left side, and the corpse's head was placed facing Jerusalem.

---

4. Herman, *Ma'agal hayei ha-yom*.

There were professional eulogizers, and musicians played flutes. After the eulogies and laments, the women responded by clapping their hands together or slapping their palms against their thighs. Avraham Yardai adds that in the area where he lived, they used to invite professional non-Jewish mourners, because the Jewish ones were not professional enough.[5]

Past and Present in Talmudic Halakhah

Rabbinic Judaism outlined a framework for the character and period of mourning, recognizing the importance of granting expression to human loss and defining legitimate boundaries for the expression of this pain.[6] There are two main reasons for this. First, "to make it easier for the individual to cope with the new reality, and second, to teach him faith and the religious consciousness that every individual has a role and purpose, and that when his time comes, God returns the deceased to Him. This follows the verse, 'The Lord gives, and the Lord takes away; blessed be the name of the Lord' (Job 1:21). Judaism forbids mourning customs that were accepted in the pagan world, such as tattooing, and cutting or scratching one's body."[7] The general rule is that respect for the living is greater than respect for the dead.

Nevertheless, Judaism still preserves respect for the dead, and mandates various actions that should be performed to honor the deceased. "We wait twenty minutes to half an hour.... Lay the corpse on the floor on its back and place it facing the door, so that the legs are pointing toward the door. Place the legs together, and place the hands together and rest them on the chest. Then close the eyes and cover the corpse with a white sheet. Light candles around the corpse. We do not leave it alone, but instead stand around it and recite Psalms.... Why do we not leave it alone?... There are two reasons for this: to prevent damage to or desecration of the corpse..., and out of respect for the dead person, so that he will not sense that he is unwanted."[8]

Out of respect for the deceased, the Torah forbade leaving a corpse unburied, and so the dead must be buried on the day of death. But if the family wishes to wait in order to honor the deceased, such as to permit a relative to arrive from a distance, or to enable greater attendance, then it may be permissible to delay the funeral. Before the funeral, the corpse is purified by washing and immersion in

---

5. Ibid.
6. *Ma'agal ha-hayim*, 266.
7. Ibid.
8. Ibid., 269.

the *mikveh*, and is dressed in white clothing (*takhrikhin*), symbolizing forgiveness and atonement, just as the high priest wore white when entering the Temple on Yom Kippur to ask God for forgiveness. When the grave is sealed, it is customary to ask the dead for forgiveness by reciting the following text: "So-and-so, son of [father's name] and [mother's name], we ask for your forgiveness. Perhaps we have not behaved respectfully toward you, yet we have done everything according to the custom of our Holy Land. May you serve as an advocate on high for the Jewish people. Go in peace, and rest in your resting place in peace, and meet your fate at the end of days."

It is a mitzvah for the relatives who are mourning to eulogize the deceased as appropriate and to mention his or her name, but one must not exaggerate in praise of the dead. In the eulogy, people should say things that arouse the listeners to reflection on the essence of human life and its significance, based on the life and behavior of the deceased. The custom of eulogizing the dead is ancient. Abraham eulogized Sarah (Genesis 23:2). Ya'akov was eulogized at length at the threshing floor of the thornbushes (Genesis 50:10). Customarily, eulogies are recited during the funeral and before burial. During Mishnah and Talmud times, there was a regular location for eulogies located next to the cemetery, called a *beit hesped* (eulogy house). During the post-biblical era, professional mourners sang laments (Jeremiah 9:16). This custom was popular throughout history until recent generations, particularly in the Eastern communities.

The Recommended Custom in Israel

Among Ethiopian Jewry, it is customary for people from all over Israel to attend the funeral of an acquaintance from the Ethiopian community. This is a beautiful custom, and should be continued. At the funeral, only four people are permitted to handle the corpse. These four people are not permitted to return home, but are considered impure for seven days. On the seventh day after immersion in a river and the purification ritual performed by the *kes*, they may return to their homes. The *kesim* do not accept the principle of *mikveh* as in rabbinic halakhah. In their view, it is preferable to immerse in the ocean or a river. If no rivers are available, as in Israel, it is preferable to immerse in a bathtub with flowing water, rather than in a *mikveh* where the water stands and does not flow. For this reason, some *kesim* have instructed their community to avoid touching a corpse. They permit the *hevre kadisha* (burial society) of non-Ethiopian origin to handle the corpse. The *kesim* do not accept the rabbinic approach that everyone today is impure due to contact with corpses. The Ethiopian custom is ancient, and we must not force the Ethiopian Jews to change their custom. They should be permitted to continue their traditional practice.

Impurity of Death

Ethiopian Halakhah

Due to careful observance of laws of impurity and purification, the job of preparing the corpse was given to a small number of people, and only they were allowed to touch it. After the funeral, they had to purify themselves so that they could return to their homes. The purification process lasted for seven days. On the third and seventh days, the priests sprinkled them with water called *hamenza* – this was the ashes of the red heifer mixed with spring water. At the end of the seventh day they immersed themselves, and then they were permitted to enter their villages.

Past and Present in Talmudic Halakhah

In rabbinic Judaism, the issue of purity in connection with burial is applicable in our times only to a *kohen*, whose purity requirements are more stringent than those of other Jews. A *kohen* may become impure (by contact with the dead) for seven types of relations: his father, mother, wife, brother (defined as a son of the same father), sister (from the same mother, but only if she is unmarried), and son and daughter (Leviticus 21:1–3). This is on condition that the corpse is whole. If any part of the body is missing, he may not become impure, but if the limb was missing while the person was still alive, then he may become impure.

The Recommended Custom in Israel

According to Talmudic halakhah, the only remedy for the impurity of death is purification with the ashes of the red heifer. Since the destruction of the Temple, there is no possibility to carry out this procedure according to Talmudic law, and therefore all people today are impure due to contact with death. By contrast, Ethiopian tradition has continued to observe biblical laws of purity and impurity, and the idea that all people are affected by the impurity of death is not accepted by the Beta Israel community. Ethiopian Jews are permitted to continue observing their traditions in all matters of purity and impurity such as impurity of death, impurity of childbirth, and so on, at least in the first generation. The second generation may also continue to observe Ethiopian customs in these matters, so long as it does not cause any problems with community unity or peace in the home. If there are any difficulties in these areas, however, one should immediately cease observing the Ethiopian traditions.

The Mourning Period

Ethiopian Halakhah

After the deceased was buried in the ground, the grave was marked with a pile of stones or a tree – but without any particular epitaph. Then the family went home and sat on the ground for seven days. Relatives and friends visited in order to comfort them. Each time a new visitor entered the home, those gathered wept and sang special lamentations. Neighbors and relatives prepared the food throughout the week of mourning.

Past and Present in Talmudic Halakhah

"God formed man of the dust of the ground, and breathed into his nostrils the breath of life" (Genesis 2:7). Adam and his descendants – all of humanity – were granted eternal life, in which the body serves as a dwelling place for the Divine Presence, the Shechinah. Human beings were given the mission of purifying their bodies and raising them to a high spiritual level, and through their bodies, uplifting daily life, the life of practical action and material objects.[9] Every human being is a unique creation, adapted to the time and place of his appearance in the world in order to fulfill its unique role. After the first sin in Eden, as soon as an individual fulfills his mission and destiny in the world, the body returns to the earth for purification and reprocessing, "and the spirit returns to God Who gave it" (Ecclesiastes 12:7), to provide God with an accounting of its actions. If a person is judged favorably, he will be resurrected in the future messianic age. The empty space that a person leaves after he departs from this world is painful for his family, and so they mourn and weep. Judaism has determined a framework and time frame for mourning, out of recognition of the importance of giving expression to mourning. Judaism forbids a person from mourning beyond the fixed framework, for two reasons: first, to ease the individual's coping with the new reality, and second, to educate the individual for faith and the religious awareness that every person has a role, and when his time comes, he is taken by God, as the verse says, "the Lord gave, and the Lord has taken away; blessed be the name of the Lord" (Job 1:21).

Judaism forbids mourning customs that were practiced in the pagan world,

---

9. Herman, *Ma'agal hayei ha-yom*.

such as making bald patches on one's head (Leviticus 21:5), tattooing (Leviticus 19:28), and cutting oneself (Deuteronomy 14:1).[10]

For the first meal after the funeral, a mourner does not eat his own food, but rather his neighbors and acquaintances bring him food. The source for this custom is in the words of the prophet Ezekiel, who was forbidden to practice mourning customs after his beloved was taken from him: "Sigh in silence; make no mourning for the dead; bind your glory upon yourself, and put your shoes on your feet, and do not cover your upper lip, and do not eat the bread of men" (Ezekiel 24:17). From this the Sages derived that on the first day after returning from the cemetery, a mourner eats his first meal of food prepared by others. This meal is called *se'udat havra'ah* – from the root v.r.h., meaning "food which is given to the mourner" (II Samuel 12:17; 13:5). Others reason have been given for this practice. First, the mourner may lose the will to live. When neighbors and friends bring food, this shows that they care about him and that he is important to them. Another reason is to intensify the mourner's grief, for a person who eats others' food feels humiliated.

The *se'udat havra'ah* is not an obligation, and it is held only if the mourner wishes to eat after the burial, before nightfall. If he wishes to eat after nightfall, he may eat his own food. During the periods of the Geonim and the Rishonim, it was customary for the mourner not to eat his own food throughout the seven days of mourning (*shivah*). This custom prevails today in a number of Jewish communities. At the *se'udat havra'ah*, traditionally the mourners are served foods that are round in shape: eggs, round cookies, chickpeas, and lentils. One reason for this is to recall the continuity of life, symbolized by the circle. During the Talmudic period, the Jews usually ate meat and drank wine, symbolizing that death was not caused by the deceased's sins but by the first sin in Eden, and that the deceased was in fact a righteous person. Tunisian and Libyan Jews do not eat meat or drink wine during the *shivah*, but other communities do.[11]

The seven-day mourning period was mentioned in the Torah regarding mourning for Jacob (Genesis 50:10). This custom was popular throughout Jewish history, and is mentioned in the pseudepigraphical literature (Judith 16:24; Ben Sira 22:11). According to the Sages, the *shivah* was instituted by Moses. During these seven days, mourners follow a number of practices. They sit on the floor – Ashkenazic Jews on a low stool or chair, up to three *tefahim* above the floor, and

---

10. Ibid.
11. Ibid.

Sephardic and Eastern Jews on a carpet or pillow on the floor, or on a chair up to one *tefah* above the floor. Mourners do not wear leather shoes, only shoes made of cloth, rubber, or wood. Bathing is forbidden, even in cold water, except for washing the hands and feet in cold water. One may also wash in order to remove dirt or sweat. One may not shave or cut the hair, nor cut fingernails, and sexual relations are forbidden.

The mourner must not wear clothing that has been freshly washed or ironed, nor may he participate in joyous celebrations. He may not study Torah, except for the laws of mourning and reading passages on destruction and lamentations from the Prophets and Writings. A rabbinic authority on whom the public relies is permitted to teach halakhah. A mourner may perform all necessary household duties, but he may not work or have business dealings, except for work that would cause financial damage if not done. But in the first three days of mourning, it is preferable that such work be performed by others, and that the mourner himself abstain from working. Throughout the seven days, the mourner must not leave his house, except for an important activity such as prayer in a *minyan*, and if he does so, he must put some sand in his shoes when he leaves the house. The mourner is permitted to spend the night in his own house and return to the *shivah* house the next morning.

During Mishnah and Talmud times, the Jews followed other mourning practices that were discontinued over time, such as placing ashes on the head as a sign of mourning. This custom ended in the early centuries CE. Another custom practiced was turning over the beds in the house, in order to remember the mourning period during the day as well as at night. In addition, they practiced "wrapping the head" as a sign of mourning. A remnant of this practice still exists today in many communities, particularly among the Sephardic and Eastern Jews – the mourner wears a head covering during the *shivah*, until the *shloshim* (thirty days after burial), or even longer. Among the Ashkenazic Jews, the mourner's extended family, such as the grandchildren of the deceased, follow some mourning practices, such as refraining from attending celebrations until after the Shabbat of the *shivah*.[12]

It is a mitzvah to comfort mourners during their time of sorrow. This mitzvah is included in "You shall love your neighbor as yourself" (Leviticus 19:18). During biblical times, this mitzvah was considered an act of kindness toward the living, meaning the deceased's family (II Samuel 10:1–2; I Chronicles 19:2). From

---

12. Ibid.

Talmudic times onward, this mitzvah was considered kindness toward the dead as well as the living. In biblical days, visits were made mainly by close family (Genesis 27:35; Isaiah 66:13). In the late Second Temple period, the circle was widened to include the entire community, and there were groups of people who took it upon themselves to comfort mourners. The Sages emphasized the importance of this mitzvah, saying that by doing so, the individual followed God's example, as He visited Abraham after the death of his wife Sarah (Genesis 21:11), and that the reward for this was cancellation of punishment in Gehinnom.

The mitzvah of comforting mourners begins in the cemetery immediately following the burial, and continues throughout the seven days. During Talmudic times in the Land of Israel, in the third century CE, the Jews comforted mourners beginning on the third day. The reason is that on each of the first three days, the mourners went to the cemetery, to check whether the dead might really be living. Today some follow the practice of going to comfort mourners immediately, while others wait until after the third day, if possible.[13]

After the seven-day mourning period has ended, the thirty-day period (*shloshim*) begins, in which the mourner must abstain from three things: cutting the hair, shaving, and cutting fingernails. Other customs have been added to these, depending on the community. Among Ashkenazic Jews, the mourner avoids washing his entire body all at once – this means he does not take showers, but he may wash face, hands, and legs in cold water. Further, they do not wear new clothes or clothes that have been freshly washed or ironed, unless another person has worn them previously for an hour or so (except for socks and undergarments). One may buy shoes, eyeglasses, and new household utensils, without a person using them previously as with new clothes. One is permitted to paint the house, but not listen to music. Sephardic and Eastern Jews are lenient with washing and wearing washed and ironed clothes.

In all communities, mourners do not participate in celebrations, even for a mitzvah. Thus the mourner may not attend a *brit milah*, redemption of the firstborn, bar or bat mitzvah, engagement, marriage, *sheva berakhot* or other celebration. However, for a celebration for a close family member, the mourner is usually permitted on condition that the mourner assist with serving the food and leave the hall while the band is playing. The practices when mourning one's father or mother are more severe, and in this case, the mourner should attend the event but leave immediately following the *chuppah*, the act of circumcision, or other

---

13. Ibid.

mitzvah. If the father or mother of a bride or groom are in mourning for a parent, they may participate in the *chuppah* and the wedding meal, and assist in serving the food, "but it is difficult to permit them to be present while the band is playing, and so it is preferable that they remain at the meal for only a short time, and the band should begin to play after they have left."[14]

On Shabbat, the mourner may participate in Shabbat meals with friends, but not a festive meal such as *sheva berakhot*. If his absence will be significant, he may participate in these as well, so that it will not seem like mourning in public, which is prohibited on Shabbat. Throughout the *shloshim*, it is customary to keep a candle lighted, for the ascension of the deceased's soul. On the last day of the *shloshim* after dawn, the mourning customs of *shloshim* end, following the halakhic rule "part of the day is considered the entire day," but mourning for a parent lasts for twelve months. At the end of the *shloshim*, the mourners go to visit the grave of the deceased, and some hold the stone-setting ceremony at that point.[15]

When mourning for a parent, mourners (both men and women) do not cut their hair during the *shloshim*, until "their comrades admonish them" – when they see that the mourner's hair has grown long, and they remark about it, or else tell the mourner explicitly that he or she should get a haircut and/or shave. But if they do not actually admonish the mourner, he is permitted to shave and cut his hair after waiting for the period of time in which they might do so. The Sephardic and Eastern communities usually do this immediately following the *shloshim* period, but if many days have passed and no one has remarked on it, he may cut his hair and shave at the end of two months, even without an admonishment. Ashkenazic Jews do not admonish before the end of three months. Former Chief Rabbi of Israel Mordechai Eliyahu, of blessed memory, ruled that an Ashkenazic Jew may also cut his hair and shave after the *shloshim* plus one day, if his friends admonish him. He adds that the mourner may also hint to his friends that they should admonish him, and his wife and family may also give the admonishment.[16]

The Recommended Custom in Israel

Because every community upholds different mourning practices, the Beta Israel should follow the instructions of their own spiritual leaders, the *kesim*. Mourning

---

14. Rabbi Haim David Halevi, *Shulhan Arukh*, Makor Haim 5:415.
15. Ibid.
16. Herman, *Ma'agal hayei hayom*.

customs help the mourner to confront the new reality. How should this be done, and in what way? The answers to these questions seem to depend on cultural context. Thus Ethiopian Jews can continue to follow their practices. Still, it is possible and desirable to follow local practice, no matter what that practice is – unity is of overarching importance.

✤ Marriage during Mourning

Ethiopian Halakhah

According to Beta Israel custom, one must not get married for one year after a relative has died.

Past and Present in Talmudic Halakhah

If a man gets married, and during the seven days of celebration, one of his relatives for whom he is required to mourn dies, he must complete the seven days of celebration, and only afterward begin the mourning period with *shivah*. A mourner may not get married during the *shloshim*, but if he has not yet fulfilled the mitzvah of procreation, he may marry after the *shivah*, with music and dancing. A widower may remarry after three pilgrimage holidays have passed. Rosh Hashanah and Yom Kippur are not considered in this count, but according to Rabbi Ovadia Yosef, "In modern times, the practice is for a widower to remarry after the death of his wife after thirty days, and rabbis and wedding registrars must not delay marriage until three pilgrimage holidays have passed."[17] A widow must wait three months from the day of her husband's death, not counting the date of death and date of marriage – meaning ninety-two days of widowhood, in order to avoid any possible doubt about the identity of the father in case of pregnancy.

The Recommended Custom in Israel

Some of these customs are preserved by Ethiopian Jews in Israel. I am aware that many Beta Israel who wish to marry and establish a Jewish home postpone the date of marriage to one year from the date of death of any relative. We must work to find an agreeable compromise between family members in such a case, at least ending the practice for distant relatives. In my opinion, preserving these customs entails a certain level of harm to the power of regular life. For all questions on this issue, one must remember the important rule that in the Jewish world, the power of life is stronger than the power of death.

---

17. *Yalkut Yosef* 7:160.

❧ Kaddish

Ethiopian Halakhah
In Ethiopia, the Beta Israel did not recite Kaddish for the deceased.

Past and Present in Talmudic Halakhah
As per tradition, the Kaddish recited by the deceased's relatives, especially his children, is beneficial for the soul and has the power to atone for it. Reciting Kaddish was practiced in the Geonic period. The custom was for the sons to recite, and if there were no sons, other male relatives did so: brothers, parents, or sons-in-law. Some think that in such cases, it is preferable for a daughter under age twelve to recite the Mourner's Kaddish from the women's section. If there is no relative to recite the Mourner's Kaddish, the family may pay someone to do so. An adopted child does not follow the mourning practices, but if there is no one else to recite the Mourner's Kaddish, it is appropriate for him to do so. A person whose parents are still living should not recite Kaddish for family members or other people. Some authorities rule leniently on this if the parents give him permission to do so.

Although the mourning period for a parent lasts for twelve months, we do not recite Kaddish in the twelfth month, because the strictest punishment given to *resha'im* (the wicked) is twelve months in Gehinnom, and because it is not respectful to parents to consider them wicked. Among Ashkenazic Jews, the mourner leads the prayer service for all the services throughout the year, except on Shabbat and holidays, and he is considered obligated in this. In Sephardic and Eastern communities, the mourner also acts as *hazzan* (prayer leader), but he is not obligated. Sephardic Jews end recitation of the Mourner's Kaddish for one week at the beginning of the twelfth month, and then they recommence recitation until the end of the twelfth month of mourning. One who is certain that his parents were considered wicked should recite Kaddish for them throughout the entire twelve months.[18]

The Recommended Custom in Israel
The Mourner's Kaddish was accepted throughout all Jewish communities, and so the Ethiopian Jews must learn it thoroughly and recite it. For all other mourning customs they must follow the instructions of the Chief Rabbinate of Israel. Those

---

18. Herman, *Ma'agal hayei ha-yom*.

of the first generation who find it difficult to adapt to new customs may continue the Ethiopian custom, without instigating unnecessary conflict.

❦ *Yahrzeit* (Annual Memorial Service)

Ethiopian Halakhah

On the seventh day and on the last day of the year following the death of a relative, the family held *tizkar*, a memorial service. This included a sacrifice and prayers by the *kesim*. This ceremony had great significance among the community, and they observed it strictly. However, they did not go to the cemetery – in fact, it was absolutely forbidden to go there and to visit the grave. There was a separation between the world of the dead and the living. Thus the *tizkar* ceremony was usually held in the home of the deceased's family.

Past and Present in Talmudic Halakhah

The annual memorial service is held each year on the Hebrew date of death, even if the deceased was buried on a different day. If the individual was buried three days or more after death, in the first year the memorial day is observed on the day of the burial, and in subsequent years on the day of death. On the Shabbat before the memorial day, except for in the first year of mourning, the mourner acts as *hazzan* for all the Shabbat services. He reads the *maftir* (portion from Prophets), and before the Musaf (additional) service he holds the Torah scroll and recites a special prayer in memory of the dead. The mourner does not recite this prayer on days when there is no recitation of Tahanun (supplication) on a weekday, nor on the Shabbat preceding Rosh Hodesh, nor on the four Shabbatot when special Torah portions are read (Shekalim, Zakhor, Parah, ha-Hodesh).

From the start of the memorial day until its end, the children of the deceased are forbidden from listening to music or participating in festive meals, such as weddings. The mourners light a memorial candle that should remain lit until the end of the memorial day in the evening, because this is comforting to the soul, "and it advances in majesty and joy, and expands in enjoyment of its light."[19] The child of the deceased serves as *hazzan* for all the services – Arvit, Shaharit, and Minhah, and recites the Mourner's Kaddish then. Sephardic and Eastern Jews recite the Mourner's Kaddish beginning from the Arvit service of Shabbat preceding the memorial day until the end of the memorial day. The custom is to light two candles throughout the services and place them on the podium in the

---

19. *Mateh Efraim*.

synagogue. If the memorial day falls on Monday or Thursday, when we read the Torah in the synagogue, a son goes up to the Torah (has an aliyah) and recites the Half Kaddish after the Torah reading, and some recite a special prayer for the deceased. If the memorial day falls on another day of the week when the Torah is not read, the mourner must go up to the Torah on the Monday or Thursday that is closest to the memorial day.

At the end of the Shaharit service, the custom is to give the congregants some alcoholic drinks and baked goods – Hassidic Jews call this a *tikkun* (repairing), as the blessings recited over the food and drink serve as "reparation" or "healing" for the soul, which rises to higher spiritual worlds. The mourners also go visit the grave. They do not do this on Shabbat, Yom Kippur, holidays, or festivals, and if the memorial day falls on one of these days, they advance or postpone the date of visiting the cemetery. Some do not visit the cemetery on Rosh Hodesh, Hanukkah, or days when Tahanun is not recited, but postpone until after those dates. In addition, some do not visit the cemetery the entire month of Nissan, only on the eve of Rosh Hodesh Nissan.

Some fast on the memorial day, and it is commendable to give charity and study Mishnah for the ascension of the soul of the deceased. The reason for this is that the letters that form the word Mishnah, *mem, shin, nun, heh*, are the same as those in the word *neshamah* (soul), and by studying Mishnah, which is the Oral Torah, one causes the soul to ascend, thereby shortening the process of atonement. If there are no children to recite Kaddish for a deceased person or to observe the annual memorial day, it is commendable to dedicate a Torah scroll or books on halakhah to the synagogue in his name, following the words of the Prophet, "I will give them in My house and within My walls a monument and a memorial better than sons and daughters; I will give them an everlasting memorial, that shall not be cut off" (Isaiah 56:5).[20]

The Recommended Custom in Israel

The Beta Israel are permitted to follow any custom they choose – there is no preference for one custom over another.

---

20. Herman, *Ma'agal hayei ha-yom*.

In Memoriam

❧ El Malei Rachamim

In memory of those who lost their lives on the way from Ethiopia to Jerusalem

God full of mercy, Who dwells above, grant rest on the wings of the Divine Presence, among the holy, pure, and glorious who shine like the sky, to the souls of our holy brothers and sisters of Beta Israel – the Jews of Ethiopia, the four thousand Jews who met their deaths on the way to Jerusalem, who died for the Sanctification of Your Name, through torment and sickness, slaughter and suffocation, by thirst, starvation, and execution by the Ethiopian and Sudanese authorities and their henchmen. Accept our prayer for the ascension of their souls. Therefore, the Master of Mercy will protect them forever in the hiding of His wings, and will bind their souls with the rope of life. The Everlasting is their heritage, and they will rest in the Garden of Eden. They will rest in peace in the place where they lay, and they will stand for their fate at the end of days. And let us say, Amen.

Prayer for Peace for the Missing Jews of Ethiopia

May He Who has blessed our ancestors Abraham, Isaac, and Jacob; Joseph, Moses, Aaron, David, and Solomon, bless the sons and daughters of the Ethiopian Jews who were kidnapped and taken captive by Ethiopian and Sudanese enemies and unknown enemies, or who were lost on the long and dangerous journey.

[Insert names of the missing.]

May the Holy One, blessed be He, guard them and rescue them from all trouble and distress, harm and disease. May He be filled with mercy for them to heal them, strengthen them, and revive them, and take them out speedily to everlasting freedom, back to the bosom of their families.

May they merit long lives and many years of strength and peace. May the merit of our ancestors bring salvation to the children, and may the verse be fulfilled in them – "Bring my soul out of prison, that I may give thanks to Your name" (Psalms 142:8).

For our brothers and sisters of all the children of Israel who are in distress and captivity, whether they be on sea or on land, may the Omnipresent have mercy on them and bring them out from distress into tranquility, from darkness into light, and from slavery to redemption, speedily and in our days – and let us respond, Amen.

Hatarat Nedarim (Release of Vows)

Hear, all –

All vows, oaths, and prohibitions, or any law or custom that I vowed or swore, whether awake or asleep; all types of ascetic practices that I took upon myself; any prohibition, or any acceptance of mitzvah, custom, or halakhah that I took upon myself, whether in the terminology of a vow, voluntary practice, or oath, whether in the terminology of an asceticism or any other statement; any custom or mitzvah that I practiced, or any statement I made, or swore or made the commitment to perform a mitzvah; any beneficial custom or good practice that I followed since I made aliyah to Israel; any practices I followed that I learned from my teachers, friends, or spiritual or community leaders, and for which I did not specify the condition that it was not a vow; anything I did for myself or to others, whether known to me or that I have forgotten – all these will all be permitted.

I ask and request of you [people of the *beit din*] that you release these, for I fear that I may fail and be trapped, God forbid, in the sin of vows, oaths, ascetic practices, prohibitions, proscriptions, consecrations, and agreements. I am not referring, God forbid, to the performance of good deeds, fulfilling laws and customs that I observed. I only ask to return to the Beta Israel traditions of Ethiopia. Therefore I ask for complete annulment, and I request permission for those customs, laws, and traditions that I took upon myself in the Land of Israel, and observed them until now, and I intend to observe them again, according to the custom of the Beta Israel in Ethiopia.

I repudiate all of the above-mentioned, whether they were things related to property, or things related to the body, or things related to the soul. I repudiate all of them, because when I came to Israel, I did not know which path to take. According to law, one who regrets and asks for release must describe the vow, but please be aware, congregants, that it is impossible to describe them, because they are many. I do not ask for annulment of those vows which should not be annulled. Therefore please consider it as if I had described them.

THOSE WHO ARE ANNULLING RECITE THE
FOLLOWING RESPONSE THREE TIMES:

All is permitted to you, all is forgiven you, all is cancelled. There is no vow, nor oath, nor ascetic practice, consecration, prohibition, excommunication, curse, or damnation. However, there is forgiveness, pardon, and atonement. Just as the earthly court grants annulment, so may they be annulled in the Court of Heaven.

THE INDIVIDUAL RECITES:

All the curses, damnations, excommunications, censures, and bans that I cursed, damned, excommunicated, or assessed, of myself, my wife, my family, or others who are members of the Jewish people; or others who cursed, excommunicated, censured, or assessed, myself or my wife, my children or my family – May it be Your will, God and God of our forefathers, our God in Heaven and on earth, that these will not govern us, they will make no impression. All curses will be transformed into positive declarations and blessings, as it is written, "So the Lord your God turned the curse into a blessing for you, because the Lord your God loves you" (Deuteronomy 23:6).

THE HOLY CONGREGATION RECITES THE
FOLLOWING RESPONSE THREE TIMES:

All are annulled for you, all are valid for you, all are forgiven you. Just as the earthly court grants annulment for you, so may they be annulled in the Court of Heaven. May all curses be transformed into positive declarations and blessings, as it is written, "So the Lord your God turned the curse into a blessing for you, because the Lord your God loves you" (Deuteronomy 23:6).[1]

---

1. I wish to thank my teacher Rabbi Yehuda Brandes, who proposed the addition of the release of curses and checked the text of the release of vows.

Reaction to the Book

The following are excerpts from letters received by the author and comments made upon publication of the original version of this book in Hebrew.

D.A.: "The book you have written (with excellent timing) was like a drink of cold water for a tired soul. Your interesting and fluent writing granted me continuous enjoyment in reading this book, and inspired me to read it again. I learned new things about the sources of Talmudic customs and general Jewish history. I was particularly impressed by your worldview, traditional and based on the Torah, yet Western. I was pleased to discover that you work in educating youth and a generation of educators."

W.A.T.: "What Rabbi Sharon Shalom has attempted in *From Sinai to Ethiopia* is to preserve the most ancient tradition among the Jewish people, from the period preceding the Sages. It will form part of the mosaic of Jewish culture and enrich it. For many years, I desired from the depths of my soul to preserve our beautiful tradition, but I did not find anyone who shared this wish. Our people only tried to distance themselves from every sign of tradition, and to imitate other communities or at least to ignore ours. After reading Rabbi Sharon's book, I was filled with joy. Only He Who knows all secrets is aware of the inner happiness and pride I felt. From that moment, I felt that our tradition had legitimacy, and there was no more need to hide it in the depths of our souls. On the contrary, we Ethiopian Jews have traditions that should be expressed in everyday life, and not remain in books or museum exhibits. Until now, the concept of traditions has been applied only to communities such as the Yemenites, Sephardim, or Ashkenazim. None of these customs has any basis in the text of the Torah, nor in the Talmud, and yet they wave the flag that bears the slogan of 'Jewish custom is Torah,' and the verse 'Do not foresake the Torah of your mother.'

"In a *shtiebl* in Bnei Brak, I once saw a sign with directives for the *hazzan*: 'The *hazzan* will wear a hat, a suit, and *gartel* [belt that separates between the heart and the lower part of the body]. He will pray according to Nusah Sefard with Ashkenazic pronunciation. Before prayer he must immerse himself in the *mikveh*. He must not shave, following the custom of our holy rabbis.' I am certain of one thing: 'the custom of our holy rabbis' is not the Tannaim or the Amoraim, not the Rishonim or the *Shulhan Arukh* or the Rema. Rather, these customs were developed by communities in Eastern Europe, but they still use the term 'our holy rabbis' even though this list of rules has no relation to halakhah, and they preserve their customs punctiliously. However, when it comes to the customs of Ethiopian Jewry, these sayings do not apply. All of our customs are deemed in error, and we should be subject to the *Shulhan Arukh* and *Yalkut Yosef*. (I do not know what source in the Tanakh or Talmud says we should be subject to these.) Naturally, this leads to loss of respect for parents, *kesim*, the entire Ethiopian community, and to slander of our ancestors who followed and preserved the customs. How sad it is to see some of the negative responses of members of the Ethiopian community toward the book, which are shallow and lacking in content. This demonstrates self-degradation, and when a person does not respect himself, others do not respect him and even belittle him. Today we see that communities who ingratiate themselves to other communities are not received in a welcoming manner, and all the more so, are derisively rejected.

"We may argue about the significance of this book, but the discussion should be topical and respectful, with proofs from the texts, as the rabbis have done throughout history. I have also heard positive responses, some from rabbis representing other communities, on the importance of preserving our tradition. This is very uplifting, and gives us strength to continue preserving our customs. One example: a Yemenite Jew who read the book told me that he regretted his grandmother was no longer alive, so that he might ask her about the customs of the Jews in Yemen. Since our aliyah, finally I feel proud to be a Jew. In Ethiopia I felt proud to be a Jew, but here I was always made to feel that our Judaism was in doubt, and that we were outcast refugees…"

Rabbi R.T.I.: "This is the first time that the halakhic and legal worlds have encountered an organized halakhic work, with citations and explanations, about Ethiopian Jewry. Until this book, no one has presented our tradition in Hebrew. From this aspect, this is a historical as well as a halakhic breakthrough. No one before him has ever done this."

Rabbi M.S. expressed opposition to the book. His main argument was that the book would lead to isolation of the community, while for the last thirty years, the community has integrated religiously. According to him, the book takes us backward in time. He explains his dissatisfaction: "Most painfully, the author is an Ethiopian rabbi, who should ideally act to connect the Ethiopians with the rest of the Jewish people. But here he is actually doing it a disservice. I have no doubt that the author's intention was positive, but from my point of view, it has led to a negative result. As Rabbi Judah Halevi stated in the Kuzari, 'Your intention is desirable, but your actions are undesirable.'"

D.C.: Rabbi Shalom proposes a path beyond accepted halakhah, divided according to generations – the older generations should continue to follow the ancient customs, while the younger generations should gradually adopt mainstream halakhah.... In certain places in the book, Rabbi Shalom seems to be speaking in an apologetic tone. On one hand, he agrees that the Ethiopian community must move within a few generations to *pesika* (implementation or practical application of halakhah) based on the *Shulhan Arukh* (Ashkenazic, Sephardic, or similar). But against the insult and humiliation suffered by members of the older generation, who are unable to change their practice, he provides a proud and courageous defense. The book raises and addresses difficult questions that demand a broader platform – on the difference between the unity and the uniformity of the Jewish people.... But more than this, he gives the Ethiopian community reason to be proud of its customs, with the knowledge that the custom in the remainder of the Jewish world is different. The non-Ethiopian public will also be very interested in this book, and may achieve a better understanding of the customs of the Beta Israel community, which perhaps seem strange at first glance, but most of which rely on sound inner logic."

Y.S.: "First of all, I congratulate you on *From Sinai to Ethiopia*. Undoubtedly, this book is a precious asset and treasure for the entire Jewish people. In particular, it grants Ethiopian Jewry a place within Israeli society. In my opinion, the response that the book has generated in the various communities of the Jewish world is proof that the Jewish people are alive and well. You have made an impressive achievement in questioning.... I would like to encourage you, and to say thank you for the wonderful gift of your book."

At a conference about the book at Yad Ben Zvi Institute, Rabbi Dr. Daniel Sperber said: "The praise that the author of this book deserves is endless. Thanks to this book, a new field of study has been created surrounding the topic of

Ethiopian Jewry. It must be studied, added to, and expanded, and most importantly – defended."

At the same event, Kes Samai Elias stated, "This evening, I am full of pride. In Ethiopia, during hundreds of years of journeys and hardships, we remained strong, because we preserved tradition that distanced us from assimilation and Christianity." He added, "For thirty years, we have been trying to defend the assertion that we are Jews in the full sense of the word. Now Rabbi Sharon Shalom has arrived and put our community on the map, our customs in the center. Ethiopian Jews will continue to observe the traditions that our ancestors observed in Ethiopia. Even if other [Jews] do not accept this, they will have to live with it."

Rabbi Yosef Hadana, chief rabbi of Ethiopian Jewry, praised the book, but noted that "the Jewish community of Ethiopia came [to Israel] with sources and traditions, but in my opinion we must decide according to the *Shulhan Arukh*."

Rabbi Reuven-Tal Iasso, who sat on the panel at the event, said, "The real question is whether or not the Ethiopian community belongs to the Jewish people. If we follow those who believe that the Ethiopian Jews are not part of the Jewish people, then there is no reason to study their tradition. If we follow the opinion that the roots of the Ethiopian Jews are within the Jewish people, this changes the entire *pesika*. Rabbi Sharon Shalom has paved a new road. He has shaken the rabbinic world by forcing it to confront Ethiopian tradition in rabbinic language, the language of halakhah and Jewish law."

Rabbi Yehuda Brandes, head of Beit Morasha *beit midrash*, added, "One of the important points of this book is to prevent the ancient tradition of Ethiopian Jewry from being swallowed within the world of modern halakhah, which has undergone two thousand years of transformation.... Someone had to translate the Ethiopian language, and to state that Ethiopian tradition is not just folklore, but tradition."

To conclude the discussion, Shula Mula, chairman of the Israel Association for Ethiopian Jews (IAEJ), stated: "In my opinion, *From Sinai to Ethiopia* is the most important book I have ever encountered." Shula shared her experience as a new immigrant who denied her tradition in order to blend in. "*From Sinai to Ethiopia* teaches us that we must not smother the practices we used to follow. We must not be embarrassed by the way we were educated. The book does not hide the arguments and the conflicts, but rather asserts that *elu ve-elu divrei Elokim hayim* – both of these are the words of the living God."

Approbations

৺ Rabbi Dr. Nachum Rabinowitz

BS"D Monday of Parashat Naso –
"And he heard the voice speaking to him," 5771

In the miracle of the ingathering of exiles that we have witnessed since the revival of the State of Israel, the most impressive event is the aliyah of the entire Beta Israel community from Ethiopia. This Jewish community was almost completely disconnected from the body of the Jewish people for two thousand years, to the extent that they forgot the holy language of Hebrew. However, they strictly preserved ancient traditions and practical mitzvot. Despite temptation on one side and torture on the other, this community adhered to its faith and to the hope of returning to Zion. Surprisingly, the aliyah to Israel of this community literally fulfilled the words of the prophet, "Who are these that fly as a cloud, and as the doves to their windows?" (Isaiah 60:8). Many lost their lives in the attempt to reach Israel, and could not fulfill the verse "When you pass through the waters, I will be with you, and through the rivers, they shall not overflow you; when you walk through the fire, you shall not be burned, neither shall the flame kindle on you" (Isaiah 43:2). The sacrifice of those who did not survive will stand forever in the merit of the entire Jewish people.

However, the difficult trials have not yet ended. The absorption of the Ethiopian Jews into Israeli society raises particularly thorny issues, even more so than those faced by multiple immigrant groups from other countries. Some thought that we could bring in all the immigrants and combine them as in a pressure cooker, annulling the barriers and particular traditions of each group. This concept is invalid ethically and has proven impractical in Israeli life. We cannot expect believing Jews who are faithful to their own tradition to abandon the customs they inherited from their ancestors, all at once, and to adopt the manner of worshipping God and the way of life of one or another Jewish community, following recent rabbinic authorities. But undoubtedly, somehow we must reckon with the many fundamental *halakhot* that the Sages determined, and which bind the entire Jewish people.

Rabbi Sharon Shalom, *shlita*, is a descendant of spiritual leaders of the Beta Israel community who has studied Torah in yeshivas in Israel, and thus exemplifies the Beta Israel tradition along with the complete history of Torah. He has taken upon himself a weighty and sacred project, to create a kind of *Kitzur Shulhan Arukh* that will bridge the gap between Jewish communities – "The end of the matter, everything having been heard: fear God and keep His commandments, for this is the whole man" (Ecclesiastes 12:13). Through this book, Ethiopian Jews will find a way to connect to their past as a distinct community, Beta Israel, as well as to the past and present of the entire Jewish people as it returns to its land.

May it be His will that he enjoy success, and that his work will serve to enlighten many. *Ve-yizkeh le-hagdil Torah u-le-ha'adirah* – May he be privileged to teach and strengthen Torah study.

Written and signed on behalf of the honor of the Torah and its students,
Nachum Eliezer Rabinowitz

❧ Rabbi Shabtai A. Hacohen Rappaport

B"H
Shabtai A. Hacohen Rappaport
Purim 5771

To: Rabbi Sharon Shalom, *shlita*, a respected member of our *beit midrash* and a diligent student of Torah, who studies in order to teach.

I congratulate you on the publication of your book. I observed close at hand how you labored at it, and how you searched for and compiled, with your characteristic thoroughness, the customs practiced by our brethren in Ethiopia. In the past generation, these fellow Jews have been permitted to make aliyah to the Holy Land, their ancient heart's desire, and we, the rest of the Jewish people, have benefited from their return to live among us. Due to the long years of disconnection between those far off in the land of Cush and the remainder of exiled Jewry in distant lands, many of their customs are different from those of the remainder of Diaspora Jewry. As Ethiopian Jews are introduced to the customs that are common among their Jewish brethren, their original traditions are gradually disappearing.

The river of explanation and documentation that springs from the fountain of Jewish custom divides into four streams, or four reasons for the importance of research and knowledge of customs.

First: customs reflect ancient halakhic decisions. Although we may not know the identity of the *posek*, it is important to verify the underlying reasoning, as the Gaon Rabbi Moshe Feinstein, *ztz"l*, explained in detail in *Dibbrot Moshe*, Shabbat par. 10. Unique customs of a particular Jewish community require study of their origin, if we can identify it, as you have assiduously attempted to do in your book.

Second: customs are a source of identity and belonging. Although most people do not usually know the true reasons for their customs, they characterize their life as individuals, families, and communities, and represent the infrastructure of ancestral tradition. An accurate concept of the "I" is an important foundation for worshipping God (see Rabbi Avraham Yitzhak Hacohen Kook, *Olat Ra'ayah*, on the prayer *Modeh ani lefanecha*). Therefore, as you have written, it is vital that Ethiopian Jews know themselves through the customs that their ancestors practiced.

Third: Jewish customs differentiate between Jews and non-Jews. Our fellow Jews in Ethiopia were extremely careful not to intermingle with non-Jews, and not to marry non-Jewish women. Thus we have eternal appreciation for the customs that enabled our brethren to preserve their uniqueness and their Judaism throughout thousands of years of disconnection from the majority of the Jewish people.

Fourth: accurate appreciation of these customs enables reexamination and adoption of necessary changes. It is very difficult to change a custom whose origins and reasons are unknown. Therefore, publicizing the customs and investigating the reasons behind them represents an important beginning on the basis of which we may correct what should be amended. The individual and the community should be moving forward, not standing in place.

From all of the above aspects, your work is deserving of praise. May it be His will that your labor succeed, and that your work will open an ever-expanding space for acquaintance with the customs of a community that had disappeared from the view of most of our people. May we have the merit to observe the virtues of our brethren, and not their shortcomings.

With true admiration,
Shabtai A. Hacohen Rappaport

✺ Rabbi Yosef Hadana

B"H
Bureau of Religious Services
Branch of Religious Services for the Ethiopian Community
Office of the Chief Rabbi of Ethiopian Jewry – Rabbi Yosef Hadana

BS"D, 12 Iyyar 5771
May 16, 2011
Letter of Recommendation
Rabbi Yosef Hadana, *shlita*

To my dear friend of many deeds, Rabbi Sharon Shalom, *shlita*, author of the book *Shulhan ha-Orit*:

I am overjoyed to see this book, which is written in clear and elegant language. The book encompasses the yearly cycle with refinement and wisdom. I reviewed the book, with particular attention to the description of the customs of Ethiopian Jewry as they were actually practiced.

It is true that the Oral Torah was not available in written form. We had no books. Everything was passed from the spiritual leaders to the public, from parents to children. For this reason, we did not have clear, organized *halakhot*. We did have the written Torah, the entire Tanakh, and it was studied with great care. We did not use the terms "religious" and "non-religious." Every Jew had to keep the Torah and mitzvot. Whoever did not keep Torah and mitzvot was considered a non-Jew. Each family had a connection to the *kes*. They accepted him as their spiritual father, and followed his instructions.

I was born in the village of Ambober, which together with the nearby villages served as the largest Jewish center. There were three *kesim* in Ambober, all given the honorary title *lika kahanat* (high priest): High Priest Taube Malko, High Priest Kes Barhan Baruch, both of blessed memory, and High Priest Kes Hedna Refael Tekoya, may God grant him a long life. They were the accepted authorities for all Ethiopian Jewry.

Shulhan ha-Orit, which is written in clear, pleasant language as mentioned, describes many of the customs of Ethiopian Jewry, in a wise and well-informed manner. The author advances one step beyond the labor of collecting the customs. He compares them to *halakhot* in the Talmud, and thus offers a halakhic way to worship God for the generation of Ethiopian Jews living in Israel. Naturally, some Ethiopian Jews will disagree with one custom or another, because in their village they behaved differently. Some Ethiopian and non-Ethiopian Jews will question the method of halakhic decision making proposed by the author. Personally, when I read about the customs, I noticed, as a friend who respects the author, that some of the customs recorded here were practiced differently in Ambober. Following are several examples:

1. Prayer: "Prayer was accompanied by…lying on the stomach and spreading the hands on the ground." I visited many villages and participated in prayer services, but I never saw or heard that the Jews were praying in this manner. Rather, they bent their knees and bowed down with their foreheads, as other Jews do on Yom Kippur.

2. Injera: This is a national dish in Ethiopia, made of teff flour. Teff is a high-quality, nutritious food. It is unrelated to legumes such as peas or chickpeas, nor is it one of the five types of grain defined in halakhah. I checked about the appropriate blessing for before and after eating injera, and the conclusion is that it is like rice. Thus one should recite *borei minei mezonot* before eating it, and *Borei nefashot* afterwards.

3. Beginning and end of Shabbat: Following a well-known custom among Ethiopian Jewry, shortly after noon on Friday, we cease all physical labor, such as field work, making clay pottery, weaving, and sewing. We make preparations for Shabbat until just before sundown. Then we douse the coals – "You shall not cause a fire to burn throughout your habitations on the Sabbath day" (Exodus 35:3). On Motzaei Shabbat we wait until the stars come out. After we see three stars, inside the home we prepare a new fire by rubbing two sticks together. We make a fire, and from it, each woman takes her own flame. When she enters her own home with the flame, each woman ululates and recites a special prayer for the coming week to be blessed and successful. She then begins to boil *buna*, coffee. On Motzaei Shabbat as well, women and men refrain from physical labor.

4. Drinking wine: You wrote that there is a complete ban on drinking wine. In Ambober, we received matzot for Passover and bottles of wine for Seder night. On the evening of Seder night, after the holiday prayer service, the entire community went out of the synagogue to the courtyard and stood. The oldest of the *kesim* blessed the community and the matzot. He gave everyone pieces of matzah and a sip of wine in the cap of the bottle. People waited with excitement and great anticipation. No one ever asked if it was permitted to

drink wine or not. Therefore, we should instruct members of the community to make Kiddush over ordinary wine, as in halakhah.

5. Giving charity on Shabbat: In Ethiopia, certain communities used to give charity offerings on Shabbat. This custom originates in error and ignorance of the many *halakhot* of Shabbat. The problem is not only giving money in synagogue, but also involves laws of *muktzeh*, carrying, and other issues. Therefore, every spiritual leader bears the pleasant obligation of explaining and instructing in order to annul this custom, even for the older generation. With regard to the halakhic decision, my opinion is that we should follow the *Shulhan Arukh*, like the majority of the Jews.

At any rate, the power of this unprecedented work is as a foundation for the discussion, comments, and clarification that will follow.

May it be His will that you continue to rise up on the ascent of Torah, fear of God and good qualities, *le-hagdil Torah u-le-ha'adirah* – to teach and to strengthen the study of Torah.

With friendship and deep respect,
Rabbi Yosef Hadana
Chief Rabbi of Ethiopian Jewry

❧ Rabbi Reuven-Tal Iasso

B"H
Sunday, 30 Adar I, 5771

To Rabbi Sharon Shalom, light of Israel, greetings and blessings.

First of all, I must admit that I am delighted and moved, *sheheheyanu ve-kiyemanu ve-higianu la-zman ha-zeh* – Blessed is He Who has granted us life, sustained us, and enabled us to reach this occasion.

As a child alone, you traveled through the forests of Ethiopia to the deserts of Sudan, where you wandered from one refugee camp to another. Only those who have experienced this journey personally can relate to the suffering and uncertainty you felt during this time.

This book is a first, a pioneer at the frontier of the field of halakhah. The world of halakhic decision making has a number of methods, of which I will note two. The *posek* can never be immune to the obstacles confronting him when he attempts to make practical halakhic decisions, as every method of *pesika* has its advantages and disadvantages.

One method of halakhic decision making is:

We begin with the original source (the oldest one), follow the issue to modern times, and then reach a practical halakhic conclusion. The problem is, a halakhah or custom that is found in ancient sources but missing in recent literature lacks status and validity. Is its absence in recent literature evidence that this custom was rejected from the body of Jewish tradition for various reasons? Or does its presence in the early and most ancient sources represent proof of its authenticity and status as practical halakhah? Further, under this method, the approach to oral tradition and custom is unclear.

A second method of halakhic decision making is:

We begin with the halakhah as practiced, and follow it backward in history to the most ancient source. The problem with this method is that it does not give expression to *halakhot* or customs that are absent from the ancient sources. What is the status and validity of such a custom? Does its absence from our ancient sources prove that it originated among foreign peoples (this has halakhic implications)? Further, when we cannot explain why the halakhah or custom no longer appears in the sources, should we assume that more recent generations objected to these sources, and decide according to the rule of *halakhah ke-batrai*, following the later authority?

And under this method, what is the approach to oral traditions and ancient customs?

In addition, we must ask, who are "our sources"? Ashkenazic customs are different from Sephardic ones, and so forth. And what about *halakhot* and customs of one community that conflict with customs of another community – can a custom of Middle Eastern Jewry conflict with and negate a custom or halakhah of Ashkenazic Jewry, and vice versa? Is the status of customs and *halakhot* practiced in the hassidic world (in its various streams) equivalent to the customs of other communities? In addition, we must inquire as to the customs of the Beta Israel community, whose unique practices are known from the period of the Ridbaz, and some of which are foreign to what is accepted today in the world of Talmudic tradition. May we view these customs as an integral, inseparable part of Jewish tradition? In general, is their status equivalent to that of other customs?

Rabbi Sharon Shalom, light of Israel, has chosen the path of integration, searching for shared aspects that unify Ethiopian Jewish traditions with those of the general Jewish public. The advantage of this method is *shalom* (peace), like the author's name – unity among Jews that stems from what is shared and connects, and little or almost no attention to what separates and opposes. I have known Rabbi Shalom closely for thirty years, and this is his path and worldview – the path of peace. He has chosen this path for good reason. In this work, we find methodical, consistent work of many years – this book was not written in one morning, nor in one week. We can also recognize that the individuals and authors that the author mentions and cites are people whom he has met over the years.

In writing and publishing your book, Rabbi Shalom, you are privileged to fulfill the verse, "But your servants will cross over, all who are pioneers [*halutz*] in combat before the Lord, for the battle, as my master has spoken" (Numbers 32:27).

Ashreinu, mah tov helkeinu, u-mah naim goraleinu – "We are fortunate, how good is our portion, how pleasant is our lot."

Reuven-Tal Iasso
Beit Shemesh

Priest Kes Mentosnot (Eli) Wende

Itbarech Egziabher amlake Israel – With blessings to the King of Israel – I have reviewed the book *Shulhan ha-Orit*, and I was particularly inspired by its title. It has great significance, since our entire world of tradition in Ethiopia was based on the Orit and on a long history of oral tradition, which was passed from *kes* to *kes*, father to father, and generation to generation. In addition, when I made aliyah to Eretz Yisrael, I learned that Oraita in Aramaic means Torah, like Orit.[1]

This composition is very important. In a clear and exact manner, the author records the customs of our community that have been practiced for thousands of years. As soon as I received the book, I read it together with my children. It inspired them to ask questions, and I felt that finally I had a shared language with them. Thus I may say that this work brings together the younger generation, which was born and grew up in Israel, and the adult generation, which made aliyah. This book is a link that connects between past and present, a continuation of the long chain of our tradition, this time a written tradition. The fact that it is written has particular importance since until now, the tradition of Ethiopian Jewry was transmitted orally and thus was endangered due to the changes that the community is experiencing in Israel, our generation's unwillingness to listen and learn, and the deep damage to the status of our spiritual leadership.

---

1. The word *Orit* in Ge'ez means "Torah" (the Five Books of Moses). The scroll of the Torah is placed in the ark in the synagogue or in the home of the *kes*, and is read on holidays and festivals. Some use the term *Orit* to refer to the entire Tanakh. The Tanakh of Ethiopian Jewry includes all the books recognized as canonical by other Jewish communities, as well as non-canonical books.

Regarding the comparison to Ethiopian customs and Talmudic halakhah, I was pleased to discover that the similarities are greater than the differences, at least for the period close to when the Talmud was written, such as in the areas of family life and holidays. I was moved to learn that there are customs preserved in our tradition that the Talmudic tradition did not preserve, such as the Sigd holiday, a custom related to bride and groom, one day of Rosh Hashanah, and some Rosh Hodesh customs. When we research the issue, we find that all customs are derived from one origin. In actuality, today some of our customs are very different from what is practiced among other Jewish communities. Things are not so simple – such as the laws of *muktzeh*, *tumah ve-taharah* (ritual purity), burial, praying at the graves of the righteous, sexual relations on Shabbat, holidays, *brit milah* that falls on Shabbat. Most of these issues are covered in this work.

The halakhah proposed by the author is an attempt to preserve the traditions we practiced in Ethiopia, but also to find a way to enable the new generation to preserve our tradition and at the same time, to become part of the Jewish people of Jerusalem.[2] Truthfully, there is no reason to change anything. As a spiritual leader, I will continue to instruct according to the customs in Ethiopia, as this has been our tradition for thousands of years. Still, I am aware that we face significant difficulties and problematic questions. After reading this book together with my children, I believe that it offers a solution to this challenge. Despite the significant differences in certain areas between our traditions and Talmudic halakhah, this is the place to request that members of our community be permitted to continuing observing their customs. I ask for understanding, even though our customs may seem foreign and far from accepted practice. Just as there are many traditions here in Israel – Ashkenazic, Sephardic, and Yemenite – I believe that all of them are performed in the Name of Heaven. To return to Eretz Yisrael is the fulfillment of the vision of our prophets, and now we can continue to stride toward the coming of the Messiah, with mutual respect and understanding. We hope that we will have the merit to witness the rebuilding of the Temple. Because our community has preserved the customs of *tumah ve-taharah* as practiced in the Temple, undoubtedly we will be the ones to teach the rest of the Jewish people how to perform the Temple rituals.

In conclusion, in these lines I wish to bless the esteemed Rabbi Sharon Shalom, *shlita*, who toiled in order to publish *Shulhan ha-Orit*, which describes the

---

2. Jerusalem in Ethiopian tradition refers to all of Israel and is a spiritual reality that extends beyond the physical city of Jerusalem.

halakhot followed by Ethiopian Jewry before they made aliyah, and proposes a method for halakhic practice in Eretz Yisrael. This book will facilitate those who study the issues of Shabbat, *tumah ve-taharah*, and holidays, among others. Such books are worthy of publishing. I hope that his book will be accepted enthusiastically, and I wish him success in all his endeavors. May all his efforts be blessed, *she-yizkeh le-hagdil Torah u-le-ha'adirah* – May he be privileged to teach and to strengthen the study of Torah.

Be strong and of courage,
Yours sincerely,
Priest Kes Mentosnot (Eli) Wende

✡ Priest Kes Tefesahaku Malki Tzedek

In the Name of God, King of Israel, King of Abraham, King of Isaac, King of Jacob and Israel.

I have seen the book *Shulhan ha-Orit*, which describes the customs of our community, the Jews of Ethiopia. I did not read it, but I have heard it described by the author, my son, Rabbi Sharon Shalom. I listened closely to his explanation of the contents, and I emphasize that it is a blessed act, as these customs were our way of worshipping God. These customs are very special, and we have an emotional connection to them – they are our life. Through our prayers, we have succeeded in reaching God. These customs breathed life into us; they are like the pillar of fire and pillar of cloud that guided the Israelites on their journey from Egypt to Jerusalem. Thus my son Rabbi Sharon has achieved a great deed. I was pleased to see this book, and very moved. It has also given me new inspiration to study and pass down our tradition to the younger generation. I am certain that many will refer to this book. I therefore bless my son, Rabbi Sharon: May He who has blessed our ancestors bless you as well. As Moses the Prophet and Aharon the Kohen were able to guide the Israelites, so may you merit through this work to be a guide for the many. Amen.